Rutherford Studies in Contemporary Theology

Editors

DAVID F. WRIGHT
*Professor Emeritus of Patristic and Reformed Christianity,
New College, University of Edinburgh*

ROY KEARSLEY
*Lecturer in Christian Doctrine and Theology of Mission,
South Wales Baptist College, Cardiff*

THE SACRAMENT OF THE WORD MADE FLESH

The Eucharistic Theology of Thomas F. Torrance

THE SACRAMENT OF THE WORD MADE FLESH

The Eucharistic Theology of Thomas F. Torrance

Robert J. Stamps

WIPF & STOCK · Eugene, Oregon

Wipf and Stock Publishers
199 W 8th Ave, Suite 3
Eugene, OR 97401

The Sacrament of the Word Made Flesh
The Eucharistic Theology of Thomas F. Torrance
By Stamps, Robert J.
Copyright©2007 by Stamps, Robert J.
ISBN 13: 978-1-62032-836-1
Publication date 7/29/2013
Previously published by Rutherford, 2007

To my wife, Ellen,
my son, Peter-John,
and my daughter, Johanna

CONTENTS

Foreword	ix
Preface	xiii
Abbreviations	xvii

1 THE THEOLOGICAL AND COSMOLOGICAL FRAMEWORK FOR TORRANCE'S EUCHARISTIC THEOLOGY — 1

    The Necessary Epistemological Determinants — 2

    The Theological Basis for God's Interaction with the World — 29

2 SACRAMENTAL SIGNIFICANCE: THE ANALOGY OF THE SACRAMENT — 59

    Rationale for Subsequent Outline — 59

    The Rejection of the Augustinian Approach and Attitude to Symbolism — 61

    The Nature of Analogical Knowledge — 67

3 SACRAMENTAL MATTER AND ACTION: THE OBJECTIVE CHRISTOLOGICAL GROUND AND POTENTIAL FOR THE SACRAMENT — 98

    The Theological Basis — 98

    'The Paschal Mystery of Christ': The Eucharist's Objective Reality — 99

    Further Ecclesiological and Eschatological Implications — 129

    Sacramental and Non-Sacramental Participation — 137

4 SACRAMENTAL EFFECT: THE SUBJECTIFICATION OF THE OBJECTIVE CHRISTOLOGICAL REALITY — 143

    Rationale for Subsequent Outline — 143

    The Real Presence within the Church's Sacrament — 145

    The Eucharistic Sacrifice within the Church's Sacrament — 192

5 AN APPRAISAL OF TORRANCE'S EUCHARISTIC
   THEOLOGY WITH OPEN QUESTIONS   239
      A General Assessment   239
      A Question of the Doctrine of God and a Latent
         Augustinianism   253
      Questions as to the Legitimacy of Various Responses
         to God   266
      A Question of the Meaning of Grace   278
      Questions of Style, Metaphor and Appeal   282
      Questions of 'Imageless Images' and Aesthetics 291
      A Further Question   304

Bibliography   319

FOREWORD

The history of theology has been largely a chronicle of controversy. That peculiar perception of theology's progress through the ages has had two unfortunate consequences. First, there has been insufficient appreciation of the way in which the story of theology over the centuries is one of growth. It was not until the nineteenth century that such a view became common and even then it needed the genius of Newman to grasp not only the truth of this but also its implication with regard to the nature of doctrinal truth. Little wonder that he wrote in his notebook about the great venture he undertook in his *Essay on the Development of Doctrine*, 'Write it Historically'. He had grasped very clearly that a historical view of doctrine could not treat it as if it were a matter of abstract proportions whose relations to one another would be merely that of formal coherence. It is this lack or inadequacy of understanding which accounted for the neglect of the context in which theology is done. For too long the history of theology has been content with stereotypes, so that, for instance, our only understanding of the profound impact of the ancient tradition of logic on the development of theology was the disparagement of much medieval theology as pointless sophistry. It is perhaps ironic that the recognition of the development by philosophy, as one of its debts to theology, was the stimulus to a better understanding. Secondly, there was generated by this concentration on controversy a tendency to neglect issues that were not matters of controversy. One has only to think of the way in which discussion of the doctrine of creation received prominence only with reference to such dramatic and controversial issues as evolution. While it is true that any age's theology cannot expect a greater longevity than the fashions of thought or the particular preoccupations of the period, it cannot be true that only what was controversial was significant. In fact the reverse is more often the case, for just as the debate about the Darwinian hypothesis is now a dead issue so the problem of what the doctrine of creation means has been given new and greater urgency by the development of cosmological science.

These thoughts are prompted by Dr Stamps' welcome contribution in this book because eucharistic theology has received all too little attention in the twentieth century. In Protestant theology Brilioth's great – and for its time magisterial – work remained the only guide to issues posed by what was recognized as a mark of the church, viz. its eucharistic praxis. It is interesting, for example, to note that one of the main features of Nonconformist reaction to the Oxford Movement was its rejection of the 'Roman' view of sacraments it revealed, as has been pointed out by recent historians of the period (see M. Walker, 'Baptists and the Tractarian Eucharist – a Study in Opposition', *King's College Theological Review*, 1988, 4–10). Yet very little creative sacramental theology resulted. In the first quarter of this century almost no reference was made by Reformed theologians to the subject; there might have been a general assumption that sacramental theology was the province of the Catholic-minded. This meant that its issues were distinct and limited if not indeed esoteric. Certainly they were viewed as of concern only to those who wished to claim a special status *vis-à-vis* Rome. To comment on the irony of this in the light of recent Roman Catholic eucharistic theology is both to confuse the issue and run ahead of the story. For the point is that such neglect was typical of neither the emergence of modern Protestant theology nor its Reformation roots and tradition. Thus Schleiermacher, fairly described as the father of modern Protestant theology, in his classical work, *Christian Faith*, was as much concerned with the problems of sacramental theology as with the more obvious traditional problems of creation, christology and soteriology. The discussion of the Eucharist – as that of Baptism – forms a significant part of the ecclesiological section of the second part of the system of doctrine. However, if I may borrow a half-joking comment of Karl Barth's (from his gloriously eirenic essay on Bultmann published in English in *Kerygma and Myth* (ed. H.W. Bartsch), vol. 2): 'Who now reads Schleiermacher?' And if that is the fate of this prince of theologians what hope is there that any notice will be taken of lesser luminaries of the Reformed firmament such as R.W. Dale who made it abundantly clear to his contemporaries that the Reformed tradition was in theology as in churchmanship a matter of word and sacrament? More recently there has been all too little interruption of a misleading silence.

If there have been all too few contributions of any kind to eucharistic theology from Protestant theologians, it must also be said that until Schillebeeckx's fundamental challenge to received notions Catholic contributions too were rather limited. Thus magisterial as was Francis Clark's correction of mistaken opinion in his *Eucharistic Sacrifice and the Reformation* it did little to advance the theological effort within the new ecumenical situation. The time has come, then, to talk in the new-found accents of ecumenism, and to few theologians has it been given to do this in so many contexts as T.F. Torrance. So Dr Stamps' task was evidently worthwhile if only because he set out to concentrate on this conjunction of Torrance's theological and ecumenical concerns. No ecumenical effort will be of any value if it fails to identify that mainspring of doctrine, from which all kinds of difficulties emerge, which are all too easily seen as merely practical issues. One of the values of this work is that it has deliberately sought not so much to discuss a particular problem or a collection of issues as to identify Torrance as an example of an archetypal Reformed theology of the Eucharist. To say that Dr Stamps has been industrious is patently an understatement: the truth is that he has been indefatigable in his search for the least morsel that Torrance offers. Yet it is not so much as a study of Torrance that this book is to be commended: its great value is that it offers a contextualization of Torrance's thinking on the Eucharist – in ecclesiology, the more general dimension of an incarnational theology – as well as his understanding of cosmology and epistemology. Also it is a very timely reminder as well as contextualization of the range of problems we face in eucharistic theology. To look with Dr Stamps at these issues is to engage in a theological effort that is as old and as perennial as the church. It is to appreciate anew that theology is a particularly lively understanding, sharing at once the subtlety of mathematics as logic and the creative perception of the poet for whom the 'Flower in the Crannied Wall' is both a symbol and an example of the universe's Mystery. Too often theologians bandy words such as 'mystery', 'transcendence' or even 'creation' and forget that what it is that we *know* of these things is given us in that feast which as a creation of time and eternity presages in time what we can expect eternity to be. This is why I hope that Dr Stamps' book will not only find grateful readers but will be repaid by profound reflection on this symbol of the heart of faith.

John Heywood Thomas
Emeritus Professor of Theology
University of Nottingham

PREFACE

The Very Reverend Professor Thomas F. Torrance has been widely acclaimed as scholar, author, leading churchman, and ecumenist, no less since his retirement in 1975 than during his long tenure as Professor of Christian Dogmatics, New College, Edinburgh. His academic interests have been notably broad; he has covered such areas as patristics, the Reformation, the theology of Karl Barth, ecclesiology, eschatology, anthropology and, most especially and recently, the philosophy of science. Although these pursuits may appear purely academic to the detached observer, Torrance has always been eager to stress the unity between Church and Academy. One comment familiar to all his students at New College is that 'theology is... a worshipping of God with the mind' (*KBI*, 215). It is therefore imperative for the reader to recognize that the man we are here considering is not only arguably the greatest living British theologian but also a man of deep spirituality. Such a unity of scholarship and devotion is perhaps nowhere more visible than in Torrance's writings on the Eucharist. He has written that his own confession of faith is 'bound up in the Nicene Creed and the Eucharistic Liturgy', that the Nicene Creed for him represents 'Faith Given' whilst the Eucharistic Liturgy represents 'Faith At Worship' (Preface to *The Centrality of Christ*). Indeed, theology, says Torrance, 'has its place within the whole complex of the Church's response in worship, obedience and mission' (*TS*, 55). Already we may suppose that our study will carry us right to the very heart of Torrance's theology.

There has only been a handful of theses written exclusively on Torrance's theology and only one, to our knowledge, concerning his eucharistic theology. This is Sister Mary Agnew's study in 1972 of the concept of sacrifice in the eucharistic theology of D.M. Baillie, T.F. Torrance, and Jean-Jacques von Allmen, but, even here, Torrance is not the only theologian under scrutiny. A still more important rationale for our study derives from the simple fact that in no one book does Torrance order his thinking on the Eucharist into a single, systematic treatment (although he has published three major essays devoted purely to the subject[1]). Rather, we find that he includes

---

[1] 'Eschatology and the Eucharist' in *Intercommunion* (1952), 'Toward a Doctrine of the Lord's Supper' in *Conflict and Agreement in the Church* (1960)

thoughts on the Eucharist in contexts concerned with much broader subjects, such as the Reformation and eschatology (*Kingdom and Church*), the vicarious role of Christ (*God and Rationality*), the ascension (*Space, Time and Resurrection*), the incarnation (*Space, Time and Incarnation*), and ecclesiology (*Royal Priesthood*). For example, although *Space, Time and Resurrection* is a book concerned with the resurrection, ascension and final parousia of Christ, it is precisely in a chapter about the ascension and parousia that Torrance deals with – in this instance – 'The Sacramental Relation to the Crucified and Risen Jesus Christ'. Our main task in the present work has therefore been to locate, systematize and evaluate critically Torrance's comments on the Eucharist within one, coherent study. In this endeavour we have necessarily had to be selective about how much of the general contexts of these comments to include, remembering always that it is Torrance's sacramental thought which is our principal concern and only secondarily the broader canvases on which he paints it. This has also meant only limited allusions to Torrance's sources (most notably the Eastern Fathers, Calvin and Karl Barth), his scientific works, and to his general comments concerning Western Christian thought (especially Medieval cosmologies and sacramental theologies), each of which might have merited a thesis on its own. Finally, even though we acknowledge the inseparability of Baptism and the Eucharist in Torrance's sacramental thought, we have had to recognize that the former is deserving of an entirely separate but equally rigorous study.

The sporadically expressed nature of Torrance's eucharistic theology has certainly made our task much more difficult than it might otherwise have been. However, there have been two important factors which have facilitated the project. The first of these is unquestionably the fact that T.F. Torrance is a living writer. C.S. Lewis once wrote that 'a man is ill-advised to write a book on any living author. There is bound to be at least one person and there are probably several who inevitably know more about the subject than ordinary research will discover.' 'Far better', he concluded, 'to write about the unanswering dead' (cited by B. Sibley in *Shadowlands*, 1985, 9). This has most certainly *not* been the case in the context of the present work; we have had two highly profitable interviews with Professor Torrance himself, as well as substantial correspondence in which parts of the present work have been discussed. The second

---

and 'The Paschal Mystery of Christ and the Eucharist' in *Theology in Reconciliation* (1975).

facilitating factor has been the consistency of Torrance's entire theological method and thought, including his eucharistic theology. Although there has certainly been some development, as we shall point out, his most important ideas all appear incipiently from his earliest works. This has enabled us to extract comments on the Eucharist from different books written at different stages on different subjects without having to spend pages describing how each year has brought with it a new perspective.

The consistency of Torrance's theology is to be found in the undergirding principle of all that he writes. This principle is reflected in our title, *The Sacrament of the Word Made Flesh*. It is that Christ is the primal sacrament of all God's truth to the Church, that the historical and risen Christ is the physical objectivity through which God speaks and interprets his Word to man. Hence it is Christ who makes our sacraments vital and efficacious; that is to say, it is Christ who makes the Eucharist refer to him, witness to him and a place where he encounters man. This being the case, we can see how this project has inevitably become as much an exercise in christology as it is in eucharistic theology.

In the final analysis, the usefulness of a thesis such as this is to be found in the fact that Torrance never works out his theology in a vacuum, or for its own sake. As we pointed out at the beginning of this preface, Torrance's theology is integrative in so far as it does not divorce scholarship from spirituality. It is also integrative in the sense that the theoretical is never divorced from the practical, just as Christ is never divorced from his Church. Nothing illustrates the pragmatic orientation of Torrance's theology more vividly than the fact that he wrote all three of his major essays on the Eucharist in books which had ecumenical objectives. The intention he stated for his eucharistic theology as early as 1960 underlines this; he said then that his desire was to build a theological bridge for 'the fullness of sacramental communion' between the Churches (*C & A* 11, 10f.).

ABBREVIATIONS

Books and Articles by T.F. Torrance

Books

C & A	*Conflict and Agreement in the Church* (vols I and II)
DCO	*Divine and Contingent Order*
CDOM	*Calvin's Doctrine of Man*
CFOM	*The Christian Frame of Mind*
DOG	*The Doctrine of Grace in the Apostolic Fathers*
G & G	*The Ground and Grammar of Theology*
G & R	*God and Rationality*
KBI	*Karl Barth: An Introduction to his Early Theology 1910–1931*
K & C	*Kingdom and Church*
Manual	*A Manual of Church Doctrine According to the Church of Scotland*
MOC	*The Mediation of Christ*
Orth & Ref'd	*Theological Dialogue between Orthodox and Reformed Churches*
R & E	*Reality and Evangelical Theology*
R/n	*Theology in Reconciliation*
RP	*Royal Priesthood*
R/st	*Theology in Reconstruction*
SOF	*The School of Faith: The Catechisms of the Reformed Church*
STI	*Space, Time and Incarnation*
STR	*Space, Time and Resurrection*
TS	*Theological Science*

Articles and Lectures

'Arnoldshain'	'Doctrinal Consensus on Holy Communion: The Arnoldshain Theses' (*SJT* 15, 1–35, 1962)
'Comments'	'Comments on Eucharistic Practice in the Church of Scotland' (*ChSSR* 5, 1983)

'GT'	'The Paschal Mystery of Christ and the Eucharist: General Theses' (*LitR* 6, 1976)
Inter	'Eschatology and the Eucharist' (*Intercommunion*, London, SCM, 1952, 303–50)
'Israel'	'Israel: People of God – God, Destiny and Suffering' (*ThRen* 13, 1979)
'New College'	'The Church in the New Era of Scientific and Cosmological Change' (*N Coll B* 7, 1973)
TL	*The Addresses at the 6th Presentation of the Templeton Foundation Prize for Progress in Religion*
'Trinity'	'Toward an Ecumenical Consensus on the Trinity' (*ThZ* 31, 1975)

Other Abbreviations

AmBenR	*American Benedictine Review*
CD	*Church Dogmatics* by Karl Barth
ChrA	*Christian Arena*
ChrG	*Christian Graduate*
ChSSR	*Church Service Society Record*
CR	*Corpus Reformatorum Joannis Calvini Opera quae supersunt omnia*
EvQ	*Evangelical Quarterly*
Exp Tim	*Expository Times*
Inst	*Institutes of the Christian Religion* by John Calvin (Unless otherwise indicated all citations are from the 2 volumes published by Eerdmans, 1957, translation by Henry Beveridge.)
IrBSt	*Irish Biblical Studies*
JChSS	*Journal of the Church Service Society*
JEH	*Journal of Ecclesiastical History*
JRel	*Journal of Religion*
JTS	*Journal of Theological Studies*
LCC	*Library of Christian Classics*
LitR	*Liturgical Review*
LitSt	*Liturgical Studies*
N Coll B	*New College Bulletin*
NPNF	*Nicene and Post-Nicene Fathers*
PSCF	*Perspectives on Science and Christian Faith*
RefTR	*Reformed Theological Review*
RMS	*Renaissance and Modern Studies*

RSCF	*Research Scientists' Christian Fellowship Newsletter*
SJT	*Scottish Journal of Theology*
StPatrist	*Studia Patristica*
Summ. Theol.	*Summa Theologica by Thomas Aquinas*
TFOC	The Fathers of the Church
Th	*Theology*
ThRen	*Theological Renewal*
ThSt	*Theological Studies*
ThZ	*Theologische Zeitschrift*
TI	*Theological Investigations by Karl Rahner*
TT	*Table Talk by Karl Barth*
USCF	*University Staffs' Christian Fellowship Broadsheet*

CHAPTER 1

The Theological and Cosmological Framework for Torrance's Eucharistic Theology

It is imperative for an understanding of Torrance's eucharistic theology that we first set out the basic precepts and working principles of his theology. We will begin with an overview of his epistemology not just because the knowledge of God and man's reception of it are fundamental to any subsequent theological formulation but because 'the knowing relation' is for Torrance a model for, and includes, all other relations between God and man. After this we will discuss Torrance's assumptions regarding God's interaction with the world. Whereas in the latter section the implications for sacramental theology will be more obvious, in the former they will be sometimes rather broad and indirect, only finally becoming clear as the dissertation unfolds. In both sections, however, wherever possible the place and function of the Eucharist will be pointed out. In any case, the chapter which follows should demonstrate beyond any doubt that the Eucharist belongs at the heart of Torrance's theology and serves as an indispensable part of his theological method as a whole.

THE NECESSARY EPISTEMOLOGICAL DETERMINANTS

I. The Reception of the Knowledge of God

(a) *The Ontological/Epistemological Equivalents: The Grace of God, The Incarnate Word and The Knowledge of God*

Torrance has said that if he were ever to write a systematic theology he would formulate it under the three headings of the Pauline benediction:

> The grace of the Lord Jesus Christ,
> And the love of God,
> And the fellowship of the Holy Spirit
> (2 Cor. 13:14)[1]

This represents, he says, 'the actual order in which the Gospel is presented', meaning that God's grace is always prior and foundational to any act of personal faith.[2] 'It is the grace of God that creates in man the capacity to receive and grasp [grace].'[3]

From his earliest writings Torrance has argued for an understanding of grace which does not 'detach the thought of grace from the *person* of Jesus Christ', i.e. one that would make God's gracious act of self-disclosure co-incidental with the life, word and deed of Christ.[4] When he refers to the 'grace of the Lord Jesus Christ' in the benediction above, he interprets the genitive τοῦ Κυρίου Ἰησοῦ Χριστοῦ as being in apposition to ἡ χάρις. Torrance never diverges

---

[1] Comment made during Lectures, Edinburgh, Michaelmas Term, 1963: 'Christian Dogmatics', New College.

[2] Thomas F. Torrance (ed. and intro.), *The School of Faith: The Catechisms of the Reformed Church* (London, James Clark & Co., 1959), xxi.

[3] Thomas F. Torrance, *Karl Barth: An Introduction to his Early Theology 1910–1931* (London, SCM, 1962), 93.

[4] Thomas F. Torrance, *The Doctrine of Grace in the Apostolic Fathers* (Edinburgh, Oliver & Boyd, 1948), V. Torrance here follows Barth in his identification of the Word of revelation with '*the Being of God in his Act*' in Jesus Christ (Karl Barth, *CD*, II.1, ch. VI, para. 28 as cited by Torrance in *KBI*, 146). This is one of the great rediscoveries of the Reformation, Torrance claims: 'In grace the Gift which God bestows is identical with himself the Giver – concretely, this meant Jesus Christ, for he is the Deed of God identical with himself, and in him God gives none other than himself to men' (*DOG*, 146).

from this distinctly christological interpretation of grace. A definition from his doctoral dissertation published in 1948 is typical:

> *Charis* refers to the being and action of God as revealed and actualized in Jesus Christ, for He is in His person and work the self-giving of God to men.[5]

---

[5] Ibid. 21. It is important for our inquiry into Torrance's eucharistic theology that when he defines grace formally, he usually makes explicit reference to the way in which the Church has often misrepresented grace in its sacramental theology. The so-called 'Biblical' definition of grace cited here was set out in contrast to the church's notion of it from the second century as a 'semi-physical substance' or 'spiritual power' to be dispensed by the Church 'in a sacramentalist fashion' (*DOG*, 12, 140–41).

In 1964 he put forward a similar definition contrary to the medieval Church's conception of grace as a 'divine power filling the Church', deposited particularly within her sacraments, 'by which nature unceasingly transcends itself and is made participant in divine nature'. 'In the New Testament grace is regularly associated with the Person and work of Christ... [it] is Christ giving and communicating himself to us unconditionally in his own sovereign love and freedom' ('The Roman Doctrine of Grace from the Point of View of Reformed Theology', *The Eastern Churches Quarterly*, Oct. 1964, reprinted in Thomas F. Torrance, *Theology in Reconstruction* (Grand Rapids, Eerdmans, 1975), 175, 172, 186–7. Page references to this work here and following from *Theology and Reconstruction*).

Again in 1975, once more to counter the identification of 'sacramental grace' with 'a realm of intermediate causality between God and the world', he wrote: 'Grace' is to be identified with 'the self-giving of God in Christ, that is, with Christ himself' (Thomas F. Torrance, *Theology in Reconciliation: Essays Towards Evangelical and Catholic Unity in East and West* (Grand Rapids, Eerdmans, 1976), 126).

Unfortunately, as Torrance notes, Calvin compromised this strict interpretation of 'the Grace of the Lord Jesus Christ' and fell into the use of the inappropriate phrase 'the grace of the Spirit'. Torrance disparages such an idiom for two reasons: firstly, because it ignores the formal identity of the content of grace with the person of Christ, and, secondly, because it implies an autonomy to the Spirit's operation as though it could circumvent the work of Christ. He observes that historically 'it was through the association of grace with the Spirit that grace came to be detached from Christ and thought of as 'something' communicable and transmissible and which could be channelised and infused' as a spiritual substance separate from the real human person and deed of Christ. This could never have happened, he says, if 'the inseparable association of the Spirit with the Royal Person and Office of Christ... [had been] carefully preserved' (*SOF*, CV). Torrance comments: 'Grace is to be understood as the impartation not just of something from God but of God himself. In Jesus Christ and in the Holy Spirit God freely gives himself to us in such a way that the Gift

Broadly speaking, like the Reformers, Torrance defines grace in terms of God's disposition to his creation, as 'the turning of God toward the world', e.g. in his will to create and preserve the natural order.[6] He completes this definition of grace dynamically and personally with the concept of God's decision to reconcile the world, despite its estrangement from him, i.e. in terms of God's dispensation of himself 'into the world' in Jesus Christ.[7] He says, '*charis* seems to pass from the aspect of disposition or goodwill which bestows blessing to the action itself and to the actual gift, but in the New Testament neither the action nor the gift is separable from the person of the giver, God in Christ.'[8]

It is obvious that 'the order of the Gospel', encapsulated in the Pauline benediction, represents for Torrance more than just a delineation of the chronological order in which man is brought to personal faith. Torrance is clearly setting out an ontological equivalence between God as he is in himself and his gracious act of self-revelation in Jesus Christ, that is, between ἡ χάρις τοῦ Κυρίου Ἰησοῦ Χριστοῦ and ἡ ἀγάπη τοῦ Θεοῦ. There naturally follows from this a corresponding epistemological identity which affirms that our apprehension of 'the grace of the Lord Jesus Christ' is the basis for our acquisition of knowledge or 'the love of God'. This represents for Torrance the essence of the divine economy with respect to man's

---

and Giver are one and the same in the wholeness and indivisibility of his Grace' (Thomas F. Torrance, *Reality and Evangelical Theology*, The 1981 Payton Lectures (Philadelphia, The Westminster Press, 1982), 14-15; cf. *R/st*, 172; *DOG*, 76-7, 139-40).

[6] Thomas F. Torrance, *Theological Science*, based on the Hewett Lectures for 1959 (OUP, 1978), 67. Torrance continues, 'God the Creator turns in Grace to create and preserve a world utterly distinct from himself' (*TS*, 67). Having therefore established that grace is equivalent to 'the being and action of God', it is axiomatic that grace should remain absolutely free in relation to the world, i.e. under no natural or ecclesiastical necessity. The ramifications of this for Torrance's sacramental theology will become increasingly evident as this dissertation progresses (*KBI*, 146). These thoughts are all characteristic of the early Barth to whom Torrance is indebted. As Barth put it: 'Grace is the generous and free will of God... its necessity proceeds from him and from him only... all this necessity is the majestic pre-eminence of grace.

Grace is, then, no spiritual power residing in the man of this world; no physical energy residing in nature; no cosmic power in this earth. Grace is and remains always the Power of God' (Karl Barth, *Epistle to the Romans*, ed. Edwyn C. Hoskyns (London, OUP, 1933), 102-3).

[7] Grace is thus defined 'as God in his turning toward man to be man's God' (*KBI*, 212).

[8] *DOG*, 21.

knowledge of God, viz. that its content and means are identical with the word and person of Christ. He says Jesus Christ is 'the Object of theological knowledge... at once [God's] Person and Word, who communicates himself to us as the Word addressing us, and who communicates his Word to us in the form of his personal Being'.[9] This epistemological identity Torrance translates into an epistemological exclusivity. 'Theology cannot, and must not try to seek knowledge of God apart from His whole objectivity, divine and human, in Jesus Christ.'[10] The Incarnate Word is the sole source of the divine wisdom; there is no other witness to God. This has all kinds of implications for Torrance's doctrines of creation and of man, which we will explore more fully later.

(b) The Knowledge of God through the Word and in the Spirit

(i) A Knowing in Relation

A Personal Relation. The nature of the truth dictates the way it will be received. God chooses to communicate himself to us, Torrance says, 'in the form of personal Being', specifically, 'in the form of active life and being in our historical existence... revealed in Jesus Christ'.[11] Because the truth of God is manifest and given temporally in this 'intensely and supremely personal' manner, it requires 'in our knowing, relationship to it in time'.[12] God addresses us 'in Person', as 'Person to person'.[13] On the basis of the equivalence of God's personal word and act our knowledge of him must be construed in terms of an encounter with him, as *Ereignis* with a speaking God, as Barth termed it.[14] God's word is never to be thought of apart from his act of speaking it.[15]

While Torrance insists that God communicates himself principally to his Church within the context of the proclamation of the Holy Scriptures, even in that association, God's Word cannot be

---

[9] *TS*, 133.
[10] Ibid. 138.
[11] Ibid. 143.
[12] *R/st*, 187; *TS*, 154. 'God's revealedness makes it a relationship between God and man, the effective meeting between God and man' (*CD* I.1, 381ff.).
[13] *KBI*, 104, 100; *TS*, 29.
[14] *KBI*, 98–9.
[15] Ibid. 104; cf. *TS*, 12, fn. 2. 'The Word of God [is] backed with God's own ultimate Being. It is not only God's Word but God's Word as God himself says it' (*KBI*, 96; cf. *CD* I.1, 490ff.). 'God's Word is not only object of our knowing but Subject. As Word of *God* it is never object without being Subject' (*KBI*, 104).

abstracted from his act of speaking and cannot be heard except in relation to the God who speaks it. However God speaks and acts, wherever he speaks and acts, he will speak for himself and by himself.[16] The Word of God is never the object of revelation without being its Subject.[17] Any knowledge of God attained in the Scriptures is not envisaged as imparted by the Scriptures *per se*, but by God making himself known through them. Likewise, however God is shown to communicate himself to us through the sacrament, his personal act there will itself constitute that communication.[18] This comprises what in Barthian terminology is an 'actualist' understanding of God's Word. It is based upon the proposition that what God is in his act of revelation he is in himself. Our encounter with God in whatever revelatory context he chooses to address us is 'pure act of God unqualified by anything outside of it' or instrumental to it.[19] Any distance ontologically or experientially between what God is in his revelation and what God is in himself is unthinkable for both Barth and Torrance. Any such distance would only lead to theological agnosticism, making theology itself a delineation of our experience of God instead of the knowledge of God given in experience.

A Relation in Being. The stark objectivity of the Word *vis-à-vis* the knowing subject which Torrance projects is not meant to diminish the intimacy of the knowing relation. For all its identity with God in

---

[16] Cf. Calvin, 'God himself [is] the only fit witness to himself' (*Inst* I.11.1).

[17] *KBI*, 104-5. God speaks to us uniquely 'out of the Holy Scriptures'. They are the 'frame and the earthen vessel of the Word'(*KBI*, 104-5). 'The Word of God... encounters and addresses us in and through the Holy Scriptures', Torrance says (*SOF*, XLV). 'The creaturely correspondence of Holy Scripture to God's Word is so miraculously assumed and used by the divine revelation... [and] adapted by the Spirit not only to mediate the Holy Word of God but to be the expression of that Word in human form.... The Word has so imprinted its own image upon the human word as to make it a faithful reflection of its own revelation' (*R/st*, 139; cf. Steven Sykes' comments on the 'epistemological relevance of the Holy Spirit' for Torrance's doctrine of Scripture, in *Karl Barth – Studies of his Theological Methods*, ed. S.W. Sykes (Oxford, Clarendon Press, 1979), 25-6). While the Word has its 'propositional' character, Torrance says, because the nature of the truth is understood as 'Person and Message in one', the Word can never be thought of as separated from God's being (*TS*, 148). Torrance reiterates in all his writings that in Jesus Christ 'The actual *Being* of God [came] to man as Word' (*KBI*, 145).

[18] 'His Word is His Person in communication, for in His speaking He Himself is personally present communicating Himself' (*TS*, 147).

[19] *KBI*, 98-9.

his being, the Word is not distanced from man in his being. Knowing the truth involves what Torrance calls 'a relation in being to it'.[20] By this he means an experience in which God out of the depths of his own reality, and without compromising what he is, penetrates to the depths of the created reality in man, without compromising what we are. It is at this depth in man and from out of this depth in God that God communicates himself. Torrance works this out in sacramental terms, although without specifically referring to the sacraments as such. Such a relation in being, he suggests, 'constitutes the sacramental area' where the knowledge of God is personally conveyed to man.[21] In another context, he states that it is precisely this kind of relation that constitutes our Eucharist. 'The Church', he says, 'is given through the Eucharist a *relation in being*, beyond its relation to Christ through faith'.[22] It would therefore be entirely correct to assume that the sacramental relation serves a vital role in the economy of this knowing in relation as Torrance expounds it.

From what has been said, it should be clear that for Torrance the Church's knowledge of God does not consist merely in its apprehension of correct propositions about the Truth, but rather in personal relation with it. It is at this point that Torrance's epistemology calls for the sacramental relation and, in so doing, gives the first indication of an inter-dependent economy existing between the Word and the sacrament. The relation with itself which the Word requires of the Church in order to demonstrate its (the Word's) personal inherence within the Truth of God determines, as he puts it, 'the place of the sacramental relation in the very heart of Christian theology'. The sacraments, however, are not just given to the Church to describe visually what cannot be expressed in words. His point is that the words themselves must defer to relation or find their proper place in the Church in partnership with the sacrament. This is not a deference of 'the language of words' to 'the language of

---

[20] *SOF*, XXXVII. 'Knowing in Truth must involve a relation in being to it as well as a relation in cognition.' Torrance insists, however, that our knowledge of God never bypasses the mind (*KBI*, 100; *TS*, 154). The knowledge of God is inclusive of every aspect of man's person, implying a oneness of knowing and becoming on the part of the believer which corresponds to the oneness of truth and being in Jesus Christ (*SOF*, XXXVII–XXXVIII; cf. *TS*, 153). Just as the truth of God was manifest in the life and deed of Christ, so it ought to take like form in us, 'so that we may be true as God is true, and learn to do the truth as he does the truth' (*TS*, 143).

[21] *TS*, 150.

[22] Thomas F. Torrance, 'Eschatology and the Eucharist', *Intercommunion*, eds Donald Baillie and John Marsh (London, SCM, 1952), 335.

vision', but the deference or knowledge as purely rational comprehension to knowledge as relation.[23] He follows through this thought: the sacraments 'will not allow us... to respond to the proclamation of the Word of God only in some intellectual or merely Spiritual way, for in and through them the movement of faith reaches its fruition as lived and acted response to the coming of the Word of God into our space and time'.[24]

In the knowing relation God is said to communicate his Word immediately to man. In whatever manner the creaturely words and/or actions of the Church's sermon and sacrament are employed to serve him they do not obstruct the immediacy of this relation. Torrance contrasts the disposition of God's word and grace to the Church with anything 'mediate'. The Word of God needs no mediators. Even so, he contends with Barth that there can be no unmediated knowledge of God, i.e. divine knowledge without an organic correlative to sense experience in space and time.[25] Man does not know God in sheer or ultimate objectivity, i.e. not as God *simpliciter*.[26] 'The only knowledge possible for us is that which he mediates to us in and through this world.'[27] It is only through created objectivity that we meet the divine objectivity.[28] This is true in a primal sense in the creaturely objectivity of Jesus Christ.[29] The Word made flesh, he insists, is 'the source and basis and norm of all God's revelation of himself'.[30] Jesus' humanity is 'the real text of God's Word addressed to us'.[31] Torrance, with Barth, speaks of the divine humanity of the Word as 'The Sacrament', or of the whole revelatory event of the Incarnation as 'itself the all-inclusive Sacrament of the

---

[23] *TS*, 24, cf. 23-5. This is not to say that the sacramental relation is itself another relation properly speaking apart from the spoken word, or 'wordless'; 'for it is the relation created by the Word that is fundamental even to the sacramental relation' (*TS*, 24-5; cf. *KBI*, 98).

[24] Thomas F. Torrance, *God and Rationality* (OUP, 1971), 161.

[25] Roger J. Newell, 'Participatory Knowledge: Theology as Art and Science in C.S. Lewis and T.F. Torrance (unpublished doctoral thesis, University of Aberdeen, 1983), 187; cf. *TS*, 136-7.

[26] Cf. *TS*, 56.

[27] *R & E*, 24-5.

[28] *TS*, 136.

[29] Ibid. 137. It is 'in the objectivity of His particular and historical humanity [that] we encounter the eternal objectivity of God himself' (*TS*, 150).

[30] Ibid. 150.

[31] Thomas F. Torrance, *The Mediation of Christ*, The 1982 Didsbury Lectures (Exeter, Paternoster Press, 1983), 88; *R & E*, 89.

Word made flesh'.[32] As we will see, the 'sacraments' only claim this title for themselves because of their relation and service to Christ who is himself the primal sacrament of God's communication to man.

In asserting that all man's knowledge of God is mediated knowledge, however, Torrance means not only that it is revealed through 'the primary objectivity' of the Incarnate Word but also that it is correlated with the broader 'media' of this created order.[33] He says, 'our knowledge [of God] is correlated with the world as His creation and the appointed medium of his self-revelation and self-communication to mankind'.[34] The sacraments belong to this 'secondary form of objectivity'. The sacramental relation as such is therefore not an anomaly or an exception in God's economy of revelation, but constitutes in itself the basic kind of knowing relation between God and man, i.e. one involving created instrumentality – of which the incarnation itself is the fundamental example.[35] Torrance refers to the sacraments as 'created mediations' through which God speaks understandably to our 'creaturely conceivability'.[36] This does not contradict his insistence that all knowledge of God is immediate, for neither the human words of scriptural proclamation nor the creaturely acts and elements of the sacraments qualify God's presence to man. They are manifest, tangible forms under which God's grace personally apprehends us, albeit invisibly. Though it has its created instruments, grace itself can in no wise 'be regarded in an instrumental sense'.[37] For quite the opposite is true:

> Grace [is] Christ giving and communicating himself to us unconditionally in his own sovereign love and freedom, [therefore] its mode and activity can be thought of only as intensely and supremely personal. It is grounded in the living relations of the Person of the Holy Trinity, and its operation is never one that breaks connection with that ground. Rather it is one in and

---

[32] *TS*, 150; Thomas F. Torrance, *Royal Priesthood*, SJT Occasional Paper, no. 3 (Edinburgh, Oliver & Boyd, 1955), 75. 'In the full sense Jesus Christ is Himself the Sacrament for it is in Him that the One Truth of God comes to us in creaturely form and existence, so that in the objectivity of His particular and historical humanity we encounter the eternal objectivity of God Himself' (*TS*, 150).

[33] *TS*, 136.
[34] *R & E*, 24–5.
[35] Cf. ibid. 49.
[36] *R/n*, 132; *CD* I.1, 426–7.
[37] *R/st*, 187.

through which God the Father, the Son and the Holy Spirit are operative together in the divine Love.[38]

'From the beginning to end in grace', Torrance asserts, 'God is immediately present and active as living Agent'.[39] At no point does the Word of Grace lose its ontological, personal identity with God; at no point does it cease to be what it is within the Trinity in order to become something else to us in the world or in association with its sacramental instruments. Just as the created matter of Christ's humanity did not remove God further from us, but rather was the form his presence took among us, the sacraments should not be thought of as intervening between God and man, but serving his presence in the world. God imposes no 'intermediaries' between himself and man. He apprehends us immediately in Christ and, corresponding to this, immediately in the world through the agency of Christ, though in the context of secondarily objective instrumentation.[40]

A Dialogical Relation. Torrance goes on to describe the character of this knowing relation in being between the Word and man as 'dialogical', or 'real conversation with the living God'.[41] He says, 'His word is always God speaking to us in Person in an ever-renewed encounter of speaking and hearing, of giving and receiving.'[42] In this conversation with God he 'breaks into our monologue with ourselves and assumes us into dialogue with himself'.[43] However, what Torrance means here by 'dialogue' is not what the word usually implies. Since all knowledge about God ultimately proceeds from him, the questions man raises independent of God's revelation will be naturally void of any relevance to the truth. Therefore Torrance maintains that 'Christianity does not set out to answer man's questions.'[44] Christ himself is 'the proper question', 'the great

---

[38] Ibid. 186-7.

[39] Ibid. 187.

[40] *R/n*, 131-2. Torrance could, in the terminology of John Baillie, be said to hold to a kind of 'mediated immediacy' (John Baillie is so quoted by J.B. Torrance in his article, 'The Vicarious Humanity of Christ', *The Incarnation: Ecumenical Studies in the Nicene-Constantinopolitan Creed AD 381*, ed. T.F. Torrance (Edinburgh, Handsel Press, 1981), 136).

[41] *SOF*, XLIX.

[42] *KBI*, 104.

[43] Ibid. 98; cf. *SOF*, XLIX. 'So long as I am simultaneously questioner and answerer I cannot know personal Truth', Torrance states (*TS*, 133, fn. 1).

[44] *SOF*, XXVI.

question of God to us', which searches out every aspect of man's life, bringing all to light.⁴⁵ The fact that in Christ man confronts a revelation which he has no part in formulating, which comes to him as totally given and to which he cannot add, 'questions' or passes judgement on man, denying in him any prerogative or capability to interrogate God.⁴⁶ Before the objectivity of the word of God in Christ, man is 'questioned... down to the very roots of his being until he is set free from himself, from his own preconceptions and self-deception, from self-willed... thinking, from pride of reason and desire to control the questioning of God'.⁴⁷ Looking at it this way, 'the question' then which must be answered is 'the question' which man is himself.⁴⁸ Man shapes his answer to God's question by allowing all that he understands as the knowledge of God to be constantly called into question, and by willingly offering himself, in his vacuity and disorientation before the truth, so as to be informed by it.⁴⁹ In this kind of dialogue man is opened up more and more to the total objectivity of the Word. Therein man receives the proper questions he should ask in order to be brought in thought and life into conformity with the Word. Indeed, Torrance says, they are 'put into our mouths'. Theology, then, is seen as an exercise in 'hearing'.⁵⁰

Although the Eucharist has to do fundamentally with visual expression, its principal role in Torrance's sacramental theology, as we have indicated, is not to reproduce the truth in pictorial form but to manifest the nature of that truth as action. On the one hand, it affords God (at his ordinance) an act within the Church through which he can demonstrate the active nature of his love towards us, and, on the other hand, it offers us the opportunity to respond or dialogue with him in an act corresponding to his. For Torrance worship is itself 'essentially a dialogical activity in which we stand over against God even when we draw near to him, distinguishing his transcendent nature from ourselves'. In our eucharistic act we relate ourselves appropriately to his holiness and majesty in a glad and thankful response for the mercy he extends towards us. Worship is

---

⁴⁵ *KBI*, 96.

⁴⁶ Cf. Barth on 'Revelation as Judgement', *CD* I.1, 183f. 'By his judgement and his grace... every private canon [is] wrested from our grasp and every private measurement spoiled' (*CD* I.1, 510).

⁴⁷ *TS*, 125; cf. 119–26.

⁴⁸ *KBI*, 96. 'Ultimately', Torrance says, 'we ourselves... are the question'(*KBI*, 96). Torrance identifies the above statement in Tillich, *Systematic Theology*, vol. 2, 14f.: 'The question, asked by man, is man himself' (*TS*, 120).

⁴⁹ *TS*, 120, cf. *G & R*, 8–9.

⁵⁰ *TS*, 120, 124, 182.

then integral to the 'answer' which God's Word of grace 'asks' of us, viz. the repentance and obedience of thankful hearts.[51]

A Reconciling Relation. The difficulty which arises in man's dialogue with God, as what has been said suggests, is not that God is in himself incomprehensible, but that man is essentially and noetically disoriented to the truth about him.[52] At the outset of this chapter we spoke of God's prior act of grace being necessary for man to receive the truth. This means more than that man must simply rely upon God for the content of his knowledge; he must also be enabled by him to receive it. There is in the mind of man an epistemological

---

[51] *G & R*, 157.

[52] Torrance will speak of God as 'the unknowable God' (*R/st*, 226). He stresses God's 'unknowability', not only to emphasize his inaccessibility through the world or by the mind of man, but to underline that man must wait upon God for knowledge of him. 'In himself God is incomprehensible to us, and unapproachable in thought but he has condescended to come down to our weakness to reveal himself to us and to redeem us in and through the humble ministry of Christ' (*R/st*, 37). He points to some Jewish and Moslem thinkers who argue 'that strictly speaking, theology is not possible, for God is essentially ineffable, unnameable and unknowable in himself'. He admits that there is a basic truth in what they say, viz. 'that the God whom we know [can only be known] through his self-communication to us' and when he is known, he always remains 'infinitely greater than we can conceive' (Thomas F. Torrance, 'Israel: People of God – God, Destiny and Suffering', *ThRen* 13 (1979), 6). He concurs with Ockham's understanding of the 'ultimate inscrutability of God', viz. that God is unknowable 'through the discursive reason', yet certainly to be known 'through divine revelation and "infused faith"' (*TS*, 63). With Thomas Aquinas he can say that 'as the reason is given knowledge of God... it acquires that adaptation by and through which it may think of him and reason toward him' (*TS*, 104). This is not to say that God possesses some sort of ultimate ineffability, as in the apophatic theology of the Eastern tradition. Reflecting upon the Eastern notion, Torrance suggests instead 'an unknowing due not to ignorance but to an excess of knowledge'. Our knowledge of God, he says, 'is a knowledge of God in his unlimited and eternal reality... one in which we know that he infinitely transcends our conceptions of him' (Thomas F. Torrance, 'Toward an Ecumenical Consensus on the Trinity', *ThZ* 31 (1975), 341–2). What he is saying is that God cannot be known by the active reason (cf. *TS*, 75ff., 96–7). 'We do not know God by acting upon him but through being acted upon by him' (*R/st*, 70). Knowledge of God cannot be extracted or wrested from the divine object by man. 'In the God/man relationship created by grace, there does not arise a reciprocity which enables man to lay his hand upon God as God lays his hand upon man' (*KBI*, 93). Before the compelling objectivity of the truth 'man himself inevitably comes... as servant not as master' (*R & E*, 31).

impasse as regards the truth of God.⁵³ As Torrance puts it, 'In his very existence [man] is imprisoned in the closed circle of his own estrangement and self-will... shut up to believing only in his own possibilities' and not in the possibility of a word from God.⁵⁴ The situation is so grave that man's mind must be thoroughly reconditioned, not just reinformed.⁵⁵ God must come 'in Grace to draw us out of our frailty, to lift us above ourselves, and create within us the capacity to know him'.⁵⁶ This further suggests that any revelatory relation, including the sacramental relation, is necessarily also rehabilitative.⁵⁷ Such an idea is already implicit in the 'relation in being' which Torrance insists that the knowing relation must be. A oneness of knowing and becoming on the part of the believer is called for in this relation, corresponding to 'the oneness of Truth and being in Christ'.⁵⁸ The knowledge of God does not take form in us merely as right thinking about God, but as our becoming like him, being conformed to his image in mind and character. Torrance speaks of our *reconciliation with the Truth*.⁵⁹ 'Revelation and reconciliation are inseparable', he says, therefore the relation in which God reveals himself must itself be a reconciling relation.⁶⁰ When Torrance asserts that 'knowing' the truth and 'becoming' like

---

⁵³ 'Yet in knowing God I am deeply aware that my relation to Him has been damaged, that disorder has resulted in my mind, and that it is I who obstruct knowledge of God by getting in between Him and myself, as it were' (*TS*, v). 'We are opposed to the Truth', Torrance says, 'and the Truth is opposed to our untruth'. Stressing that we did not lose our minds and wills in the Fall, he cites *John Craig's Catechism* (1581) as to what was forfeited: 'We... lost a right mind and a right will' (*SOF*, XXXVI-XXXVII).

⁵⁴ *TS*, 50.

⁵⁵ Man must be 'adapted to the Truth by the Truth' (*SOF*, XL). Therefore, when he says God must 'create within us the capacity to know him', Torrance is not saying simply that man's capacity must be 'enlarged' or that new mental categories for understanding have to be constructed, rather that that very capacity must be literally created (cf. *TS*, 132-3). 'A radical change', he says, must take place in 'the structural capacities of our reason'. The 'whole shape of our minds [must be] altered', so that we can recognize and comprehend the knowledge of God (*TS*, 49). God must '[create] in us the capacity to hear and see him' (*R/st*, 226).

⁵⁶ *TS*, 132-3.

⁵⁷ 'We cannot think out the mediation of revelation apart from the mediation of reconciliation' (*MOC*, 34).

⁵⁸ *SOF*, XXXVII-XXXVIII; *TS*, 153.

⁵⁹ *SOF*, XXXVI.

⁶⁰ The full quotation: 'Revelation and reconciliation are inseparable, and communication and healing cannot be divorced from each other' (*SOF*, XXXVI).

the truth cannot be separated, it is the process of sanctification which comes to mind. Accordingly, it is within that aspect of the saving economy of God that Torrance places the sacrament of the Eucharist. It is the sanctification of the Church to which the Eucharist witnesses and intrinsically belongs.[61] Indeed, Torrance says the Holy Communion may 'be spoken of as the Sacrament of Sanctification'.[62] Consequently, it should be assumed that when God approaches man in the sacramental relation he is at the same time conditioning him for the reception of his truth. Torrance suggests that this kind of inward transformation occurs in the Eucharist when he says 'the Church must nevertheless reckon that it is dead to the old life and alive in the new, for that is what actually takes place in the Eucharist'.[63]

(ii) A Knowing by Participation

We will next consider what is perhaps the single most important factor (other than the incarnation itself) in Torrance's understanding of man's knowledge of God, namely, participation in Christ. Though only an element in the overall christocentric structuring of his thought, it is nevertheless a vital one. Knowledge of God is not seen to be *fundamentally* revealed in the context of *our* relation to God at all, but rather as given and received for man, within what he calls 'the dialogue of the divine-human life of Jesus'.[64] It is the Son's personal and dialogical relation with his Father *as man* which forms the ground, the primary context, from which our knowing relation with God is informed and sustained. A discussion of such a key element in Torrance's epistemology at this point will serve our purposes as an introduction to his christological systematisation of

---

[61] Cf. *Inter*, 312–13, 320–21.

[62] Thomas F. Torrance, *Space, Time and Resurrection* (Grand Rapids, Eerdmans, 1976), 150.

[63] *Inter*, 321.

[64] *SOF*, LXVI. Not only is the Incarnate Son seen as the speaking subject of revelation to mankind, but the hearing subject as well. The knowledge of God is not only given in Christ, but is also received in him. 'Jesus Christ is himself both the word of God as spoken by God to man and that same word as heard and received by man, himself both the truth of God given to man and that very truth understood and actualised in man. He is the divine and human truth in one person' (*TS*, 50). 'God the Logos... assumes our human being and reality into such an inseparable union with himself, that in and through Jesus there takes place a real communication of God himself to us and at the same time a real reception and appropriation of that divine self-communication by man' (*R/n*, 255).

theology, and it will ultimately disclose the principle of connection between the objective and subjective elements of the christological mystery in his eucharistic theology: the Holy Spirit.

In Jesus Christ the knowledge of God is already a human experience. In him that knowledge has been perfectly realized in our humanity; 'In him the revealing of God and the understanding of man fully [coincide]'.[65] It is, therefore, upon Christ's knowledge of God that all possibility for our knowing God rests. Torrance perceives the actual realisation of that knowledge in us in terms of our participation or sharing in the Son's knowing relation with his Father. It was suggested earlier, in reflecting upon the identity of truth with the being of Christ, that 'theological knowledge... involves knowing and becoming in inseparable unity'.[66] This is true for man in his relation to God because it reflects the nature of the truth itself in Jesus Christ. For in him

> God has condescended not only to objectify himself for man and to bestow his truth upon him, but also to provide from the side of man, and from within man, full, adequate and perfect reception of that truth. Both of these have been fulfilled in Jesus Christ, for he is not only God objectifying himself for man but *man adapted and conformed to that objectification*, not only the complete revelation of God to man, but the appropriate correspondence on the part of man to that revelation, not only the Word of God to man, but man obediently hearing and answering that Word.[67]

As we suggested, man's knowing of God demands a definite breaking-down of all barriers to its reception, particularly the noetic ones. Hence, 'it is the alienated *mind* of man that God laid hold of in Jesus Christ in order to redeem it and effect reconciliation deep within the rational centre of human being'.[68] In the divine-human person of Christ revelation and reconciliation meet and are made to serve each other. In him the whole epistemological inadequacy and arrogance of man is overcome. God and man know each other freely and fully in Christ, and at an ontological depth beyond anything that we can comprehend. It is from what may be called the vicarious subjectification of the knowledge of God within the man Christ Jesus – 'Christ Jesus... whom God made our wisdom' – that our knowledge

---

[65] *MOC*, 19.
[66] *SOF*, XLIII.
[67] *TS*, 50, italics mine.
[68] *MOC*, 49.

of God has its fountainhead.⁶⁹ 'Only at that point where in Jesus Christ the Incarnate Word is *homoousios* with us in our nature and *homoousios* with God in his divine Being', Torrance contends, 'is there a real revelation and therefore a knowing of God, which really derives from the eternal Being of God as he is in Himself'.⁷⁰ 'The *homoousion* is the ontological and epistemological linchpin of Christian theology.'⁷¹ If a 'relation in being' with God is required for an appropriate understanding of him then surely that relation which inheres in the person of Christ – *homoousios* with us in our nature and *homoousios* with God in his – must be the *plenus locus* of that knowledge. In the divine-human life of Christ, the divine object reveals himself in a manner that permits man to know him not only from man's side, but also from God's side.⁷² In Christ 'the revealing of God and the understanding of man [have] fully coincided'.⁷³ Torrance says, 'It is, therefore, in the hypostatic reality of Jesus Christ who is consubstantial *(homoousios)* with the ultimate being of God as he is in himself, that human theological inquiry may by the grace of God find its *point of entry* into genuine knowledge of God.'⁷⁴

The question of our own personal 'entry' into the knowledge of God is that which concerns us and sacramental theology most acutely. For it is one thing for the human mind of Christ to be informed by the divine mind, quite another for us to know God in this way. From man's perspective this knowledge is 'closed to him' because he is 'imprisoned in the closed circle of his own estrangement and self-will'.⁷⁵ There can be then 'no possibility for man to really know God unless he can be taken [by God] into [this] closed polarity where such knowledge is to be realised'.⁷⁶ Torrance, however, insists that this has now been opened for us in two respects: first, as we have just indicated, by God himself, who through the incarnation has broken into the 'closed circle' of our epistemological inability and inadequacy and from 'within our alien condition achieved and established real knowledge of himself'; secondly, by enabling us personally and 'freely [to] participate in the

---

⁶⁹ 1 Cor. 1:30.
⁷⁰ *R/st*, 214.
⁷¹ Thomas F. Torrance, *The Ground and Grammar of Theology* (Belfast, Christian Journals Ltd, 1980), 160-61.
⁷² Cf. *TS*, 165.
⁷³ *MOC*, 19.
⁷⁴ *R/n*, 255, italics mine.
⁷⁵ *TS*, 50.
⁷⁶ Ibid. 50.

knowledge of God as an actuality already translated and made accessible for us by his grace'.⁷⁷ How Torrance conceives the means whereby we 'actually' participate in the knowledge of God will demonstrate the essential role that the doctrine of the Spirit plays in his overall epistemological method and ultimately as well in his sacramental theology. This knowledge is gained 'only through sharing in the knowledge of the Son by the Father and the knowledge of the Father by the Son'.⁷⁸ Man's knowledge of God is never more or other than Christ's knowledge of God. Our participation in this knowing relation between the Son and his Father is based on the work of the Holy Spirit, who is given by the Father and proceeds into man from out of the depths of Christ's own knowledge of God. Torrance asserts that 'how we know God and what we know of Him are inseparable'. He speaks out of a pneumatology which understands the act and being of the Spirit as indivisible from that of the Father and the Son. For man thus 'to *be* in the Spirit is to *be* in God, for the Spirit is not external but internal to the Godhead'.⁷⁹

It is the Spirit who speaks the truth of God within man directly from the knowing of God in the mind of Christ. He it is who, according to Torrance, specifically creates in us 'the capacity to hear and see' the things of God.⁸⁰ 'The Creator Spirit is God in his freedom to be present to the creature and to realise the relation of the creature to Himself in being and life.'⁸¹ Formally, however, that relation as such is created or constituted not in the Spirit, but in

---

⁷⁷ Ibid. 51.

⁷⁸ Ibid. 138. Torrance points out that for Athanasius it was uniquely the relation between the Father and the Son that constituted the 'epistemological heart of... theology' (*R/n*, 240). We know God only as we share with the Incarnate Son his knowledge of God. Man's knowledge is a participatory knowledge. Our knowledge of God cannot be said to be precisely equivalent to Christ's knowledge of God in his humanity, due to our creaturely limitations, but it is exclusively restricted to *his* knowledge of God. He says, 'Knowledge of God the Father and knowledge of Jesus Christ the incarnate Son of the Father arise in us together, not one without the other. We do not know the Father apart from the Son, for there is no Father but the Father of the Son. Nor do we know any Son of God apart from the Father, for there is no Son of God but the Son of the Father.... Thus we come to know the Son and the Father, the Father and the Son, in one indivisible movement of knowing... grounded in and governed by the mutual relation in being [and] in knowing which the Father and the Son have with one another' (*MOC*, 65).

⁷⁹ *R/n*, 239.

⁸⁰ *R/st*, 226.

⁸¹ *RP*, 23; cf. *SOF*, LVI; *CD* I.1, 515ff.

Christ. In the economy of God it is the Spirit who enables man to know and enjoy God out of the knowing relation Christ has with his Father. It is this christological relation that the Spirit 'realizes' in us. This demonstrates what Torrance calls 'the simultaneity of knowledge of God in his Son and the enlightenment of the Spirit'.[82] In this relation to God through Christ and in the Spirit the ontological and intellectual aspects of truth are held inseparably together, i.e. what God is really like and our thinking about him, respectively. Torrance says, 'It is from the Son that the spirit *shines forth* and *in the Spirit* that God is known.'[83]

Man's knowledge of God is conceived and sustained within the relation in being which Christ has with his Father.[84] Hence, Torrance says, it is 'open to all men, but... accessible and communicable only through a relation of each to Him'.[85] His doctrine of participation in Christ through the Spirit reveals the completion of this thought. The Spirit is himself the presence of God to us in his own being, proceeding out of his relationship with Christ. Consequently, by his relation with us in our being, he affords us access to God as he is known in the mind of Christ. By participation in Christ Torrance never means more than this kind of relation or *koinonia* but never anything less than a relation in being as we have defined it.[86] 'To know the Truth', he insists, is 'to be actively participant in it' and it is just such a mutual and personal indwelling as this suggests which the Spirit offers us in the sacrament.[87] The Eucharist parallels that aspect of the Church's relation to God which Paul describes as 'Christ in us'.[88] From his earliest writings on the subject, Torrance delineates his eucharistic doctrine in terms of the Church's intimate participation in Christ through this 'communion in the Holy Spirit'.[89] Torrance draws eucharistic and knowing participation together explicitly, commenting on the economy of the Church's being united in its worship with the rational worship of the ascended Christ: 'Through his vicarious self-consecration and oblation on our behalf... we are enabled to *share with him his mind*, and be associated with him in his priestly presentation of us in and through

---

[82] *R/st*, 224.
[83] Ibid. 215.
[84] *MOC*, 63–4.
[85] *TS*, 302.
[86] *R/st*, 185–6, cf. 215; *TS*, 143.
[87] *TS*, 87.
[88] *Inter*, 305.
[89] Cf. ibid. 311; *R/n*, 109.

himself to the Father.'[90] Eucharistic participation may thus be seen to play a significant role in the whole process of the Church's assimilation of truth.[91]

2. The Systematic Ordering of the Knowledge of God

(a) The Intuitive Apprehension of the Truth

As Torrance understands it, 'theological science shares with other sciences a generally recognised scientific procedure based on the principle of objectivity'.[92] The scientist is radically committed to the facts as they are set out in the object of inquiry. Such 'objective thinking' implies, on the negative side, a refusal to bring to the object any foregone conclusions or external hypotheses that would prejudice the inquiry. On the positive side, it requires an exclusive devotion to the inherent evidence offered by the object.[93] 'It is the very devotion of theology to its proper object', he says, 'that is the scientific passion of theology'.[94] Though all sciences have a general procedure in common, the dissimilarity between the nature of the objects proper to the physical and theological sciences requires different kinds of interrogation. It is the difference, he says, between 'discovery' and 'revelation'. In the natural sciences the object is speechless, the scientist being obliged to frame not only the questions put to it, but its answers back as well. In theological science, however, it is all very different. For 'we do not have to do with a mute or dumb reality (that would be an idol), but with one

---

[90] *R/n*, 113, italics mine.

[91] Cf. *TS*, 148.

[92] *TS*, 112; cf. *CD* I.1, 315ff., esp. 316. All sciences are pledged to keep faith with their object. Further, 'in proper theological thinking we have to act within the boundary imposed upon us by the nature of the object' (*TS*, 129).

[93] *TS*, 129.

[94] Ibid. 55. Torrance qualifies the use of the term 'objectivity'. He contests its usual connotation implying 'detachment' from the object of enquiry. The scientist is to be 'detached' certainly, but from his own predispositions towards the object. In fact, the word 'objectivity' indicates for Torrance a rigorous commitment to the object itself, restricting scientists' judgement to only that which the object itself evidences. As he puts it, what the theological or physical scientist does is to 'subject to doubt... his own assumptions about the object and so... allows *attachment* to the object to help him detach himself from his own presuppositions'. This is what Torrance means by 'objective thinking' (*G & R*, 8, italics mine).

who acts upon us and addresses us in his word, where the expressions "reveal itself" and "declare itself" are really in place'.[95] For Torrance the divine-human person of Christ, the Living Word, stands as the sole object of theological investigation; there can be therefore no positivistic mastery of the human subject over the divine-human object.[96]

Man's knowing of God is for Torrance 'essentially a rational event' but one which originates not in the power of the mind of man to know God but in God who makes himself known.[97] It is 'Reason [communicating] itself to reason'.[98] The *logos* or reason of God prescribes for our thinking about him unique and precise modes out of, and corresponding to, his own 'intelligible, specific reality'.[99] To know... God is to partake of his rationality', Torrance says. It is in this sense that he can speak of the theological scientist becoming 'more fully rational' and the theological exercise itself possessing a supremely rational character.[100]

'Intuition' is the term which Torrance uses to connote man's apprehension of the truth of God, or, more appropriately, the apprehension of man by that truth. It does not indicate, as the word itself might suggest, any autonomous power of the mind – the *'intellectus agens'* – or some innate, supra-rational faculty to assimilate truth by sudden mystical insight.[101] There is no abrogation or 'diminishing of rational powers' in our acquisition of theological knowledge.[102] The term underlines the noetic surrender of the knowing subject before 'the sheer weight or impress of external reality upon his apprehension'.[103] However, this is not meant to imply that 'intuition' consists merely in our being suddenly grasped

---

[95] *G & R*, 200.

[96] Theology 'must not try to seek knowledge of God apart from His whole objectivity, divine and human, in Jesus Christ.... We are concerned with only one of its kind – *deus non est in genere*'. The Incarnate Word alone is the object of a scientific theology (*TS*, 138-9).

[97] *TS*, 11.

[98] *KBI*, 100.

[99] *TS*, 292. 'Theological activity is a rational act', he says, one 'answering to the nature and rationality of its object' (*KBI*, 187).

[100] *TS*, 11, fn. 1. In the theological endeavour 'we behave rationally' when we start to think and to 'act in accordance with the nature of the object' (*G & R*, 199).

[101] *R/st*, 68.

[102] *TS*, 54, cf.11; Thomas F. Torrance, 'Reason in Christian Theology', *EvQ* 14 (1942), 29-30.

[103] *TS*, 111.

by the obviousness of the truth. For Torrance truth is not so much intellectual material but rather a living intelligibility in dialogue with us. Theological truth is self-evidencing, not just obvious. This suggests a decisive, revelatory act by God upon the human mind.[104] Man intuits knowledge when the Word finally 'seizes our minds and sets up within them the law of its own rationality'.[105] Although he is never 'coerced' in the knowing relation, the force of the truth is such in its self-evidence that man is brought under, what Torrance calls, 'the compulsion of [God's] divine Being... coming to view and becoming in our understanding and knowledge of Him what He is consistently in Himself and in all His relations with us'.[106] The term 'intuition', then, finally implies both the 'intelligible self-evidenc[ing] of the divine reality' and the 'apprehension and intellectual consent which [that] compels in us'.[107]

Although the self-disclosing character of the truth requires a corresponding personal reception of it, that truth also demands that the divine objectivity should not be submerged or lost in the subjectivity of the knower. For all the necessity of an internal apprehension of truth on our part, no matter how intimate the relation between God and man becomes in its communication, the truth itself always remains external to our knowing faculty. When Torrance speaks of the 'sheer objectivity' of God, he is highlighting two facts: first, the radical self-existence of God's truth in revelation, and secondly, the unyielding transcendence of that truth in relation to the human mind. Torrance cannot contemplate 'the activity of the knower entering into the actual content of the knowledge of God itself'.[108] The Word of God to man is and will remain, he insists, 'a word... from *beyond* our subjective experience'.[109] At the same time, however, he insists that 'our activity in knowing the truth is part of that knowledge'. Such a statement simply reinforces his point that

---

[104] Cf. ibid. 29–30; *KBI*, 111.
[105] *G & R*, 21; Roger Newell, 'Participatory Knowledge', 196.
[106] *TS*, 143.
[107] *G & R*, 21.
[108] *TS*, 85.
[109] Ibid. 30, italics mine. Statements like this make it patently clear how wrong Mary Agnew, a researcher into Torrance's eucharistic theology, is in her assessment of Torrance's epistemology: '[For Torrance] the fundamental source of the content of theology is the personal experience of God in faith' (Mary Agnew, 'The Concept of Sacrament in the Eucharistic Theology of Donald M. Baillie, Thomas F. Torrance, and Jean-Jacques von Allmen' (unpublished doctoral thesis, The Catholic University of America, Ann Arbor: University Microfilms, 1972), 198).

our vital participation in the knowing of God in Christ is essential to our reception of that knowledge. We cannot know God 'outside' of the one in whom it is given.[110]

(b) The Christological Pattern of the Truth

The controlling fact of the *homoousion* – that God is in Christ what he is inherently and eternally in his own Being – coupled with Torrance's understanding of the intuition of the knowledge of God, has profound implications for the definitive formulation of doctrine, and, as we will see, especially for the doctrine of the sacrament.[111] For if that which is presented to us objectively in the act of revelation is really subjective to the being of God, then our intuition of that revealing Word is equivalent to our minds being informed by the inward logic and coherence of the mind of God itself. Torrance therefore believes it is actually possible for the human mind to be taught to order its thoughts so that they manifest a rational uniformity and consistency corresponding to that which is immanent to the divine *Logos*. This is not achieved by our intellectual ability to order information but by the Word ordering our thoughts according to his own inherent order. 'The order', Torrance says, 'is in the Object before it is in our minds, and therefore it is as we allow the Object to impose itself on our minds that our knowledge of it gains coherence.'[112] In the divine-human person of Christ we 'penetrate into the inner *ratio* and *necessitas* of the object of our knowledge..., into the ontic *ratio* which is both created truth within our world and yet the uncreated truth of God, the *ratio fidei* and the *ratio veritatis* in one'.[113] The concept of participation explicated above facilitates in Torrance's method just such internal access to the truth suggested by this notion of 'penetration'. Parallel to this, but employing stark connotations of ecclesial passivity, Torrance states that the Church is to 'come under the power of the inherent rationality of the *Logos* of God' and begin to think 'from a centre in God' by its intuitive interaction with the divine mind in Christ. Such a theology of the Word, therefore, manifests its own 'inner rationality' derived from the Word.[114] The

---

[110] *TS*, 87; *R/n*, 239; cf. *TS*, 100.

[111] Cf. *G & G*, 40–41.

[112] *TS*, 138.

[113] *KBI*, 195.

[114] *R/st*, 55; *KBI*, 100; *TS*, 29, 199; Thomas F. Torrance, 'Hermeneutics of St. Athanasius', *Ekklesiastikos Pharos* 52 (1970), 446–8; cf. *G & G*, 155.

goal of a scientific theology, he says, is 'to develop from within the actual content of theology its own interior logic and its own inner criticism'.[115]

To order our reason after the inner *ratio* of Christ means more for Torrance than just to systematize the teachings of the historic Jesus, or even to discover a cohering principle inherent within those teachings as such. Neither is he interested in the formal ordering of truths about Jesus by the imposition upon them of 'alien principles' originating outside the ontic reality of Christ himself. Although all scientific, theological thinking has a 'systematic interest, for it must attempt to order the material content of its knowledge... into a coherent whole', our statements about the truth must always be checked and refined by strict and continual reference to the truth itself.[116] To think otherwise is to reduce the truth to ideas and thus to distance the truth from the person of Christ.[117] In the final analysis, Torrance conceives the intention of systematic theology not as the systematization of the truth (for the truth does not lack order), but the systematization of our thinking about the truth through intuitive interaction and dialogue with it.

Torrance demonstrates the result of this kind of thinking by the historical development in the Church of the doctrines of the *homoousion* and the Trinity. He speaks of these as the basic 'grammar of theology', by which he means the way God speaks to us about himself and hence the way we should form our thoughts and speech about him.[118] These two doctrines comprise for Torrance the most essential statements by the truth about itself and from which

---

[115] *TS*, 7. Systematic truth must never be thought of simply as 'the logical-syntactical relation of statements' about it, for the logic of our statements about the truth is determined only by strict and continual reference of those statements to the truth itself (Roger Newell, 'Participatory Knowledge', 194). Theology is '*theo*logical', Torrance insists, meaning that its inner coherence actually obtains in the inherent logic of God himself (*TS*, 29). In a truly '*theo*logical' theology we are obliged to 'use only those concepts which can be co-ordinated as truly as possible with the given reality' (*TS*, 119).

[116] *TS*, 138. Torrance speaks in the same language with respect to natural science: 'Science can be described as the activity in which we investigate things and events for the order or regularity they manifest in their interconnections in the attempt to reduce the manifold of relations in the world, or at least in some field of experience, to some kind of uniformity, and if possible to penetrate down to a unitary logical basis in our understanding of them through which the whole field of our experience can be illuminated' (*G & R*, 11).

[117] Roger Newell, 'Participatory Knowledge', 194.

[118] *G & G*, 155.

the Church can think out the broader implications of God's activity in the Church and in the world – 'paradigmatic concepts', he calls them.[119] It might be thought that in elevating these doctrines to such a plenary interpretative position above the rest he is committing precisely the error he warns against, viz. shaping theology by imported principles. On the contrary, he argues that these systematic and systematizing ways of thinking about God arise from the subject matter of theology itself, being 'forced upon the understanding of the Church' as it allows the self-interpretation of God through the 'biblical witness to imprint its own patterns upon its mind'.[120]

In the divine-human objectivity we find ourselves confronted with the very subjectivity of God to himself, i.e. not only the relation of the Word as man to the Word as God, but also the Incarnate Word within the inner relations of the Holy Trinity.[121] This however is not conceived as a quiescent fact simply to be contemplated but a vital revelatory act into which we as subjects of revelation are caught up. God's self-disclosing movement in the world is a multi-relational, inter-personal event – 'from the Father, through the Son, and in the Spirit'. Correspondingly, we apprehend the knowledge of God through an epistemological excursion into the inter-relations of that operation – 'in the Spirit, through the Son, and to the Father'.[122] Torrance insists that it is imperative for the theological scientist to let his mind '[fall] under the inherent pattern (εἶδος) of the Godhead

---

[119] Cf. *TS*, 239.

[120] *R/st*, 40.

[121] 'We are given to share in the knowledge which God has of himself within himself as Father and Son or Son and Father, which is part of what is meant by our knowing God through the Spirit of God who is in him and whom he sends to us through the Son' (*MOC*, 65).

[122] *G & G*, 155. 'We may know only in accordance with the steps he has taken in revealing himself to us and the steps he has taken in reconciling us to himself, through the incarnation of his Son within the ontological structures of our human existence in this world, in such a way that he sets up within it the laws of his own internal relations and our rational understanding takes on the imprint of what it is given to know, the triune Reality of God himself. To know this God, who both condescends to share all that we are and makes us share in all that he is in Jesus Christ, is to be lifted up in his Spirit to share in God's own self-knowing and self-loving until we are enabled to apprehend him in some real measure in himself beyond anything that we are capable of in ourselves. It is to be lifted out of ourselves, as it were, into God, until we know him and love him and enjoy him in his eternal Reality as Father, Son, and Holy Spirit in such a way that the Trinity enters into the fundamental fabric of our thinking of him and constitutes the basic grammar of our worship and knowledge of the One God' (*G & G*, 155).

as he is in his own interior relations'.¹²³ 'The Object... must prescribe the mode of activity of the reason directed toward it.'¹²⁴ We must learn to think from the Trinity in its act (economic Trinity) to the Trinity in its being (immanent Trinity), i.e. to formulate our patterns of thought about God himself in a way appropriate to the active nature of his revelation. This is what Torrance calls 'thinking inside the inner-movement of the Truth'.¹²⁵ Hence Torrance is bound to couch his theology as a whole and his sacramental theology in particular in immanent and dynamic categories.¹²⁶

3. The Implications for the Eucharist

It is the incarnation, therefore, considered, as suggested above, analytically or in terms of its 'own interior and active logic', which provides for Torrance 'the systematic principle' for arranging the Church's thoughts and exposition about God and his involvement with his creation. His engagement of this principle is nowhere more obvious or exemplified than in his eucharistic theology.¹²⁷

At this point, however, Torrance issues a predictable warning against reductionism of two kinds. In the first place, while admitting that 'some formal use of Christology is necessary in systematic theology', Christ must not be, indeed cannot be, reduced to a formal abstract principle. When he speaks of systematic principles he is never thinking of formulae which can somehow be abstracted 'from direct dialogical encounter with God in Christ'. Scientific theology is systematic, he insists, because rational man abides in personal

---

[123] *R/n*, 251.

[124] *TS*, 139.

[125] Ibid. 127-8; cf. *TS*, 7.

[126] In saying this it should not be thought that in Torrance's method the doctrine of Christ ever 'graduates' into the doctrine of God or only takes us so far in order to deliver us to a higher or deeper way of thinking. The Church never takes its eyes off the Incarnate Word to gaze upon the Godhead. He is our window into God. 'The incarnation', he says, 'constitutes the epistemological centre in all our knowledge of God, with a centre in our world of space and time and a centre in God himself at the same time' (*G & G*, 165). We have no other way to behold God and cannot look upon him except in the person of Christ. Torrance puts it: 'Now it is because we do not know the Father or the Son except through the revealing and reconciling work of Jesus Christ, that our knowledge of the Father and the Son and of the Holy Spirit is, as it were, a function of our knowledge of Jesus Christ' (*MOC*, 65).

[127] *R/st*, 39; *SOF*, L; *TS*, 138-9; cf. *SOF*, LXI.

relation with Christ and learns in that relation to think with him his thoughts his way.[128] Systematic theology, then, corresponding to the 'logic of grace', is seen not as the static possession of the Church, but as a vital, rational gift, given within man's perpetual relation and dialogue with God.[129] Secondly, Torrance warns the Church against 'the reduction of every other doctrine to Christology'. Although he never qualifies his axiom that 'Christology is all determining in the knowledge of God', he insists that what is being put forward here as a systematic principle is not meant to transform all theological questions into christological ones. He draws a fine line between making every theological issue a statement of christology and allowing christology to comment upon and emerge as finally decisive in all these issues. Torrance speaks of christology employed in this way as 'an interpretative frame (or)... instrument' in our ordering of the knowledge of God.[130] His sacramental thought will demonstrate this very well. It will also put his theological method rigorously to the test; for if a theology is so totally preconditioned by and preoccupied with christology can it keep from collapsing altogether into it? Though such an overview at this juncture will raise many questions prematurely, let us nevertheless preview how Torrance will implement this normative incarnational principle in resolving some of the basic issues raised by sacramental theology. As to the interaction of divine and creaturely realities in the sacramental union, it is the relation of those realities in Christ which will tell the possibility and set the limits. Torrance will qualify the historic question of *Res* and *Signum*, first by discarding any notion of unreality or symbol in Christ's humanity, and then by positing the whole divine-human person as the living referent and active witness to himself in the sacramental analogy. The sacrament's matter and action he will define as the salvation constituted and completed by the Word in his divine humanity and now incorporated in his risen life. With respect to the real presence, it is the enduring integrity of

---

[128] *TS*, 138. A systematic theology can only be developed in the Church, as we have observed, through continual dynamic interaction with the person of Christ. Therefore, neither can the Church's knowing relation to Christ, nor the christological formulations annunciated within that relation be 'turned into an independent systematic principle by means of which we can form the whole of theology into one definite and fixed pattern' (*TS*, 138).

[129] Cf. *KBI*, 186. 'Revelation', Torrance says, 'must be continually given and received in a living relationship with God' (*R & E*, 16). 'The creature does not have a continuity in relation to God that belongs to the creature in itself, for this is continuously given and sustained by the presence of the Spirit' (*R/st*, 223).

[130] *SOF*, LXIII; cf. *The Incarnation*, XII-XIII; *TS*, 127.

the ascended Christ in his human as well as his divine natures which will both require for the sacrament the presence of *totus Christus* and condition the manner of that presence. Finally, concerning the Church's eucharistic sacrifice, Torrance will delineate the perfect human and doxological response of the Incarnate Word to the love of the Father as that which both embodies the objective reality of the Church's worship as well as calls forth and realizes its subjectification in the Church.

These are ways in which Torrance applies his basic christological frame of reference to different areas of eucharistic theology. However, just as formative for our discussion are the two primary incarnational models around which he systematically constructs his sacramental thought. The first pattern, observed from Torrance's earliest works on the Eucharist and never discarded, is that of 'union with Christ'. In the incarnation, he says, Christ is united to us; in the sacrament, we are united to him.[131] These are properly speaking not two unions but one, the latter being understood as the re-presentation in the life of the Church of the former. In the *unio hypostatica* Christ has brought all men vicariously 'in his flesh and blood' into reconciling relation to God. In the *unio sacramentalis* that christological union is reiterated 'in our flesh and blood', in the mutual relation of brothers to God in Christ. The Church's union with Christ is realized because of and out of his union with us through the gift of the Holy Spirit. Torrance will speak both of that christological union being given to the Church in the sacrament as well as of the Church being united to it through sacramental participation.[132] Either way the sum of it is the same: our holy communion consists in the uniting of the Church in space-time with the Holy Communion of God and man embodied in the ascended Christ. In this tableau the Church in its union with God is set in relief against the primary union of God and man in Christ, with the Holy Spirit being the divine co-ordinator between them. The Spirit is he who unites the earthly and heavenly realities, the one who realizes among us a communion which is already a vicarious fact in Christ.

Most recently Torrance has preferred a second model by which to frame his eucharistic theology, viz. 'the mediation of Christ', specifically as it is accomplished within his divine-human person. The sacramental union, he says, is best understood by thinking of it in relation to the reciprocal movement of Christ's priesthood, viz. as

---

[131] *MOC*, 101.
[132] Cf. *Inter*, 320.

God to man and as man to God. The central 'events' of the sacrament, the real presence and the eucharistic sacrifice, are said to correspond to these two dispositional aspects of Christ's mediation. However, the relation is not just a comparative one. Indeed, he insists that the Eucharist takes its impetus from the strength of that mediation. God's gift of himself through Christ in the sacrament (the real presence) as well as the gift of ourselves to God through Christ there (the eucharistic sacrifice), he suggests, are both offered as the Church is drawn right into the inner operation of Christ's priestly work and hence into the inner relations of the Trinity itself, which inhere within the person of the High Priest.

When first observed, these two models might appear to have little in common, but in fact the first is foundational for the second, its underlying assertions always presumed. They both arise, as Torrance would put it, from the same 'centre'.[133] While neither of the patterns can be said to be static or external to the person of Christ, the first focuses primarily upon the union of the divine and human natures in the incarnation over against our sacramental union with him, whereas the second is concerned more with the inter-relations immanent in his divine-human person and the involvement of the Church in its sacramental union in them. When Torrance employs the earlier model he seeks to discern and explicate meanings from the incarnation considered in its related 'parts'; in the latter he does so as it were from within the dynamic life of that mystery itself. This demonstrates a growing preference in Torrance's theology for more internal and active metaphors with respect to Christ. It is also consistent with his requirement, just laid down, that an inquiry into the revealed reality is only correctly carried out when done so in conformity with 'the inner relations', or after 'the interior logic' of the living objectivity.

The contrast between these two models here also illustrates the increasing significance of the concept of the mediation of Christ as a theme in Torrance's eucharistic theology, as well as the growing importance rendered to the humanity of Christ within that mediation. These, however, have always been crucial in the explication of his epistemology. From his earliest writings Torrance has spoken of the mediation of knowledge within the person of Christ. In 1955, in *Royal Priesthood*, he suggested that God and man know each other in a primal sense through the mediation of God's Word to man and man's response to that Word (as our word to God)

---

[133] Cf. *G & G*, 165.

within the person of the High Priest.[134] A decade later, in *Theological Science*, he observed 'a twofold movement' of knowledge inhering in the Incarnate Son, 'from the side of the object known and from the side of the knower'.[135] Revelation and the reception of that revelation have always been for Torrance 'a bi-polar act of the God-man', with the initiation of God and the response of man gathered up, united and mediated, all within the person of Christ.[136] This dynamic mediatorial model, employed early on in his epistemological thought, does not in fact find its way fully into his sacramental theology until the mid 70s. Earlier works on the sacrament do indicate, however, that he had begun to think in this direction. In *Conflict and Agreement*, published in 1960, he spoke of our eucharistic communion having 'two "moments"': 'the first... is that of the receiving [God's] gift of Himself in all that He has done on our behalf', and the second 'involves a union with [Christ] in the whole of His obedient Self-oblation to the Father'.[137] Undoubtedly, the idea is already incipient here, but these 'two moments' in the Eucharist took nearly twenty years to be expanded into the 'two-fold movement' already explicit in his epistemology. By the writing of 'The Paschal Mystery of Christ and the Eucharist' in 1975, however, this formal mediatorial theme is fully integrated into his eucharistic theology.[138]

THE THEOLOGICAL BASIS FOR GOD'S INTERACTION WITH THE WORLD

I. The Christological Ground and Implications for Sacramental Theology

The fact of God's interaction with the world is fundamental to sacramental theology, since any view of the Eucharist which would

---

[134] Cf. *RP*, 15.

[135] *TS*, 45.

[136] Cf. *R/st*, 130.

[137] Thomas F. Torrance, *Conflict and Agreement in the Church* (London, Lutterworth, 1960), vol. 2, 147.

[138] The essay 'The Paschal Mystery of Christ and the Eucharist' represents Torrance's latest and most fully developed major work on the sacrament. It was originally prepared for the Reformed/Roman Catholic Study Commission in 1974 and was then published as a chapter in *Theology in Reconciliation* in 1975.

aspire higher than 'bare symbolism' presupposes at least some degree of intercourse between the Creator and his creatures. For his part, Torrance holds to a mutual interaction of these realities within the sacramental relation, one that is both real and intimate, indeed unparalleled in the Church.[139] Although, as we will discover, he is preoccupied primarily in the *unio sacramentalis* with the personal relation between God and his people, that relation is envisaged as inclusive of other created constituents. Torrance states: 'We are concerned [in the Eucharist] with the real presence of Christ... in the spatial and temporal conditions of our bodily and historical existence.... There are spatial and temporal ingredients in a proper understanding of the real presence which have to be taken seriously.'[140] By 'spatial and temporal ingredients', he undoubtedly means more than (from the Church's side) 'the bread and wine of the table', or (from Christ's side) a presence considered only 'in... body and blood'.[141] What he is saying is that a proper understanding of the Eucharist does not ignore any of these. For, as will become clear, there is nothing in the nature of God that is revolted by the lowliness of his creatures and nothing in the Eucharist that is not open-ended towards its Creator and through which he cannot move to apprehend his people.

The fundamental difficulties in western eucharistic theology, as Torrance sees it, result from the Church's understanding the sacraments on the basis of the preconceived notion of a dualism between God and the world.[142] Consequently, the Church has often found itself lacking adequate theological and/or cosmological categories with which to conceive a Creator/creation relation in which God is ontologically and maximally free to interact with his people. For Torrance everything depends upon this divine prerogative. Indeed, the very 'possibility of our knowing God is grounded in His divine freedom to cross the boundary between himself and us and give himself to be known by us within the

---

[139] Cf. *Inter*, 337.

[140] *R/n*, 121.

[141] Ibid. 121.

[142] Indeed, Torrance will go so far as to say: All theologies 'may be divided into two distinct types which... may be called 'inter-actionist' and 'dualist'. By an interactionist theology I mean one in which God is thought of as interacting closely with the world of nature and history without being confused with it, and by a dualist theology I mean one in which God is thought of as separate from the world of nature and history by a measure of deistic distance' (Thomas F. Torrance, *Transformation and Convergence in the Frame of Knowledge* (Belfast, Christian Journals Ltd, 1984), 285).

conditions of our frailty on earth'.[143] Similarly, the meaning and efficacy of the Church's Eucharist within that knowing process also depends upon it. 'A damaged understanding of the relation of God to the world', he asserts, 'affects our understanding of the self-giving of God to us in Jesus Christ, for it refracts the inherent oneness of the Giver and the Gift, and so alters the way in which we conceive the real presence'.[144] In other words, unless the Church's understanding of God and creation can facilitate a personal encounter with God in his being and act in the world, that which will be perceived as present in the sacrament will necessarily be something different from God in his self-giving and therefore something less than grace. Moreover, if the Church's theology in general does not allow God to be actively and substantially present in his world, then its eucharistic theology will make the bread and wine in the context of the Church's sacramental action a substantial 'substitute' approximate to his presence, or a 'created intermediary' of it.[145] He further states that if the Church does not profess a genuine meeting in the sacrament between God and his Church, then it will inevitably attribute the significance of the sacrament to either 'the rite itself and its performance or [to] the inward and moral experience of the participant'.[146]

Dualism and real presence are mutually exclusive ideas, the former only being uprooted by a sound, christologically based affirmation of the latter. The question of the real presence is at the heart of the problem – not just the real presence of Christ in the Eucharist but rather the reality of God himself coming into the world and co-existing with it whenever and wherever he will without compromising his own or the created integrity.[147] In the incarnation that fact was established and in the resurrection and ascension has become an enduring reality. 'The Incarnation of the Son of God in our human being and existence... is', he says, 'the direct interaction (*energeia*) of God himself within our creaturely world, and the real presence (*parousia*) of his eternal being within space and time, in Jesus Christ'.[148] Furthermore, just 'as the Incarnation meant the

---

[143] *TS*, 49–50.
[144] *R/n*, 131.
[145] Ibid. 131.
[146] Ibid. 130–31.
[147] Cf. Thomas F. Torrance, 'Doctrinal Consensus on Holy Communion: The Arnoldshain Theses', *SJT* 15 (1962), 12–13; Thomas F. Torrance, *Space, Time and Incarnation* (OUP, 1978), 30.
[148] *R/n*, 130.

entry of the Son into space and time without the loss of God's transcendence over space and time, so the Ascension meant the transcendence of the Son of God over space and time without the loss of his incarnational involvement in space and time'.[149]

Accordingly, the divine/creaturely interaction claimed for the Church's Eucharist is understood by Torrance 'from a point of central reference in the Incarnation of the Word or Son of God' in the same way as it gives 'inner cohesion and structure to all Christian understanding'.[150] This is consistent with his methodological principle just related, viz. that all theology must be formally shaped in concepts consonant with God's self-disclosure in the Incarnate Word. Torrance singles out 'the doctrine of the Sacraments' as being especially served by what he calls 'Christological correction'. He narrows it further, saying that it is particularly the relation of 'The Divine Presence and the worldly element in the sacrament' which can be determined from this 'central relation and union of God and man of which every other relation must partake'.[151] The incarnation, then, serves eucharistic theology both as the guarantor of vital intercourse

---

[149] *STI*, 31. Torrance sees Luther's eucharistic theology as a clumsily alien, albeit courageous, attempt to 'nail' together ontologically 'the two kingdoms' of God and the world, the visible and the invisible ('The *hoc est corpus meum...* became for him the ontological nail that held the two kingdoms together, and made possible real participation of one in the other', *STI*, 34). The great German Reformer was forced to such radical measures by the equally radical conclusions in the other directions drawn up by the sacramentarians. The latter, as Torrance sees it and as we will discuss presently, made their deductions from an inveterate Augustinian dualism and an Aristotelian view of space and time (cf. *R/n*, 127-8; *STI*, 30-31). Unfortunately, Luther's sacramental theology was allowed to dictate his christology, rather than the other way round, as it should have been to Torrance's mind. This was a common approach already in Western medieval theology, which tended to think out its understanding of God's presence in space and time 'not primarily as in the East from a consideration of creation and incarnation but from a consideration of the real presence of Christ in the Mass on the one hand and from a consideration of cosmology on the other hand' (*STI*, 25, cf. 32, 34). Luther's doctrine, for its part, was formulated in a decidedly Monophysite complexion, after that manifest in his doctrine of the real presence (*STI*, 62). In contrast to Luther, who thought out God's interaction with the world from his interaction with his people in the Sacrament of the Altar, the incarnation is Torrance's standard. That mystery for Torrance, however, is no artificial clamp holding God and his world together. Indeed it is, as we have indicated, a statement of the way God is disposed toward the world in creation and redeeming grace, as well as the way the world is made to interact with him (cf. *TS*, 67).

[150] *R/n*, 264.

[151] *SOF*, LXII; *R/st*, 114.

with God within the sacramental relation, and as the standard for measuring the limits of that relation.

(a) Some Hebraic and Patristic Groundwork

It is a neo-Platonic/Augustinian style dualism, which Torrance sees as impairing the Western Church's doctrines of God and creation in general and its sacramental theology in particular. The specifics of this sort of disparity between God and the world will be addressed more fully later. Generally speaking, it arose from the notion of a God handicapped by his inability to create reality wholly independent of himself and therefore to act personally or objectively upon the world. In such a view God tended to be understood as only abstractly related to creation and creation in turn only symbolically related to him. In the Church's eucharistic theology these ideas presented themselves in the form of a severe transcendentalism which set the material element of the sacrament over against the so-called spiritual element in wholly symbolist and subordinationist categories.

Torrance counters these misconceptions from a wholly different, non-Hellenic base, viz. out of what he understands as a Hebraic and patristic world-view. He insists that formative Jewish thought and, subsequently, that of many early Greek Fathers, most notably Athanasius and Cyril of Alexandria, allowed for 'God's providential interaction with the world of nature', working as they did from a 'unitary, non-dualistic understanding of the universe'.[152] In order to grasp the full implications of this with regard to God's intercourse with the world – 'The closest possible relationships between divine and human activity' – he contends that the Church must interrelate 'conceptually the complementary meanings of a decidedly Jewish doctrine of creation *ex nihilo* with a decidedly patristic doctrine of the incarnation'.[153] Such a doctrine of creation establishes that the Creator Word did not call the world into being out of any primordial substance, either divine or previously created, conferring upon it a unique identity distinct from his own. The doctrine of the incarnation, while establishing the intensity and extent of the inter-relations possible between God and creation, also demonstrates the impossibilities within such a relation. For even in the innermost reaches of the hypostatic union, neither reality is submerged or lost

---

[152] *R/n*, 28–9; 'Israel', 6.
[153] *R/n*, 28; 'Israel', 6–8; cf. *R/n*, 126.

in the other.¹⁵⁴ The incarnation has demonstrably and stubbornly upheld each reality in its own dignity in relation to the other.¹⁵⁵ Only when these two doctrines are considered together, says Torrance, can the distinction God has established between himself and the world and the freedom he has to interact with it be held jointly and without contradiction. The doctrines stand, as it were, at either end of creation, delineating together the bounds of the Creator/creation relation.¹⁵⁶

Torrance is convinced that the Reformation (he means primarily the Calvinist Reformation) sought to reclaim the prerogatives and restraints implicit in both these historic doctrines.¹⁵⁷ Even 'the resurgence of Augustinianism' in Reformation thought he does not see as contradicting this thesis. For it had a laudable motivation, viz. to reassert the clear ontological difference between divine and creaturely realities confused at the hand of the Aristotelians/Thomists.¹⁵⁸ This was, he claims, 'an Augustinianism with a difference', as it tended 'to move from mainly ontic to mainly dynamic modes of thought, evident in [the Reformation's] stress upon the interaction of the living God with the world of space and time'. For example, he shows how the Reformers re-stated the patristic identification of God's grace with the person of Christ, and the gift of his grace, whether in the sacraments or otherwise, with God's self-giving act in the world.¹⁵⁹ Torrance sees his own task, as

---

¹⁵⁴ He says there is 'a unity of Logos and Being in God in accordance with the unique nature of God, and [a] unity of logos and being in man in accordance with the utterly different creaturely nature of man'. 'What we are concerned with in theology is a field created by the interaction of the divine Logos who inheres in the Being of God and the world of created being on which God through creation has conferred intelligibility in such a way that there too, form inheres in being, and logos inheres in human being' (*R/n*, 249).

¹⁵⁵ *R/st*, 64; *R/n*, 137.

¹⁵⁶ 'Israel', 7.

¹⁵⁷ *TS*, 61, 68, 101; *R/n*, 126; *STI*, 37.

¹⁵⁸ Torrance will also commend the worthy intentions of the Thomists/Aristotelians in their attempt to hold form and matter, idea and event, concept and image together in the face of early Augustinian dualism (cf. *R/n*, 123; *TS*, 18).

¹⁵⁹ Cf. *TS*, 68. Torrance generally downplays the affect of Augustinianism upon Calvin's theology. He seems to be among the few Reformed scholars who does not see an implicit transcendentalist/voluntarist bias as a profound conditioning factor in Calvin's overall theology, and especially in his eucharistic theology. He contends that, for Calvin, 'The creation was not just the utterance of a rational fiat upon the part of God, which then left created being with an existence in itself, even if it was a derived existence. He thought of creation as

Calvin's before him, to maintain, on the one hand, the distinction between God and his creation, while, on the other hand, to uphold the optimal possibility for God's objective, personal act within it.[160] Let us then briefly and systematically restate those premises which Torrance says guided the Reformation's theology of nature and consequently conditioned its doctrine of the sacraments.[161] They will prove foundational for the rest of this chapter as well as crucial for our understanding of Torrance's sacramental theology as a whole.

(b) Some Reformation Premises

(i) The uncreated and created realities exist each in its own being distinctly, though the latter in a contingent way.

In the Reformation, Torrance says, men learned to think of the world as 'something utterly distinct' from God.[162] The Athanasian conviction that 'there is no likeness between the eternal Being of God and the being of created reality' was reclaimed and reasserted.[163] God was seen as beyond all created being, yet remaining being in his own

---

continuous and as continually depending on the communication of the divine Word, in such a way that it was maintained in being, and governed by immediate relation to the will of God' (*R/st*, 103). Torrance would, therefore, identify the symbolist and depreciatory motifs used by Calvin when referring to the relation of the material substance of the sacrament to its spiritual factor, as an employment of Augustinian language without its usual Augustinian connotations (e.g. *Inst* IV.14.3). Calvin's use of such an idiom would seem reasonable since the Augustinian terminology was acceptable on all fronts in his day and, for his purposes, most effective in the debate over what he considered a capitulation by the Lutherans and Roman Catholics to Monophysitism.

[160] *R/n*, 126. 'Reformed theology sought to assert the relation between Creator and creature, Grace and nature, in such a way as to repudiate any confusion or reversibility on the one hand and any separation or dichotomy on the other, for it took as its guide in understanding that relation the fulfilment of God's Covenant of Grace in Jesus Christ' (*TS*, 68).

[161] When Torrance speaks of 'the Reformation' in contexts such as these he is referring primarily to the Calvinist Reformation; the 'high Reformation' he calls it elsewhere (cf. Thomas E. Torrance, 'The Church in the New Era of Scientific and Cosmological Change', *N Coll B* 7, 1 (1973), 23).

[162] *R/st*, 63.

[163] *R/n*, 221. Torrance cites Athanasius, *Ad Serapionem*, 1:9. The actual quotation: 'It is absurd to name together things which are by nature unlike. For what community or what likeness is there between creature and Creator?' (Athanasius, 'Epistle I. A Letter of Athanasius to Bishop Serapion Concerning the Holy Spirit', *The Letters of St. Athanasius Concerning The Holy Spirit*, ed. C.R.B. Shapland (London, The Epworth Press, 1951), 80).

transcendent way as Creator of all other beings.¹⁶⁴ Created being, though retaining always its ontological distinction from its Creator, retains as well its dependence 'upon his will for its being and ultimate order'.¹⁶⁵ In other words, when Torrance classifies the world as 'utterly distinct' from God, he is not saying that God has left the creation sufficient in itself to operate independently from him. He refers to this ontological, operational freedom or creation conferred upon it by God as *contingency*. The term carries its usual connotation, viz. 'transience', 'temporal finitude', and 'having a beginning and end in time', as well as a freedom from all external, rational necessity, particularly that inherent within the being of God.¹⁶⁶ 'Contingent things do not have to be and contingent events do not have to happen.'¹⁶⁷ The implications of the cosmology which he is proposing entails, without contradiction, a world utterly distinct from God only because it is totally dependent upon him.¹⁶⁸ Distinction then must never be misconstrued as dichotomy, for contingency obtains in a relation between the Creator and the creature, 'freely maintained by him and preserved in his love'.¹⁶⁹

---

¹⁶⁴ *R/n*, 218.

¹⁶⁵ *R/st*, 63.

¹⁶⁶ John Hick, 'God as Necessary Being' in *God and the Universe of Faiths*, revised edition (London, Collins, 1977), 80.

¹⁶⁷ Thomas F. Torrance, *Divine and Contingent Order* (OUP, 1981), 85.

¹⁶⁸ Thomas F. Torrance, Lectures at Nottingham, 27 February 1986, no. 3, 'Time in Scientific and Historical Research'. 'God the Creator turns in Grace to create and preserve a world utterly distinct from Himself, but because it is utterly distinct, although entirely dependent upon His free will and wisdom, it is to be interpreted aright in its utter distinctness, that is, its natural and material processes without direct reference to God' (*TS*, 67). This suggests that the world could not operate as it does, distinct from God, except for its dependence upon the free act of his grace to keep it that way. He says, 'The only principle of order that pervades the whole of the universe is utter dependence on the mercy of God' (Thomas F. Torrance, *Calvin's Doctrine of Man* (Westport, CT, Greenwood Press, 1977), 47). The implication in all of Torrance's writings is that except for precisely the kind of relation God keeps with this order, ensuring the integrity of its rationality and operation, the whole world would either fly apart or collapse into absolute necessity (cf. esp. *R/st*, 103, 105, 110; *G & R*, 144; *TS*, 101).

¹⁶⁹ *R/st*, 65. Torrance admits that there is always the risk that a deistic world-view might be thought to be implied by such a liberation of nature. It is a risk worth taking, he insists (cf. *TS*, 67, fn. 1). Once, in fact, in *Space, Time and Incarnation*, he speaks of a 'proper dualism' as opposed to a 'radical one', the latter inhibiting any real intercourse with God and the world, and the former permitting it. 'God's interaction with the world he has made', he says, 'maintains a proper dualism between [the world and himself]' (*STI*, 71).

(ii) The created and uncreated realities each possess their own distinct rationality, and each their own mode of intelligibility, neither being essentially definitive of the other. The integral being and rationality of each reality must then be scrupulously upheld and never confounded.

God and his world are both 'inherently apprehensible' by men, but each in its own way. As we have noted, God's perceptibility is grounded in the fact of his own self-disclosure in the world. The universe, on the other hand, is intelligible by the fact that God has made it 'in such a way that it can bring forth and articulate knowledge of itself', that is, with rational man understood as its mouthpiece.[170] 'The Reformers', he says, thus 'release a nature for empirical investigation out of itself while reverting to the Patristic insight that the rationality inherent in nature is conferred upon it by God's creation of the world out of nothing'.[171] God made the world in such a way that it 'tells its own story'. It cannot out of itself reveal the truth or logic of its Creator; that is his prerogative and his only to disclose. God's rationality is only explicable from his side.[172] But neither does the knowledge of God *per se* disclose the nature of the created reality.[173] God in his creation of the world has endowed the universe with its own created being, whose integrity he respects and whose secrets he has left reposited in that reality to be discovered by rational, scientific man. Divine and created things are known each according to their own respective natures. Torrance deems highly 'unscientific' the transferral from one field of reality to the other 'the distinctive mode of rationality that develops within it'.[174]

---

[170] *G & G*, 5, 30-31. The intelligible structure inherent in the universe is to be apprehended through immediate intuition of its reality. Torrance means a *real* and substantial kind of knowing that defies any structure/being, matter/form, phenomena/noumena disparity.

[171] *STI*, P 37.

[172] Cf. *R/st*, 64-5.

[173] He says the world 'is to be interpreted aright in its utter distinctness, that is, in its natural or material processes without direct reference to God' (*TS*, 67). 'The whole world of nature, is entirely contingent upon God, and it cannot be known through knowledge of the divine Being' (*SOF*, LXXIV).

[174] *G & G*, 8-9. Torrance nevertheless has tended to write more and more of the 'creation's indefinite range of intelligibility' which, he says, is 'open-ended at the top', intimating a praeternatural rationality outside itself (Thomas F. Torrance, *The Addresses at the 6th Presentation of the Templeton Foundation Prize for Progress in Religion* (Dublin, Lismore Press, 1978). For example, he says that in our examination of the world 'we are faced with a mysterious intelligibility of indefinite depth which precisely in *its* intelligibility demands completion beyond itself'. The spontaneity and order of the created universe

2. The Aversion: 'An Inherent Correspondence'

Torrance has an antipathy for any notion of a 'sacramental universe'; in his view, the idea is a shibboleth of natural theology. At worst, it implies a theological cosmology of the Stoic sort or a cosmological theology which leaves God incomplete or incapacitated without the world-processes to assist him. At best, it still leaves the door open to synergism. Torrance's basic opposition to the concept is directed toward the presupposition that all being ultimately can be referred to one category, principle or substance. There is no intrinsic connection with or participation in divinity at any depth or height within the created order.

Underlying all this is the basic commitment of his theology, namely to guard at once 'the Godness of God' and 'the naturalness of nature'.[175] One would think that as a theologian his arguments would be weighted more heavily toward the former, but this is not the case. In fact, in his more recent writings, he just as avidly insists upon a created sort of 'transcendence' proper to nature.[176] For if divine substance or principle is forced upon nature, if even the slightest possibility of that remains, nature will always be the loser.[177] For the better part of the last twenty years Torrance's primary writings have sought to 'think out the interrelations of theological and natural science', by demonstrating the creative integration possible between the disciplines, all the while grounding his dialogue upon an assumed natural distinction between the modes of rationality proper to each. For all of Torrance's interest in defending the transcendence of God from domestication at the hands of the natural theologians – 'Let God be God!' – he is just as vitally interested in preserving the God-given freedom of nature to be itself – 'Let nature speak for itself out of itself!' – free of any determinism or divinisation.[178]

'cries out for a transcendent ground in the unlimited reality and freedom of God' ('Israel', 8). No matter how this created order might suggest or even 'demand' another order above it, however, Torrance will never allow that indication to become assertion. The inviolable maxim is that 'nature in itself is silent as to God' (*TS*, 101).

[175] *TS*, 66.

[176] Ibid. 30. 'By meeting us and entering into dialogue with us through His Word the transcendent God creates space for our "transcendence" over against Him and at the same time creates between us and Himself the rational continuity in which reciprocity and communion can take place' (*G & R*, 157).

[177] Cf. *TL*.

[178] Ibid.; *KBI*, 52; *TS*, 101. 'We must learn to give... to nature what belongs to nature', he insists (*TS*, 104). 'We... cheat by secretly importing "divinity" into

On both these counts, Torrance considers the medievalist attempt at an integration of being and structure along Aristotelian lines as having failed. Though it certainly brought form and matter together, the natural reality was left no formal rationality of its own. God was left impersonally related to the world, in a rationally substantial kind of way, which confused his being and act with that of the world, relegating any special revelation on his part merely to high points of a general revelation synonymous with the rational order of the world itself.[179] The inherent likeness or 'pre-established harmony' between the Creator-Logos and the natural order of the universe was thus retained. God had created the world and imposed upon it an all-embracing *divine* order so that the world could only be understood in reference to a rationality which was not its own.[180]

In his creation and sustaining of the world, God was seen 'to provide necessary causes for effects which he willed to be necessary', with every effect ultimately traceable retrospectively to God himself as First Cause. For medieval theology, then, the world was seen as impregnated with final causes, so that not only could an eternal pattern be read off the face of nature, but apart from the understanding of the eternal pattern in God, there could be no ultimate knowledge of nature. Contingent things and events were

---

it' (*TS*, 101).

[179] With all the heroic attempts at synthesis, there persisted in the medieval mind a sense that the dignity of the world would be forfeit if its ontological ties with divinity were broken. To have made the break, as Torrance says, within the framework of medieval theology, would have implied a creation 'deficient in reality and rationality' (*DCO*, 85).

[180] *DCO*, 86. Torrance admits that formally 'medieval theology quite definitely rejected the conception of the world as an emanation of God and therefore the linking together of the necessity of the world with the necessity of the divine nature, but nevertheless it held on to a (modified) notion of a hierarchy of being, embracing both the lowest and the highest being, which seriously blurred the Biblical distinction between the Creator and the creature, and introduced into its doctrine of God an unfortunate ambiguity' (*TS*, 59–60). Oliver O'Donovan points to Torrance as typical of Protestant thinkers who 'claim that the freedom of God was inadequately respected in pre-Reformation Christian thought'. Citing this passage from *Theological Science*, he commends Torrance's 'moderately-phrased judgement'. Nevertheless, he contends that 'this kind of characterisation of the high Medieval theology hardly does justice to the astonishing insistence on the freedom of God which marked, not merely the late-medieval voluntarism of Duns Scotus and William of Ockham, but the whole scholastic tradition from Peter Lombard' (Oliver O'Donovan, *Resurrection and Moral Order: An Outline for Evangelical Ethics* (Leicester, IVP, 1986), 40).

seen to 'obtain only under condition of extrinsic relation to what is necessary', having no true identity or freedom in themselves.[181]

In the late Middle Ages, the metaphysical, causal bridge thrown up across the chasm separating God and the world took a definitively logical shape. Incredibly complex syntactical sequences and *ratio*-deductive systems were developed which sought to demonstrate logical and necessary truths through logical and necessary argumentation, in effect positing that truth as man could deduce it was commensurate with the thought of God.[182] Man sought 'to exercise a determinative power over all the apprehension of Truth', rather than being bound and subject to it. For if the world's rational order is ultimately reducible to the divine rationality, it is a short journey indeed from that to presume a natural correspondence between active human reason and that of the Logos. And following upon that, it is but another short step to assume that which Torrance calls 'the *particular form* [of] the principle of the sacramental universe': 'the Church regarded as a sacramental institution of grace grounded upon and continuous with the Incarnation, as its extension into space and time'. 'It was on this ground', he says, 'that the Church itself came to assume supreme authority, for the expression of the mind of the Church in its dogmatic definitions was held to be the expression of the nature of the Truth'.[183] This led to God's revelation, already rendered to mere particulars in a general field of divine procession within the world, becoming more and more associated with the pronouncements of the Church.[184]

In the midst of this whole complex of cause and effect, Torrance observes, the sacraments became attached to a deficient concept of grace associated with the operation of the Church, which projected divine being as cause related to creaturely being as effect. This set up the creaturely action and element – e.g. those proper to the Church's sacramental union – as 'intermediating' God. This was totally in

---

[181] *DCO*, 86–7.

[182] Ibid. 87–8.

[183] *SOF*, XLIV–XLV.

[184] The Doctors of the late Middle Ages, though appearing to lean toward a more empirical approach to nature (perhaps because they gazed ever deeper into it, seeking its 'true nature'), still could not refer 'immediately' to contingent things and events, but rather transposed them into 'second order terms' which only indirectly represented things, not identifying them explicitly. The exteriority of a thing still could not be countenanced as having direct relation to the interior rationality of the thing itself. To this 'algebraic' way of thinking, then, these symbolic propositions about things were requisite to their intelligibility (*DCO*, 86–7).

order, of course, within a world already itself the effect of the divine cause, and within a Church itself the objectification of the Incarnate Word. On the surface this might be thought to comprise an exchange of God's transcendence for his immanence, opening the way for some form of panentheism. Indeed, some modern so-called Thomists, further removed from their Aristotelian sources, have developed their thoughts in this direction.[185] Torrance, however, is quick to point out that the Aristotelian container view of the universe – viz. space understood as a compartment containing all created reality with God exterior to it – coupled with the Aristotelian concept of God as unmoved mover had just the opposite effect. For God himself, the unmoved mover, remains quite transcendentally, impassibly, aloof from the world, and only 'inertially determines the whole cosmic order'.[186] With regard to real and personal divine interaction with the created world, therefore, the doctrine of God was seen to fare no better at the hands of the Thomists than at the hands of the Augustinians. Though God's presence was immediately perceptible as an impersonal, rational principle, it was extremely difficult for the medieval mind to think of him as actually present 'from the outside', without an immanent, created intermediary 'on the inside'.[187] The natural world of the medievalists, though suffused throughout with the rational imprint of God (the *signum*), cried out for God himself (the *Res*).

3. The Option: 'A Covenanted Correspondence'

Against all this, Torrance contends for God's real involvement with a world thoroughly itself and capable of relation to him out of no integral necessity, but simply at his word. God does not 'intrude' in his own world.[188] There is no natural barrier in creation that would hinder him, no inherent aversion to God in nature itself. But neither is there a *cursus naturalis* for the revelation of God intrinsic to the world's structure, that is, a capacity in nature for conveying God's word. This is not only due to the fact that 'God holds Himself at a distance' from the world since the fall of man, or because of the

---

[185] E.g. the 'convergent evolutionary' thought of Pierre Teilhard de Chardin.
[186] *DCO*, 86–7; TS59 ; cf. Thomas F. Torrance, *The Christian Frame of Mind* (Edinburgh, The Handsel Press, 1985), 25.
[187] Cf. Thomas F. Torrance, 'The Paschal Mystery of Christ and the Eucharist: General Theses', *LitR* 6, 1 (1976), 7.
[188] *TS*, 135.

insidious effects of natural depravity.[189] It simply follows from the way the world was made.[190] God may come to man through nature but never by it. His relation with the world, particularly in his act of revelation, is not an unnatural one, i.e. not an act out of character with either his own nature or the nature of the created order. His way to man in the world is in harmony with his relationship to created reality generally. He comes to man and speaks to him only out of his eternal word. His way and his word are purely his own, not that of the world.[191] Regardless of how closely God is involved with the created instrument in the revelatory act, the created element as such never becomes substantially part of the content of revelation. The created intelligibility is God's servant, never his consort. God's revelation is wholly a self-revelation.[192]

When seeking to place his theology of nature and revelation within a classical framework, Torrance calls upon the traditional Reformed doctrine of 'the Covenant of Grace'. In contrast to the medieval idea of a sacramental universe, or a natural correspondence, he proposes a 'covenanted correspondence' – what Barth terms a 'created correspondence'.[193] The concepts of covenant and correspondence thought out together suggest that God's relations with the world are based not upon, what Torrance calls, some 'imaginary inherent relation of likeness', but solely upon the

---

[189] *SOF*, CI. Torrance takes natural depravity quite seriously; e.g. 'The harmony between heaven and earth is broken. Even nature is cursed, so that it is impossible to hear the Word of God in it' (Thomas F. Torrance, *The Apocalypse Today* (Greenwood, SC, The Attic Press Inc., 1960), 180; cf. *CDOM*, 164).

[190] *TS*, 101-2.

[191] Cf. *KBI*, 95f.

[192] D.M. Baillie speaks of nature being naturally 'fitted to speak to us of [God]' (Donald M. Baillie, *The Theology of the Sacraments and Other Papers* (New York, Charles Scribner's Sons, 1957), 46). This is not broad enough for Torrance. Indeed, if he had so desired, God could have 'fitted' specific places or passages through which to proceed into this order; but this was unnecessary. The world is not 'fitted to speak for God, it is made to have relation with him and in that relation he may move in creation wherever he likes and speak through any part of it. However, Torrance would insist emphatically that God must be the subject of the verb 'to speak'. God may indeed speak through the world, but the Word remains God's Word. If the world is 'dumb' without rational man to give it word, it is 'twice dumb' to the things of God, devoid not only of content but of expression. At best, the world is but a channel through which God speaks his Word to man, but in no wise itself formative to its content or delivery. Torrance says: 'The works of creation teach us, doubtless by their "mute expression", but all this is of no avail apart from the Word' (*CDOM*, 40).

[193] *CFOM*, 23. Torrance cites Barth, *CD* III.1, esp. para. 41.

free decision of his grace to be so related to it. Although he will speak of the Creator/creation relationship as 'a two way relation', that connection itself does not, indeed cannot, arise from the world. The initiation belongs wholly to God; in this sense it is 'irreversible'.[194] Neither can the created proportion in the relation, as we have shown, account for its part in it. It is axiomatic that in any Creator/creation relation the world is interpreted in terms of God's action upon it.[195] With respect to the covenant, these relations are said to be ancillary to his revelation of himself to man in order to redeem him.[196] As he puts it: 'The whole world of signs which God in His Covenant mercy has appointed to correspond to Him only has revealing significance and therefore can be interpreted only, in relation to His Covenant will for communion with man and in the actualization of that Covenant in the course of His redemptive acts in history.'[197] This means that God has not created the world simply to exist for itself or its own ends, but to serve his covenantal purposes for man, to be 'the appointed theatre of his revelation'.[198] God in his covenant, Torrance says, 'embraces not only man but the whole of creation', assuming it 'beyond anything it possesses in itself into such a relation to Himself that He may use it as the instrument of His glory, and as the sphere within which He creates fellowship between man and Himself'. It is wholly in line within the earthly nature of God's covenant that his relation to man should involve 'created objectivity', in this way. Indeed, it is inconceivable that in the election of man this world order, man's assigned dominion, should not be elected as well, not only to serve God toward man's redemption but also to be renewed with him. Torrance thus expands the thought that the world can only be interpreted in the light of God's act upon it, proposing that 'creation cannot be understood in abstraction from God's Covenant purposes, but only as the instrument of his purpose in revelation and reconciliation'.[199]

It is not, however, in 'created objectivity' broadly speaking that God's covenant with man and his world has been fulfilled, rather in the particular, historical objectivity of Jesus Christ. The natural implements thus serve the Word of God as pointers toward his own divine humanity in which he is formally disclosed. Torrance states:

---

[194] *TS*, 67.
[195] Ibid. 67.
[196] *SOF*, LI, LIII.
[197] Ibid. LIII.
[198] Ibid. LI; *TS*, 68, 43, 137; cf. *R/n*, 222.
[199] *SOF*, LI–LII.

'the object of theological knowledge is creaturely objectivity bound to divine objectivity, not just creaturely objectivity in general but that specific creaturely objectivity which the divine objectivity has assumed, adapted and bound to himself, Jesus'.[200] The incarnation thus models God's larger implementation of the natural world.

To summarize: creation cannot be understood in its relation to the Creator apart from an understanding of his covenantal relation to it for man's sake. The world is made to correspond delightfully to God, but has no revelatory significance or power apart from the explicit light of God's word upon it.

4. The Way of God into the World: 'Through the Incarnate Son'

We have seen how the incarnation, God's fullest statement as to his interaction with the world, dictates the nature of all the relationships he has with his creatures. However, the Creator/creation relation in Christ is not merely exemplary for all God's relations with the world; rather it is the source from which they proceed. Torrance sums this up:

> The Spirit and the Word cannot be interpreted in terms of immanent principles or norms within the creaturely processes, but as the power and presence of God the Creator supervening upon the creaturely world in transcendent personal fashion, through the commanding Word of God, through the incarnate Person of the Son.[201]

An analysis of this passage, in the light of what has been said thus far, will help us to understand the economy of the 'new' relation God maintains with the world since the incarnation. The text speaks of God's transcendence over against the world. We have seen that this does not imply spatial distance or any lack of immediacy between God and his creation. The distance is ontological. God will not be anything less than or become anything different from himself in his relation to us. Transcendence and immanence are not mutually

---

[200] *TS*, 137. He continues: 'Thus theological activity is concerned with that special creaturely objectivity *in its relation* to divine objectivity, and therefore with that creaturely objectivity as it is given ultimate objectivity over against all other objectivity within the created universe', viz. with 'the creaturely objectivity of God in the incarnation of His Word in Christ' (*TS*, 137).

[201] *SOF*, XCVII.

exclusive predicates of God in Torrance's view. He may he both at once so long as he remains God. In the incarnation the transcendent God is seen to be immanent in creation, whereas, in the ascension, creation in its natural 'transcendence' is found to be immanent to God.[202] The passage above refers to God's presence proceeding 'upon' the world. Torrance often characterizes the disposition of God toward the world in this way. Although he will say that God's act is 'not simply a mighty act... done *upon* us', he never abandons the use of the preposition.[203] While this might imply a commandeering or condescending relationship, as though God were forcing the world to do something unnatural to it, what is 'natural' to the world must be understood to mean that which it can naturally become in relation to its Creator.[204] Torrance's use of this preposition underlines the fact that God's act proceeds directly out of his being and not by any circuitous means or secondary causality. God's act *ad extra* is identical with his act *ad intra*; it shares God's objective relation to his creation.[205] No secondary objectivity through which God might mediate himself qualifies this fact. This is hardly the language of interventionism. God acts 'upon' the world, for he cannot act as integrally part of it.

The word 'supervening' in the quotation we have cited can also be misleading. It too accentuates the sovereign nature of God's act but is not meant to suggest that his act within creation is an alien one. Nor does it imply that God's activity there abides in a merely 'vertical' relation to the world or as necessarily proceeding in a discontinuous way within the natural order. Indeed, Torrance has said explicitly that God's presence and act in the world are

---

[202] 'The Incarnation of the Son of God in our world falls within and not without the inner life of God... the creation must [therefore] be regarded, in a certain way as in God and our understanding of it have a trinitarian structure' ('Trinity', 349).

[203] *R/n*, 117.

[204] Torrance derides the inherent disjunction between the *natural* and *supernatural* implicit in the Augustinian Western dualism (cf. *R/n*, 222; *STI*, 69). It precludes the possibility of any genuine ontological interplay between God and his world, and thus disallows nature's facilitating the divine presence however he should choose. Though God's acts in the world might sometimes appear as contradicting nature, they are in fact grounded upon his relation to it, a relation in which the natural order remains totally in harmony with itself. No 'miraculous activity' of God in the world transgresses the integrity of nature when understood within the context of its relation to the Creator.

[205] 'Trinity', 338.

'continuous with space and time'.²⁰⁶ In another place he writes 'the operation of the Spirit in creation and in nature is to be regarded as the presence of God with the creation'.²⁰⁷

The key phrase in the passage, however, is 'through the incarnate Person of the Son'. God does have a 'way through' into the world, certainly once in time from above, but now through Christ's continuing humanity by the gift of the Spirit. Christ's breathing the Holy Spirit upon the disciples out of his own regenerate humanity depicts for Torrance this new way or dispensation of God's gift of himself in the world. This is not to say that the economy of God's operation has not always been 'from the Father, through the Son and in the Spirit'. Now however it is 'through the Son' who is in unseverable, reconciling and hypostatic union with us. Earlier we stated that this union was the source from which all God's relations with the world proceed. This is so much the case that Torrance can speak of the presence of God in the world as the presence of that union; for God will never be without it. He can never be among us except as the incarnate God. All that the Spirit accomplishes in the world and, in the light of the covenant, all that he does for man in relation to man is ordered by the incarnation. This is what Torrance has in mind when he says 'Now that the Incarnation has taken place... theology... is prevented from thinking of a relation of the Spirit to the creation or to men except in and through the Person and Work of the incarnate Son.'²⁰⁸ Technically, then, it can be said that God no longer comes 'down' upon creation; he comes to us as from within our order, as one belonging to our order.²⁰⁹

---

²⁰⁶ Lectures at Nottingham, 27.2.86: No. 2, 'The Legacy of Karl Barth'; cf. R/n, 137.

²⁰⁷ SOF, CII, italics mine.

²⁰⁸ Ibid. XCVIII.

²⁰⁹ This raises the whole question of Torrance's choice of framework and procedure. Our study thus far shows that he is following Barth in his preference both for what is commonly referred to as an 'above and below' pattern in the development of his cosmology and for a 'descending mode' in doing christology. The remarks which need to be made here, however, will be neither exhaustive nor conclusive, for it is not the business of eucharistic theology to argue cases which are strictly pertinent to other disciplines of theology and which are not ultimately decisive in the context of the sacrament. While our comments will suggest how Torrance might answer his critics, they are intended primarily to clarify his position rather than weigh its strengths.

First, with regard to structure: Despite Torrance's wholesale rejection of all the underlying dualistic presuppositions of classical Platonism, his eucharistic theology betrays certain necessary assumptions which can only be made intelligible by a quasi-Hellenistic contrast of transcendent/divine and immanent/created dimensions. Following the lead of his christology, Torrance's eucharistic theology paradoxically demonstrates at once the integral difference between these realities and the integral freedom they have to relate to each other. Even after the genuine ontological intersection of these realities in the sacrament is established, this kind of model remains intact. It is predictably when Torrance seeks to underline the element of distinction that 'the above' and 'the below' are brought into sharpest perspective. Torrance speaks of a natural tension that always exists between the divine and contingent orders, of an 'asymmetric' relation that persists between God and any created thing he assumes in the revelatory or sacramental relation (*R & E*, 94–5). In fact, it could be argued that in Torrance's cosmology there is a degree of differentiation made between the two orders that neither Plato nor the neo-Platonists could have countenanced. In any form of Platonism the basic theme of metaphysics is monistic. Plato could at least speak of the phenomenal world as an 'ectype' of the Ideal, the Stoics could point to the *logoi spermatikoi* creation and Augustine to the *rationes aeternae*. Torrance, however, as we have seen, declares unequivocally that the two realms bear absolutely no similarity to each other, that there exists no 'natural' link between these whatsoever (*R/n*, 221). His point is that the divine operation in the world is free of all alien necessity, that it arises purely out of God's 'ontic necessity', that it is something God must be or do only by virtue of his being God. (Cf. Steven Sykes, 'Barth on the Centre of Theology', *Karl Barth – Studies of his Theological Methods*. He comments on the concept of 'ontic necessity' in Barth, which he defines as 'the impossibility of the object of faith being other than it is'. He cites Karl Barth, *Anselm*, 49ff.). Torrance's eucharistic theology guards this fact and thereby promotes this kind of framework. However much the created element in the sacramental relation might qualify the way God is present to his Church, it does not qualify that presence itself. Factors such as these prescribe to God's operation in the world quite naturally the disposition of an act 'upon us', of an accommodating act which descends, and thereby recommends this kind of above/below framework. Even if this so-called 'platonic' phenomenal/Ideal model did not exist, something like it would be required to represent the unyielding ontological distinction in Torrance's theology.

However, it is the way Torrance structures his thought that has left him open for criticism. It must be said that his choice of motif is only secondarily 'platonic', and primarily biblical. This is a particularly relevant observation in the light of his repeated references to the Book of Hebrews which itself depends greatly upon both late Hellenistic imagery as well as the contrast between 'the heavenly' and 'the earthly' implicit in the doctrine of the ascension. It will become increasingly clear as this thesis unfolds just how determinative the doctrine of the ascension is for every aspect of Torrance's eucharistic theology. Whereas an appropriate transcendent/immanent model was needed to underline the strict ontological distance that obtains between God and the world, so the ascension requires a similar framework to accentuate Christ's physical separation from his Church and his present relation with man from 'the innermost seat of the Godhead'. It seems probable, therefore, that his choice of an above/below model is demanded as much for these reasons as by any latent platonic disparity between God and the world which has not yet been dispelled.

Secondly, with regard to procedure: Whatever his causes for choosing an 'above and below' model for his eucharistic theology, Torrance dismisses out of hand this sort of contrast in christology (*MOC*, 65). Despite his rejection of a 'descending christology' formally, however, it would appear that he persists with this kind of reasoning himself. While, as we have said, his sacramental thought is not directly affected by his choice of method, his theology overall is regulated by it and his theology of the sacrament, as much as any area, worked out in a classically descending style.

Since Torrance's methodology constitutes a virtual restatement of Barth's approach to christology, we usefully examine his views with respect to this question by applying Pannenberg's now famous criticisms of Barth (Wolfhart Pannenberg, *Jesus - God and Man* (London, SCM, 1968), 34-5; cf. Nicholas Lash, 'Up and Down in Christology', *New Studies in Theology*, eds Steven Sykes and Derek Holmes (London, Duckworth, 1980), vol. 1, 31-46; Colin E. Gunton, *Yesterday and Today: A Study of Continuities in Christology* (London, Darton, Longman & Todd, 1983), 33-55, esp. 43-51).

First, Pannenberg questions the validity of any theology which 'presupposes the divinity of Jesus'. He thinks it begs the central question of Christian theology, precisely by answering it, albeit prematurely. Secondly, following upon this first point, he objects to theologies which assume Christ's pre-existence since, being preoccupied with the stupendous implications of the incarnation, they tend to recognize 'only with difficulty the determinative significance inherent in the distinctive features of the real, historical man, Jesus of Nazareth'. Finally, he faults Barth's approach because it supposedly only makes statements about God upon the ground of what God has said about himself. For Pannenberg this is tantamount to circular reasoning and proposes an inaccessible and therefore impossible position for the Church to do theology, that is from God's side. (Pannenberg, *Jesus - God and Man*; cf. Richard H. Roberts, 'The Ideal and the Real in the Theology of Karl Barth', *New Studies in Theology*, eds Steven Sykes and Derek Holmes (London, Duckworth, 1980), vol. 1, 165.)

Pannenberg has certainly not misunderstood the direction the Church's theological thinking ought to take according to either Barth or Torrance. The former says, 'The real difference between the philosopher and the theologian [is] not in their subject matter, but in the "order" and "sequence" of their concern for knowledge. As he strives for knowledge the theologian thinks from above (from God) downwards (to man) and only in this way from below upwards, whereas the philosopher adopts precisely the opposite approach... Jesus Christ is the one and entire truth through which [the theologian] is shown how to think and speak, just as strictly as the philosopher is given his task' (Eberhard Busch, *Karl Barth* (London, SCM, 1976), 435. Busch cites Barth's 'Philosophie und Theologie' in *Philosophie und Christlicher Existenz*, Festschrift fur Heinrich Barth, 1960, 93ff.).

Barth, of course, is not proposing, as Pannenberg suggests, that the theologian must somehow get to God's side in order to understand truth about

God, but that he must get truth from God's side. This does not preclude an historic revelation, or advocate one that is only tangential to our existence, rather it anticipates God's word being spoken to us on this side. Rahner, sharing Barth's view, suggests that a so-called '"descending" type of christology' is 'in some sense logically contained... all along' in a christology developed from below (Karl Rahner, 'The Two Basic Types of Christology' in *Theological Investigations* (London, Darton, Longman & Todd, 1975), vol. 13, 218). In other words, the concept of revelation *per se*, no matter how materially or historically contextualized, contains implicitly the notion of God's witness to his own transcendence.

Torrance's theology does, as Pannenberg suggests, assume the divinity of Christ, and not only that but the Chalcedonian definition of his divine-human person. For Torrance it is not the duty of every generation to rewrite the *prolegomenon* of Christian faith. Now, though it is true that whatever christology Torrance would have adopted would have formed the basis for his eucharistic theology, as we have already pointed out, there is something terribly 'safe' about arguments from presuppositions, especially 'inaccessible' ones involving pre-existent being. Richard Roberts' sweeping criticism directed at this kind of thinking, particularly that of Barth, can be applied as well to Torrance. Simply stated, he contends that Barthian theology purposively protects itself from external criticism by its retreat into its presuppositions, or by a convenient deference to 'the divine side'. He calls this an 'illusory security' (Richard H. Roberts, 'The Ideal and the Real', 164–5, 167). Although we must not presume to accuse Torrance of an intentional evasion of issues as Roberts does Barth, we will on several occasions observe how he does tend to avoid important metaphysical questions, like Calvin, through invoking the *sursum corda* or by appealing to the inscrutability of the work of the Spirit. For example, Torrance speaks of the *sursum corda* and the doctrine of the ascension as 'guarding the mystery of the sacramental relation' (*C & A* II, 142). In recent times the statement by the Calvin scholar John Dillenberger, with regard to this aspect of Calvin's method, has become a standard one; 'Calvin calls upon the Spirit to rescue him in... dilemma. In one sense his conception of the Spirit is his escape hatch, but from another standpoint it is the pivot upon which everything turns.... At the edges and limits of Calvin's thought the Spirit takes over. The Spirit is so self-evidently the pivot of his apprehensions that it frequently operates as a *deus ex machina* in his thinking' (John Dillenberger, *John Calvin: Selections from his Writings* (New York, Anchor Books, 1971), 18).

Regardless of how questionable his presuppositionalist method might be, however, Torrance's eucharistic theology, as we have stated, must be examined primarily not with respect to questions related to methodology, but in the light of issues directly related to it.

As for Pannenberg's second major criticism, it is already clear that Torrance's theology, his eucharistic theology not excepted, will depend for its meanings not nearly so much upon the observable reality of Christ, that which history would expressly record, as upon the unobservable theoretical side, or upon the interpretation of that historical reality by the theology of the Church (Rahner acknowledges a basic weakness in what he calls, 'metaphysical

Christology', viz. christology convinced of the 'self-evident reality' of Christ's relation to the Trinity, which 'does not need any further recourse to the experience of Jesus in saving history', K. Rahner, *TI*, vol. 13, 214).

Torrance undoubtedly would not see any conflict here. He is, as Pannenberg contends, gripped by the profound implications of the incarnation, but not as a reality separated from real history. For Torrance the knowledge of theology is mediated through the particular, 'temporal, worldly creaturehood' of Jesus of Nazareth and never loses its direct contact with him or his history, even in his ascension (cf. *TS*, 312ff.). As we will see, the Eucharist affords the Church real contact with the Jesus of history, but by virtue of the resurrection and ascension, which, as prevailing events, still belong to time as well as eternity. Some might say that an encounter with 'the historical Jesus' understood in this way is at best an abstraction and really disconnected from our history both past and present, a kind of 'timeless event' which Torrance warns against in his eucharistic theology (cf. *SOF*, XCIV; *TS*, 312). Torrance would reply that it is no less an abstraction than the historical, though risen, person of Christ and no more removed or alien to our present history than God's act upon us in his world. Indeed, all theological activity proceeds from 'direct personal dialogue between ourselves and God', as well as 'by constant reference to its (historical) source and sole norm' in the historical record. These are parallel points of reference in Torrance's thought; they do not intersect each other at right angles. (*TS*, 307; As far as the historical investigation of this event is concerned, Torrance contends that the positivist – 'operating from a classical continuum of cause and effect and the disparity of Historie und Geschichte' – would have the same difficulty apprehending the mystery of who Christ was 2000 years ago as he would today. That is to say, his presuppositions would preclude any observations except those 'in the flat', *TS*, 320).

Nevertheless, Torrance himself is sometimes so keen to penetrate to the internal meanings of Christ's historical life, which transcend history as well as belong to it, that the actual succession of the events of that life become like figures in a surrealist painting, only conveying meaning if one understands the meaning first. The human history of Jesus for Torrance can never be said to be an irrelevance, as Pannenberg's criticism might imply, but it also cannot be said to have meaning, not in the fullest sense, except for its involvement with one who infinitely transcends it.

The final criticism is the one most pertinent for our study. For Torrance, as for Barth, every true thing that can be said about God depends upon the self-revelation of God and our willingness to be apprehended by it. The Theo-logic of Torrance is the so-called 'vertical' logic of Barth (Richard H. Roberts speaks of Barth's 'vertical' logic by which 'the validity of cohering assertions is given by the quality of purported witness each makes to the divine being' (Richard H. Roberts, 'Karl Barth's Doctrine of Time: Its Nature and Implications', *Karl Barth – Studies of his Theological Methods*), 112). In Torrance's theology everything relevant to the doctrine of the Eucharist is obtained from the christological reality, not in some analytical sense – i.e. by the probing of the theology of the Church into the interior reality of Christ – but by the Word himself informing the mind of the Church out of his own inner being. As we will see presently, it is

He says,

> This world of ours in space and time is actually intersected and overlapped, so to speak, by the divine world in the *parousia*, or advent and presence of Jesus Christ. He was acknowledged and adored, therefore, as one who is

the Living Word interpreting himself through his real humanity who calls for the sacramental analogy or relation in the world. He it is who will prescribe the promise of his presence within that analogy and then come to perform it. By his coming that Incarnate Word summons the Church to 'lift up its heart' in thanksgiving and by his prayer in our midst realizes the analogy between our liturgy and that of heaven. The sacramental analogy will be seen to have its meaning and legitimacy wholly by its reference, or more precisely, by its deference to the Word's self-reference manifestly present within it, though infinitely transcendent to it. This will all be evident from the central place Torrance accords to the *sursum corda* in the liturgy, which he understands as the Church's acknowledgement and answer to the transcendent reality confronted in its sacrament.

For all its transcendence, however, the word of God is not only a word from 'above'. The unmitigated reality of God coming to man, speaking to man 'through the incarnate Person of the Son', a fact uncompromised by the distance (aboveness) of the ascension, renders, to Torrance's mind, the whole characterization of 'a Christology from above' inappropriate. It is the *homoousion* which for Torrance cements together the 'above' and 'below' forever. In the Incarnate Word the heavenly (eternal) and earthly (temporal) revelation have been made to coincide and to complement each other. With respect to his being and origin God's Word is essentially and always a word 'from above' but with respect to his relation to us he is a Word 'from below' or 'through Jesus Christ' who is forever *God with us* (*SOF*, XCVII). Torrance says, 'Because God has revealed himself to us and given himself to us in him, Jesus Christ constitutes in his own Incarnate Person the mediating centre of that revelation whereby all our knowledge of God is controlled. It should now be clear that in the nature of the case it is theologically quite improper to contrast a christology from above and a christology from below, for our knowledge of God the Father and our knowledge of God the Son perfectly coincide in our knowledge of the one undivided reality of God's *self*-revelation in the Person of Jesus Christ, the Mediator' (*MOC*, 65).

Richard H. Roberts is quite right then to suggest that, given their presuppositions, one cannot conclusively argue with either Barth or Torrance except in dialogue with revelation as well, which precisely the engagement they prescribe. Roberts cites Torrance who concludes, 'Barth rightly insists that in the knowledge of God we cannot raise questions as to its reality from some point outside of it.' (Richard H. Roberts, 'The Ideal and the Real', 178, he cites Torrance, *STI*, 54; Bonhoeffer referred to this aspect of Barth's method negatively as 'a positivism of revelation', which makes 'a law of faith' and thus begets a system as closed on the size of faith as traditional positivism is closed against it. Dietrich Bonhoeffer, *Letters and Papers from Prison*, ed. Eberhard Bethge, enlarged edition (London, SCM, 1971), 286).

God of God and yet man of man, who in his own being belongs both to the eternal world of divine reality and to the historical world of contingent realities.[210]

This so-called 'overlap' is still in place in the humanity of the ascended Christ.

The Word bears our nature through death unto resurrection and ascension and therefore has representatively elevated all creation to a higher coherence in union with God. He states: 'The Biblical teaching is quite explicit that in Christ all things are really involved in reconciliation, that He is not only the Head of believers but the Head of all creation and that all things visible and invisible are gathered up and *cohere* in him.'[211] In his creaturely nature, that is, in its re-constituting relation with God, the whole of creation has proleptically entered into a totally different relation to its Creator. He states:

> It belongs to the very essence of the incarnational life and work of the Son that in him redemption penetrates back to the very beginning and reunites man's life to God's creative purposes. Redemption is no mere after thought on the part of God, for in it the original creation comes to a transcendental redemption, and the one Covenant of Grace made with all creation is fulfilled.[212]

'With the Incarnation and the finishing of Christ's work', Torrance writes, 'the whole relation between the Spirit of God and his creation [has undergone] a change'. It is a change that has transpired in the very flesh of Christ by virtue of his relation to God and man as 'the First-Born and Head of all creation'.[213] 'In some real sense', he says,

---

[210] *G & G*, 39.

[211] *SOF*, CXIII.

[212] Ibid. CXII–CXIII.

[213] Ibid. CII. 'Without the incarnation of the Creator Word the fallen world would crumble away finally and irretrievably into nothingness, for then God would simply be letting go of what He had made and it would suffer from sheer privation of being. But the incarnation has taken place. Once and for all, the Creator Word has entered into the existence of what He has made and bound it up with His own eternal Being and Life embodied in Jesus Christ, yet without violating its creaturely nature. In this union of the Creator with the creature the eternal Word of God who is the ground of man's existence from beyond his existence has now become also the ground of his existence within his existence, undergirding and sustaining it from within its natural process in such a way as to establish his reality and meaning as human being and to realize his distinctive

'the *creatio continua* is even now conditioned by the Incarnation and Atonement, and... the whole universe pivots upon Jesus Christ'.[214] God's entire operation in creation must be thought of as issuing from his reconciliation with created being in him. The Spirit comes forth from God in Christ to stand 'with the creation' because in Christ God has brought forth a creature to stand creation blamelessly before him. With the incarnation, death, and resurrection of Christ the new creation has already interpenetrated the old order 'so that it is already the fulness of time'.[215] No longer does the world order as it were move toward its reconciliation, rather that reconciliation moves towards it in the approach of the second advent and the full disclosure of the glory of Christ's created humanity. It is specifically with this interpenetration of God with our order, Torrance says, that the Church's Eucharist has to do.[216] These thoughts will be further developed in later chapters.

---

response toward God in the fulness of his creaturely freedom and integrity' (*G & R*, 144).

[214] *SOF*, CIII.

[215] *Inter*, 309; *SOF*, CII.

[216] If an exact delineation of the implications of the incarnation for creation as a whole seem to be lacking in this section, if basic questions appear to be raised but not answered, this seems to be the way Torrance has left it. He insists that with the incarnation of God into our humanity the whole relation and economy of the Creator toward his creation has changed. His writings are full of inferences of great affects upon the created order resulting from God's unparalleled and lasting embrace of it in Jesus Christ. Some of them we have already observed, e.g. 'with the Incarnation... the whole relation between... God and His creation [has undergone] a change.' 'In some real sense', he says, 'the *creatio continua* is even now conditioned by the Incarnation' (*SOF*, CI-CII). Among those which we have not noted, perhaps the most intriguing is one from *God and Rationality*: 'In Jesus Christ the transcendent Rationality of God has planted itself within the created order where its bounds, structures and corrections break down under the negation of evil, in order to reintegrate spiritual and physical existence by setting up its own law within it and restore it to wholeness and integrity in the form, as it were, of a meeting of the Rationality of God with itself in the midst of estranged existence and in the depths of its disorder. In this way, the Incarnation has affected the whole creation, confirming the primordial act of the Word in conferring order and rationality upon it' (*G & R*, 162-3).

Just now the relation between God and the world has been 'changed' by the fact of the incarnation, or in what 'real sense' that enduring event now 'conditions' the ongoing of creation is still very much an open question. The quotation immediately above is typical. He speaks of God 'reintegrating spiritual and physical existence' in Jesus Christ, of God's maintaining the world order now as it were from within it and by that fact confirming the conferral of

5. The Eucharist: 'A Sacrament of God's Interaction with our Physical Existence in Jesus Christ'

By describing the sacraments as 'God's interaction with our physical existence in Jesus Christ' Torrance implies several things.[217] First, it should be said that the Church's sacraments are given for the period in which a 'world already redeemed by Christ' awaits its full realization 'in the future consummation when he will return to make all things new'.[218] They are sacraments of God's involvement with the world in as much as they witness to these two facts: on the one hand, to the final restoration of harmony between God and his creation in Jesus Christ and, on the other hand, to the incomplete, cumbersome kind of interaction that characterizes the Church's relation with God in a world still estranged from its Creator. With regard to the latter point, both the fragmented way in which the physical ingredients of the sacraments express spiritual reality, even at the word of God, and the limited nature of the sacramental union itself demonstrate the restraint of God's power and activity in the world. This is evidence that the new creation is not yet a universal reality, nor is it a full reality in either the Church or its sacraments. The sacramental rites, he says, testify to this 'tension between the physical and spiritual' which characterizes 'a world waiting for the redemption of the body'.[219]

---

contingent rationality upon the world at creation. But what all this means Torrance never explicitly says. He cannot possibly be suggesting that the created world as we know it was lacking in order before the incarnation, or any less 'fallen' since. Surely, the world's order is no more efficiently maintained now that God belongs to it.

There is certainly no lack of clarity in his writings, however, as to the consequences for the new heaven and new earth of this incomparable restoration of harmony between divine and created being in Christ. What has transpired between God and creation in Christ's humanity will bring about at the *parousia* nothing less than the reversal of the effects of the Fall and the reconstitution of all things. Torrance is explicit with reference to the new creation brought about proleptically in Christ and just as clear when expounding the outworkings of this eschatologically, but scarce on anything but inferences for the creation prior to the *eschaton*. He states that Reformed theology has never fully worked out 'the doctrine of the relation of the incarnate Word, crucified, risen and ascended, to the whole creation' (*SOF*, CII–CIII). In his own theology of incarnation and creation Torrance has made an attempt at it, but it cannot be said that he has 'fully worked it out' either.

[217] *G & R*, 161.
[218] Ibid. 161.
[219] Ibid. 161.

The sacraments can also be referred to as 'Sacraments of God's Interaction with our physical existence' in that they constitute such an interplay themselves. Just as the hypostatic union demonstrates in a primal way just how divine and contingent realities are free to interact and co-exist, so the sacramental union demonstrates in the Church this same freedom, though not in the same way or depth. The sacraments both 'call for and provide', Torrance says, a response in which 'the interaction of the spiritual and physical is exhibited here and now'.[220] Far from denying the world's estrangement from God or seeking to promote the spiritual reality 'over the head', as it were, of physical reality as it exists, the sacramental union is erected in the midst of history and created things to be the appointed sign of God's covenant. As such it embraces those tensions and holds them in relation to Christ in whom they have been taken up and resolved. The sacramental relation therefore modifies those tensions in the world, not 'allowing them to become radical breaks which would plunge us into chaos and futility' but instead making them to serve the covenanted purposes of God.[221] He says,

> The Sacrament of the Eucharist then is the form which our sacramental union with Christ takes within the brokenness and the divisions of history, and yet mediates the wholeness of that union as such an abiding reality that the brokenness and the division of history, in which the church inevitably partakes, are revealed to be but the shell of the old life which passes away.[222]

The sacraments are signs of God's interaction with creation in Jesus Christ also in that they are the counterparts in human experience of God's miraculous works in the gospel. Just as those mighty deeds performed at Christ's hand represented God's healing the brokenness of creation and his reversal, at least in part, of the rule of decay, so the sacraments are 'prophetic signs that have to do with the saving of creation' in a universal sense. As we will see, Torrance frequently links the sacramental signs with the miraculous signs of Christ.[223] They are signs of God's healing of creation, however, not just with reference to that final restoration of all things at the *eschaton*, but also as 'active signs' of God's presence here and now in

---

[220] Ibid. 161.
[221] Ibid. 161.
[222] *Inter*, 321.
[223] *G & R*, 161, cf. 143–4.

the world, through which he continues to heal and renew his creation in union with Christ.[224]

We have already observed briefly that the sacraments are 'Sacraments of God's interaction with our physical existence *in Jesus Christ*' because they witness to the supreme and reconciling intercourse of God in Christ with the contingencies of our human life. This, more than anything else, is what Torrance indicates by the expression. The sacraments represent concretely God's having broken into the world in Christ and his ongoing solidarity with it in the continuity of the incarnation.[225] By their ordinary, earthly properties they evidence the sheer, unabashed physical reality of God in the flesh. For as much as the sacraments speak of the union of God and man in Christ they also demonstrate the difference between that unique and inimitable relation and the profoundly limited one which they afford. Torrance speaks of the former as a *unio consubstantialis* and of the latter as *communio substantialis*.[226] In the incarnation the life and word of God and the life and word of man coinhere or subsist together in a single, new identity in the person of Christ. In the sacrament, on the other hand, while there is comprised '*a true and substantial union*' between Christ and his church, an 'ontological relation' between divine and created being, the two realities are seen as subsisting separately. Though the presence and act of God in the sacramental union is said to be concurrent with the presence and act of the church, with all the material ingredients this involves, there can never be a common identity.[227]

Nevertheless, these so-called sacraments of God's intersection with his world, particularly the Eucharist, offers the Church the ultimate manifestation of the natural, ontic relation possible between God and his creation within the world. We said earlier that since the presence of God in Christ embodies the hypostatic union, his presence in the Church's sacrament was seen as equivalent to that union impinging upon the Church's historical existence. It is 'that union' which, Torrance says, the Holy Spirit inserts 'as an abiding union into the heart of our estrangement'.[228] It is in this sense that

---

[224] Ibid. 161; *Inter*, 310.

[225] Cf. *Inter*, 311–12.

[226] Ibid. 311–12.

[227] Ibid. 336, 312.

[228] Ibid. 320, cf.323. The salvation which has been achieved for man in Christ is set out by Torrance in terms of a relation of 'healing reconciliation between God and man' (Thomas F. Torrance, *The Centrality of Christ: Devotions and Addresses: The General Assembly of the Church of Scotland, 1976*

The Theological and Cosmological Framework 57

the sacrament ultimately anticipates the restoration of the world order in unhindered relation with God, i.e. by affording the Church real contact with Christ's humanity, in which, by virtue of its healing union with God through death and resurrection, God has fully renewed created being. This too is what Torrance has in mind when he says that the new order interpenetrates the old in the Eucharist, viz. that this present world, at least in its microcosm, the Church, is being constantly renewed in eternal life by communion with Christ in his new humanity.[229] It is because of the presence of the christological union in the midst of the Church's sacrament that he can make his superlative claim for the sacramental relation, viz. that

> no union, save that of the Persons of the Holy Trinity, could be closer, without passing into absolute identity than that between Christ and his Church as enacted in the holy Eucharist.[230]

If the Eucharist takes its model after the hypostatic union, though without duplicating it, then every other relation which the Church has with God takes its model after the Eucharist, though also without duplicating it.

§

Our immediate task in this first chapter has been to examine, from the perspective of the sacramental doctrine, the fundamental

---

(Edinburgh, The St. Andrew Press, 1976), 15). This is an accomplished fact. Yet this reconciliation, while constituted in Christ, is not to be thought of statically as existing only within the circumference of his human body, but dynamically as extended into the world in the movement of the Spirit. This very relation, Torrance says, is 'inserted as an abiding union' into the world 'from God the Father' by the Spirit, who himself effected the virginal conception, which was itself the historic insertion of 'that holy union... into our flesh and blood' (*Inter*, 320). Just as the Spirit was sent from the Father to enact once in history the union of the Word with our humanity in the womb of the Virgin Mary, so it is the Spirit who enacts within the continuity of space and time, this 'abiding union' in the Church. The Spirit draws man to God, restores him to divine communion and there lavishes upon him the diversities of the one gift of grace in Jesus Christ. Torrance asserts that this relation is concretely manifest and realized within the Church in the Holy Eucharist (cf. *Inter*, 320-21). Still the fact that Christ is present among us only in the mode of his Spirit, as well as in the sacramental manner, indicates that we do not yet enjoy the fullness of the new heaven and the new earth, but only a foretaste.

[229] *Inter*, 319.
[230] Ibid. 337.

structure and effective precepts of Torrance's theology. Although our discussion has not been exhaustive, all the essential and pertinent ingredients of his theological method have been touched upon and the Eucharist itself shown to belong naturally to the whole. The remainder of this dissertation will exhibit how Torrance fully and consistently engages these in the delineation of his eucharistic theology.

CHAPTER 2

Sacramental Significance: the Analogy of the Sacrament

RATIONALE FOR SUBSEQUENT OUTLINE

T.F. Torrance has no single, standard way of approaching the sacrament. In his earlier writings he developed his eucharistic doctrine in conjunction with discussions of eschatology and the theology of the Church, later around the central theme of the mediation of Christ. In the earlier works also he tended to deal with the Eucharist within the context of his theology of the *kerygma*, or 'under the rubric of proclamation', as he put it. Later the Eucharist was dealt with in its own right, though never so as to suggest that it could be understood except by the light of God's Word upon it.[1]

Because of the variety of settings and explication which Torrance gives his theology of the Eucharist, it is difficult to find one outline in terms of which his thought can be presented systematically. For our purposes, the outline Calvin most frequently employed has been selected.[2] This does not mean that Torrance always agrees with Calvin's material, but the headings are sufficiently

---

[1] *Inter*, 328.
[2] *Inst* IV.17.1.

broad to contain all the divergent aspects of his theology. They are also arranged in such a way as to correspond with the movement of his thought. Furthermore, in *Conflict and Agreement*, in the section 'The Formulation of the Doctrine of the Supper', Torrance himself employed Calvin's outline, though with considerable difficulty.[3] We will therefore enlist it here, but not without our own alterations.

Calvin arranged his eucharistic theology under the headings:

Signification,
Substance or Matter,
Effect or Action.

In any presentation of Torrance's thought on the subject, his own re-interpretation of the material indicated by these classical divisions must be taken into consideration. Corresponding to Calvin's outline, *Sacramental Signification* can be dealt with first, as it highlights the relationship of Word and sacrament. With regard to *Sacramental Substance or Matter*, however, the absolute identity in Torrance's theology between formal substance (God's Being) and formal action (God's Act) in Christ requires that we join under the same heading what Calvin separates in his second and third divisions. *Sacramental Matter and Action* thus becomes the second title in our outline. This coincides with what Torrance calls 'the objective ground of the sacrament', constituted formally in the person of Christ. Calvin's last heading, *Sacramental Effect*, compares precisely with what Torrance designates 'the subjectivication of reconciliation' constituted in Christ.[4] Our revised version of Calvin's outline becomes:

Sacramental Signification: The Analogy of the Sacrament,
Sacramental Matter and Action: The Objective Ground and Potentiality[5] of the Sacrament,
Sacramental Effect: The Subjectification of the Sacrament's Objective, Christological Reality.

---

[3] Cf. *C & A* II, 140ff.

[4] Cf. *SOF*, CV.

[5] The term 'potentiality' is employed here at some risk. Torrance never uses the word. It is not meant to invoke its classical Aristotelian connotations (cf. *G & G*, 63). Neither does it carry the slightest implication of an 'impersonal *res* or *potentia*' in the Thomist sense, that is, something distinguished or separated from the personal work of Christ (cf. *R/st*, 182). The word is chosen for its common meaning as 'the source of all possible effect' within the sacrament, thus applying exclusively to Christ himself, the divine-human Potentiary of all God's action in the world.

THE REJECTION OF THE AUGUSTINIAN APPROACH AND ATTITUDE TO SYMBOLISM

Torrance's non-dualist thinking prohibits him from formulating a sacramental theology which treats the Eucharist as symbol over against the Christ who is symbolized. Torrance departs from Calvin here in his understanding of metaphor, for Calvin did not hesitate to speak in symbolistic categories.[6] He sees, in this concept of symbolism, the manifestation of a cosmological/epistemological bifurcation between spiritual and material realities. Such a cleavage of the totality of existence, he contends, issues indirectly out of a neo-Platonic cosmology promulgated in the Western Church for over 1500 years by a generally accepted Augustinianism.[7] The neo-Platonic division, which Augustine revised, between the *mundus intelligibilis*, the world which we perceive with our mind, and the *mundus sensibilis* or that which we perceive with our senses, suggests more than just two different ways of gaining knowledge of the world.[8] For Augustine, as for the neo-Platonists, the world existed on two different planes of reality, viz. the formal, rational dimension of the Ideal, on the one hand, and the material, sensible antitypical dimension, on the other.[9]

Torrance will not entertain such a division, as we have indicated, for it was precisely this kind of thinking which laid the conceptual foundation for the dualism between 'the ultimately real and the world of the finally transient', i.e. between God and his world. In such a framework the material world can have little more than symbolic reference to reality, a reality subsisting ultimately not in its

---

[6] E.g. *Inst* IV.14.1, IV.14.4, IV.14.15, IV.17.24.

[7] Torrance notes the damage inflicted upon the Church's 'theology and experience' from such a dualistic outlook. He cites particularly the rift made by Kant, working from Augustinian premises, between the 'noumenal' and the 'phenomenal', between the hierarchical dimension of reality (things as they are in themselves) and the earthly dimension of sensory perception (things as they appear to us) (cf. *G & R*, 4, 17; *ST1*, 43-4, 48; *R & E*, 39).

[8] *R/st*, 175.

[9] One of the few things Torrance ever ventures to commend about the Aristotelian/Thomist synthesis of the late medieval period was its attempt to hold together 'concept and image, ideas and events', though he is never happy with its solution (*TS*, 18).

own manifest substance but in another dimension altogether.[10] Torrance comments further:

> In the Augustinian tradition... the universe was regarded as a sacramental macrocosm in which the physical and visible creation was held to be the counterpart in time to eternal and heavenly patterns. Thus the world of nature was looked at only sacramentally, i.e. looked *through* toward God and the eternal realities.[11]

Augustine's world was, to Torrance's way of thinking, thus doubly cursed: once for its inability to speak for and about itself, or to be understood except by taking a reading from its so-called higher pattern, and again for its lack of categories by which God's real interaction with it could be explained.

Under the influence of this kind of thinking, the Church was driven to invent 'an intermediary realm of grace' between the Creator and his world. The sacraments played their role in this intermediation as 'outward and visible signs of inward and invisible grace'.[12] In this context, the sacraments could at best only be symbol-signs of a divine reality which was incompatible with their physical, outward manifestation. Neither could the inward 'grace' represented by the sacraments really be identified with any kind of personal act by such an abstract deity, except in a purely 'instrumentalist' sense. In this view grace itself is the instrument of God, possessing inherent causality, and manifest under naturally comparable physical signs. The sacraments are thus twice removed from that which they signify, once from grace and yet again from God himself.[13] It is precisely this sort of fractured thinking, Torrance insists, which has robbed the Church's faith of vital encounter with God in the sacraments, and also prevented her from being able to rethink the theology of the

---

[10] Cf. *R/n*, 122.

[11] *TS*, 66. 'So long as man look[ed] only away from the world to God to find its meaning in its particular divine patterns' the development of modern science was fundamentally impeded, he says (*TS*, 67).

[12] *R/n*, 122; cf. Augustine, 'Letter 98', *Letters, vol. II (83–130)*, TFOC 18 (Washington, DC, The Catholic University of America Press, 1953), 129–38. Harnack quotes Hahn's definition as Augustinian: 'The Sacrament is a corporeal sign, instituted by God, of a holy object, which, from its nature, it is adapted by a certain resemblance to represent, and, by means of it God, under certain conditions, imparts his grace to those who make use of it' (A. Harnack, *History of Dogma* (London, Williams & Northgate, 1898), vol. 5, 157; he cites Hahn, *Die Lehre von den Sakramenten*, 1864, 12).

[13] *R & E*, 29; *R/n*, 123.

Eucharist in the direction of a sacramental realism, which recognizes that in the sacramental communion man truly and immediately meets God in the presence of Christ.

Torrance also rejects this sign-as-symbol mentality for epistemological reasons. As far as our knowledge of the natural elements is concerned, to speak of the sacrament as an 'outward and visible sign of inward and invisible grace' suggests a world depending on another reality for significance. What Torrance wants to say is that the natural element in the sacrament is truly significant in itself. The natural element considered alone will never say anything out of itself about him.[14] The sacramental universe of the Augustinians made the created order significant of a lofty reality but one exterior to itself, thus denying the world its proper dignity. For all of his emphasis on sacramental realism, Torrance is also emphatic that in the sacrament man will truly meet the natural element, manifesting its own created integrity even in the intimacy of sacramental relation with its Creator. In that relation there must never be a mistaking of one element for the other.[15]

Augustinianism relegated the sacraments merely to sign-symbols among a whole universe of these. Consequently, man was left epistemologically disorientated in a sea of divinity, where everything in general but nothing in particular signalled God's presence. He thus turned into himself to find God, and was left, as Torrance says, to grope in 'the vague mists of... [his own] vaunted self-understanding', for signs of the numinous.[16] There, however, he could only reflect upon himself; hence his theological formulations were determined by primary reference to his own thoughts and experience. For this reason, Western man, throughout the centuries, has projected upon God an image after his own (man's) image and construed his own thoughts as those of God.[17]

Torrance sees one of the most exciting trends of our day in the attempt being made in both the physical and theological sciences to 'think symbol and concrete reality together' (see below).[18] This

---

[14] Cf. *TS*, 101.

[15] He says, 'Theology will [not] confound knowledge of God even in his relation with creatures with the knowledge of creatures in their contingent relations' (*TS*, 57).

[16] Hence, for the Kantians, Torrance suggests, this meant that for man 'the one fixed point is his self-understanding. Theologically... there can be no God for man outside of himself or independent of his consciousness' (*STI*, 44).

[17] 'New College', 21.

[18] *TS*, 17.

denotes for him a fundamental breakdown of the Augustinian world view. On the one hand, it suggests a discarding of the notion of any inherent likeness between the earthly and the divine realities. On the other hand, it represents an overcoming of the need for the symbol to 'identify' God's presence and/or to afford that presence 'contact' with the world, thus precluding the need for 'intermediaries'. It also indicates the emergence of a corrective re-thinking of the basic relation of cosmology with theology, delegating to each field its own identifiable way of reasoning, with divine and contingent reality each being apprehensible without direct reference to the other and each representing (or 'symbolising') only that which it is in itself.[19]

This fundamental re-appraisal of the overall nature of reality Torrance perceives as occurring simultaneously today within the natural and theological sciences. Both disciplines have found themselves opposing the same unnatural disjunction of substance from structure, intelligible reality from sensible reality. With regard to epistemology, each independently of the other has arrived at similar conclusions as to how to apprehend knowledge in its

---

[19] In *Ground and Grammar of Theology*, Torrance points out that in valid scientific observation the 'visual image' of things, or things as they are outwardly observed, should not be conceived as symbolically representative of another reality or subjective states within the observer, but 'precisely in their objective reference to the invisible and intangible realities [proper to the larger reality of the thing in question] at levels beyond appearances and observations'. He speaks of the relation between the outward and inner character of the world as an *analogical relation*. He prefers 'analogy' to 'image' because of the latter term's symbolist connotation. This analogical relation is a genuine relation between the surface level and deeper level of *the same reality*. He says, 'In scientific operations, analogical relations are not relations in which we compare things with one another on one and the same level, but are relations in which the pattern of thought or image on one level is semantically significant when it refers beyond itself to a correlate on a higher [or deeper] level, which may well not be picturable at all, but may instead be inherently unobservable, as in quantum or in relativity theories.' The implications of this for Torrance's eucharistic theology will be seen presently (*G & G*, 115–16).

Torrance illustrates the unity of 'sign' and 'thing signified' in his epistemology, comparing it to the mutual inherence of form and matter. Form represents the rationality of matter or its inherent intelligibility. Our minds do not invest form into the object. 'We must distinguish the formal pattern of *our* knowing (relations of ideas) from the material in what we know (relations in matters of fact).' 'The formal pattern' *itself* or rationality of the object is the 'sign' of the 'thing signified' and inheres within it. It is the means by which we construct knowledge of that thing out of its own objectivity. By 'sign' in this context Torrance means that thing itself considered in its rational self-manifestation by which we intuit its fundamental reality (*TS*, 171–2).

respective field, based upon the rejection of dualist presuppositions. In physical science, the new physics is seen as displacing the old Newtonian physics which, as Torrance sees it, was founded upon an Aristotelian cosmology. Newton, working also from the presuppositions of Hellenic dualism, imposed an unnatural wedge between a world of rigid natural laws and that which could not be codified.[20] Torrance comments on the unseating of these sacrosanct modes of thought:

> Christian theology is confronted [today] with a scientific culture which is non-dualist and which breaks down barriers between the empirical and the theoretical, the tangible and the intangible, the visible and the invisible, and which does not automatically call in question a continuous dynamic interaction between God and the universe.[21]

He recognizes on the theological side a corresponding development countering the long-accepted Augustinian-Kantian disjunction between what we might think about ultimate reality and reality as it truly is. He discerns at the root of Kant's noumenal/phenomenal hiatus the conditioning of the Augustinian world-view. This gap is being bridged cosmologically, as well as epistemologically today, he attests, by theologians intent upon radically revising their understanding of created reality and the Creator's prerogative to interpret himself within the created order, viz. in the light of the incarnation. Torrance singles out the teachings of Barth among Protestants and Rahner among Roman Catholics as representative of this conceptual reassessment. Barth's conjunctive re-thinking of '*the being of God in his acts and the acts of God in his being*', is given special attention. Torrance reflects upon Barth's indebtedness to patristic thought, specifically for the idea of the divine word and action being united in the singular word/act of the Incarnate Son.[22] This is of especial relevance to our discussion in that God in his self-disclosure in Jesus Christ is neither distanced from, nor dependent upon, the created being in which he articulates himself. Christ's humanity does not speak for God or about God, rather God speaks through it for and about himself.[23]

In the hypostatic union of divine and human natures in the incarnation, both realities in their respective *noumenal* and

---

[20] *STI*, 40.
[21] *R/n*, 137.
[22] Cf. also Karl Rahner, 'The Word and the Eucharist', *TI*, vol. 4, 255ff.
[23] Cf. 'New College', 23ff.

phenomenal aspects are integrally sustained.[24] The divine word (the noumenal) and the divine act (the phenomenal) are coincidental in the Incarnate Son. So too, the human body (the phenomenal) and the human spirit (the noumenal) are substantiated and manifest together in him. Christ's humanity does not then finally corroborate the Kantian disjunction by itself serving as the mere phenomenal appearance of an essentially noumenal Being. The divine mind or spirit does not displace the human mind or spirit in Christ; that would be Apollinarianism. Neither does the assumption of the genuine humanity of Christ by the Word qualify the latter's divinity, as in Monophysitism. Christ is 'unqualified deity' and 'unqualified humanity', never more or less of one than the other.[25] Even in the incarnation, the humanity *qua* humanity of Christ does not serve purely as a sign of his divinity. A sign of divinity is definitely present; but only in virtue of the power and witness of the Word. The rest of this chapter will be devoted to expanding these thoughts with reference to the Eucharist.

Such incarnational thinking sets aside the possibility that God might require some secondarily effective sign external to himself to speak or act for him in the world. The Word made flesh rules out any other 'words' being definitive of what God is like. At the same time, the incarnation confirms God's constant disposition to speak his word within the conditions of space-time. The incarnation prescribes that wherever in the world God promises to speak and act, there he can, and in a way already defined in the fulfilment of all his promises in Jesus Christ.

Torrance takes all this to what he thinks is its natural, realist conclusions in eucharistic theology, something Barth will not do. Torrance criticizes Barth for his failure to shake off a lingering 'dualist orientation' in his sacramental doctrine.[26] Having dismantled the dualist construct in his realist understanding of the incarnation, Barth will not pursue its full implications for sacramental theology. Torrance insists that the incarnation instantiates the free intercourse God may have with his Church in filling all its sacraments with his presence and power. Barth hesitates in ascribing any power to the rites of the Church, even by the adventitious power of Christ. He interprets the sacraments mainly as

---

[24] These Kantian terms, replete with dualistic overtones, are employed here advisedly, simply to make a point which will in turn illustrate their irrelevance to our larger discussion.

[25] *G & R*, 138.

[26] *R/n*, 128–9; Torrance, *Transformation and Convergence*, 287.

aids for giving the believer an assurance of faith, and as 'imaging' for the Church 'the objective permanence of faith', positively realized in the 'once and for all self-offering of Christ on the cross and in the Ascension'. Instead of the Eucharist being the instrument through which Christ acts to realize his fulfilled word, as in Torrance's thought, the sacrament's efficacy for Barth is said to be laid out chiefly in terms of its 'calling... for ethical acts on our part as the appropriate mode of response here and now.'[27]

THE NATURE OF ANALOGICAL KNOWLEDGE

Torrance agrees with Calvin that 'the only knowledge of God possible is analogical knowledge'.[28] He would, however, immediately correct that statement christologically lest it be misinterpreted to mean that any natural analogy, any *analogia entis*, might exist between the divine and natural order.[29] He also denies that any residual, static analogy can be assumed between God and man based upon an ontological continuity or 'some prior relationship... on the basis of which common attribution is possible', e.g. the *imago dei*.[30] Calvin's statement is cited approvingly: 'There is no proportion nor likeness between God and His creatures.'[31] Torrance's doctrines of creation and the fall of man exclude this possibility.

---

[27] *R/n*, 128-99. Barth, especially in his later writings, deals with the sacraments chiefly in symbolical language. They are said to be 'confirmational' to faith, means to assurance in faith, but not means to the creation of it. Their most significant role is to *witness* to that which already is, 'the objective permanence of faith', viz. that the believer has 'already' entered into the fellowship of the death of Christ and is abiding in him. Unlike Torrance, Barth will not finally assign the sacraments a dynamic instrumentality through which God's Word might actually do something new (cf. Karl Barth, *The Heidelberg Catechism for Today* (Richmond, VA, John Knox Press, 1964), 106ff.).

[28] *CDOM*, 140; cf. *R/st*, 114. Cf. Calvin's statement: 'For God cannot reveal Himself to us in any other way than by a comparison with things which we know' (John Calvin, *Commentary on the Prophet Isaiah*, ed. William Pringle (Grand Rapids, Eerdmans, 1948), vol. 3, 223).

[29] *R/st*, 113.

[30] Cf. Frederick Ferré, *Language, Logic and God* (London, Eyre and Spottiswoode, 1962), 108-9.

[31] *CDOM*, 142; cf. John Calvin, 'The CLXXII. Sermon, which is the fourth upon the thirtith Chapter of Deuteronomie', *The Sermons of M. John Calvin*

All 'knowledge of God is analogical' because God has chosen to communicate himself to man within the contingencies of the created order. This is as it must be, for 'God cannot reveal himself to us in any other way than by a comparison with things which we know.'[32] Torrance's emphasis here, as we have observed, is always upon the God-givenness of this correspondence or analogy. The analogy between God and his creatures is an *analogia gratiae*; that is to say, in every divine interaction with nature it is always grace which defines that relationship.[33] The strength of any analogy is not in the likeness between nature and God but between the Word which God speaks there and the word which God is in himself.[34] Hence man's knowledge of God within the world begins not with an examination of the world *per se* but in the hearing of God's Word or the act of God's grace. For Torrance, 'nothing is prior to grace'.[35] It is the Word, or specifically God giving himself to us as Word in Jesus Christ, which is the 'given fact' of grace. God's own self-givenness in the created humanity of Christ is the final ground for analogy between God and his world.[36] Any analogy which is to refer back to God must, therefore, be erected by God himself. Only then can we be sure that our forms of thought and speech are rooted in the being of God himself, or, as he puts it, that God 'himself presides in all our judgements about him'. These are the premises at the heart of the meaning and economy of revelation for Torrance.[37]

God therefore has provided in Christ the definitive referent for the systematization of all creaturely thought about him. He is the

---

upon the *Fifth Booke of Moses called Deuteronomie* (London, printed by Henry Middleton for Thomas Woodcocke, 1583), 1065-71.

[32] *R/st*, 113.
[33] *KBI*, 142.
[34] *CDOM*, 142.
[35] Cf. J.B. Torrance, 'Covenant or Contract? A Study of the Theological Background of Worship in Seventeenth Century Scotland', *SJT* 23 (1970), 67.
[36] *TS*, 29.
[37] Cf. Ibid. 37f. Difficulties arise when man falsely thinks that he can speak of divine and created realities interchangeably, seeking to co-ordinate them 'in one and the same language': that is, without acknowledging the dependence of all thought and language about God and his relationship with the world upon the *analogia gratiae* in Jesus Christ. Inevitably, Torrance contends, man's capacity to hypothesize with respect to the infinite will collapse. He will then tend to universalize his despair, reading back into the divine–human intersection in Christ his own failure to bring into proper relation his thoughts and words about God and the world, making of the incarnation, corresponding to the inadequacy of his own statements about it, an *hoc significat* rather than an *hoc est* (*STI*, 76).

'primal sacrament' of God, so that it is through the particular creaturely form and life of this man that God decisively interprets himself to all men.[38] It is the hypostatic union of Creator and creation in Christ which is the parent analogy, 'the prime analogate', as Ferré would call it, which God has erected in the world and after which all other relations between God and his creatures are judged to be analogous to him, including the sacraments.[39] This adds yet another dimension to the meaning of Torrance's description of Christ as 'the all-inclusive Sacrament of the Word made flesh'. Indeed, it is Christ the Sacrament who ultimately 'sacramentalises the Sacraments' of the Church, i.e. it is the relation, or the interrelations between God and creation in him, that ultimately fills the sacrament with significance.[40] This has important implications for Torrance's broader understanding of sacramental signs and images.

Sometimes Torrance uses the terms 'sign' or 'image' to refer generally to the creaturely objects which can be assumed by the Word to facilitate his revelatory purposes in the world. He writes in one place that 'it is through word that the [creaturely] images are made to signify or indicate that to which they point'.[41] Therefore the whole creation is potentially 'a mirror, a theatre, a world of signs'.[42] However, following upon his insistence that creation's relation to God is not to be understood 'in abstraction from God's Covenant purposes, but only as the instrument of His purpose in revelation and reconciliation', the terms 'sign' or 'image' should technically not be applied to creaturely objects until they are actually made 'instruments of his self-disclosure', i.e. only in the context of God's direct act of revelation.[43] Though image or sign generally do not mean separate things to Torrance, the former will best be employed in our discussion of the 'reflexive' character of the revelation of God among his creatures, whereas the latter will serve most appropriately in our treatment of the dynamic nature of that revelation and the historic *Res/signum* question. We will address this issue first.

---

[38] Cf. *TS*, 150; *MOC*, 33.
[39] Ferré, *Language*, 108–9.
[40] *RP*, 77. For 'Sacrament of Sacraments' Torrance cites Aquinas, *Summ. Theol. Suppl.*, q.27.4.2–3.
[41] *TS*, 20.
[42] *SOF*, LIII.
[43] Ibid. LII–LIII.

I. The Sacramental Sign

(a) Res and Signum: Word and Sacrament

In view of his rejection of the entire symbol/reality construct, one can easily understand Torrance's hesitancy at using the word 'sign' to denote a sacrament. This is because of the widespread use of the term as if it were a synonym for 'symbol' in sacramental theology. It is precisely this kind of parallel that Torrance is seeking to avoid. On the other hand, he hesitates to give the term a sacramental connotation for fear that the contingent elements within the sacrament might be construed as other than creaturely and thus as being able to represent God in themselves. It was on these same grounds that Torrance, in his earlier writings, refused to debate the classical *Res/signum* question as traditionally framed, i.e. in terms of the natural correspondence between 'the invisible *res* or *virtus*' in the sacrament and its 'visible sign' in the created elements there.[44] The whole debate, he contended, suggested a static or purely metaphysical interpretation of the sacramental relation. The sacramental sign, he insisted, should be understood only 'in terms of dynamic movement', corresponding to the nature of the Word within it, who is himself defined in terms of the concrete act or the dynamic being of God and who cannot be 'conveyed in mere speech but has to be conveyed in saving acts'.[45] This fact determines for Torrance the inter-dependent relation which must obtain in the Church between the preaching of the word and the sacraments, and means that sacramental participation is understood as corresponding 'to the activity of the Word as Event'.[46] Torrance thus ascribes to the sacramental sign the dynamic Markan usage (cf. Mark 16:20), i.e. 'signs' being equated with the miraculous acts of the Lord, specifically those attendant on and confirming the preaching of the gospel.[47]

---

[44] *Inter*, 309; cf. *C & A* II, 142. Hermann Sasse's discussion of this question in his monumental study of Luther's sacramental theology, *This is My Body*, is most thorough and helpful, particularly for its clarification of the Augustinian roots of the issues at stake (H. Sasse, *This is My Body*, revised edition (Adelaide, Lutheran Publishing House, 1981), 19-21, esp. fn 10; cf. *G & G*, 63).

[45] *C & A* II, 142, 144; *Inter*, 306.

[46] *G & R*, 160. 'That is why the life and being of the Church are intertwined with Eucharistic proclamation, for the presence of the Living Lord in the Church, which is the very essence of the Church, is not a static presence, but is the living action appropriated by the Church in its continuous action of proclamation' (cf. *Inter*, 327).

[47] *Inter*, 309.

Correspondingly, in the sacramental sign the Word demonstrably realizes in the Church that which he promises in the sermon.[48] In the sacrament, he says, 'this Word proclaimed as divine event becomes divine event in the bodily existence of the Church and is fulfilled as Word'.[49] Strictly speaking, however, the sermon and the sacrament in

---

[48] The idea that God acts in the sacrament to fulfil what is 'symbolized' or promised there is a common one in Reformed eucharistic theology. John M. Barkley says, 'The term "symbol" in Reformed Theology is used, not in the popular but in its biblical sense, as constituting an act of God in the sacrament' (John M. Barkley, *The Worship of the Reformed Church* (London, Lutterworth, 1966), 70). Similarly, Torrance says that the sacrament 'effects that which it symbolizes because what it signifies Christ does' (Thomas F. Torrance and Ronald Selby Wright (eds. and revised), *A Manual of Church Doctrine According to the Church of Scotland* by H.J. Wotherspoon and J.M. Kirkpatrick, 2nd edn (London, OUP, 1960), 18–19. In a personal interview in Edinburgh (23 December 1985) Torrance referred to the section on the sacraments in this edition of Wotherspoon and Kirkpatrick's *Manual* as thoroughly representative of his own view. Indeed, he went so far as to say that its statement on the theology of the Eucharist, which he revised, could be considered as though it were his. All references to this work which follow therefore will be designated either to Torrance directly or, more often, to Torrance 'with Wotherspoon and Kirkpatrick'). In this he is reaffirming Calvin's own thought: 'For what is the nature of a sacramental union between a thing and its sign? Is it not because the Lord, who by the secret power of his Spirit, fulfills what he promises?' (John Calvin, *Commentary on a Harmony of the Evangelists, Matthew, Mark, and Luke*, ed. William Pringle (Grand Rapids: Eerdmans, 1957), vol. 3, 209). Torrance's identification of the sacramental sign with the miraculous signs accompanying the preaching of the gospel *as per* Mark 16:20, however, appears to be unique to his eucharistic theology. He states: 'In on-going history his healing and forgiving work is normally mediated through the Holy Sacraments which are given to the historical Church to accompany the proclamation of the Gospel and to seal its enactment in the lives of the faithful' (*STR*, 149). Indeed, he departs from Calvin in this case, who understood the sacramental signs as expressly not supernatural, but rather as 'ordinary' and containing 'no miracle' for the believer, or at least not the kind 'perceived by the eye or by some of the senses' (John Calvin, *Commentary on the Prophet Isaiah*, ed. William Pringle (Grand Rapids, Eerdmans, 1958), vol. 1, 241–2).

[49] At this point Torrance follows the early Barth, who defined a sacrament as 'an action in which God acts' or as the 'action added to the spoken word'. 'The sacrament appears... to go up to the sermon and to point out: there is not merely *speaking* here but here something is done! And what is done is just the event indicated in the Sacrament... nourishment in the spiritual life.... To the spoken word is added the action.' 'In pointing out the event-character of the Sacrament, it must not be understood as simply that the sermon as such is not event.... The sermon is also something done' (K. Barth, *Credo: A Presentation of the Chief Problems of Dogmatics with Reference to the Apostles' Creed* (London,

Torrance's thought do not stand over against each other as that which is not active to that which is, rather as heard event to manifest event.⁵⁰ Indeed it might be said that these do not stand over against each other at all, but rather both stand over against the Living Word. The sacrament represents for Torrance not merely another active way for the sermon to be reiterated, but is also a means whereby God who acts can express himself. God's Word in sermon and sacrament is one and the same Word, what he proclaims himself to be as word in the former he proclaims himself to be as action in the latter.⁵¹ Both are essential aspects of the *kerygma*, which Torrance interprets as God's active witness to himself as saving grace through the Church's preaching and sacraments. 'These may be distinguishable from each other in thought', he says, 'but are actually inseparable'.⁵²

Torrance occasionally points towards a certain illustrative element within the sacramental sign. To cite an instance: 'The Lord's Supper is', he says, 'a prayer and hymn of thanksgiving, dramatic prayer acted out in the broken bread and poured-out wine which Christ Himself puts into our hands through His ordinance'.⁵³ When he resorts to this kind of metaphor it is always the element of action within the sacrament from which he draws his parallels, e.g. as the text above emphasizes, the *breaking* of the bread and the *pouring out* of the wine.⁵⁴ Elsewhere Torrance speaks of the Church's

---

Hodder & Stoughton, 1936), 199–200; K. Barth, *The Knowledge of God and the Service of God according to the Teaching of the Reformation* (London, Hodder & Stoughton, 1938), 191). Later Barth prefers to speak of the sacramental relation to the Word as witness-signs to the nature of the Word as deed, but backs away from referring to them as comprising acts of God. Since they are characteristically acts of men, they can therefore 'only be a witness' to the divine act (cf. K. Barth, *Table Talk*, recorded and edited by John D. Godsey, SJT Occasional Paper, no. 10 (Edinburgh, Oliver & Boyd, 1963), 86).

⁵⁰ Cf. Barth's comments in the footnote immediately above. Torrance also resists any notion that the sermon should not be defined itself as action, as well as the suggestion that the sacrament is merely an addendum to the sermon and therefore of only secondary importance. The conjunction which Torrance makes of the sacraments with proclamation in this way means that 'Christ will not allow the Word proclaimed to return to him void but insists on actualizing in us the promises of redemption and regeneration that are extended to us in it' (*G & R*, 160).

⁵¹ Cf. *G & R*, 160.

⁵² *Inter*, 309.

⁵³ *C & A* II, 148.

⁵⁴ The illustrative, dramatic element in Torrance's eucharistic theology is always the *action* of the sacrament, which he understands as appropriate to the Word in a way that other created elements cannot be. In other words, it is not

sacramental communion 'pointing beyond itself to what Christ has done and does for us, ... [and] so *figures* our union with Christ'.[55] In this case, however, the sign is not merely left as a figure; it represents only in the concrete act of re-presenting' its subject. Our sacramental union 'figures' Christ's union with us precisely because our union with him is realized within it.[56] Even when Torrance is stressing their dramatic role, the sacraments never lose their dynamic, biblical quality as event. They are vital signs through which the mysterious union of Christ with his people is actually 'embodied in the Church on earth'.[57] This thought will be developed in detail in our next chapter.

In his later writings Torrance endeavours to deal more directly with the issue of *Res* and *signum* in the sacrament. What he says is characterized by a strong rejection of any dichotomy between the sign and the thing signified. All notion of symbolization is therefore dismissed outright. Indeed, Torrance seeks to relate *Res* and *signum* ontologically as well as epistemologically, which leads to his curious interpretation of signification. 'The outward sign and content belong together', he says, 'as form and content of the sacramental communion'.[58] Sign, as Torrance uses it, denotes a form of presence, a sacramental kind of presence, i.e. one which mediates itself through created objectivities. 'Sign', he says, 'is the worldly form which the Christ-event assumes in action, the point at which Revelation embodies itself actively in history'[59] It is the presence of God's word within the sacramental action of the Church which gives

---

the bread and wine *per se* that represent Christ, but the *taking, breaking, pouring, sharing* of those elements. Torrance speaks of the Eucharist as the 'sacramental enactment of the real presence of Christ' and by this he has a degree of the dramatic in mind. However, the strength of the analogy is never the Church's simulation as such, rather the act of God's Word in conjunction with the Church's act. He quotes Calvin approvingly, 'What the minister figures and attests by outward action, God performs inwardly' (*Inter*, 334; cf. *Inst* IV.14.17). Torrance even recommends a return to the old Reformation rubric at the Eucharist of performing the 'fraction' at the words of the institution, 'It is *broken* for you', and the pouring of the wine into the chalice at the words 'It is *shed* for you'. He makes a case for this on the grounds of Calvin's argument that 'almost the whole force of the Sacrament consists in the [verbs]... *broken* [and] *shed*.' (Thomas F. Torrance, 'Comments on Eucharistic Practice in the Church of Scotland today', *ChSSR* 5 (1983), 17; cf. *Inst* IV.17.2).

[55] *C & A* II, 141, italics mine.
[56] Ibid. 140.
[57] *Inter*, 310.
[58] *C & A* II, 141.
[59] *Inter*, 309.

it its significative character, so that the Eucharist is 'a sign *with* a meaning'.[60] 'A true sign', he says, 'has in it something of that which it signifies.[61] The *unio sacramentalis*, therefore, contains 'something of an identity' with that *unio hypostatica* and 'something of a difference'. There is an identity in that the divine Word is principally present and active in both and since the *genus* of humanity belonging to Christ in his union with God and that belonging to the Church in its sacramental union is the same. There is a difference in that the *unio hypostatica* is of a kind utterly unique and the particular humanity of Christ is not itself manifest in the *unio sacramentalis*.[62] Nevertheless, it is the true presence of the Incarnate Word which is that 'something [in the sign] of that which it signifies'.[63] The Word is 'the objective bond' between the sign and the thing signified.[64] In the sacramental relation Torrance is never prepared to separate form and content, for they subsist together in the Word. *Res* and *signum*, therefore, cannot be thought separately, the *Res* being the Word in his hypostatic relation with the creaturely life and deed of Christ and the *signum* being the God-man in his sacramental relation with the creaturely word and action of the Church's Eucharist.[65]

---

[60] *C & A* II, 141.

[61] Ibid. Cf. Calvin's statement: 'The thing meant consists in the promises which are in a manner included in the sign' (*Inst* IV.17.11).

[62] *C & A* II, 141; *TS*, 20. Speaking of the proposition, 'This is my Body', Torrance says, it is 'neither a proposition of identity nor of difference but of analogy; for the analogy reposes on the union wrought in Christ'. He means that the analogy is based not upon an identity of Christ's body with bread, or the symbolical 'likeness' of bread or its consumption with Christ and our partaking in him respectively (which would be in fact a statement of *difference*, according to the nature of a symbol) but rather upon the presence of that christological union in the sacramental union bearing active witness to itself (Thomas F. Torrance, *Kingdom and Church: A Study in the Theology of the Reformation* (Edinburgh, Oliver & Boyd, 1956), 144).

[63] *C & A* II, 141.

[64] 'The connection between the sign and the thing signified is the Word' (*R/st*, 20). This contrasts significantly with the early Barth who can find 'no true objectivity' in the sacrament, but who invariably contends that that objectivity resides rather 'in the Scriptures'. However, because of the presence of that scriptural objectivity in the service of word and sacrament, Barth can say that there is an objectivity at least associated with the sacramental meal (K. Barth, *Credo*, 199). In the later Barth the objective presence of Christ is still to be identified principally with the *kerygma*: 'Sacrament is included in the preached Word.' 'When we preach we do the same thing as the Roman Catholic priest when he is celebrating the transubstantiation' (cf. K. Barth, *TT*, 36, 22).

[65] *C & A* II, 141.

(b) An Active Analogy / An Active Sign

Torrance describes the Eucharist as an 'active analogy'. He prefers this to the term 'effective sign', which was popular in the Reformation.[66] One might think that this connotes a more passive role for the sacrament than the traditional understanding of 'sign', but this is only partly true. Certainly Torrance wants to dismiss altogether any synergistic implications that might be associated with the idea of sacramental signs, but he is not seeking to play down the divine action concurrent with the Church's sacramental action. To understand what he means by this new term we should recall his conception of the *analogia gratiae*. Analogy must be conceived dynamically, as we have said, or as existing within and by virtue of the Word's sovereign relation with its created instrument. What Torrance calls an 'active analogy' could just as well be deemed an 'active, analogical relation'. Once the emphasis is upon the action of God within the sacramental sign, Torrance is free to designate the sacrament as an 'active sign', but only then.[67] Indeed, after this is understood, he will go so far as to say that the Eucharist is 'an efficacious Sacrament, effective as well as signitive'; in other words, that God's word is present in the sacrament to realize, as well as declare, his promise.[68]

We have already noted in passing how the sacramental relation 'points beyond itself to what Christ has done', while stressing that its analogical function must not be conceived in some detached, abstract sense; in other words, not as pointing us away to a reality necessarily far removed from the sacrament itself. 'Distance' for Torrance in these discussions denotes ontological distinction, not spatial separation. In the analogy of the sacrament God speaks by his Word and acts in his speaking, granting the Church what the sacrament declares, namely, vital participation in Christ. Torrance, with Calvin, refers to the sacramental analogy having the power to 'conduct us upwards', to 'elevate us' or 'raise us up' to share in the life of God. The different but complementary ways Torrance has understood this illustrate the two incarnational models mentioned in the last chapter and demonstrate his dynamic understanding of the sacramental analogy. Early in his ministry Torrance, like Calvin, wrote of this 'elevation' effected by the word in the Church's sacrament as a transferral of reference from the earthly to the

---

[66] *Inter*, 309–10.
[67] Ibid. 310.
[68] *C & A* II, 154.

heavenly given by the inspiration of the Holy Spirit, or as an earthly realisation in the Church of that 'fellowship with the divine life', patterned after its heavenly counterpart in the incarnation.[69] Later on, with the benefit of patristic insight, he has begun to write more about the eucharistic worship in the Church being conjoined with that of Christ in heaven, finding the substance and movement of its own worship by virtue of that relation.[70] It is in this sense that the sacrament is finally seen to be a living analogy which leads us, as Calvin says, 'from the physical things... to spiritual things'.[71] According to both models, however, it is the presence of the Word within the sacramental analogy which effects this; in the first place, by directing our minds to the prime analogate, the christological reality, and, secondly, by uniting the Church to Christ in his worship and in that realizing his praise dynamically in the praise of the Church. It is the living character of the sacramental analogy's Subject, which not only gives the sacrament active meaning but makes it the active means by which the Church is drawn into a communion with God. Torrance says, 'Analogy without Christology is nothing'.[72]

(c) The Mystery of the Sacramental Analogy

The sacramental analogy is directly referable to the christological mystery: 'The incomprehensible union of God and man in one Person'. Since, as we have determined, it is the kind of active analogy in which God gives the Church communion in that mystery, the sacrament can be said to be a mystery itself, albeit in a derivative sense.[73] Torrance prefers the title *mysterium* above all others when referring to the sacrament because it avoids the impersonal, static categories, as well as the controversies associated with the *Res/signum* question. To speak of the sacrament as mystery is first of all to accentuate that transcendent divine magnitude associated with it, that which recedes to an infinite depth beyond the sacrament itself

---

[69] Ibid. 145; *Inst* IV.17.1-3.
[70] *R/n*, 118.
[71] *Inst* IV.17.3 (trans. F.L. Battles). See also François Wendel, *Calvin: The Origins and Development of His Religious Thought* (London, Collins, 1965), 332. He cites Calvin, *CR*, 1:119.
[72] *K & C*, 144, fn 5.
[73] *C & A* II, 141.

or our capacity to apprehend it.[74] Secondly, it underlines the dynamic nature of the divine presence there and hence of the sacramental relation itself, but of a divine action 'which is not yet fully disclosed in conditions of the fallen world'.[75] Finally, when ascribed to the Eucharist the term *mystery* stresses that the sacrament's meaning and efficacy depends utterly upon the christological mystery.[76] In Torrance's own words, ascribing the title *mysterium* to the sacrament has 'the advantage of preserving both the Christological mystery behind it all, and the dynamic character of the union and communion involved in participation in Christ'.[77]

---

[74] *Inter*, 305-6, 313; cf. *TS*, 149-50; *SOF*, LXI. 'Mystery means that our knowledge contains far more than we can ever specify or reduce to clear-cut, that is, delimited, notions or conceptions, and is concerned with a fulness of meaning which by its very nature resists and eludes all attempts to reduce it without remainder, as it were, to what we can formulate or systematize' (*TS*, 150).

[75] *Inter*, 310.

[76] It was around the question of causality or 'means' that Barth raised doubts as to the advisability of using the term *sacrament*. For Barth the whole notion of 'sacraments of the Church' inevitably denoted rites infused with the prerogative and power to 'give the immediate relation' with God themselves. Christ alone is 'The Sacrament' in this sense. The only 'means' or power which belongs to sacraments, as far as Barth is concerned, is the power to testify or witness. He therefore preferred 'to abrogate the word "sacrament" or to use "sacrament" for all ecclesiastical actions' (K. Barth, *TT*, 86).

Alasdair Heron comments on Barth's paradoxical assigning of significance to the *human* action in the sacrament precisely in an attempt to excise from the sacraments any synergistic implications! He states: 'Behind Barth, by contrast, lies a somewhat zwinglian rejection of "sacramentalism", sharpened up by Barth's own insistence that the so-called "sacraments" of Baptism and the Eucharist are not to be looked upon as vehicles of *God's* action but of *ours*: they are our witness and sign and response to the one sacrament which is Jesus Christ himself' (A. Heron, *Table and Tradition: Toward an Ecumenical Understanding of the Eucharist* (Edinburgh, The Handsel Press, 1983), 157). Torrance, in contrast to this, seeks to avoid any notion of sacramental causality by emphasizing the adventitious nature and predominance of the divine Word and Spirit in the sacramental relation. His use of the term *mysterium* demonstrates this.

[77] *C & A* II, 142. Torrance will not conjecture as to the inner workings of the *unio sacramentalis*. In the sacraments, as in the Holy Scriptures and their proclamation, it is the Word who unites the divine and the human in a true and vital union through which he communicates his truth to man. Since both content and agency of that truth are synonymous with the being and act of the Word, they both defy human explanation. Like its parent christological mystery, the mystery of the Holy Communion cannot 'be explained positively and put into precise rational terms' (*C & A* II, 142). What Torrance says regarding all

2. The Sacramental Image

(a) Reflected Images

We have indicated that in Torrance's view there is no inherent 'image' of God anywhere in creation. Neither is there any special endowment given the created proportion within the sacramental relation which alters this fact. In fact, it is the obvious creatureliness of that relation which serves the divine purpose in pointing away from itself to God. There is a built-in *sursum corda* in Torrance's theology of nature. Any likeness which might be seen between God and the creaturely image, exists solely because he has acted upon it and assumed it 'into such close relation with him that it may reflect His Glory'.[78] When Torrance uses the verb 'reflect' here he does so advisedly, implying the literal meaning of the term. Strictly speaking, the image of God resides only in God. In the Creator/creation relation, Torrance insists that 'likeness and conformity [exist solely] between God and his Word'.[79] It is thus God who must create an image of himself in the world, by assigning to objects or events meanings appropriate to, or 'reflexive' of, him.[80] The created instrument's role in revelation is simply to serve as a mirror of the Word. 'The image is always only a reflex... of his Word.'[81] As a mirror depends entirely upon its referent for what it reflects, so the

---

communication of the truth is also relevant with respect to the possibilities and limitations of the form of that communion offered in the Eucharist. 'Truth is communicated to us in the form of mystery (μυστηριον) that is in the form of a concrete fact or particular event to which nevertheless the Truth is infinitely transcendent. It is the revelation of Truth so full and rich and inexhaustible that the more we know of it the more we realise the ineffable and infinitefulness of its reality which defies complete disclosure within the limits of our experience' (*TS*, 149).

[78] *TS*, 68.

[79] *CDOM*, 142. Torrance cites J. Calvin, *Sermon on Deuteronomy*, 30:15f.

[80] Cf. *CDOM*, 35-6. Torrance's choice of the grammatical term 'reflexive' in these discussions over against the seemingly more appropriate 'reflective' is interesting. Although the latter word does designate 'action being turned back upon the subject' and thus could refer broadly to the function of a mirror, the former word better suits Torrance's purposes in that it stresses, in line with its grammatical meaning, the 'subject's action on himself or itself'. In this context then, it assigns the power of reflexion (reflection) not in the mirror (or nature) *per se* but wholly in the divine Subject (cf. 'Reflex', 'reflexive', *Concise Oxford Dictionary*, 872; 'Reflect', 'Reflex', 'reflexive', *Chamber's Twentieth Century Dictionary*, 1134-5).

[81] *CDOM*, 128.

created sign depends entirely upon the image of the Word for that which it 'images' in a secondary sense. As Torrance puts it, 'Man looks into the mirror of creation, too; and he also beholds the image of God there, only he does it through the Word, which, properly speaking, is the image of God.'[82] One notes here the ambiguity of the concept of image. This ambiguity shows Torrance's anxiety to stress the total dependence of man's perception upon God. Without the insight which the Word affords us, he says, 'the world of creation is a labyrinth in which we are only lost and swallowed up... for only by the thread of the Word can we find our way through it to the Light of God'.[83] Analogy for Torrance is always to be understood in active, relational categories, never in static ones.[84] The analogy is sustained only so long as that relation is maintained.[85]

Torrance's christological summation of all this is wholly predictable. Earlier we observed that the way divine and creaturely realities were made to 'correspond' in the incarnation should be considered determinative for all other divine/creaturely correspondence. The incarnation, considered in its interrelations, can be said to be the parent analogy after which all other analogies are given appropriate reference to God. It follows naturally that the Incarnate Son would be seen by Torrance as 'the express image or the lively image of God' in created being.[86] Although he strictly qualifies statements like this in light of God's invisible nature, as we will see, he can still say that Christ is God uniquely 'imaging' himself to man.[87]

In Christ the image and what is imaged, the mirror (the divine humanity) and what is mirrored (the divine being), as well as the power to reflect (the act of the divine being) all co-inhere and complement each other. All are manifest in Christ in a fundamental, quintessential way, so that every other divine/creaturely relation must subsequently image what he is. The Incarnate Word is the *primum exemplum* of which every other divine word in created

---

[82] Ibid. 40.

[83] *SOF*, LIII.

[84] *R/st*, 114.

[85] Cf. *CDOM*, 31, 38.

[86] Ibid. 42; *K & C*, 150; *The Incarnation*, XVIII.

[87] As we will see, this does not mean that the historical Christ actually comprised an eidetic image of God. This is an impossibility, since, in line with Anselm's thought, 'God is greater than we can conceive' (*R/st*, 19). Like all other valid images of God, the image of God which Christ connotes is one of denotation not description, indicating concepts of God's character and truth, not purporting to reproduce visibly his invisible being.

utterance is a reflection. The image of God disclosed in Christ is an enduring image by virtue of the permanence of the incarnation. In the ascended Christ God has inextricably bound himself to his creation. Though this world is still hindered in its ability to reflect God's glory because of its marred relationship with him, the intimate relation which God maintains with the world in Christ offers creaturely being a proximity to glory it has never known before and therefore a possibility for the reflection of that glory it could never imagine.

(b) Verbal and Visual Images

Torrance affirms that 'images have and must have a place in our knowledge of God'.[88] He means, in this case, all 'images' projected by the Word, verbal ones as well as visual. For man assimilates reality to his mind by both verbal and visual means and does not discern uncreated spiritual reality except through creaturely images.[89] However, Torrance highly favours the auditive image. 'The connection between the sign and the thing signified is the Word', he states, adding that this connection 'involves an acoustic not a mimetic relation'.[90] For the auditive means of communication is directly appropriate to God, whereas the visual is not.[91] God can be heard but not seen. The auditive image is preferred over the visual image also because, as speech-event, it corresponds more closely to God's dynamic nature. Furthermore, faith arises only *ex auditu*, 'not by sight'.[92] It is 'word [which] is the personal and human and historical communication through which Christ has ordained that He will be met and known, and through which He has ordained that He and His Gospel will be proclaimed to all men'.[93]

Torrance contrasts the Roman Catholic and Reformed ways of comprehending knowledge, the former in its preference for the 'language of vision', the latter for audition. He sees the former as ultimately meaningless since visual imagery must always be interpreted and informed by the auditive.[94] Human language is

---

[88] *TS*, 19.
[89] Ibid. 19.
[90] *R/st*, 20.
[91] *TS*, 19.
[92] *R/st*, 58.
[93] *SOF*, CXXII.
[94] Certainly Roman Catholic theology historically has preferred visual imagery, not only devotionally, e.g. the devotion to the Sacred Heart, but

always the ground for signification in the natural order.⁹⁵ Not only that, but visual images are incapable of communicating themselves. This inability in itself would deny their identity with a truly living God. A pictorial image without objective explanation must finally be interpreted by the viewer. This recalls Torrance's warnings against the ultimate subjectification of theology when its primary epistemological ground in Christ is lost. Nevertheless, he admits that there is an 'essential and unavoidable place' for the knowledge of God being construed 'on the pattern of visionary experience', since 'we are inescapably involved with earth and history'.⁹⁶ Furthermore, according to Torrance's own method, the Word of God Incarnate requires material as well as verbal correlates for his communication among men. He states it poignantly,

> It is, I believe, still within the matrix of Eucharistic worship and meditation upon the Holy Scriptures, and evangelical experience in the fellowship and mission of the church, that the empirical and theoretical components in

---

eschatologically too, e.g. the 'beatific vision'. (Note the discussion of the relation of the concept of love and the 'bodily heart' of Jesus in K. Rahner, 'The Theology of the Symbol', *TI*, vol. 4, 249ff.) However, there has never been a total absence among Roman Catholic scholars of those who would insist upon a necessary predominance of the verbal or auditive image in order to inform the visual image. For example, Pope Paul VI quotes a eucharistic hymn by Thomas Aquinas suggesting a preference for 'audible images' *vis-à-vis* visual ones:

> Sight, touch, and taste in thee are each deceived;
> The ear alone most safely is believed:
> I believe all the Son of God has spoken,
> Than Truth's own Word there is no truer token.

(Pope Paul VI, *The Holy Eucharist*, Encyclical letter *Mysterium Fidei* (London, Catholic Truth Society, 1965), 10.)

Further, the popular, present-day Roman Catholic convert and lay theologian, Malcolm Muggeridge has said, 'there are some forms of communication which are more clearly related to reality than others.... I would say the written word, for instance, is more effective than the visual image which is a very superficial thing and is not capable, except in very exceptional circumstances, of expressing ideas. It can only convey the phenomena of life, and to use them to express ideas is extremely difficult' (M. Muggeridge, 'A Line To Reality', interview in *Viewpoint Magazine*, vol. 32, 7–8).

⁹⁵ *G & R*, 150. Torrance states: 'Into this created rationality (or *logos*) that the Word (or *Logos*) of God enters, assimilating it to Himself in the incarnation, *in order to become Word to man through the medium of human word*' (*G & R*, 139–40, italics his, then mine).

⁹⁶ *TS*, 23, 27; *R/st*, 24.

our knowledge of God are found fused together, in a kind of stereoscopic coordination of perceptual and auditive images, and thus provide us with the cognitive instruments we need for explicit theological understanding of God's interaction with us.[97]

The Eucharist is thus envisaged as the principal visual correlate in the Church. Torrance never suggests, however, that the sacrament somehow says in pictures what the word cannot say otherwise. His point is that the sacrament enhances the Church's ability to hear God speak.

God the Word, by means of a sacramental relation with both media, informs the sacrament of the Church with meaning via the Scriptures. For it is 'the relation created by the Word (the Scriptures in this context) that is fundamental... to the sacramental relation'.[98] By this, Torrance is not setting word against sacrament, as if the former had more efficiency than the latter. Nor is he saying that there is more efficacy in the word by virtue of the sacrament's being added to it. 'God is equally active in word (the Scriptures and/or preaching) and in the Sacrament', he insists.[99] Neither the secondary objectivity represented in the bare words of the Bible and/or in its proclamation, nor that proper to the sacrament convey any power of their own. Both the Scripture and the sacrament depend upon a sacramental relation for their power. All potentiality in such relations inheres solely in the uncreated Word.

Though the proclamation of the Church is never dissociated from the sacrament, and though the sacrament depends upon the spoken word for explanation, efficacy in the sacrament is not to be identified with the verbal image any more than with the visual image. There is no vestige in Torrance of a latent 'secondary causality' reposing in the written or spoken word, as can be detected in some of the writings of the Reformation. Efficacy exists in the person of

---

[97] *R & E*, 49. Whereas 'it is through the Word (the word as preaching, though within the Eucharistic celebration) that Christ comes to us personally and worship reaches its focal point and culmination in personal encounter with the living Christ... [it] is then that holy Communion has its rightful place crowning faith with vision and enacting in our flesh and blood the real presence of Christ' (*C & A* I, 55-6).

[98] *TS*, 25.

[99] *G & R*, 160. 'Apart from the Word', he says, 'sacraments cannot exist. Apart from the Word there is only an empty sign that is nothing but a ceremony' (*Inter*, 313). 'Just as the head without the body is useless, so the Word without the Sacraments is an abstraction, and the Sacraments without the Word are a torso' (*RP*, 101).

the Word himself who is related to both verbal and visual signs in an adventitious way – although, admittedly, the verbal form lends itself more suitably to his service. The Incarnate Word is 'equally active' in sermon and sacrament.[100] This does not mean, as one might think, that the activity of the Word is equal in both, but that it is equally the Living Word who is active in the sacrament as well as in preaching. Though Torrance would agree with Rahner and Barth that the proclamation of the Church is itself- technically a sacrament, he never puts it like this.[101] He also resists Barth's later tendency to emphasize the divine Word's sacramental activity in preaching to the near-exclusion of everything else.[102]

Torrance repeatedly stresses that all images, both verbal and visual, finally break down in their attempt to express their inexpressible Object. As we have implied, the goal of theological knowledge, for Torrance, cannot be a description of the truth in either words or pictures, for divine truth by its nature precludes this. Neither is the goal ultimately understanding as such. The end as well as the means of theological knowledge is participation. It is in order to facilitate this participation that the sacramental relation, entailing the spoken word, the bread and wine of the table, and all other creaturely aspects of the Church's active response to God's gracious invitation, is placed 'at the very heart of Christian theology'.[103] The sacramental relation underscores the participatory nature of our knowledge of God and itself offers to the Church a form of that knowledge as participation.

(c) 'Imageless' Images

'Images', Torrance says, 'have to be taken, not in a descriptive but in a *paradigmatic* sense, that is, as aids to our human weakness in apprehending the indescribable God.'[104] By insisting that God must employ created images to be understood by man in his weakness, Torrance does not imply that God is thereby catering for man's addiction to sensible reality. Torrance does not fall into the depreciatory notion typical of the sixteenth-century sacramentalists who insisted that the believer should be weaned from the material element and satisfied only with the purely 'spiritual factor' or its

---

[100] *G & R*, 160.
[101] 'Sacrament is included in the preached Word' (K. Barth, *TT*, 36).
[102] Cf. K. Barth, *TT*, 86.
[103] *TS*, 24.
[104] Ibid. 20.

corollary in the Church, the auditive witness. Torrance's non-symbolist understanding of created reality prevents him from devaluing the material element in revelation. The sacraments are not second best. There can be no adequate comprehension of God in space-time without them. Whether strong or weak, in the economy of revelation man only knows God by sacramental means, by word *and* sacrament, not by the spoken word alone.

In the above statement Torrance is not just stressing the limitations of the verbal image compared with the visual image. Before the indescribable God *all* images ultimately fall short. For 'God is not imaginable'.[105] The Church therefore is bound to rethink the role of its 'signs' or 'images', so as not to suggest that they actually portray God. Images are to serve as 'paradigms' of the Word, i.e. as 'pointers' specifically to the Word in his divine-human reality. He says, 'Granted that images have and must have a place in our knowledge of God, are they not tools rather than pictures, pointing to a reality they do not describe?'[106] The created image thus points to God in such a way that 'we may have some hold in our thought upon his objective reality, but without actually imaging him', and we might add, by drawing as little attention to themselves as possible.[107] 'The likeness or comparison the images entail is to be regarded *as helpful to man rather than as fitted to God*, since they suggest or indicate and do not exhaust him.'[108]

Torrance speaks of Christian theology's communication of the truth of God by 'imageless imaging', complying with the interdiction placed upon the Hebrews against the fabrication of effigies of God.

---

[105] *R/st*, 90.

[106] *TS*, 19.

[107] Ibid. 20. In another context Torrance gathers many of these familiar metaphors together to explain the function of images with regard to theological statements. Theological statements are 'reflexive statements'. They are 'analogical statements', i.e. 'they are genuine statements so far as they *derive from* [the] Word and *refer back* to it' (*R/st*, 33, 36). Analogical statements, words or ideas 'correspond' to God only as they 'refer back or upward [and] to God', i.e. to his own self-interpretation by the Word from which all theological language has its meaning (cf. *R/st*, 33). The function of theological images is not descriptive but 'ostensive and persuasive', underlining their unique instrumental relation to the Word in his act. Their role is not to convey creative ideas detached from the divine existence but to *direct* us beyond ourselves to the divine existence and to bring our minds under his reality (*R/st*, 91, italics mine).

[108] *TS*, 20. Torrance quotes Hilary here and in another place again: 'There can be no comparison between God and earthly things, but the weakness of our understanding forces us to seek certain images from a lower level to serve as pointers to things of a higher level' (*ST1*, 20–21, *De Trinitate*, 1:19).

The Bible prohibits 'images of the imagination as well as of clay or metal'.[109] For while God is unimaginable, he is not unknowable.[110] He therefore acclaims the Jews' unique ability to intuit the word of God auditively, without the aid of visual images. They learned to 'think without images', he says, or to hear without seeing.[111] This does not imply that they could somehow think without the assistance of 'word-images' or intuit God 'above and beyond the Word' in some fanciful 'wordless vision'.[112] They had acquired, however, the ability to cognize in words without pictures. When mimetic images did arise in their minds they learned to qualify them immediately as essentially unrepresentative of the One who defies description.[113]

We might think that all of this is said finally to make the point that our images are not in themselves constitutive of that which they reflect, viz. Jesus Christ who is 'in his word and act... the image of God'.[114] But Torrance is saying more than this, for even in the Incarnate Son, the human aspect does not replicate the 'imageless' God who is united to it. Even in Christ God prohibits us from identifying the distinctly human with the distinctly divine element. In other words, the differential remains; the 'ineffable and infinite fullness of [the Word's] reality defies complete disclosure within the limits of our experience'.[115] This is not to introduce an inscrutability in God, rather it accentuates his inexhaustibility even in Christ.[116] There is not some feature of the Godhead which cannot be known or could not be present to man. That would be tantamount to saying that there still remains something in the depths of human or divine being which makes for a divide or prevents an unfeigned knowing relation. This cannot be, since in Christ 'unqualified Godhead' is immanent to 'unqualified humanity'. God has not left hidden some

---

[109] *R/st*, 90.
[110] Ibid. 20.
[111] '*Israel*', 5.
[112] *KBI*, 98.
[113] He contends that 'there will always remain an element of impropriety in human statements about God' (*TS*, 86). He therefore draws the parameters carefully for the words by which we think of the Creator: they must not be pushed 'beyond the boundary of creaturely being', for 'God reveals Himself to man in such a way that he does not need to stretch himself beyond his humanity to know Him'. Otherwise they take on 'a mythological form' and we project 'the creaturely content of our statements as such on to God' (*STI*, 19; cf. *TS*, 86).
[114] *G & G*, 40.
[115] *TS*, 149–50; *G & G*, 167; cf. *STI*, 67.
[116] Cf. *G & G*, 163.

dark aspect of his being. There is not, as he says, 'another God behind the back of Jesus'.[117]

In Christ the fullness of the Godhead dwells bodily in all its integrity, but certainly not in its entirety. Torrance is attempting to prevent the Monophysite heresy being committed again. The finitude proper to our humanity must also be respected in Christ and at every level of his being. Even at the depths of the *hypostatic union*, the adventitious nature of the divine Word's relation to his creaturely being remains. The incarnation has not modified God's being; it has added human being to it.[118] Therefore in our reflection upon the humanity of Christ we must be careful not to

> [read] back into God himself the material or pictorial images that arise out of the reciprocity he has established with us through the incarnation of his Son in space and time, for through the oneness of the Son and the Spirit the iconic images of God in the Son are made to refer imagelessly to God.[119]

For all his insistence upon the validity of the *communicatio idiomatum*, Torrance always maintains a real, though necessarily abstract, distinction between the being and operation of divine and creaturely realities in Christ. Thus, strictly speaking, even the humanity of Christ does not image God. By Torrance's own definition, the image of God which Jesus Christ manifests is also constituted only in its relation with the Word. The divine-human relation, like all other images, has divine significance only by virtue of the Word's act upon created being there. Even in the Incarnate Son, *essential* likeness exists solely between God and his Word.[120] He too is an Imageless Image.

---

[117] *MOC*, 69f.

[118] 'If we are to take seriously the fact that God became man in Jesus Christ, really became man once and for all, without of course ceasing to be God, then must we not ask what that imported for God himself? Does it not mean that to all eternity God has ceased to be God only, since he has taken up human nature into himself and maintains it there to all eternity, so that there is no God for us now except this God who is exclusively bound to Jesus Christ' (*Transformation and Convergence*, 288).

[119] *G & G*, 166. While Torrance is making the point here that in Christ we do not have the impossible, that is, an image of the Unimaginable, he is also reiterating the lessons learned in his epistemology and recalled in this section, viz. that we must 'obstruct ourselves from projecting our subjectivities into God or from confounding God known by us with our knowing of him' (*G & G*, 163).

[120] Torrance speaks of the Spirit making the so-called 'iconic image of God in the Son... to refer imagelessly to God' (*G & G*, 166). By this he is saying that the Spirit allows us to penetrate beyond the outward structure or manifestation of the incarnation to its inner structure, to the objective interrelations of the

In the light of the full scope of God's Word, the Church is able to translate, as it were, the human life of Jesus from that which is only visible into meanings appropriate to his transcendent identity, and which defy 'perceptible expression'.[121] The vital centre of God's communication to us is not in the humanity of Christ *per se*, but in the relation of that humanity to God, i.e. in the divine humanity. Neither is it in the historical thirty years of Christ's earthly life only, for that was removed from us in the ascension.[122] God continues to communicate to us today from the depths of that relation in the ascended Christ, and he does so invisibly by the Spirit. This does not imply a circumvention of any created aspect of the incarnation in the Spirit's communication of knowledge to us, 'for that knowledge does not allow us to leave the *man* Jesus behind when we know Him in his divine nature'.[123] He says, 'The very humanity [of Christ] embedded in our knowledge of God is an essential part of that knowledge, for it belongs to the essential nature of the Truth.'[124] However, the participatory knowledge given to man by the Spirit, corresponding to

---

hypostatic union, there to discern the true meaning of relation to God. Everything in the human life of Christ must come to be understood as an outworking of this most basic statement of his being. Torrance warns the Church against the tendency in modern theology of viewing Christ's objectivity only in terms of the exterior life of the historical Jesus without proper attention to the dimension of depth within that phenomenon, i.e. that mystery of the incarnation discernible only by the light of the Word. He comments: 'The aspects of the life of Christ that have to be interpreted in the language of vision, have their full meaning as predicates of the Word made flesh, the Son of God become incarnate. This is precisely the aspect of Christ that cannot be seen, but can only be heard.... We hear a word from beyond, the eternal Word of God from beyond the observable, a Word which, while it is made flesh at this end, yet recedes into the eternity of God at the other end' (*TS*, 24).

[121] *TS*, 23. *G & G*, 49–50.

[122] *G & G*, 163. Torrance is not indicating that knowledge of God is possible apart from the humanity of Christ, or indeed the historical Jesus, for 'it is in and through persistent attention to the empirical (or historical) correlates of theological knowledge... that the theologian [maintains] his orientation to objective reality' (Thomas F. Torrance, *Christian Theology and Scientific Culture*, Theological lectures at the Queen's University, Belfast, 1980 (Belfast, Christian Journals Ltd., 1980), 111). 'There is an inevitable and proper element of [the] anthropomorphic in our knowledge of God' (*G & G*, 163). He says further, 'The humanity of Christ is 'embedded' in our knowledge of God [and] is an essential part of that knowledge, for it belongs to the essential nature of the Truth' (*TS*, 86-7).

[123] *TS*, 149, cf. 146.

[124] Ibid. 86-7.

both the inward and primal knowing relation in Christ and the Spirit's own invisible nature, is itself conveyed to man in an unseen Way.[125]

The place of the formal sacramental relation in this emphasis upon paradigmatic images is interesting. The sacrament, joined analogically as it is with the ultimate paradigm of the incarnation, can be said to be *an image of the Imageless Image*. However, for the Eucharist to be in such a relation with the christological mystery means that it must serve the truth vitally, not just as its static illustration. The analogical relation proper to the sacrament is an analogy which offers dynamic communion with invisible reality. The Word by the Spirit in the sacramental relation is said to communicate invisible truth invisibly and so enhances the Church's ability to think correctly about God. The Word 'makes us look through the images and hear past them to what God has to say, and so apprehend Him in such a way that we do not have and are not allowed to have any imaginative or pictorial representation of Him in our thought'.[126]

Torrance has a predilection for theoretic, abstract models, which are 'free from representational qualities'.[127] His whole approach to reality gives rise to this. The concern of natural science, he insists, is to understand physical reality ontologically, or from the most essential, yet invisible, statement of its nature. He sees common ground existing in this method between pure science and pure theology, or dogmatics, in that both reject the assumption that all knowledge must be 'describable in terms of perceptible expression'.[128] Quite the opposite is actually true.[129] 'Relativity theory', for example, 'shows that what is observable cannot be represented with scientific precision without reference to what lies outside observation altogether.'[130] Similarly in theology, we have seen how the christological mystery must not be considered only from its outwardly observable form, but from the innermost centre of its reality, at that intangible depth revealed solely by the Word.[131]

Predictably, when Torrance illustrates truths in the area of pure theology from the natural world, he does so from the field of pure

---

[125] Cf. *G & G*, 166.

[126] *TS*, 20.

[127] Cf. 'Abstract-Art', *Concise Oxford Dictionary*, 5.

[128] *TS*, 23; cf. *G & G*, 49–50.

[129] 'The real force of analogical relations in scientific operations', is, as he calls it, 'the cross-level reference, in which images on one level refer to what is imageless on a higher level, but which from that higher level controls meaning on the lower level' (*G & G*, 116).

[130] *STI*, 83.

[131] Cf. *Christian Theology and Scientific Culture*, 110.

science. For example, he demonstrates the importance of theology thinking 'imagelessly', by referring to quantum theory and its concern 'with objective realities that are quite non-observable, and where we have to decipher the information content of invisible light signals that pervade and illuminate the whole universe'.[132] The highly abstruse 'particle theory' demonstrates for Torrance the necessity for non-partitive thinking relative to God, i.e. understanding the nature of all things, even the persons of the Trinity, in their interrelations with each other.[133] He also substantiates how imperative it is to achieve a unitary or non-dualist outlook upon reality by the new understanding in physical science of 'the mutual interaction of the space-time metrical field and all matter-energy in the universe'.[134] Furthermore, he compares the relationship between the theology of the Church and its divine object with that between geometry and physics. Just as geometry cannot operate as an independent science apart from physics or 'the science of its inner rational structure', so a natural theology is impossible apart from its *natural*, proper subject matter – the 'actual knowledge of the living God as a prior conceptual system of its own'. The Church's definitive apprehension of the knowledge of God within the human being and word of Christ, functions as a sort of 'theological geometry', says Torrance, to determine 'the *inner* material logic of the knowledge of God'.[135]

It is more in method, however, than in a commonality of models, that Torrance's theology parallels the new physics. For just as the pure scientist seeks to penetrate beneath surface phenomena in order to understand the created order and calculate according to its intrinsic structure, interconnections and inner-coherences, so Torrance, in line with the principles laid down in his pure science of theology, seeks to apprehend the Incarnate Word beneath the outward form of his self-disclosure, i.e. in the inter-relations of his divine and created proportions which inhere within the very inner-relations of the Trinity itself. The theological scientist, no less than the philosopher of science, can say 'that our knowledge... is not cut short at appearances or what we can deduce from them, but is a grasping of reality in its ontological depth, and that we are unable to pierce through appearances and apprehend the structures of reality unless we operate with the ontological integration of form and being'.[136]

---

[132] *MOC*, 30.
[133] Ibid. 58–9.
[134] Cf. *DCO*, 12ff.
[135] *STI*, 69–70, italics mine.
[136] *G & G*, 162.

(d) Transparent Images and the Sursum Corda

The word of God is that divine objectivity 'indefinitely transcending' the sign. Apart from the divine Word, the created signs or images are 'opaque' and naturally disoriented to uncreated reality, having only creaturely reference.[137] However, as the Holy Spirit appropriates them to function within God's revelatory purposes, they are made, in Torrance's terminology, 'transparent', i.e. windows through to God. Such a transference of reference is imperative, since an understanding of the universe in any of its relations to God can only be perceived out of God himself.[138]

True images of God then must point away from themselves and point us away from ourselves, 'as they direct us to look at God or rather listen to him' instead.[139] Torrance has already been shown to

---

[137] R/st, 93–4.

[138] G & G, 83.

[139] R/st, 91; MOC, 100. Torrance draws two illustrations from either side of the Church which highlight the necessity for the Church at large to perceive the spiritual depth behind its outwardly visible or audible images. He offers first an example from the iconology of the Eastern Church. Normal pictures, even the most abstract ones, are usually painted so as to present their subjects to the viewer in as nearly life-like, 3-dimensional proportions as possible, that is with their subjects appearing larger nearer, as it were, to the observer. In these kinds of paintings the focal lines of the pictures' subjects actually meet at a central point in the picture itself.

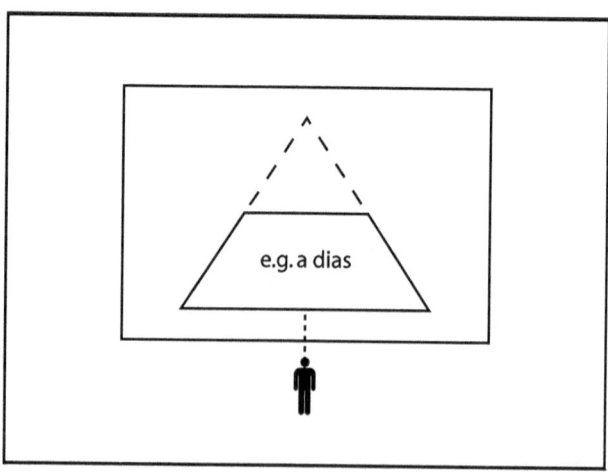

In pure Byzantine iconography, however, this natural plane of perspective is reversed. The objects in the picture are turned around in their

use the example of a mirror to stress the reflexive relation of the image to its subject; now he seeks to clarify further the reflexive character of analogy, insisting that the image should be seen through as a window.[140] The Word sounds through the images out of its own reality and thereby makes them instruments through which we perceive the knowledge of God.[141] It is the Holy Spirit who 'makes the content of what is revealed (by the Word) burst through the forms (e.g. the Church's words and sacraments) employed so that our acts

disposition to the viewer, so that he seemingly observes them backwards, or with the objects appearing smaller nearest him.

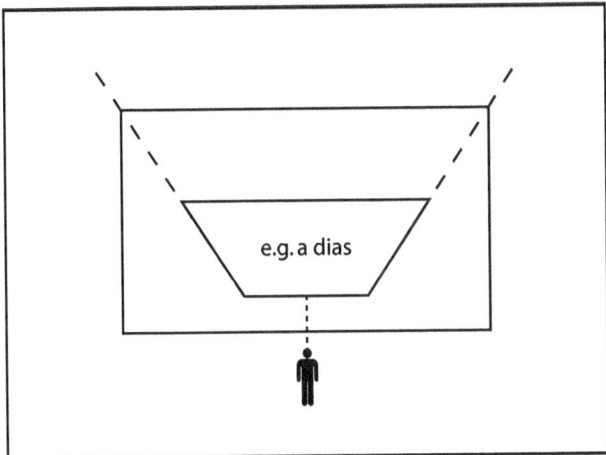

This, in effect, gives the icon an abstract depth with its focal lines being projected to infinity outside it, thus directing the worshippers beyond the visual image to their depth and meaning in an infinite God. Torrance makes the point that 'The range of vision [was opened out] from the spacial and temporal into the infinite and eternal, from the material and visible into the immaterial and invisible Majesty of God Pantocrator' (*STI*, 83, cf. 18).

He makes the same point from the Western Church, which has historically been associated with devotion to verbal images, e.g. to the Bible and preaching. This illustration Torrance uses in the form of a corrective. It must be remembered that the Word of God always 'transcends our speech'. We should never think that our words, even the inspired words of the Bible, actually contain God's Word, rather they convey it. The Word of God is not given to us in the Bible 'in the form of delimited and tight propositional ideas but only in verbal forms that always point away from themselves to the Word itself, that is to the Word speaking in Person'. Thus, our 'words about the Word' should be malleable in his hands, always remaining open to the mystery that speaks within them but lies beyond them (*TS*, 40).

[140] Cf. *R/st*, 89.
[141] Ibid. 94.

of cognition are formed from beyond us by the reality disclosed in the very act of disclosure'.[142]

We have already observed the place Torrance assigns in his epistemology to primary and secondary objectivity. The role of secondary objectivity is mediative, but only in the sense that it affords the Word creaturely correlative material or 'media' through which to speak his message. Only then in relationship with the Word can images attain transparency, so enabling us to look through them and understand the reality to which they refer.[143] Their meaning in reference to God is not found at some remote depth proper to their own reality, or even in their relation to the Word as such. Torrance makes precisely this point when referring to the sacramental images' relation to Christ: 'The analogical relation by itself tells us nothing, for that is just the bare form of the sacramental relation; but the content of it is Christological, that is, union with Christ, and, as we have seen, such a union that it reflects in itself the nature of Christ.'[144]

All images realize their function vitally as they become part of God's act of self-disclosure to man. Likewise the sacramental images' significance and purpose lie entirely in their function to point us to Christ. Therefore 'a proper understanding of the Eucharist', Torrance says, is not to be gained by looking at the Eucharist *per se*, or formulated 'in terms of external relations between Christ and the Eucharist', but wholly in the Word's act within the sacramental relation directing our attention away to Christ.[145] The Word, from his incorporation of all men in Christ and within the eucharistic sign of that incorporation in the Church, acts sacramentally to effect that which is signified, viz. a vital union of the Church to Christ in one body. It is then in this dynamic sense that we are to understand how images finally become transparent, i.e. precisely as they are made sacramental or communicative of the reality they signify. It is from this active understanding of the transparence of images that we can perceive the place which the *sursum corda* has for Torrance within

---

[142] Ibid. 94.

[143] *TS*, 20; *R/st*, 91.

[144] *C & A* II, 141. It is not the relation of the Word to the visible material or action of the sacrament, neither is it the relation of the Word to the Church in the sacrament, which interprets the Eucharist. In other words, the sacramental relation does not finally interpret or 'objectively control' itself. The Word in his hypostatic union with man *in Christ* – the divine-human objectivity – alone defines the sacrament (cf. *G & G*, 120).

[145] *GT*, 6.

the Eucharist. The Church does not 'lift up its heart' or 'look away from the sacrament to Christ' by the power it can muster out of its own memory or experience. It does so by the light of God's Word. The Word of God is at once both the means and the object of the *sursum corda* of the Eucharist. He is the source of the Eucharist's transparency, as well as the object observed through it. It is the Church's part, he says, to purify and adapt its 'liturgical language until it becomes, as far as possible... a transparent medium for communion with God in which we do not obstruct discourse on His part'.[146] However, such 'refined activity' by the liturgists only serves to facilitate transparency, it does not effect it. No amount of polishing the mirror evokes a reflection. The Church's sacraments 'window' Christ by the Word's reference to himself through them. It is he who, in the midst of the sacramental action, eclipses the Church's act, precisely by realizing in it the gift of the real presence of him who is its subject. The full significance of this for Torrance's eucharistic theology will be shown in our discussion of his doctrine of the eucharistic sacrifice.

The presence of the Word in the context of the creaturely elements of the Eucharist allows these eidetic 'images' to witness to their subject by virtue of what they cannot be in relation to him, viz. anything other than created being. The images' incapacity to speak of the mystery which they signify apart from the Word, accentuates that mystery's divine magnitude.[147] The stark contrast between the created elements within the eucharistic image and its divine Creator-Subject is in itself the built-in *sursum corda* mentioned earlier, which leaves no doubt as to whom the glory belongs.

It is not, however, only the material elements in the Eucharist which cry *sursum corda*; the very nature of the sacramental union between Christ and his Church speaks of a mystery which it cannot reproduce. 'In the Eucharist', Torrance says, 'the wholeness of its union in Christ is received *only sacramentally* in brokenness of time'. The limitations and discontinuity of this 'sacramental' kind of relation, when compared to the inimitable depths, permanence and completeness of the Church's union with God embodied in Christ, demands that all reverence be given to the latter. The sacramental sign, he says, is 'such an embodiment in conditions of time as to point beyond itself to an infinite fulness'.[148]

---

[146] *G & R*, 157.
[147] *Inter*, 313.
[148] Ibid. 309, italics mine.

Torrance seldom mentions the *sursum corda* except in the context of the ascension. We have already established that the analogical relation of the sign to the matter of the sacrament depends entirely upon the nature of the matter, so that sacramental relation is 'determined by the nature of Christ Himself, who is the substance of the matter signified'.[149] Thus far we have focussed attention primarily upon Christ's nature considered in its most essential form, viz. in the hypostatic union. The sacrament's christological matter, however, must not be construed only in terms of that ontological state, as though the hypostatic union existed as a distinct entity, as some removable factor within the God-man. Indeed, it is in and by that union that the divine-human person of Christ exists, and is now ascended to the manifest glory of God.

Christ's ascended state then should also be taken fully into account when the Church expounds the nature of its sacramental relation to him. The sacrament must be understood as an image of a mystery glorious both for the depth of the divine-human union and for the height to which human being has been raised in Christ. The depths and heights of this mystery far transcend the ability of our minds to comprehend, or of the word and sacrament to communicate its significance. Torrance reiterates Calvin's emphasis; 'We must raise up our minds and hearts above' where Christ is, seated on high.[150] By this Calvin and Torrance both insist that the Church should order its thoughts about Christ and the theology of its eucharistic communion in him, taking into careful consideration the implications of the 'distance' of the ascension. This so-called 'distance' accentuates the transcendent element in the Christ-event. The ascension for Torrance always highlights the uniquely divine nature of that event as well as underscores the fact that explication of the 'act of communion in the Body and Blood of Christ' lies 'beyond our senses and our abilities to provide [explanation] in rational categories' and must be given to us from the side of God.[151] This suggests in turn the operation of the Holy Spirit and the whole doctrine of participation in Christ through communion in him.[152]

---

[149] *C & A* II, 141.

[150] Ibid. 142.

[151] Ibid. 142.

[152] The understanding of the role of the Holy Spirit, which Torrance inherited from Calvin, is given prominence in his doctrine of the *sursum corda*. What is said here with reference to the Spirit's place in the economy of revelation could have as easily been said in the context of his eucharistic theology: 'The Spirit stands for the ultimate majesty of God, the ultimate

The ascension manifests the ultimate intellectual inaccessibility of the Incarnate One by accentuating the divine character of the Christ-Event. He can therefore say it 'guards the mystery of the sacramental relation'.[153] For Torrance the *sursum corda* highlights this, serving as an exercise by the mind of the Church in epistemological deference to God who must always finally explain the mystery of his ways among men.

We can thus see the crucial place of the *sursum corda* in the light of Torrance's overall theological method. Not only does it uphold the basic premise that the world in its relation to God must be interpreted by God's action upon it, but it also reasserts the necessity for 'epistemological repentance' on the part of the would-be knower of God, and indeed provides in the midst of the eucharistic knowing-relation an exercise of intellectual submission by the Church to the grace and Word of God.[154]

(e) Redundant Images

Torrance has his own way of stating the final design for all visual and/or verbal signs before the mystery of the ascended Christ. All forms or signs which the Church brings to God, even those brought at God's direction, exist in a state of tension with the Word in his Spirit. This is not to suggest that there is anything intrinsically repugnant to the divine Spirit in the natural element. Rather, there is, as Torrance repeatedly affirms, a created dissimilarity between the natural order and the revelation of God. Hence, 'the Spirit of Truth... resists the forms we bring to him'.[155] He means that the Spirit of revelation naturally throws off any attempt to be contained or 'spoken for' by the created sign, and immediately empties them of any pretext of 'telling the glory of God' in and of themselves, precisely by speaking through them his own unmistakably divine word.

For Torrance the sacramental images exist in the Church so that the Word may speak through them and be heard 'past them'.[156]

---

objectivity in which we are carried over from ourselves to knowledge of God out of God, and not out of ourselves. The testimony of the Spirit is essentially that which inheres in the objective truth of God, and when it echoes in our hearts it directs them *away from themselves to God* in his own eternal Being' (*R/st*, 96, italics mine).

[153] *C & A* II, 142.
[154] Cf. *TS*, 122; *C & A* II, 142.
[155] *R/st*, 96.
[156] *TS*, 19–20; cf. *R/st*, 91.

Therefore, when the Word is recognized in its relation with the created image or sign, and heard to speak there, a radical 'conversion of analogies' takes place.[157] That is, the church makes 'a transition from the observable to what cannot be observed but may be heard, and from the world of created realities to the Creator Himself'.[158] He could have called it a silencing of our analogies. For the message spoken by the Word immediately gives the lie to any attempt to make any analogy, taken by itself, archetypical (in the Platonic sense) or anything more than an ectypal analogy, albeit a dynamic, active one.[159] The sacramental analogy tells a story in which it has no direct part to play. When that story is told its work is done. After conclusive reference to the parent analogate is made the sacramental sign has no further service to render. Hence, the final duty of all significative instrumentalities in the Church is to make themselves redundant, or, as Torrance puts it, 'in a real sense *dispensable* as they do their work and we apprehend the reality through them'.[160]

For Torrance the ultimate goal of the sacramental sign is to empty itself of significance, i.e. so thoroughly to ascribe its meaning to another that his word and presence ultimately displaces the sign altogether in the mind of the Church. We have illustrated how fundamental it is in Torrance's theology that the Church recognize that the created element within the sacramental analogy, 'the thing brought into comparison with God[,] is nothing'.[161] By this, Torrance is not bringing the created substance into disrepute. On the contrary, he is seeking to maintain its integrity before the predominant majesty of God. This simply means that 'in comparison with God' there is naturally no comparison, no point of proportional identity.[162] Neither is Torrance emptying the sacramental analogy of importance, rather he is saying it is empty, impotent, indeed non-existent, except for the Word's appropriation of it to his service. Our thoughts, he insists, must never 'terminate at the image but at the reality itself which we perceive through and beyond the image'.[163] Even in the closest embrace of Christ within the sacramental union,

---

[157] Ibid. 133.
[158] *G & R*, 205.
[159] Cf. *TS*, 133; *R/st*, 133.
[160] *TS*, 19, italics mine.
[161] *CDOM*, 140.
[162] Ibid. 139; *STI*, 86.
[163] *R/st*, 89.

the Church is not permitted to equate its relation there with its primal relation with God in and through Christ.[164]

We next turn to examine with Torrance the exact nature of that christological objective reality itself, the Paschal mystery of Christ, which it is the goal of every sign to reflect, and upon which the mystery of the Eucharist is grounded.

---

[164] Cf. *C & A* II, 143.

CHAPTER 3

Sacramental Matter and Action: the Objective Christological Ground and Potential for the Sacrament

∽

THE THEOLOGICAL BASIS

The union of God and man in Christ demands that we think conjunctively and christologically of the matter and the action of the sacrament. With regard to God himself, as we have shown, there remains no ontological distinction, no temporal or spatial distance, between who he is and what he does in creation. All divine power in the world resides in and proceeds directly from God himself. This means that if God's power is effective within the sacrament, he himself must be there, for God and his power are one. This divine reality, in the unity and freedom of his being and act, has joined himself to man in Jesus Christ in such a way that, while not divested of his identity as God, he assumes real human identity. Although ontologically the divine and human dimensions in Christ must be distinguished, they must also be regarded as existing together in a new, singular identity in him, since it is God who acts from within human being as human word and deed.¹ In Christ 'God and man *completely concur*, so that the same person is at once God and man.'² This was observed at the very outset of this dissertation as the most fundamental assertion of Torrance's theology. In that context we noted its profound epistemological implications; it has equally profound ramifications for his sacramental thought, for God cannot be known in the revelatory 'sacramental relation', either in word or formal sacrament, except from the integrity of his incarnation. The divine Word-Act is apprehended in the world only in dialogue with the creaturely being of Jesus Christ.³ Torrance states: 'There is an indivisible unity in the ultimate Fact of Christ, true God and true Man. Theological knowledge rests upon and partakes of that duality-in-unity in the Person of Christ.'⁴ What this suggests is that if God's being and operation are one and if they are to be identified formally and inextricably with the single life and work of Christ, then his presence manifest in the sacrament (sacramental matter) and his power demonstrated there (sacramental action) must also be a singular entity, identified with the mystery of the Incarnate Son.

'THE PASCHAL MYSTERY OF CHRIST': THE EUCHARIST'S OBJECTIVE REALITY

I. 'The Mystery of the Eucharist', Soteriologically Defined

(a) A Comprehensive Interpretation of 'The Paschal Mystery of Christ'

A year after the publication of his most comprehensive treatment of eucharistic theology, 'The Paschal Mystery of Christ and the Eucharist', Torrance was commissioned to prepare a summary

---

[1] This means that 'in what he is and what he says he is creative Act of God, so that we have to think of him as Person and as Word only in an active sense, for his Word does not fall short of what he is or does, and his Person does not remain uncommitted in his Act any more than he is uncommitted in his Word' (*R & E*, 143).

[2] *R/n*, 157; cf. *C & A* I, 242–3.

[3] Cf. *R & E*, 21.

[4] *TS*, 149.

statement of his eucharistic thought. He did this in the form of a 'General Thesis' or condensed version of the previous work.[5] He further reduced that abbreviated statement to a single, opening sentence. It would be difficult to find a proposition which more efficiently draws together the major themes of his thought:

> The mystery of the Eucharist is objectively grounded in the Paschal mystery of Christ which gives it its meaning.[6]

In the light of what we have said already about the things of God being revealed to the Church always out of the 'inner logic' of Christ, we would be correct to assume that when Torrance here refers to 'the Paschal mystery of Christ' as affording objective meaning to the sacrament he is speaking of the christological mystery considered at a profound ontological level. We would be incorrect, however, to think that in seeking to interpret the Eucharist from a study principally of the interior reality of Christ's person, we will be preoccupied only with the finer points of Chalcedonian christology, that is, with drawing implications for the sacrament purely from a union of *phuseis* or from the relation of human *ousia* with the divine *hypostasis*, *anhypostasis* and *Enhypostasis*, as finally codified by the Second Council of Constantinople. Although Torrance is firmly committed to these conciliar definitions, he regrets that they were formulated in almost entire abstraction from the salvific life and work of the historical Jesus. The hypostatic union is not just a formal statement of christology but a working soteriological principle. Reconciliation, he contends, is not something accomplished simply by the interpenetration of natures within the hypostatic union, or something merely added to it, but is that union 'itself at work in expiation and atonement'.[7] Therefore, when Torrance suggests that it is a 'Paschal mystery' which affords meaning to the Eucharist, he is underlining the sacrament's principal soteriological orientation based upon the saving disposition of its object. In other words, the meaning of the sacrament reflects the meaning of the gospel. The Eucharist, he says, is a 'sacrament of the Gospel'.[8]

---

[5] The abbreviated version was published in 1976 (*GT*, 6–12).
[6] Ibid. 6.
[7] *C & A* I, 239ff.
[8] Cf. *MOC*, 105. 'The Gospel as it is proclaimed in and by the [sacrament] belongs to evangelism as much as the Gospel proclaimed in the Word. Christ communicates himself to us through both and through both together' (*MOC*, 107).

In spite of this corrective, we might still be led to think that by the phrase 'the Paschal mystery' Torrance is suggesting that it is exclusively the passion events in Christ's life which interpret the Eucharist. The adjective 'Paschal' could refer merely to Christ's historical *pesah*, or those happenings stretching from the final celebration of the Passover with his disciples through his sufferings and death on the cross to his resurrection.[9] Indeed, in line with what he sees as the Passover-context of the Lord's Supper, and in agreement with the Reformers, Torrance insists that the Word presents Christ in the sacrament as one sacrificed.[10] It must be remembered, though, that however the Word 'presents' Christ to the Church, he does so in person. Therefore, when Torrance seeks to secure the historical event of Christ's death for the Church's Eucharist, he begins with the Easter event, the fact of the Living Christ.[11] Taking the implication of the resurrection fully into account, therefore, Christ's sacrifice can be understood as present in the sacrament simply by virtue of the presence of the risen Christ there 'as one sacrificed'. The resurrection guarantees, for Torrance, that what Christ has done for us will not be lost to either his past or ours, for Christ 'cannot be separated from what he did'.[12] The Church is confronted in its Eucharist with 'not merely a piece of past history' but with Christ's historical *pesah* as living event.[13] For Torrance, Christ's sacrifice is contemporaneous with the Church's ongoing life.[14] Hence he can say it is 'at the Cross' where Christ meets and

---

[9] Cf. *STR*, 49–50; *C & A* II, 134–5.

[10] *C & A* II, 134ff. Cf. J.D. Crichton, 'A Theology of Worship' in C. Jones, G. Wainwright, E. Yarnold (eds) *The Study of Liturgy* (London, SPCK, 1978), 11–12. It is in the light of his foremost act of self-giving on the cross that God draws all to himself. In his passion 'in the fullest sense the divine Word and Act were one in the person of Jesus Christ' (*Inter*, 306). Here the identity of God's Word and Act with the word and act of Jesus Christ reached the ultimate depth of expression. God and man were never more noetically congruent than in the perfect obedience demonstrated on the cross. Paradoxically, it is at the cross also, at the very point of mankind's greatest disobedience, that God brings man in the person of Christ to the perfection of obedience in perfect love. Cf. Hebrews 5:8-9: 'although he was a Son, he learned obedience through what he suffered; and being made perfect he became the source of eternal salvation to all who obey him'.

[11] 'The New Testament', he says, 'does not present us with a message of Good Friday and *then* with a message of Easter, but always and only with the Easter message of Christ crucified [and] risen again, the Lamb who has been slain but who is alive for evermore' (*STR*, 49, italics mine).

[12] *R/n*, 120.

[13] *Inter*, 306-7.

[14] Torrance can speak as though we were actually in contact with the

gives himself to man in the sacrament; 'we make contact with him', he says, 'only through His wounds'.[15] On this basis he identifies 'the form of [Christ's] actual and active presence among us', the peculiar 'eucharistic form' of his presence, as 'the form of his humiliation'.[16] It is the real presence of one who brings his sacrifice with him in his flesh and blood. Although Christ's passion finds its fullest expression in the crucifixion, it cannot be thought of as only there, i.e. separated from the saving significance of the rest of his life, either before or after his death. For Torrance that which saves us is never envisaged as an event encompassing only a single moment of time in the life of Christ, but rather 'the whole action of Christ for us, in His Incarnation, obedient life, His Self-sacrifice for us on the Cross, His Self-offering to the Father in His ascension on our behalf and His eternal advocacy of us or intercession on our behalf'.[17] While he never diminishes the importance of redemptive deeds, the all-inclusive salvific event is the event which the Incarnate Son of God was and is himself. It is in these terms that Torrance provides us with his most thorough definition of the Paschal mystery:

> Jesus Christ was regarded as constituting in himself the great Passover from death to life, from man-in-death to man-in-life of God.... It is, then, in that profound unity and continuity, ontologically structured in and through the Person of Christ as Mediator, that the resurrection was understood as forming with the crucifixion the great *Paschal Mystery* of our salvation.[18]

Torrance is fond of quoting Calvin's phrase, 'Christ clothed with his Gospel'.[19] 'Christ and his Gospel belong ontologically and inseparably together', he says, 'for that is what he is, he who brings, actualizes and embodies the Gospel of reconciliation between God and man and man and God in his own Person.'[20] His desire is to give the whole human life of Christ its rightful redemptive significance.[21]

---

historical happenings themselves: 'The People of God from generation to generation continue to participate in the once and for all events of the birth, life, death, resurrection and ascension of Christ' (*SOF*, LVIII).

[15] *R/n*, 121; *RP*, 58. 'In [the Lord's Supper] He who was crucified comes to show us His wounds in His hands, feet and side, to give us peace and forgiveness through His passion' (*C & A* II, 138).
[16] *R/n*, 120–21.
[17] *C & A* II, 144; cf. *SOF*, xx.
[18] *STR*, 49.
[19] *R/n*, 120; *TS*, 146; *SOF*, LVIII.
[20] *MOC*, 73.
[21] *SOC*, LXXXVI.

We are reminded of his criticism of classical christology, that it was formulated with little reference to Christ's historical life and deed. Torrance's argument with Reformation and post-Reformation soteriologies (with the exception of Calvin) is that out of the magnitude of Christ's earthly life they isolate only certain days or events as having redemptive importance. Contrary to this, he insists that each day of Christ's life had salvific significance; every prayer was an offering of love made for us; every temptation comprised its part of what Calvin called that 'perpetual Cross' which he was obliged to carry, in that he made atonement by 'the whole course of His obedience', i.e. the offering of the totality of his life.[22] 'Throughout the whole life and mission of Christ', he says, 'hypostatic union and reconciliation, incorporation and atonement, involved each other in redemption and new creation.'[23] 'The Paschal mystery *of* Christ', then, becomes 'the Paschal mystery that *is* Christ'. It is the saving mystery understood in this way which Torrance suggests must objectively control our thinking about the Eucharist.[24] He gathers these thoughts in a single statement: 'The Eucharist by its very nature points us beyond itself to its constitutive reality in Jesus Christ himself, to the saving mystery which he is in the unity of his person and work and word as the one Mediator between God and man.'[25] It is Jesus Christ, he affirms, who 'constitutes himself in his paschal mystery as [the Eucharist's] objective reality'.[26] The Eucharist is but the 'foreground' then of the saving event of Christ who is 'the objective ground', from whom and by whom all God's Power moves upon the Church.

(b) *The Christological Nature and Fulfilment of the One Covenant of Grace*

Torrance expounds 'The Paschal mystery' in terms of God's working out his covenanted purposes in Jesus Christ, or, more specifically in the terminology of classical Reformed theology, as 'the One Covenant of Grace and its total fulfilment in the Person and Work of Jesus Christ'.[27] From the guidelines which he has set out we can be sure

---

[22] Cf. George S. Hendry, *The Gospel of The Incarnation* (London, SCM, 1959), 35; Hendry cites Calvin III.8.1.
[23] *C & A* I, 241.
[24] *G & G*, 120.
[25] *R/n*, 108–9.
[26] Ibid. 119.
[27] *SOF*, LII; cf. *TS*, 68. We have already noted his reference to this covenant

that what it entails and how it is brought to completion will have direct bearings upon what the Eucharist means. It must therefore be examined carefully. The Covenant of Grace fundamentally involves God's will to have personal communion with man and his establishing man in a knowing relation with himself. As the title suggests, it arises from and is framed in God's disposition and act of grace. Grace is central to the whole idea of covenant in Torrance's thought, implying the predominance and unilateral nature of the divine operation in its transaction. God's way to fulfil his covenant is to fulfil it himself. God has in Jesus Christ entered into relationship with man irrespective of his acknowledgement and acceptance of him. He 'was incarnate by the Holy Ghost of the Virgin Mary'. He has entered into an ontological relation with all men in the assumption of our human flesh.[28] The election of man, the seal of the new covenant, has been cut 'into the flesh of Christ'.[29]

Although affirming that God's covenant originates and is executed solely at God's initiative and by his power, Torrance contends that every covenanted relationship has its reciprocal aspect, that it 'asks for [a] response'.[30] However, this part too, that is, man's part, God undertakes to fulfil for us as a man himself. In other words, he fulfils the covenant 'from both sides'. The Incarnate Son, he says, 'takes over responsibility for us' in the divine-human relation to know, love and serve the Father in a way that belongs to a genuine filial relationship between man and his God.[31] It is in this sense that the incarnation is said to be 'the goal of the Covenant', for it constitutes the realization of God's will to have fellowship with man to be our God and that we be his people – in that man is brought in Christ into an ongoing dialogue and intercourse in being with God of the most intimate kind.[32] In this the covenant is fulfilled and 'the great act of salvation' accomplished. Consequently, God is already and always will be, in the words of *The Westminster Larger Catechism*, 'a God in Covenant' with man.[33] To speak of God having

---

in his exposition of the Reformed doctrine of creation (cf. Chapter 1, section B8). Torrance contends that if Reformed theology has a 'systematic principle, it is to be regarded as deriving from this Covenant [of Grace] and its fulfilment in Christ and as such derives from the very substance of the Gospel' (*SOF*, LII).

[28] Cf. ibid. CXXII.
[29] *RP*, 6; cf. *SOF*, LXXXVIII.
[30] *SOF*, L.
[31] *MOC*, 86-7; *R/n*, 158; *SOF*, LXXXVI-LXXXVIII; *STR*, 115.
[32] *SOF*, LIII; *MOC*, 86-7; cf. *R/n*, 157-8.
[33] *SOF*, 207; cf. *DOG*, 35. Torrance cites *The Westminster Larger Catechism* in *SOF*, LXXIII.

reciprocally secured the covenanted relationship in this manner introduces the radical substitutionary base which underlies Torrance's eucharistic theology and must be taken fully into account if the latter is to be rightly understood.

(c) *The Essential Substitutionary Presupposition*

We have indicated an ever-increasing significance being delegated in Torrance's theology to Christ's role as mediator between God and man, as one who represents the things of God to man and the things of man to God, e.g. in his understanding of the mediation of revelation.[34] This notion is implicit in his concept of a two-way fulfilment of the Covenant of Grace. The 'controlling centre' in the covenant action is always located in the act of God, specifically in what he accomplishes for us as man in Jesus Christ. Torrance seeks to explain Christ's vicarious ministry by combining the concepts of representation and substitution. Christ is The Representative Man, he says, echoing Barth; he is the one sent by God who stands for the many.[35] However, he asserts that the concept of representation by itself does not sufficiently depict the intensity of Christ's internal embrace of our humanity. It only addresses the salvific deed in exterior categories.[36] Already his eucharistic theology has shown that such superficial relations will not suffice. We cannot, he contends, 'think of what Christ has done for us only in terms of representation, for that would imply that Jesus represents, or stands for *our* response, that he is [merely] the leader of humanity in humanity's act of response to God.'[37] Torrance goes beyond this to address Christ as the Substitute Man, though avoiding the legal connotation which is sometimes associated with this idea, a connotation which makes Christ one who is merely accounted in our place.[38] He states that 'if Jesus is a substitute in detachment from us, who simply acts in our stead in... [a] formal or forensic way, then his response has no ontological bearing upon us but is an empty transaction'.[39] God in his saving deed does not remain aloof from us, he does not save us, as it were, from a distance. 'Substitution is possible only on the grounds of incorporation', he insists, and 'we are unable to regard

---

[34] *MOC*, 86–7; *R/n*, 201.
[35] *Inter*, 317, 330.
[36] *MOC*, 50.
[37] Ibid. 90.
[38] Cf. *SOF*, LXXVII; *STR*, 63ff.
[39] *MOC*, 90.

these two as alternatives. They belong together inseparably.'[40] The Son is made man's substitute because he is 'made man' himself; he redeems our humanity from within it.[41] In his human identity everything he does toward his Father is reckoned and received as an act of man, not by God having to think of it as something different from what it is, but because it is that in reality. Christ takes our place not just economically but immanently.

Torrance asserts that in order to approximate the scope and depth of Christ's deed the two ideas of substitution and representation have to be combined and recognized as interpenetrating each other within the controlling concept of the incarnation.[42] Christ stands for the one and the many, precisely because he is 'The One and the Many, the One who includes the many, and the Many who includes each one'.[43] God's purposes are said to be realized for all men in and through this 'one particular and individual Man', yet, his 'incarnational union with us involves all men'.[44] Torrance can speak like this because the Substitute is a divine-human person – on the one hand sharing a genuine, individual human identity with each of us, while, on the other hand, related ontologically to us all as our Creator. The substitutionary/representative act is therefore not the act of man *qua* man or God *qua* God but of the Word Incarnate acting as man from his hypostatic relation with our human being.[45]

---

[40] *C & A* I, 249.

[41] Cf. *SOF*, LXXVII.

[42] *MOC*, 90; cf. *STR*, 112 for an example of Torrance's use of 'Representative Man' in this way.

[43] *SOF*, CXXIII.

[44] *SOF*, CXXII, CXI. 'In His Incarnation the Son of God became one particular and individual Man, for that was the way in which he entered into relation with all men in the flesh... therefore the relations of God with all men are to be understood as relations through this one Man, Jesus' (*SOF*, CXXII).

[45] In his own flesh God has 'made the generations of humanity his very own' (*MOC*, 50). That is, the Son and Word of God became man by becoming one particular Man, but because He is the Creator Word who became Man, even as the incarnate Word He still holds all men in an ontological relation to Himself. That relation was not broken off with the Incarnation. It may be argued that this applies only to the eternal Son, but if we really hold that the human nature and the divine nature share in one hypostasis or person, it will be extremely difficult to maintain that Christ has only generic relation to men' (*SOF*, CXII). Christ is therefore not another man to us properly, 'Christ and his people are properly One Man' (*SOF*, CIX-CX).

(d) The Christological Nature and Fulfilment of the One Covenant of Grace (cont'd)

The way God realizes his covenant will, not only from his side but from ours, the way he substitutes for man by living as a man himself, demonstrates in Torrance's theology the essential, inextricable link which the ontology of Christ has with both the economy of salvation and the matter/action of the sacrament. The whole scheme of redemption is envisaged as unfolding and realized within the humanity of the Word.[46] By this he is not referring to the body of Jesus *per se*, although that is never excluded, but principally to his finite mind which, as Torrance understands it, is the essence of Christ's humanity.[47] At the same time he insists that the mediation of reconciliation cannot be referred 'simply to the humanity of Jesus' in either mind or body, but rather 'to the mediatorial ministry of the Son of God *within and from the side of our humanity towards God the Father*'.[48] Christ's human being is seen to serve the predominant Word as the focal centre for the two-fold fulfilment of the covenant. It is 'the all-important middle factor' between 'the two parties of the covenant partnership'. It is the fulcrum for the movement of God's covenant love.[49]

Christ's human being, however, does not just comprise the setting where the covenant is transacted but also the material out of which it is fulfilled. For in order for the covenant relation to be secured and an appropriate response to be made, man has first to be put into a right disposition toward God. Torrance is thinking both ontologically and christologically: ontologically, because this involves an integral renewal of man's mind, since it is precisely this aspect of his humanity which must frame a proper reply to God's grace; christologically, because it entails both the ministry and the mind of Christ, for he is the one who must offer such a response as man. Torrance concurs with Gregory Nazianzen and Cyril of Alexandria that what 'has not been taken up, has not been saved'.[50] It is imperative therefore that God 'takes up our estranged human

---

[46] Since in Jesus Christ God himself has come into our human being', Torrance states, 'the atoning reconciliation takes place within the personal Being of the Mediator' (*MOC*, 73).

[47] He says, 'We must think of Christ in his vicarious humanity as Mediator of our salvation in mind as well as body' ('New College', 27).

[48] *R/n*, 171–4; cf. *MOC*, 73.

[49] *MOC*, 87.

[50] 'New College', 27; *R/n*, 112, 154. Torrance cites Gregory of Nazianzus' 'Epistle 101'.

mind in order to heal and sanctify it in Jesus Christ'.[51] We have already noted the significant part this plays in the way Torrance understands man's receiving the knowledge of God out of the renewed mind of Christ. Now it emerges as an equally crucial part of God's scheme for the redemption of man. Nothing is more important; the whole validity of the incarnation for Torrance hinges on the fact that God has taken upon himself 'what needed to be saved', that he has assumed man in his fallenness, not in his innocence.

When the fourth Gospel speaks of the Word becoming 'flesh' Torrance interprets 'flesh' in the Pauline sense, i.e. as the principle of disobedience which conditions all humanity.[52] It is through unrestricted ontological interrelation with fallen man in Christ that God chooses to rectify the recalcitrance of our flesh. The Word, he says, 'has entered into and made his own that estranged and disobedient condition of our human being' and thereby 'altered [it] from within and from below in radical and complete *metanoia*, a repentant restructuring of our carnal mind, as St. Paul called it, and a converting of it into a spiritual mind', redirecting 'it back in his own human being in love and obedience to the Father'.[53] Hence we have another perspective on Torrance's notion that 'Incarnation and the Atonement are one and inseparable', for not only is the covenant negotiated at the 'centre' of the Incarnate Word, but what constitutes that centre also belongs to the content of his saving response to God, viz. the mortal mind of Christ in its union with God.[54] In the first chapter we observed how revelation and reconciliation in Torrance's theology cannot be separated. In the light of the incarnation, we can understand this now more profoundly as pertaining not only to the Church's rational reception of the knowledge of God but to the human mind of Christ which must be conditioned to receive it for the Church. The very processes integral to the intercourse of the divine *Logos* with the *logos* or reason of man in Christ are therefore shown to be themselves redemptive.

Christ's knowing relation with God, by which our humanity is given participation in the divine rationality, is thus seen to be that

---

[51] 'New College', 27. He recreates us, Torrance says, 'from within the very foundations of our existence'. (*MOC*, 73).

[52] Lectures at Edinburgh, Michaelmas Term, 1963: 'Christian Dogmatics', New College; cf. *R/n*, 155. Torrance puts it poignantly, 'God has become man in downright reality' (*R/n*, 160).

[53] *MOC*, 89, 95.

[54] Ibid. 73; cf. *SOF*, CXIII-CXIV.

which renews the human mind in obedient conformity to the divine mind and will. Similarly, the doxological relation between the Father and the Son which, as we have shown, is an essential part of that larger knowing relation, also plays a vital function in the restoration of man's mind.[55] For just as 'the mediation of truth' within the divine–human dialogue in Christ and the reconciliation of the mind is seen to be one and the same, so too is the 'mediation of prayer' and the conversion of the human spirit. The rational worship of Christ 'in Spirit and in Truth' works to reorient the distracted human mind, fixing it upon God who reorders our intellect and teaches it to heed the Spirit of Truth. Furthermore, it is the renewed mind of Christ that hears and answers the call of God's covenant 'for [man's] response in worship and love'.[56] Out of his own unsullied human mind, and conscience purified of any motivation save the glory of God, the Word returns love for love, offering man in himself back to his Father.[57] Torrance states: 'The real crux of the matter has to do with the mediation of salvation through the unimpaired humanity of Christ, in which the activity of his human mind and soul in vicarious faith, worship and thanksgiving are essential ingredients.'[58] Christ's worship thus marks the quintessence of the restoration of man's mind into agreement and covenant with the mind of God. It is obvious now what Torrance means when he suggests that the worship of Christ is the ground for the Church's worship.[59] We can also understand why the Eucharist in his theology, answering as it does the worship of Christ, should be central to the life of a reconstituted, new humanity.

Torrance has all these noetic and doxological elements interwoven and complementing one another when he says, 'Jesus Christ constitutes in his own self-consecrated humanity the fulfilment of the vicarious way of human response to God promised under the old covenant.'[60] Salvation is not merely a new state of affairs existing between God and man due to Christ's salvific work, it is a new state of being: the reconciliation of God and man inhering within the very framework of Christ's reconstituted rational

---

[55] Cf. 'New College', 27; *R/n*, 175ff.
[56] *SOF*, L.
[57] *G & R*, 151–2.
[58] *R/n*, 201. Christ's worship on earth is thus seen as 'an essential part of his saving and vicarious work in the form of a servant which he fulfilled... on our behalf' ('New College', 27; cf. *R/n*, 113).
[59] Cf. *R/n*, 175ff.
[60] *MOC*, 86.

humanity. Christ is, Torrance asserts, 'even in His human nature, the Source and Substance of [our salvation]'.[61] His divine humanity is 'the great *paliggenesia*' of our salvation, the imparting principle of grace for the world.[62] Consequently, conversion means not only a sharing in the *divine* reality in Christ, but an actual partaking in his humanity, which has been 'converted back to union and communion with God'.[63]

All these ontologically reconstructive factors must be taken into account in our explanation of the Eucharist out of its objective christological ground. The profound ramifications they have for the way Torrance conceives the formal matter and action of the sacrament are immediately clear. We observed at the outset of this chapter how the *homoousion* requires us to think as one the Act and Being of God and the act and being of man in Christ Jesus. Now we can understand just how vital and indispensable the human act and being is in the economy for the accomplishing of the will of God. Torrance has implied as much already in his suggestion that what grace does arises immediately from what grace is. It would now be impossible to conceive of the effective presence of Christ in the sacrament, as it were, without his humanity, as it is part and parcel of the whole work of salvation. Hence, Torrance's sacramental theology will require nothing less than the presence of the *totus Christus* in the sacrament. Furthermore, his presence there in his new humanity demands that the Eucharist never be conceived of as anything less than a 'converting ordinance' itself.[64] It follows,

---

[61] *SOF*, LXXXII.

[62] Ibid. XXXVIII; *MOC*, 95. The Incarnate Word is the regenerative source, he says, from which the Church 'draws all its life and all its understanding' (*SOF*, LVIII).

[63] *C & A* II, 144; *SOF*, XXXVIII.

[64] *MOC*, 107. Most point to John Wesley as the originator of the phrase 'converting ordinance' (Graham Pigott in his *Christian Liturgy as Education*, (unpublished M.Phil. thesis, University of Nottingham, 1984), 205, fn. 72 cites the work of Sr. Benedicta, S.L.G., *Liturgy Today*. Sr. Benedicta notes the use of the phrase 'converting ordinance' by Wesley in his preface to *A Collection of Hymns for the Use of the People Called Methodists of 1799*). In fact, Wesley himself indicated that '*many have affirmed*, that the Lord's Supper is not a converting, but a confirming ordinance.... But experience shows the gross falsehood of that assertion, that the Lord's Supper is not a converting ordinance' (John Wesley, *The Journal of the Rev. John Wesley, A.M.*, ed. Nehemiah Curnock (London, Charles H. Kelly, 1909), 361, entry for Friday, June 27th, 1740, italics mine). This would seem to indicate that the term itself was part of the conventional jargon of the mid eighteenth century. Whatever the case, Mr Wesley and the Methodists popularized the phrase and perpetuated it. The idea however is not peculiar to

therefore, that all 'the saving acts of Christ', including those in the sacraments, 'must carry with [them] in our understanding, the whole substance of Christ's human life and nature'.[65] In formal sacramental theology this means that we cannot think of any benefits of salvation existing in the sacrament apart from the Saviour. With this, Torrance obviates from the start any possible accusations of virtualism, i.e. that what the Church receives in its sacrament is the virtue or energy of Christ but not Christ himself. He cites Calvin: 'To communicate to us the blessings which he received from the Father, he must become ours and dwell in us.'[66] In short, the absolute identity in his thought between the matter and action of salvation completely disallows any divergence of matter from act in the sacrament, for Christ in his divine and saving humanity constitutes both.

(e) *The Objective Fulfilment of the Covenant in Christ vis-à-vis its Subjective Realization in the Church: 'A Fulfilled Efficacy'*

Following this line of thought, Torrance works out his soteriology from the objective fulfilment of the covenant within the divine-human person of Christ to its subjective realization in the Church. 'Reconciliation', he says, 'has already taken place objectively in Jesus Christ.'[67] Consequently, his theology of the covenant is not so much a development from a formal concept of Covenant Theology to a particular kind of christological exposition of *that* theology as it is a progression from a general covenant theme to its all-inclusive embodiment in Christ. He has become 'the concrete universal' of what is generally promised in the covenant.[68] All that God does

---

Wesleyan sacramental theology, as Torrance's use of it would indicate. Indeed, John Paul II in his 'Apostolic Letter', *Dominicae Cenae*, suggests a more ancient source in Roman Catholic thought: 'It is not only that Penance leads to the Eucharist, but that the Eucharist also leads to Penance' (Pope John Paul II, *The Mystery and Worship of the Holy Eucharist*, Apostolic letter *Dominicae Cenae* (Preston, Apostolate of Catholic Truth, 1980), 10).

[65] *SOF*, LXXXII.
[66] *Inst* III.1.1; cf. also III.1.2-3, II.16.19. The Scottish Divine, Robert Bruce, commented along these lines in the sixteenth century: 'To the end, therefore, that this sacrament may nurish thee to life everlasting, thou maun get in it thy hail Saviour, hail Christ, God and man, with His hail graces and benefits, without separation of His substance fra His graces, or of the ane nature fra the uther' (as quoted by D.C. MacNicol, *Robert Bruce: Minister In The Kirk of Edinburgh*, London: Banner of Truth Trust, 1961, 73).
[67] *SOF*, XXXVIII.
[68] Ibid. LV.

subjectively in the Church is understood to have its objective counterpart, its formal parallel, in Christ's vicarious work. The Incarnate Son's own relation with his Father embraces every part of man's relationship with God, and, as we will see, in a very particular sense, each aspect of the sacramental relation. Hence the Church's experience of God is seen as nothing more than the discharge in its corporate, earthly life of the fullness of salvation which inheres in the life of this one man. All this is suggested when Torrance refers to the christological mystery as the *objective* ground for the Eucharist. 'With the Incarnation', he says, 'the whole economy of the Covenant changes, for here in the Person and Work of Christ the Fatherly will of God for communion with man is actualized in incarnation and reconciliation, and in the light of that fulfilled communion all else is interpreted'.[69] In this new economy of salvation, with Christ's ascension and fulfilment of the covenant and the subsequent descent of the Holy Spirit, all God's operation in the world is understood in terms of the unfolding or self-releasing of the Christ-event.[70] Indeed, he can say there are no longer any 'new or different' acts of God among men, only Christ's 'one saving action' which is 'continuously operative for our salvation'.[71]

Torrance's soteriology, and consequently his sacramental theology, operates from what he calls a 'fulfilled efficacy'.[72] This antilogous term highlights at once two mutually complementary and equally prevalent emphases. By it Torrance reiterates the point just made that God's salvific purposes have been objectively *fulfilled* in Christ, but goes on to suggest that they are realized in such a transcendent way that the *efficacy* of the fact prevails forever. Let us look at each aspect in turn. When he refers to Christ's 'finished work' he is employing both the idiom and thought pattern of the Reformation. 'On the part of God', Torrance says, 'our salvation is completed'.[73] Salvation is 'a *fait accompli*' in Christ and is 'once and for all'.[74] He uses expressions like these to communicate a sense of the 'eternal finality' of the Christ-event, emphasizing not only its decisiveness in achieving God's covenant purposes, but also its inimitable and 'unrepeatable' nature, not just in time but in character.[75] When

---

[69] Ibid. LV–LVI.
[70] *MOC*, 77.
[71] *C & A* II, 144.
[72] *SOF*, LVIII.
[73] *K & C*, 104.
[74] *SOF*, LVIII; *DOG*, 25; *Inter*, 311.
[75] *Inter*, 311, 306, 303. This notion of the 'eternal finality' of Christ's work

Torrance suggests that 'the great act of salvation has already taken place in Jesus Christ', however, he must not be misunderstood to mean that Christ's redemptive acts have terminated or that the actual *locus* of their efficacy is at some point in the past.[76] As we have seen, while Christ's saving life and deeds certainly belong to the history of man, they are not fixed there in some dormant sense. For Torrance christology qualifies everything associated with it dynamically and existentially. Christ's work is only 'finished' with respect to past history. But, as he puts it, 'this historical Jesus is no longer merely "historical" in the sense that He belongs to history that irreversibly flows away into the past forever, but within that history He is superior historical reality as actual and live happening in the continuous present'.[77] By his resurrection and ascension, all that Christ is and all that he has done 'are taken up eternally into the life of God, and remain prevalent, efficacious, valid or abidingly real'.[78] Torrance is following here the same logic we saw him employ to account for the perpetuation of Christ's historical passion.[79] The

---

suggests for Torrance the mystery of the ascension. When he speaks of 'the completed work of Christ' he has in mind a deed which has ramifications not only in time but also in eternity. That saving deed, having no identity of its own disconnected from Christ's person, is eternally vindicated and secured in that he has ascended to the acceptance and honour of the Father (cf. *STR*, 120, 114–15). But, while 'terminatory' expressions such as 'once and for all' and 'finished work' do have their eternal implications for Torrance, they also ascribe to the redemptory event a real and concrete mooring within history. In reality these two emphases are not contradictory for Torrance. It is the ascended Christ, he says, who 'sends us back to the historical Jesus Christ as the *covenanted place* on earth and in time which God has appointed for meeting between man and himself.... The ascension... means that to all eternity God insists on speaking to us through the historical Jesus' (*STR*, 133).

Thus, he asserts, we 'must give the historical Jesus Christ His full place as God's saving action' (*SOF*, XX; cf. *STR*, 147). In the incarnation God's Word has 'embroiled Himself forever with our human history' in that he has bound himself to a particular historical form in Jesus Christ, so that there is no word of God for us apart from his history in our world (Thomas F. Torrance, *When Christ Comes and Comes Again* (London, Hodder & Stoughton, 1957), 17–18; *RP*, 58). The *Heilsgeschichte*, therefore, has been grounded here and recorded here as having once really happened in our *Historie* (cf. *R/n*, 46ff.). All that was necessary for the redemption of historical man God has accomplished within the creaturely contingencies of man's time and experience 'once and for all'.

[76] *DOG*, 35; *SOF*, LVIII; *STR*, 114–15, 133.
[77] *RP*, 57.
[78] *STR*, 114–15.
[79] The truth and power of what God has done 'once and for all' in history does not bear upon the Church today simply by the strength of the inspiration of

Christ event is not 'remembered' only for having once occurred, rather encountered as a living reality. Thus Torrance's eucharistic theology offers no studied, independent treatment of the *anamnesis*. When this aspect of the rite is addressed it is always in the dynamic context of proclamation, which for Torrance primarily connotes the Incarnate Word's witness to himself.[80] We do not call him to mind, he calls himself to our remembrance, 'because... the proclaiming activity of the living Lord stands behind the Church's proclamation [and]... behind its *anamnesis*, so that it is really Christ in the Eucharist who represents to the Church and makes effective for the Church His own atoning deed of sacrifice'.[81] Consequently, what Christ 'has done once and for all in history has the power of a permanent presence in him'.[82] This is *anamnesis* in the 'eternal indicative'.[83]

Taking all this into account, we can now fully understand the text which to this point has been quoted only in part:

> The redemptive acts of God have been completely fulfilled in Christ, but Christ and His finished work, Christ clothed with His saving acts, remains [an] enduring and everlasting reality, continually and really present in the Church as its Lord and Master giving it to participate in the *fulfilled efficacy* of His atoning reconciliation.[84]

Christ thus emerges as himself the 'fulfilled efficacy' of his gospel and likewise of the sacraments of the gospel. Only from this understanding can we grasp what Torrance means when he says that the sacraments 'are sacraments of the finished work of Christ'.[85] In fact such a statement underlines Christ's real presence in the

---

the record of it having once happened or by the Church's faithfulness to remember to declare that it did.

Cf. Torrance's recent criticism of fundamentalism in this regard in *R & E*, 14ff.: 'Fundamentalism cuts off the revelation of God in the Bible from God himself and his continuous self-giving through Christ and in the Spirit, so that the Bible is treated as a self-contained corpus of divine truths in propositional form endowed with an infallibility of statement which provides the justification felt to be needed for the rigid framework of belief within which fundamentalism barricades itself' (p. 17).

[80] 'It is such a proclamation', Torrance says, 'that in and through it the Living Christ continues to do and teach' (*Inter*, 307).
[81] *Inter*, 328.
[82] *R/n*, 120.
[83] *DOG*, 35.
[84] *SOF*, LVIII, italics mine.
[85] *MOC*, 99–100.

sacrament, for the 'sacraments... have as their substance and content none other than Jesus Christ clothed with his Gospel of atoning mediation and reconciliation'.[86] When one adds to this thought the identity and simultaneity of Christ's saving life and deed the dynamic implications of Torrance's assertion become plain: 'The action of the Sacrament is none other than that which Christ has already accomplished on our behalf once and for all.'[87] He is placing the Eucharist at the total dependence and service of this 'fulfilled efficacy'. Just as Christ was shown to be the objective referent for all sacramental meaning and significance, so in his 'fulfilled efficacy' he is the objective source of sacramental efficiency. On this basis Torrance can say that the Eucharist 'continually seals our renewal in that finished work and gives us to participate in its effective operation until He comes again in power and glory'.[88]

(f) The Church's Communion in 'The Paschal Mystery' by the Holy Spirit: Inclusive of her Eucharistic Participation

Thus far we have spoken of the matter and action of the sacrament primarily in terms of the direct presence and act of the Risen Christ. The actual economy of this, however, is decidedly more trinitarian as well as more complex. How Torrance envisages the Church's sacrament being materially and efficaciously endowed by Christ is clarified in the light of the way he understands the Church itself being savingly related to him. As we have shown, salvation for man is fundamentally a relation of reconciliation and reciprocal accord between God and reconstituted humanity proper to Christ. That christological union forms uniquely the substance as well as the means of our salvation. For Torrance there is really only 'one union' with God, all 'others' are viewed as that union realizing its universal implications.[89] Salvation is effected in the Church as that 'eternal communion of love in God overflows through Jesus Christ into our union with [him] and gathers us up to dwell with God and in God'.[90] This 'overflowing' and 'gathering' suggests the procession and ministry of the Spirit within the Church. He it is who communicates salvation to men, not by 'the reconstituting of holy relations between man and God', as such, but by uniting the Church to Christ in his

---

[86] Ibid. 100.
[87] *C & A* II, 144.
[88] Ibid. 146.
[89] Cf. *SOF*, LXXXVII, CVII, LV.
[90] *MOC*, 74.

union with God.⁹¹ It is not our faith relation, either within or outside of the sacramental relation, or our relation *per se* to the Spirit which gives us access to God's grace, but Christ through whom 'we have obtained access to this grace in which we stand' (Rom. 5:2). The economy by which the Church draws its life from God is therefore said to be: '*union with Christ through the Communion of the Spirit*'.⁹² 'The "objective" union which we have with Christ through his incarnational assumption of our humanity into himself is "subjectively" actualised in us through his indwelling Spirit, "we in Christ" and "Christ in us" thus complementing and interpenetrating each other.'⁹³

The interjection of the doctrine of the Holy Spirit at any point in Torrance's theology always introduces with it the idea of participation. We have observed in the development of his epistemology how participation through the Spirit served as 'the essential bond of connection' between the knowledge of God conceived and sustained in the mind of Christ and its personal reception in the Church.⁹⁴ The Spirit was said to give divine knowledge to man by actually affording us internal access to the knowing relation between the ascended Christ and his Father.⁹⁵ Similarly, the 'mediation of reconciliation' to man, he declares, also 'takes place within the Person of the Mediator himself' so that 'men and women are savingly reconciled to God by being taken up (by the Spirit) in and through Christ to share in the inner relations of God in life and love'.⁹⁶ Salvation is given to the Church as the heart of the Church is drawn by the holy Spirit (internal both to God and man) into the processes of reconciliation and dialogue proper to Christ's vicarious humanity.

It is always within this larger concept of participation that the Eucharist in Torrance's theology finds its place as well as its explication. He states: 'A proper understanding of the Eucharist... is reached... in terms of our participation in Christ... through the Spirit he has sent us.'⁹⁷ The Church is said to know and experience Christ's presence (the matter of the sacrament) and that presence in

---

⁹¹ Ibid. 74; cf. *SOF*, LVIIIf.

⁹² 'The Communion of the Spirit', Torrance contends, 'has to be understood as correlative to the union of God and man wrought out in the Life and Work of Jesus Christ' (*SOF*, CVI). It is the Word's union with 'all flesh' that 'supplies the field of the Spirit's activity', or determines that the Spirit should be poured out upon 'all flesh' (*SOF*, CXVII).

⁹³ *MOC*, 77; *SOF*, CVI.

⁹⁴ *R/n*, 183; cf. *Inst* IV.17.10.

⁹⁵ *G & G*, 154; cf. *TS*, 49, 52, 136.

⁹⁶ *MOC*, 74.

⁹⁷ *GT*, 6.

action (the action of the sacrament) in the same participatory way as it is said to know and experience the truth of God. Just as sacramental participation was seen not to be something separate from but rather essential to the Church's knowing relation, so it must also be viewed as a vital aspect of the Church's reconciling relation. He speaks of the Church's sacramental communion as an outward form of the communion of the Holy Spirit, which is its inner reality.[98] This is not to say that there are not other manifestations of the 'Communion of the Spirit', but none where the Word draws the analogy so tightly or with such efficacy.[99] In the sacrament, he says, 'the all inclusive effect is our abiding union with Christ and through union our participation in all the benefits of Christ'.[100] The Eucharist acquires its identity as participation and its efficiency as a sacrament through the Spirit's uniting the Church's sacramental act to the vicarious act of God in Christ, lifting up the Church to her 'union with Christ' and so to 'share in the life of God'.[101] Thereby it derives its name appropriately: 'The Sacrament of the Holy Communion'. In all of this the sacramental relation in Torrance's theology never loses its absolute dependence upon the christological relation. This is as it must be if, as Torrance suggests, 'the mystery of the Eucharist is objectively grounded in the Paschal mystery of Christ which gives it its meaning'.[102]

2. 'The Mystery of the Eucharist', Explicated in Terms of the Mediation of Christ

The way Torrance proposes for the Church to ascertain a proper understanding of the Eucharist has now become clear in its fullest development. His basic principle is that all reality should be intuited and represented in a manner faithful to its own self-disclosure and by reference to the most essential statement of its being. With this in

---

[98] Cf. *C & A* II, 145. Sacramental communion does not for Torrance reinforce our objective union in Christ, either in itself or by its repeated observance. That is wholly in Christ and needs no upholding or replenishment by sacraments. Neither is 'sacramental participation' as such seen to be exactly equivalent to that 'participation in Christ' which the Spirit offers, rather it is one expression of it, albeit the most significant one to Torrance's mind.
[99] *SOF*, LVI.
[100] Ibid. 146.
[101] Ibid. 145.
[102] *GT*, 6.

mind the christological mystery is to be apprehended in the light of the relationship between God and man which inheres within it, but not without taking into account the interrelations of the Holy Trinity which also inhere there by virtue of the divine nature's participation in God.[103] It is particularly the salvific dimension of this mystery which Torrance claims finally unfolds the mystery of the Eucharist and consequently allows us to formulate a sacramental doctrine apposite to its christocentric and trinitarian revelation.[104]

All this Torrance has in mind when he suggests that it is 'in *the vicarious humanity of Jesus Christ, the priesthood of the Incarnate Son*', that 'the immediate key to the understanding of the Eucharist is to be sought'. 'A proper understanding of the Eucharist', he says, 'requires attention to be directed to *the inner relations of the Incarnate Son* and the saving work which he fulfilled (for man) in his relation to the Father.'[105] To look thus into the inner reality of Christ is to be confronted with the fullness of the divine reality, existing and acting consubstantially and co-extensively as the inter-relations of three persons. 'God makes himself accessible to us in his internal relations as Father, Son and Holy Spirit', he states.[106] It is the mediatory operations internal to Christ's life in the triune God – 'the overflowing love of God' the Father willing and acting in his Son and by his Spirit to bring man by the Spirit through the Son 'to share in His life and glory' – which provide in their order and dynamic framework for the actual structuring of Torrance's eucharistic thought.[107] Within what he calls the 'double movement' of God's love,

---

[103] As we have suggested in Chapter 1, the substance as well as the pattern of God's self-disclosure is trinitarian; however, the 'inner relations' of the Trinity are discernible only within the context of the relation between God and man proper to the Incarnate Son. There is no knowledge of the Trinity for the Church that is not at the same time knowledge of Christ and *vice versa*.

[104] *GT*, 6.

[105] Ibid. 6.

[106] *R & E*, 23. Just as sub-atomic particles do not exist to themselves as individual entities but only in their interrelationship with each other, actually *as* that interrelationship, so God cannot be known in his being apart from those 'relations in being' which inhere within him. Torrance calls these 'onto relations', i.e. 'the kind of relations subsisting between things which is an essential constituent of their being, and without which they would not be what they are' (*R & E*, 42-3). By analogy, no person of the Trinity can be known singularly, but only within dynamic relation to the whole (*R & E*, 23). God in Christ is made known to us precisely out of these kind of 'relations'. He is the Father giving his love to the Son through the Spirit; he is the Son giving his love to the Father through the Spirit.

[107] *SOF*, LI; cf. *GT*, 6-7; *SOF*, LXVI. These thoughts are not new in

God-manward, and man-Godward, already observed in our exposition of his concept of covenant fulfilment, Torrance identifies the inmost witness to Christ's salvific word and act. Here is 'the whole paschal mystery of Christ' upon which the Eucharist is objectively grounded and from which it takes its meaning.[108] This is the heart of the gospel which the sacrament must necessarily reflect.[109] It is therefore by a 'proper and profound co-ordination' of our thinking about the sacrament with the internal reality of this saving mystery, that the Eucharist can be seen to 'correspond... and participate in the whole movement of God's saving love in Jesus Christ'.[110]

From his earliest writings on the subject Torrance has invariably preferred such active categories in which to think out his sacramental theology.[111] Recently, with the introduction of this dynamic internal metaphor, he has deployed a model used earlier in his epistemology. In that context he spoke of 'one two-fold movement' of knowledge belonging to Christ's vicarious knowing-relation, 'from the side of God who gives Himself to be known and from the side of man who knows'.[112] It is in strikingly similar terms that he now formulates his eucharistic thought, i.e. according to the

---

Torrance's evangelical theology. In 1959 he suggested that the only proper way to structure our thinking about the Eucharist was to 'conceive it after the pattern of Christ himself' (*C & A* II, 142). The idea has continued to expand as his theology has developed. At that early stage Torrance was seeking simply to gain a broad understanding of what could and could not be affirmed about the relationship of created and uncreated realities proper to the sacramental relation through reference to the primal relation of those realities in the *hypostatic union*. However, paralleling the evolution of his thought around the theme of the mediation of Christ and his growing conviction that reality can only be correctly intuited in the light of its 'internal relations and intrinsic structures', the 'form of Christ' has thus come to be defined in increasingly more inward and dynamic categories (*SOF*, LXII; *G & G*, 146). In his eucharistic theology the 'pattern of Christ' has more recently been enlarged, as we can observe here, to incorporate, as his epistemology always has, the reciprocal operation of mediation within the Word's humanity (cf. *C & A* II, 142).

[108] *GT*, 6–7.

[109] Heron, *Table and Tradition*, 163.

[110] *GT*, 6–7.

[111] This is illustrated by his persistent stress on the unity of God's word and act, his early designation of sacramental sign and mystery as 'essentially event', his equation of those signs with Christ's miraculous acts, and finally his insistence that since 'union with Christ' can only be construed in terms of 'dynamic movement' the Eucharist's meaning must be couched in terms of 'active analogy'.

[112] *TS*, 45, 50.

katabasis/anabasis pattern: the descending movement of God's coming to man in his love, wholly actualized and mediated in the Incarnate Son and, inversely, that same movement of divine love translated into the form of man's response to God, turned around and 'offered back to the Father' in the ascended Christ.[113] This *katabasis/anabasis* movement of the mediation of Christ represents divine love come full circle, having achieved its purposes: perfect reciprocity of covenant-love 'within the circle of the life of Jesus Christ'.[114]

'The Eucharist', Torrance says, 'is to be understood from within this double movement'.[115] Developing this thought, he discusses the sacrament more or less exclusively from its character as real presence and eucharistic sacrifice. The former, he asserts, takes its meaning from the *katabasis*, represented in the incarnation, whereas the latter is to be understood according to the *anabasis*, represented in the ascension.[116] This illustrates the point made earlier that everything which God effects in the Church has its objective parallel directly in Christ's person and work.

(a) The Objective Ground of the Real Presence

The real presence for Torrance is a christological reality before it is a sacramental reality. In its formal conformation in Christ it is nothing less than true God and true man hypostatically present to each other in Jesus Christ; it is, as he puts it, 'the presence of man in his completeness as man in God'.[117] However, when he correlates the real presence in the Eucharist with the *katabasis* of God's love in the incarnation, he has more in mind than the bare metaphysical or historical fact of that event. As we have noted, the incarnation always implies a vital, personal relation in being. In Jesus Christ God 'assumes our human being and reality into such an inseparable union with himself, that in and through Jesus Christ there takes place a real communication of God himself to us and at the same time a real

---

[113] The incarnation and ascension are each pivotal points along this descending and ascending line of movement, depicting, as it were, its low and high points, its greatest 'reach' down to man and its greatest 'reach' up to God. They do not, as individual events, however, comprise the whole of this movement; they only trace it out. The completed circle of God's love is contained within the life and work of Christ.

[114] *R/n*, 210-11.
[115] *GT*, 6.
[116] Ibid. 6.
[117] *R/n*, 155.

reception and appropriation of that divine self-communication by man'.[118] The whole coming of God into the world, and particularly into the sacrament, is summed up and encapsulated in the Incarnate Christ, that is, in his total life as God with us. Torrance's point is that in Jesus Christ the real presence of God to man and man to God at the most profound level of ontological intercourse and personal commitment is already an accomplished fact. 'God has drawn so near to man and drawn man so near to himself, that they are perfectly one.'[119] In Jesus Christ God is 'present to himself' as man. It is precisely this objective reality which must condition the Church's thinking regarding the real presence in the sacrament.[120]

This principal *Praesentia Realis* confirms God's disposition to re-establish man and his world in their full inheritance. For God has not come to his 'place in this world where he is present in our place' in only a general sense or to no purpose, but with a specific redemptive mission.[121] 'The Incarnation, even in its narrower sense', he insists, is 'redeeming event, reaching out to its full *telos* in the death and resurrection'.[122] Christ is therefore seen to be 'the place of contact and communication between God and man in a real movement within... our estranged world... in order to bring His boundless being to bear directly on man'.[123] This is 'the real presence' in the form of 'Christ's reconciling union with us in which he becomes bone of our bone and flesh of our flesh in order to take away our sin

---

[118] Ibid. 255.

[119] *MOC*, 38-9.

[120] *R/n*, 121; cf. *STR*, 132. We recall that to Torrance's mind it was the securing of this objective presence of God within the world that was also Luther's paramount concern. The Reformer sought a way to 'nail' the two kingdoms together, ontologically, as Torrance put it, a way to maintain 'The actual presence of the Being of the Son of God in space and time..., a presence actually real of the whole Christ and in Him of the Being of God with us' (*STI*, 34; T.F. Torrance, 'Doctrinal Consensus on Holy Communion: The Arnoldshain Theses', *SJT* 15 (1962), 11, 13). Luther did this by a radical insistence and defence of Christ's 'material' presence in the 'material' of the sacrament. His stress upon Christ's physical presence in the Eucharist is seen by Torrance as wrongly placed and wrongly stated. In contrast to what he considers Luther's dualistic pre-suppositions, Torrance says that 'the two worlds came to be understood not as entirely separated, nor as only tangentially related to each other, but as actually intersecting in Jesus Christ' (*STI*, 15). For, as he sees it, only after the being of God has been proven hypostatically present in Christ can we make authentic claims about his presence elsewhere, e.g. in the Sacrament of the Altar.

[121] *STI*, 77-8; cf. *R/n*, 121.

[122] *R/st*, 155.

[123] *STI*, 78.

and guilt and pour out upon us the love of God'.[124] As we have suggested, the redemptive character of God's presence to man in Christ requires a correspondingly redemptive connotation to be ascribed to the real presence of Christ within the Church and its sacrament.[125]

In the Eucharist God and man truly meet ontologically and redemptively, but not just on the basis of God's presence to man in the sacrament but rather on the basis of the 'true relations between God and man and man and God' in Jesus Christ.[126] Torrance has an interesting way of explaining this. He suggests that the Eucharist is first and foremost the sacrament of 'Christ's... union with us'.[127] That is to say, it is upon the ground of God having come and united himself to us that we come to him. As Torrance puts it in another context, 'It is a decisive and eternal deed of God's love which makes the ground of man's approach to God an act and a promise in which he is irrevocably committed' viz. in the gift of himself in Christ.[128] It is only when the sacrament is understood thus, as Christ's 'union with us', that it can be further understood as the sacrament of our 'union with him'. For the God we meet in the Eucharist is the God who has met us already in Christ.[129] Torrance's proposition that 'Jesus Christ is the *place* (τόπος) where God and man meet' is therefore seen to be as much a sacramental statement as it is a christological one.[130] The Eucharist is designated a 'dominically appointed place' where we encounter God because Christ, himself God reconciled and united to man, meets us there. Likewise, God's presence in the Eucharist is said to be 'of the profoundest and most intense kind there could ever be' because we meet him there in the fact of his incarnation, in the person of Christ.[131] The Eucharist does not qualify the fact that Christ is the 'one place' where man meets God to know him.[132]

(b) The Objective Ground of the Eucharistic Sacrifice

Whereas the real presence in the Church's sacrament is correlated with the *katabasis* of God's love manifest in the incarnation as its

---

[124] *MOC*, 101.
[125] Ibid. 101.
[126] *R/st*, 70.
[127] *MOC*, 101.
[128] *DOG*, 16.
[129] *MOC*, 101.
[130] *R/n*, 210.
[131] Ibid. 121.
[132] *G & G*, 40.

objective pattern, the eucharistic sacrifice is said to correspond in the same way to the ascension, or with the *anabasis* of that love.[133] However, just as the objective real presence was not seen to be precisely equivalent to the event of the incarnation or to that event understood simply as an abstract fact, but rather identified with the whole incarnate life of God in his self-giving to man, so the ascension in this context means much more than a single happening at the end of Christ's earthly life. It entails the whole life of the Incarnate Son, only in the self-offering of himself as man to the Father.[134] The actual ascension event is said to epitomize this movement, as that which brings it to its consummation, for it gathers up the risen humanity of Christ into the very life of the Trinity. In that 'Place' the ascended Christ presents himself to the Father and from his reconstituted humanity offers the love and praise of a new creation. This self-oblation of Christ before God is unending even though his earthly work is completed; for what he offered 'once in time' he continues to offer in the doxology of his eternal session.[135] The fact that the integrity of the incarnation is upheld in the ascension signifies for Torrance that Christ's sacrifice prevails in its efficiency, not only in the heart of God but also in the ongoing life of the Church.

It is particularly the doxological dimension of the priesthood of the ascended Christ which represents for Torrance the objective ground of the Church's eucharistic offering. The high and holy praise of Christ is that which calls the Church to worship and leads her in her eucharistic prayer. This is not to exclude any other aspect of his sacrifice, but rather to underline the fact that all the offering of his life was and is 'eucharistic' in that it is made in no part except in a spirit of praise.[136] 'He lived in our human nature in such a way', Torrance asserts, 'that his whole life formed itself into worship, prayer and praise which he offered to the Father on our behalf'.[137] This doxological aspect of Christ's sacrifice therefore more directly and appropriately corresponds to the eucharistic sacrifice of the Church because the latter is said to be exclusively eucharistic.[138]

If the 'true relation' between God and man in Christ is the objective counterpart of the real presence of Christ in the Church's sacrament, then the 'true worship' of the Incarnate Son is the formal

---

[133] *GT*, 6.
[134] Cf. *STR*, 119–20.
[135] Ibid. 115.
[136] Cf. Ibid. 115.
[137] *R/n*, 211.
[138] *C & A* II, 148ff.

counterpart of the Church's eucharistic sacrifice. If the Eucharist can be said to be a 'place' where God meets man because Christ in whom God and man are 'perfectly one' is present there, then our eucharistic offering can be said to be 'a sacrifice', and worthy of God, because Christ has united himself to it and caused his praise to be heard within it. It is this kind of relation that fixes the analogy between his sacrifice and that of the Church. This illustrates the point made in Torrance's doctrine of analogy that true signs of God always contain 'something of which they signify'.

However, as Torrance sees it, the Church's sacrifice can never be said really to accommodate Christ's sacrifice; indeed, it is the other way round. For the vicarious human sacrifice which Christ makes constitutes a response so comprehensive as to anticipate and 'contain' antecedently the whole magnitude of humanity's response to God. There is no aspect of Torrance's theology which more vividly illustrates the point that nothing takes place subjectively in the Church which has not already transpired objectively in the life of Christ, for the worship which the Church offers is said to be that which has already been formed in the life and heard in the prayer of the ascended Christ.

(c) The Eucharist's Place Actually within Christ's 'Human Response Vicariously Fulfilled for Us'

Not surprisingly, in Torrance's sacramental theology the emphasis of the Eucharist for the Church is on the side of Christ's 'human response vicariously fulfilled for us' or that aspect of his divine life which incorporates the 'answering Word' of man to God's Word.[139] It is the man-Godward aspect of reconciliation with which the sacrament is primarily concerned. However, it must never be thought that the man-Godward movement in Christ can be separated from God's movement toward us, for man's movement toward God in Christ operates on the foundation of God's having come to man in him. Indeed, as we have seen, these constitute the two aspects of one operation. Torrance says this precisely in another context:

> The way from God to man and the way from man to God... are not two separate movements, each proceeding from its own independent ground to meet the other, but one two-fold movement, for even the movement from the side of man toward God, free and spontaneous as it is, is coordinated

---

[139] *G & R*, 159; *STR*, 119.

with the movement of God toward man, and is part of the divine movement of revelation and reconciliation.[140]

Objectively speaking, it is the *katabasis* of God's love which redirects itself as love's *anabasis*. This occurs for Torrance at 'the nadir of that whole movement', 'his substitutionary death on the Cross'.[141] As we will recall, it was this pivotal point upon which the Church's Eucharist was said to focus the mind of the Church, i.e. precisely where God's greatest act of love toward us seeks to elicit an appropriate praise. It is thus 'at the cross' that the real presence is given and the eucharistic sacrifice begins. The Incarnate One is not reckoned 'present' to us in the fullest sense until he has come finally to the limits of our retreat from him. When he says that the *anabasis* corresponds to the ascension of Christ, he is not indicating a different 'turning point', since, for Torrance, 'the ascension of Christ to heaven' begins 'not with his actual ascension or resurrection' but 'with his lifting up on the Cross'.[142] It could be depicted thus:

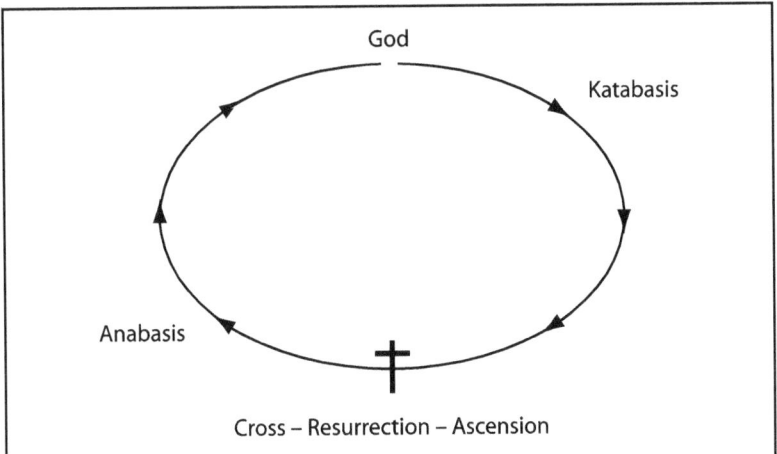

However, this diagram is by no means comprehensive, for it does not embrace Torrance's repeated assertion that God's real presence is with man, or in our 'place', as he puts it, from Christ's conception. Is this not the point he is making when he marks out the incarnation and not the crucifixion *per se* as the objective counterpart to Christ's presence within the sacrament?

---

[140] *TS*, 45.
[141] *RP*, 39.
[142] *STR*, 109–110.

There is an obvious overlap here, for although Torrance insists that the ascension event does not formally begin to transpire until the crucifixion, other comments he has made clearly indicate that the Word's vicarious human response, consubstantial with the man-Godward movement of Christ's mediation (the *anabasis*), begins at the incarnation. This suggests that the *anabasis* is already taking place from Christ's birth or simultaneously with the *katabasis*. Not only then are they different aspects of God's love moving in two directions, but are both operating at once. The man-Godward disposition of Christ's mediation is also a movement of God 'toward us', Christ fulfilling the reach of God for man in the very act of his bringing our human response to God as man. God's coming to us and his bringing us to himself in his human nature are therefore not clearly distinguishable. Torrance confirms this: 'The whole existence of the incarnate Son', he says, 'was both the fulfilled intervention of God among men [the *katabasis*] and the fulfilled response of men toward God [the *anabasis*], in filial obedience, faith, trust, love, worship, prayer, and praise'.[143] This would suggest the following diagram:

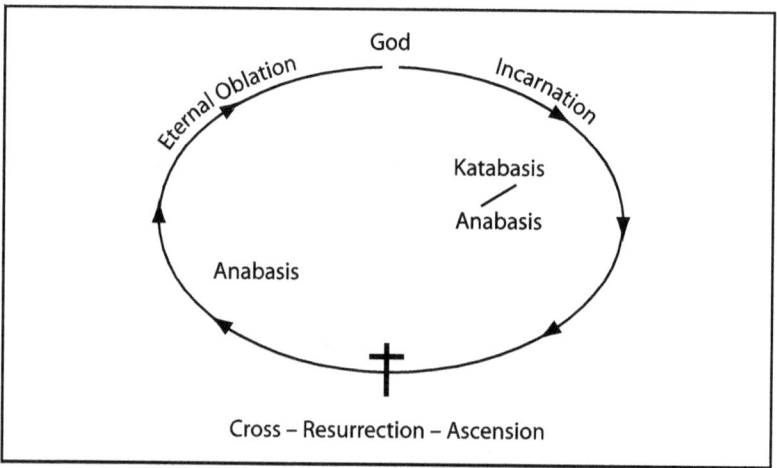

Whichever way we look at it, the God-ward aspect of the Word's saving operation cannot begin until the man-ward work is established, until 'the Word is become flesh'. Hence, the Church's Eucharist operates from the pre-supposition of Christ's presence. In Torrance's words, 'The Godward movement reposes upon the

---

[143] Ibid. 115.

manward movement.'[144] Indeed, it is the Word's presence within the Church which prescribes the sacrament, affiliates it with his saving work, thereby setting it in its God-ward motion.

The overlap mentioned above, this ambiguity on the objective side of Torrance's christology, carries over in a corresponding ambiguity in his exposition of the sacrament. Although he insists on an 'actual *katabasis* of the living Lord, and an actual *anabasis* in which he bears the Church up with Him to the Throne of God', Torrance nowhere indicates precisely where and when the Church finds presence in the sacrament or on what point in the sacramental action her praise is united to his. Just as it is hard to differentiate in the christological mystery between the *katabasis* of divine love and its *anabasis*, or to see where one becomes the other, it is likewise difficult to discern distinguishable 'moments' within the eucharistic action which can be specified exactly as real presence or eucharistic sacrifice.[145] There do remain, however, contrasting dispositions within the sacramental action of that which is 'received' and that which is 'offered'. As Torrance puts it

> The Eucharist involves a movement of *reception and communion* grounded in the self-giving of God to us in Christ – the real presence; and a movement of *thanksgiving, worship and offering* grounded in the vicarious self-consecration and self-offering of Christ to the Father which he fulfills in our human nature and on our behalf – the eucharistic sacrifice.[146]

Torrance's major emphasis in matters related to the movement of God's saving love is that God is always the principal mover. The Word, he says, has 'embodied in himself in a vicarious form the response of human beings to God, so that all [our] worship and

---

[144] *RP*, 39.

[145] *Inter*, 337. It is important to note that Torrance nowhere seeks to clarify this imprecision. Since God's coming to us and his bringing us to himself cannot really be separated in the Incarnate Son, why should it be any different in the Sacrament of the Word made Flesh? It follows then that in the Eucharist, just as in the incarnation, God's gift of himself to man and man's gift to God should be understood as given continuously and proceeding simultaneously. The whole of the Eucharist should be seen as celebrated within the real presence of God to man and man to God in Jesus Christ. Likewise, the whole of the Eucharist ought to be conceived as an offering of the Church's eucharistic sacrifice celebrated within the open, bi-polarity of Christ's life. We will discuss critically the problems which this ambiguity raises in our final chapter.

[146] *GT*, 7.

prayer [become] grounded and centred in him'.[147] No consequent or complementary act of worship by the Church has any authenticity or appeal before God except as ordered to the worshipful response for man which God has formed in Christ. The Eucharist, deferring as it does perpetually to Christ and his work, therefore provides for the Church in its own uniquely sacramental way 'the natural basis within our daily physical existence for free and spontaneous response to the Word of God'.[148] The sacraments are said themselves to constitute 'above all divinely provided, dominically appointed ways of response... sealing to us within the new covenant our sharing in the vicarious [work] of Christ'.[149] Just what kind of response this might be is suggested by J.B. Torrance in a discussion of 'the vicarious worship of Christ'. He speaks of the Church's eucharistic worship as 'a response to the Response already made for us by Christ to the Father's holy love, a response we are summoned to make in union with Christ'.[150] As this implies, however, the Church's response is not simply made as an entity set over against the response of Christ, any more than his vicarious work is accomplished in detachment from us. For T.F. Torrance the Church 'respond[s] to the love of the Father' in fellowship with the response which Christ makes to his Father for us.[151] Christ conveys his Spirit upon the Church, thereby 'drawing us into the power of his vicarious life'.[152] This is the means by which the Church in its sacramental action is assumed 'into unity with... [Christ's] self-offering through the eternal Spirit to the

---

[147] *MOC*, 96–7, 22, cf. 100.

[148] *G & R*, 159, cf. 161.

[149] *MOC*, 99–100.

[150] J.B. Torrance, 'Covenant or Contract?', 141.

[151] *MOC*, 97–8. The implications and details of the economy of this we will unravel later. At this stage it is enough to say that Christ 'carries in Himself the vicarious actuality, and conveys in Himself the active possibility, of true and faithful response on the part of all men to God's word' (*G & R*, 138). This passage indicates, albeit indirectly, the crucial role the spirit also plays in this scheme, though predictably a role subordinate to that of Christ. Torrance clarifies this: 'All is understood as having taken place within the incarnate life of the Mediator, in whom and in whose saving work on our behalf we are given participation in the Spirit who is regarded as co-active with the Son in all acts of redemption and sanctification as well as in all acts of creation' (*R/n*, 231).

The 'vicarious actuality' in the above text but one implies the vital potentiality for the Church's worship garnered in Christ's own doxological relation with his Father. The 'active possibility', on the other hand, of the Church's response – i.e. its hearing of the gospel, its obedience in service, as well as its eucharistic worship – is implicit in the work of the Holy Spirit (*G & R*, 138).

[152] *R/n*, 107.

Father'.¹⁵³ What we said above about the Eucharist being a 'response to the Response' of Christ can now be more deeply understood, not just as our response to something spiritually observed or overheard, not merely as our liturgical attempt to reply to Christ's worship, but rather as a response in the form of actual participation by the Spirit in Christ's response for us, or 'a response *within* a response'. Gathered by the Spirit within that perfect response of Christ, then, the Church is given to share in a worship which transcends all her natural capacities.

FURTHER ECCLESIOLOGICAL AND ESCHATOLOGICAL IMPLICATIONS

I. The Objective Conformation of the Church

In Torrance's theology the whole Church, and not just its sacrament, has its objective counterpart in Christ. The reconciliation of mankind within the 'One and the Many' intertwines the lives of all of us in the embrace of God's universal love.¹⁵⁴ Christ's identity in union with all men means that our 'union with him' can never be thought of merely in pietistic or individualistic categories, but must be considered instead in terms of 'mutual indwelling'.¹⁵⁵ Torrance states this clearly: we have 'no relation to Christ except in Christ's relation with all for whom He died'.¹⁵⁶ This in turn suggests the necessarily corporate nature of the Church.¹⁵⁷ When Torrance describes the Church as 'the Body of Christ' he therefore has its objective christological conformation as much in mind as any aspect of its subjective manifestation. As he puts it:

> Since the Church is rooted in the hypostatic and atoning union embodied in the person of the Mediator, the description of the Church as the Body of

---

[153] Cf. Ibid. 133; Heb. 9:14.
[154] Cf. *MOC*, 73.
[155] Ibid. 77; *SOF*, CXXIII.
[156] *SOF*, CXXIV.
[157] Hendrik Kraemer draws attention to Torrance's aversion to an individualistic concept of the Church as espoused in the Lutheran notion of the 'priesthood of all believers'. Torrance is cited as saying of the idea that 'it carries with it a ruinous individualism' (Hendrik Kraemer, *A Theology of the Laity* (London, Lutterworth, 1958), 62, fn. 1, cites TFT, *RP*, 35, fn. 1).

> Christ is not a figurative way of speaking of some external moral union between believing people and Jesus Christ, but an expression of the ontological reality of the Church concorporate with Christ himself.[158]

The fact that the concept of the Church arises definitively out of the theoretic union of divine and human natures in the incarnation does not in any way diminish the importance of the union between man and his fellow men in Christ. Indeed, that 'ontological reality' requires of us a corresponding union of the most intimate kind; it also carries decided significance for the way the Church weighs and conducts its corporate life. Humanity has been brought into such harmony with its Creator in Christ that there is prescribed an 'order' of love and justice in the world, particularly within the Church. In Christ man has been reconciled to God; it is therefore quite inconceivable that the community which is said to represent his divine-human life would not be manifestly itself a community of reconciliation, a 'House of Peace'. Torrance's definition of the Church in this context reflects this:

> The Church is the point or the sphere in human flesh where the personal union in Christ between God and man creates for itself a corresponding personal fellowship between man and man, within which the relation between Father and Son and the Son and the Father is folded out horizontally in history, or (to put it the other way round) within which men in their relation with one another in creation are given to share in the life and love of the Father and the Son and the Holy Spirit, that is in the Communion of the Spirit.[159]

For Torrance it is impossible to think of a person being united to God by the Spirit without at the same time being united by that same Spirit to his fellows. It is likewise unthinkable that one should be committed to God without this taking shape in a corresponding commitment to the brethren. The formal constitution of the Church on earth thus entails each person acknowledging his larger, plural identity in Christ and therein being joined by the Holy Spirit to all who are implicated by the new covenant. In this the reconciliation which Christ has wrought between God and mankind, and which now inheres in his divine humanity, is realized and takes corporate shape on earth. Following the thought of the Scottish catechizer M. John Craig, Torrance suggests that in the hypostatic union the Word

---

[158] *MOC*, 77–8.
[159] *SOF*, CXVIII.

was 'made flesh of our flesh', whereas in 'the corresponding union' between Christ and his Church 'we are made flesh of His flesh through being united to Him spiritually as members with the Head'.[160]

As we might expect, the way this 'corresponding union' takes manifest shape in the world is through the sacraments of the Church. The subjectifying role of the sacrament *vis-à-vis* its christological objectivity is nowhere more vividly seen in Torrance's theology than in the way the sacramental union is linked to the formal embodying of the Church. The sacramental union is said to incorporate in our flesh, that is, by the physical and corporate union of brethren in Christ which it comprises, that universal incorporation of humanity in Christ's flesh.[161] The sacraments give the relation which Christians have with Christ 'a new form in the Kingdom of God', Torrance says, 'indeed constituting them as the Church concorporate with Himself'. In this way, 'they enshrine in time the great mystery concerning Christ and his Church'.[162]

In the sacrament of Baptism the individual believer is sealed initially in Christ with the focus being upon the unbroken constancy of his personal incorporation, paralleling the eternal dimension of Christ's union with God. In contrast to this relatively individual character of Baptism, the participation in Christ which the Church is afforded in the Eucharist takes an outwardly corporate shape, as 'the personal union in Christ between God and man' 'creates for itself a corresponding personal fellowship between man and man'.[163] It is in the *unio sacramentalis*, then, that point at which every Christian is brought to the most intimately personal experience of Christ's relation with him, that God enlarges the Christian's experience to include all others who are united to Christ. However, this 'shaping' of the Church effected through the sacrament must never be considered only a perfunctory event, simply intended to give the Church outward, codified definition in the world. Although it does that, it does so in the context of a continual renewal of the Church's life in Christ. Indeed, in the Holy Communion we are brought face to face in the personal presence of Christ with the permanence of Christ's

---

[160] Ibid. CIX.

[161] Torrance works the idea in both directions: on the one hand, the sacrament is that which gathers the Church subjectively to its own objective participation in Christ, and, on the other, it is that 'sacramental infleshment [by which] the word comes to its full eventuation in our humanity' (*RP*, 101).

[162] *Inter*, 319, 309.

[163] *SOF*, CXVIII.

union with us, with the unchanging fact of God's love for all humanity. Torrance discusses the consequences of the Church's contact with the christological union in this way. He says,

> It is by the Eucharist, following upon Baptism, that that union is inserted as an abiding union into the heart of our estrangement from God the Father, and into all the conflicts of history. Here we are given the perfect union between the eternal and the temporal, between the divine and the human inserted into our flesh and blood, and it is that made flesh in the Eucharist which is the inner core of the Church's reality on earth.[164]

Christ present in the sacrament presses upon the Church the full implications of her own primal and vital form in him 'the wholeness of [her] union' with Christ in God – and therefore judges the order of her life by the rule of love which 'orders' his own.[165]

Finally, the corporate nature of the mystery of Christ requires that the sacrament in which that mystery is 'folded out horizontally' be shared also corporately. He states: 'It is the Sacrament of the communion in the Body of Christ and is therefore rightly celebrated with the whole Body of the Church in heaven and earth.'[166] As the sacrament through which God 'erect[s]... the covenanted relation appointed by Christ' with the whole world it should in no wise be contrived as 'a private rite of the few'.[167] Rather, 'it is the Sacrament of the New Covenant in which Christ gave Himself a ransom for many, and all are to eat... and drink... for there is one loaf and one cup, as there is One Lord in whom the many are reconciled to God and formed into One New Man'.[168] Although the 'human relations' with the sacramental union can never be said to be its point, nevertheless, the Eucharist is the kind of rite in which men find themselves related together and therefore ought to be considered a corporate sacrament also because of what it witnesses to on the human level, 'enshrining', as it does, 'the mutual relations in love of the members of Christ's Body'.[169]

---

[164] *Inter*, 320.
[165] Ibid. 321.
[166] *C & A* II, 151.
[167] *G & R*, 161; *C & A* II, 151.
[168] *C & A* II, 151.
[169] Ibid. 151.

2. The Objective Embodiment of the New Creation

Not only does the relation with God which Christ has won for man incorporate the objective reality of the Church, it also embodies proleptically the recreation of man's world (space) and the *telos* of his history (time). We have touched briefly upon the ramifications of this kind of eschatological thinking for Torrance's sacramental theology in our explanation of the Eucharist as 'the sacrament of God's interaction with the world'. In the ensuing chapter on his doctrine of eucharistic sacrifice we will discuss it further as part of a study of the implications of the Church's worship being intersected by one whose praise anticipates 'The New Song of Heaven'. However, before anything we have said or will say about the eschatological significance of the Eucharist can be fully appreciated, several definitions need to be clarified and the way Torrance develops his thought delineated.

Our first task is to establish what Torrance means by 'space and time'. He refuses to think of these concepts as abstract or static dimensions. While space and time do manifest differing dimensional qualities, as the terms themselves would indicate – 'three dimensional and one directional or irreversible' respectively – they are not these abstract qualities themselves, but rather that which is qualified.[170] For example, space is not envisaged as an abstract 'container' of creation as in the Aristotelian cosmology, but as 'that which occupies it'.[171] By the barest definition, then, space and time are equivalent to the whole material and temporal magnitude of existence itself.

However, Torrance takes this a crucial step further. Space and time are not just synonymous with existence as such, but with *man's* existence. They are relational concepts, he stresses, concepts relativized to man, which cannot be properly grasped outside that relation.[172] Existence does not just 'exist' to itself. It has been created for man. Torrance's whole understanding of space and time reposes upon this proposition and, following upon it, that man has been created for God. Since all things have their existence for man, or as contingencies of his world, space and time can thus be more precisely defined as categories which designate the physical and durational aspects of his life. Torrance says they represent 'the field

---

[170] *STR*, 131.
[171] Ibid. 124, 130.
[172] Ibid. 126ff.

of change and sequence of coherent structure in which [man] lives his life'.¹⁷³ Space and time refer to created things in general then only in a secondary sense, that is, because these things are themselves constitutent to man's personal existence and therefore participate in *his* space and time.¹⁷⁴

Taking this primary relation to man fully into account, Torrance insists that space and time must be explained dynamically and existentially. That is to say, space does not simply indicate the physical 'stuff' of man's existence which displaces void. It is the whole complex of his created existence, and this implies 'meaning'. Space is 'the room which [man] makes for himself in his life and movement'. But 'room for what[?]', Torrance asks.¹⁷⁵ Similarly, time cannot be 'abstracted from the purpose' of man.¹⁷⁶ It cannot be conceived only in terms of the passage of days or the succession of the millennia, but rather as the evolution of man and his world, as the meaningful unfolding of his existence, i.e. as his history. Time is an irrelevance apart from man. Man has time, Torrance contends, 'for something'.¹⁷⁷ He sums it up, 'we must think of [space] as well as time in terms of that *for which* they must exist or function'.¹⁷⁸

To speak of space and time then is to speak of the meaning of man's existence. This leads us to ask why he was created and recalls the second part of the interpretative proposition advanced above, viz. that man was created for God. Whereas the world has its existence, its space and time, its meaning, after man and for man, man discovers the purpose of his life in relation to his Creator. The world is anthropo-centric, man is theocentric. This is not to say that the world is not itself centred in God, but only after the fact that it is centred in man who is centred in God. The story, however, has not unfolded so harmoniously as this. For although the world was made for such a congruent relation with man, being given to his priestly

---

¹⁷³ Ibid. 131; cf. *STI*, 23–4.
¹⁷⁴ Cf. *STR*, 131.
¹⁷⁵ Ibid. 130–31.
¹⁷⁶ Ibid. 130.
¹⁷⁷ Ibid. 130.
¹⁷⁸ Because these concepts ask the same question of man's existence it is sometimes difficult to differentiate between them. Indeed Torrance insists that they belong together 'as temporal relation belongs to location'. However, they are thought together in Torrance's mind primarily not because of a relation they might have to each other but because of their mutual relation to man, as definitive of varying aspects of his existence. Since they cannot be separated in man's life, Torrance generally persists in addressing them singularly as space/time (*STR*, 130–31).

charge by God, it subsequently suffered for its relation to him, i.e. participating with him in his alienation from God.

In order to rectify the situation, to draw the whole contingent order back into conformity and continuity with his purposes God has come to the source of the primeval discord. In Jesus Christ, God has made the contradictions of our space and time, embodied personally in man's rebellion and manifest in his corruption and naked mortality, contingencies of his own existence. He has not released man in his dereliction but reordered and reconditioned his nature by the power of his obedience, thereby reversing the degressive flow of his history.[179] In his own holy life, by his resurrection and ascension, Christ has exalted man's existence, his space and time, to 'God's place', bringing his life to its purposive culmination in union with his Creator.[180] 'In the resurrection and ascension', Torrance states, 'our human existence and our human time, without being annihilated or disrupted, are transformed and recreated and are taken up into abiding union with God'.[181]

Given the priestly relationship which man has with creation, the charge he has been given over it but betrayed, the recreation of his nature and the fulfilment of his time cannot be contemplated without taking into full account the implications this has for the whole contingent order.[182] In God's economy for the restoration of the world creation cannot be freed from its 'bondage of decay' until man is returned to his place of responsibility over it, and this can only be accomplished when man is brought himself into right relation with God. In Christ's high priesthood both have been achieved; man has been offered to God and in that recommissioned to offer the praise of creation. This both anticipates and guarantees for Torrance 'the reconciliation of all things' (Col. 1:20). Just as 'the

---

[179] Torrance puts it: 'We believe that the Son of God took from the Virgin Mary our Adamic nature, flesh of our flesh of sin, and that in taking it He sanctified it, condemning sin in our flesh, and carrying His holy life in our flesh to its *telos* of utter obedience to the Father in His death' ('Arnoldshain', 12).

[180] *STR*, 135, 130-31. 'Man... in the ascension has a place in the innermost seat of the Godhead' (*R/n*, 175). In the ascension Christ gathers our world and its history to culmination in the very 'life and rule of God' Torrance says. (*STR*, 135, 137). In that exalted event, he states, man in his 'place' meets God in his 'place'. He defines God's 'place' 'by the nature and activity of God as the room for the life and activity of God as God. Man's 'place', on the other hand, is defined 'by the nature and activity of man as the room which he makes for himself in his life and movement' (*STR*, 131).

[181] *RP*, 49.

[182] Cf. *STR*, 131.

creation fell for man's sake and with man... it is in and with the adoption of the sons of God that the creation will receive its emancipation and renewal'.[183] He puts it even more profoundly and hints at the eschatological undertones so important for his doctrine of the Eucharist when he says,

> The resurrection and the ascension mean that he has overcome the contradiction and tension and has carried through His union with our creaturely existence and our time into a new creation in which the whole purpose of God in creation is fully realized and in which our temporality is redeemed... in union with His own eternity.[184]

In the light of the meanings we have explicated, this union which Christ has wrought between God and 'our creaturely existence and our time', and the 'new creation... fully realized' by it, can now be understood, not as some vague contact between God and abstract dimensions, but between God and real humanity. Torrance says, that in the risen and ascended humanity of Christ, the eschatological new man is already a reality. 'The New Humanity is already raised up in Christ' and 'in the establishment of human nature in an imperishable state' the new creation has already dawned.[185]

It is by union with the resurrected Christ that the Church is said to participate in a reality of creation beyond all threat of transience and decay.[186] In the presence of the risen Christ the Church's own 'new creation' with its 'new time' – i.e. that which it will surely become in the fulfilment of the purposes of God already realized in Christ presses back upon her in present time. It is this very presence which confronts the Church in the Eucharist. It is 'through the Word and Sacraments', Torrance insists, that the Church's participation in incorruptible creation and fulfilled time becomes 'a present reality'.[187] In claiming this for the sacramental union he no more has an abstraction in mind than when he claims it for the christological union just observed. This is not some nebulous conjunction with an idea but vital intercourse in the Church's sacrament with Christ's real humanity in its unhindered relationship with God. The

---

[183] *SOF*, CXXVI.

[184] *RP*, 49.

[185] *STR*, 34, 135–6, fn. 12; cf. *Inter*, 311. Torrance says, 'we have revealed the new creation in the risen Body of Jesus Christ' (*Inter*, 311).

[186] *RP*, 49.

[187] Ibid. 49.

Eucharist, Torrance says, actually affords the Church participation in its own future 'as real act in time', 'as Word-deed enacted in our flesh and blood inserted into history'.[188] 'It is by the Eucharist', he states, 'that the Church's ultimate reality stands not only at the end of time but impinges creatively upon the Church throughout history.'[189] Although she still 'partakes of decay and corruption of the world' the Church also 'participates in its new being' by virtue of its communication in 'that whole reality of the risen humanity in Christ'.[190] In the penultimate chapter we will discuss the refining influence of the presence of the eschatological Christ upon the earthly configuration of the Church. However, we can see already how Torrance can say that the sacraments are certain 'pledges' of our future participation in a Kingdom fully come, and, more than that, recalling his dynamic connotation given to the term, eschatological 'signs' by which we 'may taste the powers of the age to come'.[191]

SACRAMENTAL AND NON-SACRAMENTAL PARTICIPATION

It is now clear how in Torrance's theology the risen humanity of Christ in its hypostatic union contains not only the objective conformation of the Church but all surety and potential for the restoration of mankind and his world in union with God. We have seen as well how the sacrament of the Eucharist provides the Church active participation in that reality through faith, so that the Church in its earthly life may be shaped and constantly renewed as a living body correspondent to that of her eschatological Head. However, our attention thus far has been given almost exclusively to the role of the sacrament in this economy. What remains to be shown is the relationship the sacrament has with other means of participation,

---

[188] *Inter*, 313. The sacraments are not concerned with an abstract future in some 'timeless moment', rather 'with a [real] union between the Church in history and the new creation as an abiding union here and now in the heart of the world's estrangement' (*Inter*, 312).

[189] Ibid. 319.

[190] *STR*, 156; *Inter*, 323; cf. *STR*, 142. In the sacrament the Church is confronted with her own renewed being in the form of that 'perfect union between... the divine and human', in Jesus Christ inserted into our flesh and blood' (*Inter*, 320).

[191] *STR*, 142; *Inter*, 308–9.

what distinctions, if any, can be ascribed to the sacramental relation among these, and finally the mutual relation in faith they all share over against the christological mystery.

Thus far we have spoken of sacramental participation almost interchangeably with the Church's participation in Christ through faith. The latter, however, is much broader than the former and wholly inclusive of it. Hence when Torrance says that the Church 'feeds uninterruptibly upon Christ's flesh', it is primarily the faith-relation outside the sacrament and not the eucharistic meal as such which he has in mind.[192] 'There is an eating of the flesh and a drinking of the blood of Christ', he alleges, 'before (or apart from) eucharistic participation.'[193] In saying this Torrance is thinking of three other ways the Church communicates in Christ. In the first place, the Church is said, as it were, to 'eat' of Christ's flesh constantly by virtue of the Word's vicarious partaking of the flesh of Christ in his incarnation.[194] All the strength of our eating Christ's flesh, either within or outside of the Eucharist, rests upon this undeviating fact. Secondly, we partake of Christ's flesh through the spoken ministry of the Living Word who gives his words to us as the 'Spirit and Life' of his divine humanity. To hear and to receive his words by faith is commensurate, in Torrance's mind, with 'eating Christ's flesh'.[195] Finally, the incorporation of the Church in Christ's body through Baptism, which answers both our objective incorporation by the Word and his self-proclamation, Torrance understands as real communion in the flesh of Christ. It is this baptismal incorporation which underlines that side of our relation with God which is unbroken and thus 'reminds us that Christ dwells in us... independently of the Supper'.[196] He is alluding to this when he says, 'he who is sacramentally incorporated into the body of Christ [in the Eucharist] is already participant in sacramental communion'.[197] In Torrance's sacramental theology the Eucharist presupposes baptismal incorporation.[198]

With these various aspects of our 'sacramental participation' in mind, Torrance can say that 'faith brings to the Eucharist a continuous feeding upon the body and blood of Christ', which is only

---

[192] *Inter*, 322.
[193] Ibid. 335.
[194] *RP*, 75.
[195] *Inter*, 335; cf. *RP*, 75.
[196] Ibid. 339.
[197] Ibid. 335.
[198] Ibid. 335; *K & C*, 146.

indirectly related to our eucharistic communion.[199] The formal *unio sacramentalis* is understood as an expression of this more comprehensive faith relation, as part of it, but not a part that can ever be separated from it. 'Sacramental response', he says, 'has its place within the all-embracing response of faith' to the Word of God and 'shares with it an inner relation to the Word'.[200] It is not something different from the more general relation in faith, rather that relation given dynamic and corporate demonstration. The question remains, 'What are we then to say of eucharistic communion?' What is unique about this aspect of the faith relation? Torrance comments:

> Surely, as Calvin has made so clear in the Reformed Church..., while we can only eat and drink the body and blood of Christ through faith... by the power of the eternal Spirit, the Church is given through the Eucharist a *relation in being*, beyond its relation to Christ through faith.[201]

This passage out of context appears to contradict what we have said above, suggesting that the faith relation within the sacrament offers the Church something substantively, 'ontologically', different from that same relation outside the sacrament. However, in the same passage he prevents this interpretation, saying that 'Christ's dwelling in our hearts', which transcends formal sacramental participation, is likewise 'an ontological relation'. His point seems to be that the Church's relation to God through faith, either with or without its sacramental expression, has at its heart something 'beyond' its own subjectivity, not something more than faith can receive but something other than faith itself. He states: 'In the Eucharist believing and actual communication through the bread and wine are not one and the same thing.'[202] 'While we can only eat and drink the body and blood of Christ through faith', he says, the eucharistic communion is not 'identical with faith'.[203] The Church's faith *per se* does not erect its relation with God, neither does it substantiate that relation in itself. For Torrance faith does not create, it only receives the gifts of God. Just as Christ and not our knowing was said to be the substance of the knowing relation, so Christ and not our believing is affirmed as the substance of the faith relation.

---

[199] *Inter*, 335.
[200] *G & R*, 159.
[201] *Inter*, 335.
[202] Ibid. 335.
[203] Ibid. 335.

Torrance never explicitly answers the questions asked of Augustine and all the theologians of the Reformation, viz. how the effect or so-called 'gift' of the sacrament differs from that of the Word, or put more fully, how the relation established in association with the Word and sacrament through faith is distinguished from the faith relation associated with the Word alone. While Torrance nowhere conclusively resolves these issues there is some indication as to how he might do so in a selection of sermons on the Lord's Supper by Robert Bruce (1554-1631) which he has edited.[204] Bruce held that the presence and/or the gifts found in the sacrament are 'no new thing, nothing more... than in the Word'. 'The sacraments are given, they are added to the Word', he says (somewhat quaintly), 'that you may get the same thing better than you had it in the Word [alone].'[205] Similarly, the distinction which Torrance makes between the Word/faith relation and the Word-sacrament/faith relation is not one of content, but of form. He says, 'whereas faith corresponds more to the activity of the Word as Word, sacramental participation corresponds more to the activity of the Word as Event'.[206] While Torrance never refers to Bruce's way of contrasting these, it seems reasonable to assume from statements he has made, such as, Christ

---

[204] Full title: *The Mystery of the Lord's Supper: Sermons on the Sacrament Preached in the Kirk of Edinburgh in A.D. 1589 by Robert Bruce* (London, James Clark, 1958).

[205] Ibid. 63-4. MacNicol gives us the full quotation in Scots: 'We get no more in the sacraments', says Bruce, 'than we get in the word.' 'Quherefore are they annexed, and we get als meekle in the very simple word as we gat in the sacrament?... It is true certainly we get na new thing in the sacrament, nor we get na uther thing in the sacrament nor we gat in the word, for quhat mair walde thou crave nor to get the Sonne of God, gif thou get him weill?... Suppose thou get that same thing quhilk thou gat in the word, yit thou gets that same thing better. Quhat is that better?... we get Christ better nor we did before; we get the thing that we gat mair fullie, that is with a surer apprehension nor we had of before; we get a better grip of Christ now. For be the sacrament my faith is nurished, the bounds of my saul is enlarged, and sa quhere I had but a little grip of Christ before as it were betwixt my finger and my thumbe, now I get him in my haill hande; and aye the mair that my faith growes, the better grip I get of Christ Jesus. Sa the sacrament is felloun necessarie' (D.C. MacNicol, *Robert Bruce: Minister of the Kirk of Edinburgh*, 74).

Torrance approaches Bruce's position, gathering up several ideas discussed in this section when he says, 'the faith-union grounded upon Baptism is presupposed by the Eucharist which nourishes and increases it, so that through the sacramental communion in the Lord's Supper we are brought into *closer and more intimate union with Christ*' (*K & C*, 146, italics mine).

[206] *G & R*, 160.

'is equally active in Word and in Sacrament', that his own understanding would not be far from his.²⁰⁷ Of this much we can be certain: it is Christ whom we receive and with whom we are related both in the sacraments and in all other expressions of the relation of faith. For Torrance as well as for Bruce there is no specific sacramental gift; all gifts of God are *in* Christ and given to the Church *as* Christ. However, it is also true for Torrance that the relation with God, given to the faith of the Church in the sacrament, is the deepest, most effectual form of that relation.²⁰⁸ Christ in his sacrament takes the faith of the Church to its limits, but rewards it far beyond itself or its power to appropriate, i.e. with himself.

Furthermore, taking Torrance's general indebtedness to Calvin's eucharistic theology into account, what Kilian McDonnell says regarding the Reformer's position is also helpful to ascertain Torrance's view on the questions raised above. He suggests that the sacramental relation is 'a particularisation of [our] union with Christ in faith'.²⁰⁹ For Calvin, McDonnell says, 'the eucharistic eating becomes [a transient experience of]... that perpetual eating which takes place in faith'.²¹⁰ From what we have indicated, Torrance's position would correspond – though not precisely – with this view. Whereas the sacramental relation for Torrance undoubtedly does constitute a particular, active expression of the larger faith relation, it has considerably more to specify than this, something infinitely more certain and concrete, more 'objective', than merely our faith. In fact, the relation which the sacrament manifests has its primary identity not in apposition to the faith relation as such, but in dynamic association with the objective divine-human relation in Christ. What our study thus far has shown is that Christ, who embodies objectively our union with God, comes in the corporeal framework of the sacrament seeking to constitute a union among us – with God and with each other – correspondent to that in him. Therefore, it is not just the union *we* have with Christ by faith which the Eucharist materially re-presents, although it does accomplish that. Indeed, for Torrance our eucharistic participation constitutes in the brokenness of time a 'moment' of Christ's unvarying 'union with us', though not disclosed in some splendidly mystical sense but rather in the reality of our fallen humanity and faltering human

---

[207] Ibid. 160.
[208] Cf. *Inter*, 237.
[209] Kilian McDonnell, *John Calvin, the Church, and the Eucharist* (Princeton, NJ, Princeton University Press, 1967), 70.
[210] Ibid. 378, cf. 179.

relationships, in the actual, outward conformation of the Church.[211] Based upon the notion that Baptism and the Eucharist together represent to the Church the plenitude of our objective participation in Christ, both in its invariable continuity in eternity and in its intersection with the discontinuity of our lives in time, Torrance states: 'The two sacraments of the Gospel enshrine together the two essential "moments" of our participation' in Christ.[212]

---

[211] Josef A. Jungmann puts it graphically: 'Communion is indeed the normal, permanent condition of the life of Christians, whose duty it is to always cherish it. All their lives are lived in a spirit of communion, and it bursts into flame every time the [eucharistic] sacrifice is completed' (Josef A. Jungmann, *The Place of Christ in Liturgical Prayer* (London, Geoffrey Chapman, 1965), 258).

[212] *STR*, 150.

CHAPTER 4

Sacramental Effect: the Subjectification of the Objective Christological Reality

RATIONALE FOR SUBSEQUENT OUTLINE

As we have sought to expound Torrance's eucharistic theology within the context of his formal theological method we have followed Calvin's outline as closely as possible. However, some alteration of Calvin's arrangement has been necessary in order to adhere strictly to the progression of Torrance's thought. In his sacramental theology, as we have noted, Calvin distinguished between the sacrament's matter and action in a way that Torrance cannot. Although for Calvin the sacrament's formal substance is never less than Christ himself, the action of the sacrament is explicated in terms of the impartation of the benefits of Christ's work.[1] By

---

[1] Although Calvin insisted that Christ could not be separated from his benefits, the way he framed his sacramental theology, as well as his repeated assertion that the physical person of the ascended Christ was 'separated' from the sacrament, left room for the misunderstanding that Christ the Giver was somehow disconnected from his gifts. For example:

contrast, Torrance's eucharistic theology demands that sacramental matter and action be treated together, since the being and act of Christ are integratively conceived as different properties of 'the undivided oneness of his Person as Mediator'.[2]

Another major difference arises from the fact that Calvin dealt with sacramental action and effect together in his outline, whereas Torrance's sacramental theology separates the effect from the action. Although there is no material difference in Torrance's thinking between the act of Christ in itself and his act in the sacrament, he distinguishes between the 'action of Christ' there and 'its effect in our reception of it'.[3] This does not designate two distinct actions, but the difference between Christ's formal action and its subjectification within the Church. When discussing sacramental effect he never speaks of the reception of benefits *per se*, but of the effective manifestation of Christ's person and work within the sacrament. He sets this out as two 'moments' of our communion in Christ – the first, 'that of receiving His gift of Himself' and the second, involving 'a union with Him in the whole of His obedient Self-offering to the

---

'But though it seems an incredible thing that the flesh of Christ, while at such a distance from us in respect of place, should be food to us, let us remember how far the secret virtue of the Holy Spirit surpasses all our conceptions.... Therefore, what our mind does not comprehend let faith conceive – viz. that the Spirit truly unites things separated by space' (*Inst* IV.17.10).

'Christ does not simply present to us the benefits of his death and resurrection, but [his] very body.... Christ's body is really, that is truly, given to us in the Supper, to be the wholesome food for our souls. Our souls are nourished by the substance of the body that we may be truly made one with him or *what amounts to the same thing*, that a life-giving virtue from Christ's flesh is poured into us by the Spirit, though it is at a great distance and is not mixed with us.' (John Calvin, *Commentary on the Epistles of Paul the Apostle to the Corinthians*, ed. John Pringle (Grand Rapids, Eerdmans, 1948), vol. 1, 379).

Christ 'communicates to us from heaven the virtue of his flesh *as though it were present*' (ibid. 382, italics mine).

The above also demonstrates Calvin's method of determining the real presence of Christ 'by equivalents'. The direct presence and operation of the Spirit in the sacrament 'amounts to the same thing' as that of Christ in his very flesh and blood. The ascended Christ conveys to the Church the benefits won for us in his flesh as though that flesh were actually present. Christ's life is given by the Spirit just 'as if there were real contact between the physical reality of Christ and that of his Church (*Inst* IV.17.10, IV.17.18). While Torrance never employs this method directly himself, he does cite Calvin, albeit uncritically, when he uses it (cf. *K & C*, 130).

[2] *MOC*, 79.
[3] *C & A* II, 146.

Father'.[4] Elsewhere he treats these two aspects of our sacramental communion specifically as the *Real Presence* and the *Eucharistic Sacrifice*.[5] Therefore, we shall discuss *Sacramental Effect* under these two headings.

THE REAL PRESENCE WITHIN THE CHURCH'S SACRAMENT

I. The Divine Word: Principle of Action and Authority within Christ's own Humanity and Consequently within the Sacramental Relation

We turn now to the question of Christ's presence in the sacrament itself. In Torrance's eucharistic theology, as we have observed, it is the Word's principal relation with creation in the humanity of Christ which dictates everything that can be said about other relations he establishes with created reality. Thus it seems appropriate to begin our discussion of the Word's manifestation within the sacramental relation by examining the relationship he has with his own created being in Christ. For all his emphasis upon the essential role that Christ's humanity plays in our salvation, the 'dominant place', Torrance insists, must always be 'accorded to the Word's'.[6] The Word is the active principle within Christ's human mind and body; he is the principle of authority and personhood within his own human identity. The humanity of Christ only fulfils its salvific function towards God because God the Word so moves it. In his saving act God 'begins eternally with Himself'.[7] He does not consult or consort with man. 'The atonement is God's act', he states, 'not of the will of the flesh, nor of man, but of God.'[8] It is '*God as man*' who reconciles man to Himself, not the human factor in Christ perceived as acting in some way independently of the divine agency.[9] As Torrance puts it again, 'the flesh of Jesus Christ did what was divine

---

[4] Ibid. 146–7.
[5] *GT*, 6.
[6] *RP*, 77, fn. 1.
[7] *Inter*, 337.
[8] Ibid. 332; John 1:13.
[9] *SOF*, XCI; *Inter*, 332.

not in virtue of its own activity but in virtue of the Word united with it'.[10]

This fundamental proposition conditions for Torrance any discussion of the relation between divine and created realities in the sacrament. He sees our relation with God in the Eucharist as reflecting and imaging Christ's own nature.[11] Hence the predominant posture of the Word with respect to his human nature determines that the Word must also be the principle of authority and action within the sacramental relation. God is present to his Church in its sacrament 'through an act issuing from the Godhead'.[12] 'The ineffable mystery of the Eucharist', he says, is 'that in it God begins with Himself in the continuity of the Church's action in the creaturely world, but by virtue of His divine nature independent of it.'[13] 'In the sacraments of the Word made flesh', Torrance stresses, 'it is the Word who exercises supreme authority, or rather it is Christ in the Sacraments..., who in His real Presence commands us through His Word and gives in the Sacraments what He commands'.[14] The Word made flesh, the Word through his flesh, is 'the all-inclusive Sacrament' of the Church.[15] This means that it is uniquely through his own 'creaturely objectivity' that God gives himself to his Church. All other sacraments are therefore subordinate to this Living Sacrament, having their efficacy by virtue of his immediate presence and act within them. Hence he can say,

> It is the Word of God which gives the Sacraments their unity, and their reality, though the Sacraments are the differing forms of the Word become visible and bodily event in the midst of the Church. Because the Sacraments are Sacraments of the Word made flesh, they are nothing apart from the Word, and so Augustine used to insist so strongly that it is the Word which sacramentalizes the ordinance and turns it into a Sacrament; *Accedat verbum ad elementum et fiet sacramentum*.[16]

---

[10] *RP*, 75.
[11] *C & A* II, 139.
[12] *Inter*, 334.
[13] Ibid. 337.
[14] *RP*, 101, 76.
[15] Ibid. 75.
[16] Ibid. 75 (Torrance cites Augustine, 'Homilies on the Gospel of John', 80.3); cf. *TS*, 150.

2. The Sacramental Relation Itself

(a) Its Meaning vis-à-vis the Meaning of the Real Presence

What Torrance means by a 'sacramental relation' has important implications for his understanding of the real presence and *vice versa*. Everything of course is prefaced by the hypostatic relation in Christ being the 'primary sacramental area' where God is given to man and received for man.[17] With this in view, a sacramental relation in the Church is one in which the Word personally communicates himself to his people, 'uniting himself to them in their communication with the truth'.[18] Although any revelatory relation is by definition a sacramental one, the relation which God establishes with his people in the Eucharist epitomizes for Torrance the *unio sacramentalis*. For this discussion, therefore, we will always use them interchangeably. That relation is formed as the Incarnate Word himself comes to meet and speak to his people in the context of appointed secondary objectivities. Unless this happens, as we have seen, the sacrament has no reference to Christ. 'The creaturely objectivities', Torrance says, 'have their meaning through this relation in depth to that objectivity that indefinitely transcends them.'[19] Corresponding to the Word's communication in and through the humanity of Christ, a sacramental relation in the Church then involves a genuine relation – a 'relation in depth', as he calls it – between God and created objectivity in which he makes it 'the instrument of His purpose in revelation and reconciliation'.[20]

---

[17] *TS*, 150.
[18] Cf. ibid. 149–50.
[19] *TS*, 150
[20] Cf. *SOF*, LII; *TS*, 150, 43. We have never indicated that the sacraments of Baptism and the Eucharist constitute for Torrance the only 'sacramental relations' in the Church. Indeed, all knowledge of God has been seen to proceed to man sacramentally, that is, by the mediation of the Word correlated 'with the world as the appointed medium of his... self-communication to mankind' (*R & E*, 25). A sacramental relation, he says, is one in which 'the divine and (created) are held together in the unity of the self-communication of the Truth to us and our communication with the Truth' (*TS*, 149–50). The most obvious and important such relation is that between the Word of God and preaching. This is considered 'a sacramental relation', in that the words of men are assumed by the Word of God to facilitate his self-communication (cf. *TS*, 149). As Rahner puts it, 'In a word, for the full normal accomplishment of a personal self-disclosure of God to the personally actualised man, the inner word of grace and the external historical word come together, as the mutually complementary moments of the one word of God to man' (cf. K. Rahner, 'The Word and the Eucharist', *TI*, vol. 4,

Torrance speaks of the created elements 'participating sacramentally in the mystery of Christ'.[21] This relation, real as it is, however, is wholly incidental and functional to the personal relation which God seeks with his people. There is no formal *unio sacramentalis*, not according to Torrance's definition, except that which exists between God and his people. The Word does not 'relate' as such to static matter. The sacramental relation is a speaking-hearing relation, so that the inanimate element is never a principal partner within it. Hence that element is always designated as an 'instrument' of Christ's real presence, never properly as a bearer of it.[22] God is united to it, but only within the process of communication with his people, that is, only insofar as it facilitates the sacramental relation.[23] The Word remains transcendent to these 'created mediations' within the sacramental action and differentiated in his divine presence from them.[24]

The sacramental relation then does not exist as a static analogy, but as an active one.[25] For Torrance every aspect of the sacramental relation presupposes the real and active presence of Christ. The sacrament consists as a dynamic relation, one which is formed in a presence, operated by a presence, and through which the One present offers himself to his Church. Torrance, therefore, concurs with Calvin's refusal to treat the words of institution 'take, eat, this is my body' literally or metaphorically; instead he understands them as implying 'an analogy of participation' for the Church. Here Christ

---

259). Torrance will not speculate concerning the exact way in which the Scriptures, preaching or the systemization of scriptural teaching participate sacramentally in the divine Word so as to become the actual expression of his Word to man (*TS*, 150; *R/st*, 139). He falls back instead on its 'mystery', that is, the divine nature of the truth itself, to 'explain' why there can be no explanation. In that it is the act of the divine word which makes God's self-communication a reality within the Church, the exact process of that act remains internal to the Word himself and thus eludes the inquisitor. It remains a mystery.

[21] *TS*, 150.

[22] *Inter*, 336.

[23] A few times, when discussing Reformation sacramental theology, Torrance will use the term *unio sacramentalis* in a manner which reflects its Reformation usage, that is, as the presence of Christ to bread. On these occasions he is usually highlighting the real association the Word must have with created objectivity in order for the Church to comprehend spiritual truth. He never addresses the sacramental relation however with an exclusively *Deus-panis* relation in mind; the principal constituents of the relation are always *Deus et homines*.

[24] *R/n*, 132.

[25] Cf. *SOF*, LIII.

associates a truth about himself – viz. that he is the source of the Church's union with God – with his communion with his Church. He then acts within that communion to bring that truth to effect within the Church's experience. For Torrance the sacramental analogy is not complete until it becomes a vital sign of the active presence of God, or an instrumental means by which God gives the Church real participation in that which is signified.[26]

(b) Its Character as Mutually Inclusive Action: The Active Presence of Christ in Continuity with the Action of the Church

God's presence within the sacramental relation is a presence, as Torrance phrases it in another context, *'in actu'*.[27] God does not present himself to man except as he is, a God who acts. The sacramental relation, while not suggesting that God has no relation whatever with exanimate things, does imply that he only has such in association with the sacramental action of the Church. That relation of course contains a human action proper to it, as well as a divine action, one prescribed by the Word, appropriate to his own nature as Word/Act. It is a relation in which 'the human and the divine... are held together in the unity of the self-communication of the Truth of God to us and of our communion with that Truth'.[28] It is the Church's active response to the gospel in its 'communication with the Word of Truth' to which Christ joins himself. Torrance speaks of it in terms of a 'union between divine action and human action'.[29] The Word, exercising supremacy in the Church, commands us to make *anamnesis*, and then 'confer[s] his own *parousia* upon it'.[30] For Torrance, *parousia* always 'means both a presence and a coming', carrying with it dynamic, eschatological connotation.[31] Christ's *parousia* in the sacrament, therefore, is an active presence in the midst of an action.[32] Hence the Church 'enacts' the real presence of Christ sacramentally, outwardly, and God, by his gift of himself,

---

26 Cf. *K & C*, 144.
27 *RP*, 72.
28 *TS*, 149.
29 *Inter*, 311.
30 *GT*, 8; *RP*, 101; cf. *Inter*, 310.
31 *Inter*, 310.
32 Killian McDonnell makes a similar observation regarding Calvin's view of the real presence. 'We are concerned here not with a [material] substance in a substance but an act in an act' (McDonnell, *John Calvin*, 239. He cites J. Beckmann, *Vom Sakrament bei Calvin*, Tübingen, 1926, 151).

makes our Eucharist become 'the divine enactment of [his own] Incarnate Presence in the Church'.[33] Torrance quotes Calvin: 'what the minister figures and attests by outward action, God performs inwardly'.[34]

This sort of language, however, should not be thought to suggest in any way a cleavage in Torrance's mind between inward/divine and outward/human operations. In fact, he acknowledges the closest concurrence between the two. For example,

> What Christ has commanded to be figured and attested in this active way, He undoubtedly performs, giving His broken Body and shed Blood for our nourishment, and effectively applying His death and resurrection for our salvation.[35]

God is thus seen to work in the Eucharist, he says, 'in the continuity of the Church's action in the creaturely world'.[36] While God and his Church act together in the sacrament, their actions are always distinguishable. They never become one. The divine and human actions in the Eucharist, he says, 'can neither be identified with, nor separated from, each other'.[37]

3. The Nature of the Eucharistic Parousia

(a) A Presence Determined by the Ascension

As we saw in our last chapter, everything concerning the real presence in the sacrament is determined by the objective presence of God with man embodied in Christ's incarnation and established permanently in his ascension.[38] The presence of unrestrained Godhead to our humanity is only a reality in the hypostatic union. Only the ascended Christ 'dwells in the immediate presence of God' in this sense, that is, 'in an unbroken communion with him'.[39] It is this normative presence of God to man in Christ in heaven which now mediates the Word's presence to us in the world. Christ ascended in

---

[33] *Inter*, 334.
[34] Ibid. 334.
[35] *C & A* II, 145. 'As surely as in the Eucharist we handle bread and wine, we put our fingers into His wounds' (*Inter*, 334).
[36] *Inter*, 337.
[37] Ibid. 311.
[38] Cf. *STR*, 129.
[39] *R/n*, 140.

his flesh represents the sealing of the reconciliation of all men in 'the innermost seat of the Godhead'.[40]

Torrance says that 'the form' of the eucharistic *parousia* is 'determined by the Ascension'.[41] 'Can any interpretation of the Supper be faithful to the teaching of the New Testament which avoids this?', he asks.[42] The fact is that Christ has withdrawn visibly and tangibly from his Church, holding 'back the full power and majesty of his presence'.[43] If sacramental theology is to take the ascension seriously the manner of Christ's presence to his Church in the Eucharist must be understood consistently with his relationship to the world of space/time since his physical departure from us.[44] For Torrance, then, the real presence must be viewed so as to allow a real interval to remain between Christ's actual flesh and blood and that of the Church.[45] The mode of his eucharistic presence must not only uphold the full integrity of his promised gift of himself, but also leave his glorified state intact. We must somehow reconcile the two aspects of Christ's present relation to his Church: 'I must go away' with 'I am with you always'.[46]

Christ is present to us in the Eucharist *from* the throne of God, and that position is never surrendered. It is from there that the High Priest is present to his Church, not from the Church's altar. The ascension accentuates Christ's independence and sovereignty over against his Church, 'reminding us that the Church is other than Christ'.[47] The way in which he is reckoned present must in no wise compromise the real 'distance' imposed by the ascension between Christ glorified and his Church, that is his physical integrity distinguished from our own.[48] This prevents the Church from usurping the Lord's supreme position by falsely 'Spiritualizing' his

---

[40] Ibid. 172-3. 'He who has already bound up our existence with Himself and who as the incarnate, crucified and risen Lord present within it, ever sustains it in its reconciled relation to God' (*G & R*, 161). 'In the hypostatic union the human nature is taken up, established, secured and anchored forever in its undiminished integrity in the Son of God' (*MOC*, 80).

[41] *GT*, 8; cf. 'Arnoldshain', 14; *K & C*, 145f.

[42] 'Arnoldshain', 13.

[43] *C & A* II, 139; 'Arnoldshain', 13.

[44] The eucharistic 'presence cannot be construed as if the ascension had not taken place', he insists ('Arnoldshain', 13).

[45] Cf. *K & C*, 145.

[46] John 16:4f.; Matt. 28:20; cf. *K & C*, 143.

[47] *RP*, 46.

[48] Cf. *C & A* II, 143; 'Arnoldshain', 13.

presence, so that it could be misunderstood as being amalgamated with the flesh and blood of the Church's historical reality.[49]

The sacramental relation is therefore conditioned by the separation of Christ's place from ours. 'The sacraments', Torrance says, 'are given to us because of the ascension and cannot be made to impugn it, as if they contained a presence fully identical with that of the parousia'.[50] With respect to our place in the world, God is bound to reveal himself to man 'through creaturely forms, appointing them as signs and instruments of His self-disclosure, veiling His truth in lowly forms adapted to creaturely apprehension'.[51] This of course corresponds with the hidden character of his person 'veiled' by the ascension. Therefore Christ comes to us in the Eucharist in a form which also conceals his glory: viz. 'under the veil of bread and wine'.[52] This in turn conforms to the humiliation of his cross, viz. 'the breaking of his body and the shedding of his blood'.[53] The eucharistic form of his presence therefore manifests at once the character of his cross and the restrained disposition of his glory. As he puts it, the eucharistic *parousia* 'is the synthesis of the dialectic between the form of glory and the form of suffering'.[54]

While the ascension rules out any notion of a tangible, material presence in the sacrament, and though it always underlines the 'physical distance' that obtains between Christ and his Church, it by no means suggests an absence of Christ.[55] Neither should this eucharistic *parousia*, mediating itself as it does 'through creaturely objectivity', be misconstrued as a presence 'twice removed' from Christ himself.[56] Even though only 'the man, Christ Jesus' knows God's presence *simpliciter*, Torrance can still speak of Christ being 'directly' present to the Church within the sacrament.

> There is an element of pure immediacy in the Church's relation to the risen Body of Christ, so that his *parousia* is a presence here and now through the Spirit. But there is also an element in the Church's relation to the risen

---

[49] *K & C*, 144.
[50] *Inter*, 310.
[51] *SOF*, LII; cf. *TS*, 43.
[52] *GT*, 8; *C & A* II, 139.
[53] *GT*, 8.
[54] Ibid. 8.
[55] Torrance insists that 'the Ascension of Christ is not in order to an absence, but in order to a presence, the real presence' ('Arnoldshain', 13).
[56] Cf. *SOF*, LIII; *C & A* II, 139; *R & E*, 29; *TS*, 43.

Body of Christ which from our experience and our understanding is still in arrears and awaits a divine fulfilment.[57]

This suggests that while the sacramental relation cannot be thought to constitute a re-presentation of the physical person of Christ, neither can it be regarded as a different presence, although one certainly manifest in a different form. Torrance leaves no doubt about this. 'Though Jesus has withdrawn His visible presence from us', he insists that 'there is such an intervention by the Risen Lord as the invisible reality behind each celebration of the Lord's Supper. *Jesus Christ is as really present in the Eucharist as He was on that Easter Day to His disciples.*'[58]

This 'invisible' presence which the ascension demands suggests some kind of 'spiritual' presence for the Eucharist. By this, however, Torrance does not mean, as we have indicated, some sort of 'spiritualized' form of Christ's physical person, nor 'just the presence of his [human] Spirit or Mind' disembodied from his human body, rather a presence of Christ given in the Spirit.[59] He has said that Christ has ascended 'in order to fulfil His presence', that is to make way for his coming into the world in a manner apposite to his assumption of 'all flesh', i.e. in the outpouring of his Spirit.[60] The presence of the Spirit in the sacrament, therefore, constitutes Christ's coming to man in a way which underlines both the universal claims of the gospel for men and the pregnant but undisclosed implications of that gospel for all creation, known as yet only to Christ's ascended humanity. The presence of God within the sacramental relation is thus a presence mitigated by the creaturely sign and mediated by the Spirit.[61]

(b) No Presence of the Word apart from the Flesh of Christ, nor of the Flesh of Christ apart from the Word

For all his stress upon the *divine* initiative in the sacrament, any disincarnate action of the Word for Torrance is theologically unthinkable.[62] 'It is', he asserts, 'only as clothed in... flesh that we

---

[57] *RP*, 45.
[58] *Inter*, 334, italics mine.
[59] *R/n*, 119.
[60] 'Arnoldshain', 13.
[61] Cf. *TS*, 43.
[62] Cf. *MOC*, 80; *RP*, 69. 'His human nature was enhypostatic in the Son, and was not separated, and therefore not separable or detachable, from the

encounter Him, and only as clothed in... flesh that we can know Him.'[63] There is no experience of God *simpliciter* in the world, for there is no action of God toward us *simpliciter*. He applies this specifically to the sacraments: 'The "divine" action is the action... of the God-Man, and not of God *simpliciter* apart from his incarnation.'[64] 'In the Supper', Torrance says, Christ 'comes to us with the body in which he overcame corruption and mortality through His death and resurrection.'[65] While there is no experience of the Word except in union with his flesh, neither do we encounter his flesh disjoined from the vital presence and power of the Word. 'He does not come to us in the flesh apart from His own Word or self-revelation.'[66] Although Torrance, with Calvin, speaks of the 'vivifying flesh' of Christ as the life-bearing principle within the sacrament, that flesh gives life only because of its participation in the Word.[67]

Torrance has an interesting way of putting this, which has profound implications for his eucharistic theology. Although he insists that the relation of divine (the Word) and human (the flesh) natures in Christ is that which is determinative for the relations which God has with his Church in the Eucharist, the sacramental relation or analogy as such is not to be understood as a simple analogy of proportions. In other words, it does not strictly follow that as 'a' (divine nature) is related to 'b' (human nature) in Christ, so 'a' (divine nature) is related to 'b' (human nature) in the Church's sacrament. For Torrance, as we have suggested, it is not the divine proportion *per se* with whom the Church has to do in the sacrament, that is, with God apart from his humanity. In his eucharistic theology the sacramental analogy has its reference and the Church its sacramental relation with a divine-human objectivity; hence the analogical syllogism: as 'a' (divine nature) is related to 'b' (human nature) in 'ab' (the divine-human person of Christ), so in the sacrament 'ab' (Christ) is related to 'b' (human nature).[68]

---

hypostasis of the Son' (*R/st*, 183).

[63] *SOF*, LXXXIII.
[64] *Inter*, 311.
[65] 'Arnoldshain', 14.
[66] *SOF*, LXXXIII.
[67] As we have pointed out already, 'The flesh of Christ did what was divine not in virtue of its own activity but in virtue of the Word united to it' (*RP*, 75).
[68] *R/st*, 185. Actually, the cited reference here only indirectly deals with the sacramental union as such, i.e. as it is involved with the larger relationship which obtains between Christ and his Church. Neither does Torrance arrange his syllogism and letterings precisely as we have. We have altered these in order to

(c) No Presence of the Spirit apart from the Word, nor of the Word apart from the Spirit

We cannot partake of the Spirit of God, Torrance asserts, 'behind the back of Christ' or 'as if the Incarnation made no difference to His work'.[69] He does not now come 'to man except in and through the Person and Work of Christ the incarnate Son'.[70] 'The Holy Spirit is mediated by Christ' in the sense that the Spirit is given out of the fullness of Christ's work; but, at the same time, the Spirit 'mediates Christ to us' so that Christ's work is brought to fulfilment in the Church through the Spirit.[71] Although the depth of its meaning lies in the unity-in-being of the immanent Trinity, this for Torrance represents the economy of the *filioque*. The Spirit comes upon the Church, in Torrance's terminology, 'uttering the Word'. He does not come without the Word, neither does the Word come without the Spirit; they are, he says, 'the two hands of God'.[72] This, then, is how Torrance applies these thoughts to sacramental theology: 'In both sacraments we are told that the Kingdom of God is amongst us not in Word only with suspended action, not in Spirit only, but in deed and power, as real act in time, as Word-deed enacted in our flesh and blood and inserted into history.'[73] We will elaborate the full ramifications of the relation between the Son and the Spirit for Torrance's eucharistic theology later in this section.

(d) The Presence of the Whole Christ: Totus Christus

What Torrance says concerning the coalescence of all God's redemptive activity within the human being of Christ, as well as what he rules out by his emphasis upon the unity of the Word and the Spirit in the economy of salvation, makes it quite inconceivable that he could describe any presence in the sacrament as 'real' except 'that actual presence of the whole Son of God', wholly God and wholly

---

make Torrance's point more easily understandable and applicable in this context. In fact, Torrance in a personal interview referred us to this passage as though it pertained specifically to the Eucharist (Personal Interview, 27/12/85, Edinburgh).

69 *SOF*, XCVIII.
70 Ibid. XCVIII.
71 *R/st*, 245.
72 *SOF*, XCVII. Torrance adapts this patristic expression saying 'it is by the Word *and* Spirit that God rules and is exalted over all in His divine majesty and glory' (*SOF*, XCVII, italics mine).
73 *Inter*, 313.

man.[74] Indeed, he interprets in the most realistic terms the Church's encounter with the presence of Christ in the Eucharist. He who is present with us in the Eucharist is none other, nothing less, he says, than 'the Being of God in our physical flesh and corporeal existence'.[75] It is 'a presence absolutely real of the whole Christ and in Him of the Being of God with us, more completely present to us than He was in His incarnation before His resurrection, yet present with all His historical life and death'.[76]

That with which the Church has to do in the sacrament is not some quasi-divine substance, or any kind of 'metaphysical event but Jesus Christ Himself, the *totus Christus*'.[77] In the Eucharist, Torrance, citing Calvin, contends that the Church receives 'not a "naked Christ" but a "Christ clothed with His Promises and Acts"'.[78] The term *totus Christus*, as we have already noted, designates for him not only the wholeness of Christ's divine humanity but the completeness of his historical work integrate in his risen person and active in his Church.[79] Christ embodies his saving history, so that we address it as we encounter him, not as an abstract past, but as a person present. When Torrance says that we partake of the *totus Christus* in the Eucharist he always has in mind the Church finding in its own history its 'place', its 'share', in the redemptive history incorporated in Christ.[80] He gathers these thoughts in a single sentence:

> It is the whole Jesus Christ who makes himself specifically and intensely present to us in this eucharistic form in his oneness as Gift and Giver, the whole Jesus Christ in the fulness of his deity and in the fulness of his humanity, crucified and risen, not a bare or naked Christ, far less only his body and blood, but Jesus Christ clothed with his Gospel and clothed with the power of his Spirit, who cannot be separated from what he did or taught or was in the whole course of his historical existence in the flesh.[81]

It must be said, however, that the presence of *totus Christus* in the sacrament is not distinct from his presence generally manifest in the Church's life. Its uniqueness lies in the fact that here it is 'specifically' given, as the text above indicates, not just for a

---

[74] 'Arnoldshain', 11.
[75] Ibid. 13, 12.
[76] Ibid. 13.
[77] C & A II, 142.
[78] 'Arnoldshain', 11; cf. *R/n*, 120.
[79] Cf. *Inter*, 311.
[80] *SOF*, CVIII.
[81] *R/n*, 120.

particular task, e.g. the formation of the Church, but within a specified sacramental act. For it is here, he says, 'that the risen and glorified Christ, in accordance with his *specific* appointment in the Eucharist, comes to meet us in the Spirit'.[82] Christ's presence is manifest in the Eucharist, Torrance says, in especial 'intensity'. This does not mean that there is more of Christ present in the sacrament than elsewhere, but that there is nowhere that the Church more effectively meets him than in this sacrament.

(e) A Presence that Eludes Us

While Torrance can claim without equivocation that the *totus Christus* is truly present in the Supper, it is equally clear that this presence is not defined in such a way that it can be identified at any one point or time within the sacramental relation. For Torrance all reality at the inmost, essential statement of its being, is unobservable. However, with respect to the christological reality in the sacrament, he has never suggested that it is unidentifiable. In the case of the real presence in the Eucharist, however, it seems to be just that. His emphasis upon the nature of the sacramental presence as the presence of divine action to human action accentuates this. One does not 'fix' an action. We have just observed Torrance saying that Christ gives himself 'specifically... in this eucharistic form', but he never offers a clue as to where 'specifically' in the sacrament he can be found.

Torrance nowhere embroils himself in the controversy over consecrating words or moments. When he deals with the traditional institutional narrative he brings out its implicit 'stress upon the action of God in the Sacrament', highlighted in the words 'broken for you', 'shed for you'.[83] The traditional words of consecration, so strongly emphasized by Luther and Calvin, are for Torrance paradigmatic phrases, suggesting God's presence in the sacrament erecting a vital sign of the Church's participation in Christ.[84] But there is no indication as to when that presence breaks in upon us in the celebration. This may simply be due to the intrinsically elusive character of the transcendent in Torrance's theology, or to an emergence in his eucharistic thought of the traditional Reformed hesitancy to proffer any notion of Christ's presence in the Eucharist which would suggest that God is contained there.[85]

---

[82] *GT*, 8, italics mine.
[83] *C & A* II, 145.
[84] Cf. *Inst* IV.17.3; *C & A* II, 145.
[85] In this regard Torrance explains 'even if we could conceive of a heaven

Looking at it another way, perhaps the presence of Christ escapes our ability to apprehend it concretely simply because God wants our attention to be fixed elsewhere. Torrance says that in the Eucharist 'the emphasis is undoubtedly on the human response, vicariously fulfilled for us in Christ' and therefore has to do primarily with our 'free and spontaneous response to the Word of God'.[86] If this is true then the attention of the Church should not be upon the advent of a special presence of Christ in the sacrament. As we have just suggested, Christ's presence in the sacrament is not distinct from his presence elsewhere in the Church's life. What is important about his presence in the Eucharist is what it achieves, what Christ comes specifically to do there, viz. to unite us and our response with him in his response to the Father. If this is true, then the emphasis should not be so much upon receiving a presence as upon that presence receiving us in our worship of God. Indeed, Torrance warns us against the subjective fixation of the Church 'upon ourselves as receivers' over against a healthy preoccupation upon God as the Giver.[87] Christ present in the Eucharist is not to be looked for or gazed upon but rather acts upon us.

It should not be thought, however, that the eucharistic presence is merely functional but actually something ontological. While it is true that that presence has a larger reference than itself – the praise of the Father – it is also true that Christ's presence constitutes the immediate and personal ground for our contact with the Father. The presence of the *totus Christus*, the God-man, always contains a dual aspect, 'two sides or faces', one set towards man as God, and one set towards God as man. These are complementary dispositions, paralleling the reciprocal posture of Christ's mediation discussed at length earlier.[88] In the person of Christ man is already present to God and God present to man. With the relevant christology thus taken fully into account, we can see how Torrance conceives of the reception of that presence from our side as equivalent to being made immediately present to the Father on the other. The presence of Christ in the eucharist does not simply usher us into the Father's presence as if it were something or somewhere else. There are not two 'presences' of God, one of the Father and another of the Son;

---

of heavens we could not think of this as containing God... for God is the transcendent Creator of the whole realm of space and stands in a creative, not a spatial or temporal relation to it' (*STI*, 3).

[86] Cf. *G & R*, 159–60.
[87] Cf. *GT*, 10.
[88] Cf. *RP*, 8, 14.

rather the presence of the Son in the sacrament exists as the Father's presence there also. Neither is 'communion' in that presence something received at a specific time in the liturgy and not in another. It is rather to be received or partaken of throughout the duration of the Supper, thus formulating the christological context of our celebration in the presence of the Father. The Church's act of reception in the Eucharist is not clearly distinguishable from its act of responsive praise any more than the two sides of Christ's presence are clearly distinguishable. Our receiving of God's presence and our praise of God exist one within the other, just as in Christ the divine and human natures exist consubstantially in the singularity of his person.

4. The Way of The Eucharistic Parousia: 'Through the Spirit'

A central problem which Torrance faces in his eucharistic theology involves the historic question: how can we uphold both the real presence of the Incarnate Word in the sacrament and at the same time the integrity of the ascension? On the one hand he can say that 'in the Supper [Christ] comes to us with the body in which He overcame corruption and mortality through His death and resurrection'. On the other hand he can insist that 'now we have to think of this Jesus Christ ascended to God as "in heaven"... above all space and time without ceasing to be man and without any diminishment of his physical, historical existence'.[89] Torrance affirms with the Swiss Reformers 'the location of Christ's body in heaven', contending that in his ascension 'the body of Christ did not lose dimensional character or reality as human body'.[90] What still is at issue, however, is how this can be without compromising either Christ's 'place' as man, or without some metaphysical conjuring trick.[91]

---

[89] 'Arnoldshain', 14; *STR*, 129. 'But it [is] nevertheless the real presence (*parousia*) of the whole Christ, not just the presence of his body and blood, nor just the presence of his Spirit or Mind, but the presence of the actual Jesus Christ, crucified, risen, ascended, glorified, in his whole, living and active reality and in his identity as Gift and Giver' (*R/n*, 119).

[90] *STI*, 31.

[91] He cites for example that which intellectually enticed the scholastic school who 'distinguished a special kind of presence applicable to Christ according to which His body could be regarded as present through something else that is circumscribed in its place' (*STI*, 28).

We have already seen how Torrance deals with these apparent antitheses without wholly unravelling the paradox. As he puts it, though 'Christ has distanced His Body from us... yet through His Spirit He has come and filled the Church with His own self'.[92] The Spirit is the way Christ is present both to his Father in heaven and to the Church under the veil of bread and wine. On the surface, this proposition seems only to compound the paradox. For it appears to contradict premises already laid down requisite for any genuine doctrine of the real presence; viz. that 'it is only as clothed in... [his] flesh that we encounter Him, and only as clothed in that flesh that we can know him'; and that the real presence of Christ cannot be construed as the presence of the Spirit *qua* Spirit, or of the Spirit apart from the Word.[93] However, by suggesting that the presence of the Spirit in the Church can indeed be interpreted as the presence of the Incarnate Word, Torrance is employing much more than just his profoundly christological doctrine of the Spirit, although that is essential. Though he nowhere expressly organizes his thinking on the real presence in these categories, it is obvious that there are at least two other major doctrines behind his argument. These are intertwined, each depending upon and implicating the other. To these we now turn.

5. The Underlying Assumptions

(a) *The Extra Calvinisticum*

The *extra Calvinisticum* was the Reformation's version of the 'classical patristic doctrine', that in his incarnation the Word did not relinquish his transcendent relationship to the world.[94] For Origen, Torrance contends, this meant

> that He by whom all things are comprehended and contained by assuming a body made room for Himself in our physical existence, yet without being contained, confined or circumscribed in place as in a vessel. He was wholly present everywhere, for He became man without ceasing to be God.[95]

---

[92] *RP*, 45. 'The ascension is not only the bearing of that Word up before the Face of the Father, but that Word accepted and honoured by God, that Word fully installed in the divine Kingdom, sent back to earth through the Spirit' (*STR*, 120, cf. 129).
[93] Cf. *SOF*, LXXXIII.
[94] Cf. *STI*, 31.
[95] Ibid. 13–14.

For Athanasius it implied that the Son of God

> entered our human space (χώρα) and became man, without leaving God's 'place' and without leaving the universe devoid of His presence and rule.... Yet He did not activate the body He assumed from us in such a way as to cease to display Himself actively throughout the universe in all its dimensions.[96]

Torrance sees the Reformed theologians as having retrieved this ancient doctrine in the sixteenth century to counter the Lutheran 'kenotic theory of Christ's *self-emptying*', with its contradictory assertions that '*finitum capax infiniti*' or that the divine person of 'the Word was resolved into this Jesus without remainder', that 'the whole Son and Word of God [was] contained in the infant of Bethlehem'.[97] In his view the Lutherans could only think of the Incarnation in these spatial categories, operating as they did from an Aristotelian 'receptacle view of space', to which we have referred earlier, i.e. 'as the place containing within its limits that which occupies it'.[98] Because of these restrictions they could only understand the Word's having become flesh in terms of God constricting himself, or the Son of God emptying himself into a containing vessel.[99] The Calvinists from their perspective rejected out of hand any notion of the 'enclosure or confinement of the Son of God in a human body'. The divine nature, they said, is 'indeed beyond the bounds of the Manhood which it has assumed, and yet is nonetheless within it as well'.[100] They dismissed any understanding that demanded 'a local or spatial connection between the divine and human natures of Christ', opting instead for what we have already observed as an understanding of 'place' with reference to God defined according to his measureless and eternal being, in other words not in terms of the space that 'contains' him but rather, 'in accordance with [his] nature and activity' as God, in terms of what he is and where he acts.[101]

---

[96] Ibid. 17, 14; cf. *STR*, 124; Athanasius, *Contra Gentes and De Incarnatione*, ed. Robert W. Thomson (Oxford, The Clarendon Press, 1971), 174–5.

[97] *STR*, 124–6; *STI*, 30.

[98] *STR*, 124.

[99] Ibid. 124.

[100] *The Heidelberg Catechism*, Question 48 (cf. *SOF*, 77).

[101] *STI*, 31, 4, 14; cf. *STR*, 131. In fact, Torrance says, 'God is not contained by anything but rather... contains the entire universe, not in the manner of a bodily container [but] by His *power*' (*STI*, 11).

This kind of thinking rendered the whole spatial question inappropriate. The Calvinists could hold at once therefore that the Word with respect to his humanity, or in relation with man, assumed 'the conditions and determinations of our existence' or human being; whereas with respect to his deity, in relation to his Father, 'he did not have the same space-relation... as we creatures have, otherwise He would be quite incapable of God'.[102] In his human nature the Word lives and moves and thinks as a man, even relinquishing the exercise of his divine prerogatives, while at the same time, purely with respect to his divine nature, he never leaves his 'place' as God.[103] The λόγος ἔνσαρκος does not cease to be the λόγος ἄσαρκος. This does not mean that there are actually two Sons, one incarnate the other not, but rather that the tension between the pre-existent and the existent should not be lost.[104]

Calvin could not accept anything less than that 'the Logos was totally incarnate'; however, this was thought out in ontological not quantitative categories, in terms of God, as he is himself, being *fully* present. The Son of God was 'totally incarnate – nevertheless he remained wholly himself'. In other words, he remained transcendent even in his incarnation; he became man without ceasing 'to be what he eternally was in himself, the Creator Word in whom and through whom all things consist and by whom all things derive and continue to have their being'.[105] He 'entered space and time without leaving the throne of God', without leaving the universe devoid of his presence and rule. The God-head of the Word fills all things, and although it is joined to the humanity and dwells in it, it is not delimited or confined by that humanity.[106] The Son has come into the flesh but is not absorbed by the flesh or merged into it, but remains he who sends the Spirit. Traditionally, this argument has been summed up by saying that all that God is (*totus Deus*) has become incarnate, but not all of God (*totum Dei*).[107] For the Lutherans,

---

[102] *STR*, 124; *STI*, 15.

[103] 'He did not call in supernature to help himself, but lived and worked within the nature, weakness and limitations of the creature, to the very end' (*STR*, 149).

[104] Cf. McDonnell, *John Calvin*, 251.

[105] *STR*, 126, 124.

[106] Ibid. 126.

[107] R.W.A. McKinney, Lecture, University of Nottingham, Autumn Term, 1983. Calvin cites what he calls this 'trite distinction' among the schoolmen: 'Although the whole Christ is everywhere, yet everything which is in him is not everywhere.' He expounds the thought in his own way, 'Therefore, while our whole Mediator is everywhere, he is always present with his people, and in the

operating from their peculiar cosmology, this could mean nothing except that 'only part of the Word was contained' in Christ, that the eternal Logos became flesh in such a way that part of him was 'excluded', that 'something of the Son or Word of God was left *outside, extra* – which they dubbed 'the Calvinist extra'.[108] For Torrance this doctrine simply states in a different way the classical christological affirmation: Jesus Christ is at once both 'very God of very God, very man of very man'.[109]

This is Torrance's ground for maintaining that 'the Being of God' is present in the sacrament 'in our physical flesh and corporeal existence' without actually meaning that he is physically present there. He can say that Christ does not come to us without 'the body in which He overcame corruption and mortality' and still not presume to say that the Word literally brings 'down' his flesh as such with him in the sacrament, for the Word cannot be, as it were, 'without his body'.[110] There is no other Word to be present to us in the sacrament except the Incarnate Word. When Torrance says that the 'Being of God' is 'in our corporeal existence' he is implying that there is nothing that the Word is that does not know what it is to be also man. This is what it means for the Word to be present 'clothed in [his] flesh' in the sacrament; that he contains in his own eternal being 'all the historical life and death' of Christ. For Torrance the whole God-head is seen as 'clothed with the Gospel' of Christ. This is so by virtue of the enduring integrity of his incarnation.[111] The *extra Calvinisticum* thus provides him with a theological basis for holding that Christ is simultaneously and wholly present within the

---

Supper exhibits his presence in a special manner; yet so, that while he is wholly present, not everything which is in him is present, because, as has been said, in his flesh he will remain in heaven till he come to judgment' (*Inst* IV.17.30).

[108] *STR*, 124, 126; *STI*, 31.

[109] Torrance, however, cannot resist an occasional spatial metaphor himself, e.g. 'The whole God-head dwelt σωματικῶς in Jesus Christ, in the narrow constraint (στενοχωρία) of a particular man' (*RP*, 25).

[110] 'Arnoldshain', 13–14.

[111] Cf. *SOF*, LXXXf. Christ's saving life and death have not just made an impression upon the divine memory or mind, so that God shall never forget an event 'past' in his own experience, but, by virtue of the ascension (in which Torrance insists Christ ascends 'wearing our resurrected humanity', *RP*, 39), God wears perpetually at his heart the flesh of men; the whole God-head is thus 'clothed with his Gospel'. There is no gospel for man or for God for that matter apart from Christ's flesh. The Word now contains our 'historical life and death' by the fact of his enduring incarnation, as a part of his (God's) own life and history (cf. 'Arnoldshain', 13; *MOC*, 88).

dimensions of his ascended humanity, in the midst of the Church's sacramental action, and throughout the whole universe, yet nowhere without his human nature and history.

(b) The Perichoresis of the Persons of the Trinity

Another doctrine undergirding Torrance's understanding of the real presence is the *perichoresis* (περιχώρησις) or the 'mutual indwelling of the Father, Son and Holy Spirit in the Triunity of God'.[112] This teaching holds that 'the inter-relations [of the God-head] must be thought out in terms of 'abiding' and 'dwelling' in which each [person of the Trinity] wholly rests in the other'.[113] It highlights the shared being of all the persons of the Godhead. He explains that 'we are to think of the whole being of the Son as proper to the Father's essence, as God from God, Light from Light'.[114] Likewise, we are to think of the Son and the Holy Spirit as wholly residing within the other, as each having room fully for the other in the one God.[115]

Torrance, agreeing with Athanasius, as he understands him, refuses to think partitively with reference to the persons of the Trinity.[116] Strictly speaking, no person of the Godhead ought to be conceived solitarily, that is, as separated from his relation-in-being to the 'whole' or to his larger identity in being as One God. They are 'three Persons of one and the same Being in God', Torrance says.[117] The characteristic of 'individuality' is to be ascribed not to separate, divine persons in their distinction one from another, but to the singular divine Being these 'persons' constitute in the coincidence of their life and integral identity. He comments, 'creaturely realities are such that they can be divided up in separate places (or parts)... but this is impossible with the uncreated source of all Being'.[118]

This leads Torrance to affirm that the Holy Trinity exists as 'a Communion of Love in whom Father, Son and Holy Spirit mutually involve and cohere in one another in the profound onto-relations

---

[112] *STR*, 131.
[113] *STI*, 15.
[114] Ibid. 15.
[115] Cf. ibid. 16. Torrance says that ultimately 'place' for God can only be defined by the communion of the Persons in the Divine life – that is why doctrinally we speak of the '*perichoresis*' (from *chora* meaning space or room) or 'mutual indwelling of the Father, Son and Holy Spirit in the Triunity of God' (*STR*, 131).
[116] Cf. *R/n*, 246.
[117] *MOC*, 75.
[118] *STI*, 15–16.

of that Communion'.[119] The unity of the Trinity consists not just in a 'mutual relation in *Being*', that is, in a relation based purely upon an identity of substance, but, more dynamically, in the mutual self-giving of love. God exists in his being and his act as one. Torrance defines the threefold act of God's being, or his 'ways of being', as the persons of the Trinity.[120] The Godhead exists not as a triad of lovers, but as a triunity of love, a threefold, though uniform operation of a single love, a *perichoresis* of love. The Trinity has its oneness in what Torrance calls 'the profound onto-relations of that Communion (of love)'. 'Onto-relations' in Torrance's thought are relations within reality (relations-in-being) which are not accidental but essential to what that reality is (relations-as-being). With regard to the Trinity, he understands the 'mutual involution' or expressions of love within the God-head as 'person-constituting relations'.[121] He says, the 'relations between persons belong to what persons are in their own beings'.[122] The persons of the Trinity are, as he calls them, 'onto-relational realities in God', which effectively constitute in their interrelation of love, what God is (his being) and in the cohesion of their expression of love, the way God is (his act). In short, God is love.[123]

With regard to the presence of God in the Church's sacrament, all this 'mutual indwelling in being' and 'mutual involution' of relational realities integrative to God, suggests a three-fold kind of presence of the one divine Being. A manifestation of any single person of the Trinity would necessarily be inclusive of the others. All the Trinity will be present at once. Citing Athanasius again Torrance explains this:

> an indivisible and continuous relation of being of the Father in the Son, so that the being of the Godhead is whole or complete not in the Father alone, but in the Son and in the Holy Spirit as much as in the Godhead…. God is God the Son as much as he is God the Father, and the Son of God is God precisely as the Father is God, for each is whole and proper to the other, so that *the same things are said of each except that one is called the Father and the other Son.*[124]

---

[119] *MOC*, 59.
[120] *G & G*, 157.
[121] Ibid. 172; *MOC*, 59; cf. Chapter 3, fn. 106.
[122] *MOC*, 59.
[123] Cf. *G & G*, 172-3.
[124] *R/n*, 246.

This means that 'the whole Godhead' is complete in the Son and in the Spirit as much as it is in the Father.[125] In Torrance's own words: God's nature or being is 'simple, uncompounded and undivided'.[126]

When Torrance speaks of the Spirit in the sacrament in terms which seem to equate his presence with that of the Son, it is based upon this sort of reasoning. In his thinking the presence of that 'relation or way of being' which the Spirit constitutes, means not only the presence of the person of the Spirit as such, but the Spirit mutually indwelling the Godhead with the Son whom, on the ground of the *extra Calvinisticum*, has been shown to be the Son in the wholeness of his divine humanity.[127] The Spirit's divine presence to us thus 'contains', by virtue of his *perichoresic* participation in the Trinity, the real presence of Christ. Approaching the real presence in the sacrament from this basis, the presence of the Spirit in the Eucharist for Torrance *is* the presence of the Word who *is* the Word Incarnate. The *extra Calvinisticum* and the *perichoresis* thus form a systematic unity or whole in Torrance's methodology. With both doctrines thus employed he can speak of the presence of Christ in the sacrament as a presence 'in' the Spirit, 'through' the Spirit, or 'as' the Spirit without begging the question.

(c) Christ and Spirit

In order to understand more fully the relation of the Holy Spirit to Christ in the Eucharist, we must now expound in detail what Torrance sees as the fundamental ontological relation between Christ and his Spirit. He affirms the Spirit's 'essentially Christological relation':

> It was through the Spirit that Jesus was born of the Virgin Mary, by the Spirit that He was anointed at His Baptism, through the Spirit that He worked his miracles..., through the eternal Spirit that He offered Himself

---

[125] Ibid. 252.

[126] Ibid. 246.

[127] Torrance states: 'The hypostatic union is grounded in, derived from and is continuously upheld by what is called the 'consubstantial communion' within the Holy Trinity, that is, the mutual indwelling or coinhering of Father, Son and Holy Spirit as three Persons of one and the same Being in God' (MOC, 75).

without spot to the Father, [and] according to the Spirit of holiness that He was raised again from the dead.[128]

Indeed, that which Christ bestows on us is nothing less than that which 'He in our Humanity has received in the fulness of the Spirit'.[129] This conforms to what Torrance sees as the overall scheme of God, who has ordained that it be through the Spirit 'that the economies of God are carried out from beginning to end'.[130]

The 'indissoluble relation' between the Spirit and the Incarnate Son, however, must not be reduced to a purely 'functional' or 'instrumental' one.[131] Torrance sees the relation of Christ and Spirit as grounded upon 'the *homoousion* of the Spirit to the Son and to the Father [and carrying] with it the inescapable conclusion, that what the Spirit is in His mission from the Son He is antecedently and eternally in himself in God'.[132] The coherence of the essential and the economic relations of the Trinity is central to the progression of Torrance's sacramental theology, and particularly his concept of the real presence.

Let us look first at the economic solidarity of the Son and the Spirit. He says that 'the doctrine of the Spirit has Christology as its content'.[133] For Torrance, of course, all theology has christology as its informing object. It is that formal creative Word, which the Spirit continues to utter as 'acutely personal action'.[134] The Spirit 'does not utter Himself'.[135] Indeed, the Spirit has no other Word, no further Word than Christ. Obversely, illustrating the concurrence of the Word of Christ and the Spirit, Torrance suggests that the Spirit has been given to the Church upon the breath of Christ' or, still more graphically for our concern, breathed upon the Church by the flesh of Christ.[136] He means by this that the Spirit is 'mediated [to us] through the name and vicarious humanity of Jesus'.[137] The Incarnate word is the focal centre and form of God's saving event. The Spirit of God is therefore 'formed' in his operation toward men according to

---

[128] *SOF*, XCVIII.
[129] Ibid. XCI.
[130] *R/st*, 223.
[131] Cf. *SOF*, XCVII.
[132] *R/st*, 218.
[133] *RP*, 25.
[134] Ibid. 24.
[135] *R/st*, 214.
[136] Cf. *C & A* II, 143, 136; *SOF*, CXVII.
[137] *MOC*, 98–9.

the character and substance of Christ's person and deed. As Torrance states it: 'The creative work of the Spirit is... proleptically conditioned by that of redemption.'[138] The Spirit's presence and operation in the world remains 'intensely personal' as he supervenes upon the created order 'through the commanding Word of God, through the incarnate Person of the Son'.[139] It is through Christ that the Spirit is given to man and it is through him that he continues to come to man. On such economic grounds he can say with Paul that 'the Spirit is essentially the Spirit of Christ', or even more incisively, that he is 'Christ's other Self'.[140]

However, what underlies Torrance's understanding of the relation of the Son and the Spirit, as we have indicated, has much deeper roots than simply the unanimity of their economic roles, for any 'economic relation' in Torrance's theology is built upon the essential *perichoresis* within the Trinity. It is grounded in the indiscerptible unity of the immanent Godhead, expressing itself in 'the indivisible operations of the Trinity'.[141] This means that the Spirit does not simply repeat the Word of Christ, but rather is himself that Word still speaking. Torrance cites Gregory of Nyssa to the effect that: 'there is *no separate action* on the part of the Three Persons, for there is *one* power in the Father, Son and Holy Spirit'.[142] The Word is not strictly speaking the 'formal cause' of that of which the Spirit is the 'efficient cause'.[143] The Word's action is never 'suspended' or only latent in relation to that of the Spirit. The Spirit does not act simply for Christ or as Christ in the world, rather the Word acts in the Spirit and the Spirit acts in the Word. The Spirit is Christ continuing to work among us. It is in this light that we must understand Torrance's statement that 'the Spirit is co-active with the Son in all acts of redemption'.[144] Their acts cannot be formally separated, but are coincidental in the unity of God's being in his acts and in the unity of his acts in his being.[145] It was this kind of thinking that gave rise to the Western notion of the *filioque* which, he says, when assigned 'its full weight' prevents any cleavage between the

---

[138] *R/st*, 217.
[139] *SOF*, XCVII.
[140] Ibid. XCVIII; *RP*, 27.
[141] *SOF*, XCVII.
[142] *R/st*, 221, italics mine.
[143] Cf. Geddes MacGregor, *Corpus Christi: The Nature of the Church according to the Reformed Tradition* (London, MacMillan, 1959), 129.
[144] *R/n*, 231.
[145] Cf. 'New College', 24.

being, act or gift of Christ and that of his Spirit.[146] He refers to the East as the source for his thought, quoting Basil that there is 'one indivisible *ousia* and *energeia* of the Holy Trinity'.[147]

Torrance develops this thought in a manner directly relevant to sacramental theology. 'In Jesus Christ and in the Holy Spirit', he says, 'God freely gives himself to us in such a way that the Gift and the Giver are one and the same in the wholeness and indivisibility of his Grace'.[148] With respect to his real and active presence in the sacrament the Spirit cannot therefore be understood as merely the Giver of Christ the Gift. When viewed in the light of the essential unity of being and act within the immanent Trinity, the Spirit's presence in the sacrament IS that of Christ. For: 'God is... present to us in his person [sic] and mode of Being as the Spirit as well as in His Person and mode of Being as the Son... we [therefore] cannot separate in our thought the operation of the Spirit from the mighty acts of God in Christ.'[149] They should not be separated intellectually because they cannot be separated ontologically.

Another Reformed theologian, John Baillie, has suggested that the manner of Christ's presence in the sacrament is that of 'a mediated immediacy'. For Torrance this would mean a presence mediated to us quite literally in the immediacy of the presence of the Spirit, which, on the basis of all we have said, is not to be understood as the presence of 'another' at all but as the immediate presence of Christ in the midst of his people validating the Word of the gospel as his own and communicating himself to men through it.[150] The work of Christ and the Spirit for Torrance, as for Calvin, are not 'posterior, one to the other, but simultaneous, with the one ordered to the other'.[151] The Holy Spirit belongs to the Christ-event not just in a servitorial, external way, that is, as the mover of that of which Christ is the content (although Torrance does employ this metaphor) but as himself proper to that event.[152] The Spirit's active presence is seen as the continual unfolding of the Christ-event within the continuity of man's history, though unfolding nothing that is not already formally constituted in Christ. This is indicated when he speaks of Pentecost

---

[146] *R/st*, 172; cf. *SOF*, XCVI–XCIX.

[147] Ibid. 222.

[148] *R & E*, 14–15.

[149] *SOF*, XCVIII–XCIX

[150] *STR*, 120; cf. Chapter 1, fn. 40.

[151] McDonnell, *John Calvin*, 250.

[152] Cf. *R/st*, 187. 'We cannot separate in our thought the operation of the Spirit from the mighty acts of God in Christ' (*SOF*, XCVIII–XCIX).

as belonging to the same series of mighty salvation events as Christ's crucifixion, resurrection and ascension.[153] The communion of the Spirit, he says, within the *Heilsgeschichte*, is penultimate to the ultimate, Christ's second coming.[154]

In Torrance's dynamic definition of the *kerygma* – 'both the thing preached and the preaching of it' – one can observe at work Torrance's presuppositions as to the economic accord and essential identity of Christ and his Spirit. He states: 'It is the proclamation of the Christ-event, but such proclamation that by the Holy Spirit it becomes the actualization of that event among men. It is such proclamation that in and throughout it the Living Christ continues to do and to teach'.[155] Who then is actually the one who speaks and acts within the *kerygma* of the Church to which, as we have seen, the Eucharist is related as a further and active expression? Christ is *unus qui agit*, the Spirit is *unus in quo Christus agit*. 'It is through the Lordly presence of the Spirit that Christ clothed with His graces so gives Himself to us that He remains the Lord and Saviour.'[156]

6. The Real Presence in Participation

In the last chapter we saw that it is under the general umbrella of 'participation' or the 'communion' in Christ which the Spirit gives that Torrance explains the operation and governance of the 'ascended Christ' in his Church. It is likewise within this framework that he defines the way the Church in the Eucharist maintains vital contact with its ascended Head and hence accounts for the dynamic inner reality of its sacrament. 'The Lord's Supper', he says, is a communion with the risen and ascended Christ through the Spirit which He pours upon His Church.[157] The difficulty which

---

[153] *RP*, 23.

[154] Cf. *SOF*, P.LVIII; *RP*, 23.

[155] *Inter*, 307.

[156] *SOF*, CV.

[157] *C & A* II, 138. The sacrament is the 'outward form' or manifestation of that of which the Communion of the Spirit is the 'inner form' (*SOF*, LVI). In saying this Torrance is not reverting to a symbol/reality dichotomy with regard to the sacraments, but is suggesting that they have an outward and an inward reality which cannot be separated. He is also saying that the Communion of the Spirit has an appropriate sacramental expression. The sacrament does not belong to the Spirit's communion as *signum* to *Res*, rather '*the whole substance*' of both belongs to '*Jesus Christ Himself*' (*SOF*, LVI). We have already shown that the Eucharist, while not itself constituting the Church's participation in Christ,

'participation through the Spirit' resolves for Torrance's eucharistic theology is how 'all the benefits of the Covenant fulfilled in the flesh of Christ' are imparted to his Church.[158] This, as we will see, is tantamount to demonstrating how the flesh of Christ itself is given in the sacrament, for Torrance is adamant, *first*, that the whole source and fruit of salvation is found nowhere but in Christ's divine humanity, and *secondly*, that there can be no partaking whatsoever of the so-called benefits of Christ without real intercourse with him in his flesh. He repeats Calvin's assertion that 'the thing requisite must be not only to be partakers of His Spirit, but also to partake in His humanity in which He rendered all obedience to God His Father'. 'For [Christ's] blessings are not ours, unless He gives Himself to us first.'[159]

When Torrance says that the Church must receive 'the body and blood of Christ' in the holy Eucharist, he is reiterating this first point. If the Church is to realize its salvation, she must return to the fountain of it, to the Word's own 'vivifying flesh', as he puts it, 'to share in [Christ's] whole human life and in His death on the Cross'. Thus to participate in Christ is equivalent in Torrance's mind to partaking vicariously of the righteousness achieved in his living and dying for us, i.e. in 'His obedient self-oblation and self-sanctification which He fulfilled for our sakes' through active conformity to God's will.[160] These are the 'benefits of the Covenant' which our high Priest has gained for us literally *in* his own flesh and blood and, which now obtains in him and must be mediated to us. In saying this Torrance implies much more than the imputation of righteousness as traditionally understood by Protestant soteriology, for the fruit of Christ's 'covenanted obedience' is not some thing separated from Christ, a state or condition that could be transported from Christ to us, rather it is God's own act of reconciliation identical with the

---

establishes in the Church's life a vital 'moment' of that participation. According to Torrance, one receives the outward and inner forms of the Spirit's communion simultaneously in the sacrament.

[158] *C & A* II, 143–4; cf. *SOF*, XCVIII. He states: Christ 'sends down [the Spirit] upon us so that through the Communion of the Spirit we are made partakers in Christ of all His graces' (*SOF*, XCVIII).

[159] *C & A* II, 142–3; *SOF*, CVIII. (Torrance cites Calvin's *Geneva Catechism*, Question 342, *SOF*, 60). 'Through the Communion of the Spirit we are given to partake of the body and blood of Christ, that is to share in His whole human life and in His death on the Cross' (*SOF*, CVIII).

[160] *SOF*, CVIII.

human 'person and word and deed' of Christ and which can only be apprehended 'in him'.[161]

This leads to Torrance's second point: there is no communication of the benefits of salvation or its so-called 'graces' apart from genuine intercommunion with the Word in his incarnation. Just as there is no salvation effected by the Word except in his union with our alienated flesh, so there is no salvation *given* except in our real union with him in his flesh and blood.[162] Torrance seeks to tie our union with Christ to our justification in him, precisely because he has justified mankind in union with us. Accordingly, he states: 'It is only through union with Christ's human nature that we can really and fully share in His obedience, so that justification in Christ reposes upon union with Him.'[163] In its effect just as much as in its cause redemption is rooted in the ontic reality of Christ. This is supremely important for Torrance's eucharistic theology and consistent with his overall patristic perspective. Justification involves an imputation of righteousness, to be sure, but this is given only where it has been effected, viz. 'in the body and blood of Christ'. It is then from an understanding once again of the essential identity of what Christ did with who Christ is that Torrance requires Christ's body and blood truly to be given in the sacrament. For their part the sacraments as such do not constitute this justifying union any more than our partaking in them comprises that which justifies us. They do, however, allow the believer active, manifest participation in Christ who is our justification. Because God in his own reconciling humanity actively presents himself to the Church in the sacraments effectively to apply the power of his death and resurrection, Torrance can refer to them as 'converting ordinances'.[164]

---

[161] *DOG*, 21; cf. *R/st*, 186-7; cf. Chapter 3, section B.1 above.

[162] 'Because in Christ human nature is everlastingly united to His divine Person we are assured of everlasting life and salvation through our sharing in His human nature, so that through Christ we share in the very life of God' (*C & A* II, 144).

[163] *C & A* II, P.143.

[164] *MOC*, 107; cf. *C & A* II, 145. The Eucharist is nowhere more clearly demonstrated to be 'a converting ordinance' than in Torrance's argument for 'intercommunion' among the churches, even where differences remain as to the understanding of the doctrine of the sacrament or as to the ordering of the sacrament *per se*. 'The Sacrament of the Lord's Supper is not', he declares, 'merely a cognitive Sacrament acknowledging a prior unity, but it is an effective Sacrament enacting a real unity.' If the Eucharist is a 'Sacrament of the Body and Blood of Christ in which [Christ] gives us repentance and remission of sins', is it

In many of his writings, but particularly his earlier ones, Torrance, following Calvin, is inclined to discuss the Church's communication in the flesh and blood of Christ by implementing a basic tripartite pattern: the ascended Christ being set over against the Church, with the Holy Spirit serving as the living link between the two, as the one who unites Christ in the fullness of his grace with the Church in its poverty. We referred to this model in our first chapter simply as 'union with Christ'. From its perspective Torrance can say that 'the Communion of the Spirit means that the Church draws all its life from its sole source in the Person and finished work of Christ', or the other way round, that through the Spirit 'the supernatural life of Christ flows into the Church'.[165] When thinking purely in these terms he can even go so far as to relate 'the movement of grace to the Holy Spirit'.[166] Although this pattern has the advantage of safeguarding and stressing the 'distance of the ascension' – the fact that Christ's body does not and cannot share our place in space/time – its weaknesses are patently obvious in the light of our immediate discussion. Most notably, it would seem to relegate the Spirit's role to purely an instrumental one, which is precisely the kind of notion Torrance's doctrine of the Spirit will not allow. Moreover, it appears to leave room for the misconception that Christ's saving life or grace is after all something that can be transferred, which of course he denies explicitly.[167] It must, therefore,

---

not the most natural context for the Lord to bring 'separated brethren' to a state of contrition for their disunity? He asks, 'Can we expect to take any real step towards unity if we are not prepared to use the Holy Sacrament to apply the healing Cross to the wounds and sins of our divisions?' (*RP*, 106).

[165] *SOF*, LVIII; *RP*, 49.

[166] *R/St*, 187.

[167] Torrance cites a text from Calvin which would appear almost to demand this misunderstanding: Christ 'testifies and seals in the Supper' 'that sacred communion of the flesh and blood by which Christ transfuses his life into us, just as if it penetrated into our bones and marrow' (*K & C*, 131, he cites *Inst* IV.17.10). Such images sometimes border on relegating the Spirit's role crudely to a sort of cypher or conduit, a mere means of conveyance through which the virtue of Christ is effused. Calvin couches it in exactly these terms: the Holy Spirit is 'like a channel through which all that Christ himself is and has is conveyed to us' (*Inst* IV.17.12, trans. F.L. Battles). The weaknesses of such metaphors are clear, for they appear to presuppose the transmutation of divine grace identified with the 'whole Christ' into a kind of transferable, purely spiritual substance. This, of course, is exactly the kind of thinking Torrance is trying to avoid. Nevertheless, for all his consistency in denying separate centres of action in the Spirit and in the Son, or anything but a totally christological identity for both the substance and operation of grace, he persists, for all its difficulty, in the use of

be said that these are only appearances; it is certain that Torrance has never compromised his convictions on such matters.[168] On the other hand, in view of his heavy indebtedness to Calvin's eucharistic theology, it is really not surprising that the Reformer's standard way of framing sacramental participation should never altogether be relinquished by Torrance. In fact, this kind of imagery reappears to some degree throughout his writings.[169] In view of all the difficulties which Calvin's pattern creates, and in the light of what we have gleaned in the last two sections, how Torrance envisages sacramental participation in the body and blood of Christ can be best understood in more refined, ontological categories.

For Torrance any union which the Church has with Christ in *his* flesh begins from his side in his union with *our* flesh. Christ is 'in' the Father through His oneness with Him (*perichoresis*); he is 'in' us through (his) sharing our bodily existence (incarnation).[170] Torrance applies all this directly to the Church's sacramental participation: 'He is in the Father by the nature of His Deity, we are in Him by His [humanity or] corporeal nativity, and He on the other hand is in us by the mystery of the Sacraments.'[171] The foundation for the sacramental union then is laid on the more profound union of the Incarnate Son with the Father. This is the objective fact that the Spirit makes manifestly real in the Church. Our sacramental union is nothing more or other than the Spirit re-enacting in the Church Christ's union with us.

From both the side of God and the side of the Church then it is a doctrine of participation that defines Torrance's understanding of

---

this imagery, relating 'the movement of grace to the Holy Spirit' (*R/st*, 187). It was precisely this kind of language, of course, which Calvin insisted on using in his sacramental polemic and which caused such scandal among the Lutherans.

[168] For example, as early as 1959 he wrote warning that the association of grace with the Spirit *per se* could lead to its formal detachment from Christ and hence be interpreted as something 'communicable and transmissible' which could be 'channelised and infused' (*SOF*, CV).

[169] For example, as late as 1974 Torrance, undoubtedly still operating from this tripartite model, can write simply that the Spirit 'connects us with Christ as he [Christ] dwells in the immediate presence of God' (*R/st*, 217).

[170] *STI*, 16. For Torrance there is a relation of 'mutual indwelling' between Christ and his Church which inheres within 'the mutual indwelling of the Father, the Son and the Holy Spirit in the Holy Trinity' (*MOC*, 77). He explains: 'Christ, in whom the complete Being of God dwells, dwells in us, so that through a relation of mutual indwelling between Christ and us, we are enfolded within the infinite dimensions of the love of God' (*MOC*, 75).

[171] *C & A* II, 144; cf. *MOC*, 101.

the real presence. It is the 'participation' or *perichoresis* of the persons of the God-head in the being and act of each other which serve as the basis for his view of the presence of the Spirit *as* the presence of Christ in the sacrament. The interior reality of sacramental participation in the Church is the Spirit's drawing us into *his* participation or communion in the word, who in turn participates in our flesh. All that Torrance says about the real presence in the Eucharist hinges upon this. It is by virtue of the Word's union with the humanity of Christ that we partake of his flesh and blood in the sacrament. As we have already observed, Torrance understands the sixth chapter of John metaphorically, that is, it is *by faith* that the Church 'eats and drinks of Christ's flesh and blood'. However, the strength of the metaphor is not faith as such, but rather the enduring integrity of the Incarnation. He insists that 'we do not get the proper perspective' on what it means so to eat and drink until we comprehend this, for it is not the body and blood *per se* that we should seek and by faith receive in the sacrament, but the Word 'given this nature'. To receive the Word is to receive him in his flesh and blood.[172] As we have shown, the *extra Calvinisticum* allows us to understand this in terms of being united to the Word who is 'become flesh' but not necessarily conjoined with that material proportion itself. It is this real and necessary 'connection' with the Incarnate Word which the Spirit provides in the sacrament, understood ontologically.

As we have indicated, our union with the flesh of Christ in the sacrament then is not finally to be understood as a physical contact between two separate, objective realities – that of the ascended Christ in heaven and of the Church on earth – established by a distinct 'third party', the Holy Spirit. In the sacrament we do not and need not touch the external reality of Christ's flesh at all. Such contact would only provide us proximity to that flesh, not union with it. In our union with the Word in the Spirit we approach Christ's humanity from within, as we share in the Word's ontological relation with it.[173] For the Church to be in such union with the Word is to find

---

[172] *RP*, 75.

[173] This would at first seem to reverse Torrance's basic assumption that it is 'through our sharing in his human nature... [that] we share in the very life of God' (*C & A* II, 144). He is always clear that man approaches the Godhead or the divinity of Christ only in the context of his humanity, not the other way round. However, this is only an apparent inconsistency. For although our recourse to Christ's actual flesh and blood might be through that aspect of his divine–human person which is infinite, at no point can it be said that the Church

ourselves in the midst of his 'carnal union' already forged with us in Christ. God thus gives the Church to share in 'the benefits... fulfilled in the flesh of Christ' precisely within Christ's union with God, which is the source and sum of them. Torrance calls the abiding, objective union we have with God in Christ 'the all-inclusive effect' of salvation, and the realization of that union in the Church through our union with him in the Spirit, 'our participation in all the benefits of Christ'.[174] The fact that the Spirit affords the Church's sacrament internal access to the Word's inner relation with Christ's humanity is equivalent to saying that that created reality is really present there, as truly and immediately present as the Word is to his own flesh and blood.

In his commentary on *The Arnoldshain Theses*, Torrance speaks of 'participation and a real presence' in the Eucharist as though these were in an appositive relation to each other. In *Conflict and Agreement* he deems the real presence as a 'moment' of this participation or of 'our union and communion in Christ'. He could just as easily have spoken of a presence *in* participation, or, for that matter, of participation *in* a presence.[175] Bringing these ideas together, he says that there is in the sacrament

> an immediate self-giving of God to us in his own divine Being and life through Jesus Christ... one that takes place *in the Holy Spirit* who is not just an emanation from God but the immediate presence and activity of God in his own divine Being, the Spirit of the Father and the Son, himself the Lord and Giver of Life. Moreover this is a real presence of Christ to us, creating a union between himself and us and us and himself in the Spirit, such as he has with the Father eternally in the same Spirit; the Spirit who comes to us from the Father, through the Son, and who gives us access through the Son to the Father. Thus the real presence of him who is both Giver and Gift in the Eucharist is a real presence of the most exalted kind, one grounded in the real presence of God to himself.[176]

---

deals with God apart from the direct mediation of his humanity. For the Spirit we meet in the sacrament is himself 'mediated through the... vicarious humanity of Jesus' and the Word we meet in the Spirit is no one else but the Word Incarnate (*MOC*, 99). For Torrance, as for Calvin, the Word is 'totally incarnate'; all that God is knows what it is to be all that man is (*STR*, 126). This ontological assertion qualifies all the rest. For although we might have 'contact' with the Word's human dimension only by means of our direct contact with his divine dimension, which infinitely transcends it, there is no relation with the divine Word outside his hypostatic union with humanity in Christ.

[174] *C & A* II, 146.
[175] 'Arnoldshain', 14; *C & A* II, 146–7.
[176] *R/n*, 132.

7. Torrance's Understanding of Sacramental Realism vis-à-vis Tridentine Eucharistic Theology

For Torrance no doctrine of the real presence which fails to safeguard either proportion within the sacramental relation can be tolerated. The Tridentine doctrine of transubstantiation violates the created identity of the divine Son of God as well as the sacramental instrument. He explains,

> Precisely by refusing to preserve the distinct property of the two sides involved in the sacramental relation it [the doctrine of transubstantiation] makes it impossible for it [the sacramental relation] to image or reflect the image of Christ in whom divine and human natures, while remaining distinct, are joined in such a way that neither is converted or changed into the other.[177]

(a) Transubstantiation's Failure to Safeguard the Integrity of the Ascended Christ

Torrance thus faults the doctrine of transubstantiation for destroying the 'whole analogical relation of participation and conformity to Christ, and [so disrupting] the basic Christological nature of the Sacrament'.[178] Tridentine sacramental theology is wanting because it is unable to uphold the wholeness of Christ, particularly in the transcendent position of his ascension. He says,

> It is precisely this doctrine of identity between the bread and wine of the Eucharist with the glorified Body in the heavenly places... which the theology of Eucharist cannot allow, for that entails its destruction as a sacrament.[179]

Not only does the identity of the ascended Christ with the elements of the supper invalidate the sacrament's christological analogy, but it also removes the natural distinction between the 'media' and the matter of the sacrament, thus undermining its essential sacramental nature.

From his first attempts at eucharistic theology, Torrance has appealed to the incarnational analogy as that which must inform the

---

[177] *C & A* II, 140.
[178] Ibid. 139–40.
[179] *Inter*, 331.

analogy of the sacrament. 'The mode of sacramental relation', he states, 'reflects the mode of hypostatic union in Christ.'[180] He has in mind specifically the dynamic nature of the relation in which the divine and created proportion must coexist if the Church's sacramental relation is to be appropriate to Christ. The nature of the sacramental relation cannot be construed in terms of metaphysical or static relationship but in terms of dynamic movement. This is what lies behind Torrance's insistence that

> since the Eucharist is to be understood in a proper and profound co-ordination with the whole paschal mystery of Christ, it must be allowed to exhibit as its *essential pattern* one which corresponds to and participates in the whole pattern of the *whole movement of God's saving love in Jesus Christ*.[181]

Tridentine eucharistic theology, by refusing to allow Christ's nature strictly to dictate the nature of the sacramental relation, artificially divides the 'objective datum' of that relation from its inherent dynamic character and thus exchanges the presence of the living, exalted Lord for a depersonalized, inactive substance.[182] However much this so-called 'body of Christ' might be interpreted as containing the bare 'material' ingredients of the divine and created realities it lacks the very attribute of the christological mystery which has saved and continues to save mankind, viz. the action of God's love. Torrance sees the medieval dissociation of grace from the person and act of God in Christ as leaving no room in the Church for the active presence of God. With Christ's presence thought to be so remote, something vital and tangible was required to take its place. The concentration of the Church's life thus turned in upon itself. To compensate for the absence of the act of God, the Church reverted to the power of its priesthood and liturgical institutions; to meet the need for identifiable grace it focused its attention more and more

---

[180] *C & A* II, 139.

[181] *GT*, 7.

[182] Cf. *GT*, 7, 9. Schillebeeckx admits in his discussion of the real presence in historical Roman Catholic eucharistic theology that 'Christ's *de facto* giving of himself here and now, his real *presentation* of himself in the Eucharist... has all too frequently been lost sight of and the real *presence* as an 'objective datum' has been given one-sided attention in isolation from this event' (E. Schillebeeckx, *The Eucharist* (New York, Sheed & Ward, 1968), 80). For Trent, he says, 'transubstantiation and real presence were identical as affirmations' (Schillebeeckx, *The Eucharist*, 46).

upon 'the *corpus Christi* in the Eucharist as something in itself rather than on the personal presence of Jesus Christ in his reality'.[183]

(b) *Transubstantiation's Failure to Safeguard the Integrity of the Created Element*

Recalling Torrance's eagerness at every turn to defend the God-given independence of 'the contingent order' from divine necessity, one is not surprised that in his doctrine of the real presence he so strenuously defends the integrity of the natural element. Torrance prefaces his discussion on the subject in his article 'The Paschal Mystery of Christ and the Eucharist: General Theses' with a christological observation: 'nothing must be allowed to detract from *the perfection, fulness and integrity of Christ's human nature*'.[184] He insists on the wholeness of Christ's humanity being maintained not just to guarantee the accessibility of a 'real presence of the whole Christ including his body and blood' to the sacramental relation, but in order to ensure that the created reality in that relation is not ultimately absorbed by the predominant divine reality.[185] For if at the depth of the hypostatic relation created being is safe-guarded and kept intact, then no derivative, secondary relation (e.g. the sacramental relation) can be thought to impair it. For Torrance this is a most important issue; its implications far exceed the bounds of sacramental theology. The dignity of creation is at stake, as well as the integrity of Christ's human reality in the sacrament. Unless the rationality of the natural order can be proved to be of such worth to God that it is not violated under any circumstances, then the created order will be under constant threat by the divine order operating concurrently with it. There would always exist the possibility, even the probability, of the divine order compelling its rationality and will upon creation. In this case the created order would ultimately be lost to the divine order. Consequently also, natural science would be lost to theology and, obversely, theology would be thought out 'from the world to God', that is as informed by nature.[186] It is the uncompromised human mind and body preserved in the incarnation of the Son of God that is the ultimate assurance that God will never enact a relation with the world which would threaten the contingent order.

---

[183] *R/n*, 125.
[184] *GT*, 6.
[185] Cf. ibid. 10.
[186] *STI*, 26.

The doctrine of transubstantiation illustrates for Torrance the confusion which results from a failure to take seriously the incarnation's profoundly simple statement as to the enduring integrity of the created order in relation to God: 'In the Incarnation the presence of complete God does not mean the absence of man, or the presence of incomplete man, but rather the presence of man in his completion as man in God.'[187] While applauding the scholastic's attempt to make Christ's true presence in the sacrament intellectually feasible, Torrance, along with most sacramental theologians today, Catholic as well as Protestant, disclaims the metaphysical gymnastics involved.[188] He sees at the heart of the doctrine the same two-fold mistake, viz. the disintegration of created reality. In the first place, Christ's human reality, which the Tridentine fathers insisted must be 'truly, really and substantially' present can only be conceived as present by separating Christ from the attributes or 'accidents' of his humanity or from the proper dimensions of his ascended body.[189] Secondly, Christ's presence has its 'place' in the sacrament only by occupying that of the bread which, like Christ, becomes separated from its own accidents, losing them to Christ in exchange for his divine substance.[190] The substance of the created element for its part is thoroughly 'dispossessed',

---

[187] R/n, 155. Torrance says, 'God has become man in down-right reality' (R/n, 160).

[188] Cf. STI, 27-8. Torrance speaks of the 'impossible paradoxes and absurdities' that the 'highly artificial separation between substance and accidents' introduced into theology (STI, 27-8). Schillebeeckx calls it 'the transubstantiation of Aristotle' (cf. Schillebeeckx, The Eucharist, 58).

[189] Cf. Schillebeeckx, The Eucharist, 44. Schillebeeckx refuses to water down the Tridentine dogma, this despite his own preference. He says, 'the presence of an ontological aspect in the sacramental giving of the bread is without doubt a datum of faith and not simply an aspect of "wording"' (Schillebeeckx, The Eucharist, 81-2; cf. Heron, Table and Tradition, 166).

[190] Regarding Christ's alleged usurpation of the created 'place' of the bread in the sacrament, Thomas Aquinas has said that 'the body of Christ in some way acquires the place of the bread, with the measurements of the bread, nonetheless mediating' (Aquinas, Summa Contra Gentiles, IV, 63, para. 12. Cited in J. Heywood Thomas, 'Logic and Metaphysics in Luther's Eucharistic Theology', RMS 23 (1979), 151).

Luther develops the argument that if the theory of transubstantiation must be held in order to prevent the bread of the altar being declared the body of Christ, then is it not also necessary to ascribe to a 'theory of transaccidentation', so as to avoid 'affirming that an accident is the body of Christ'? (Luther, The Babylonian Captivity of the Church, ed. Dillenberger, 265. Cited in Heywood Thomas, ibid. 153).

obliterated.[191] Although the observable reality remains that of bread, this is illusory, for its identity, albeit now an abstract one, has totally changed. In reality, in the 'species' of the Tridentine Eucharist we have something less than the risen, ascended Christ and yet something different from bread. It is a 'presence' which belongs to neither world. In both respects the created reality involved is transgressed to the denigration of God's creation, but not to the genuine benefit or service of the Creator.

The greatest error of this sort of thinking, however, is not that which is manifest in the sacrament as such, although that is serious enough, but rather what a sacramental relation of this kind says analogically with regard to the christological relation. He states: 'If sacramental grace involves transubstantiation in the Mass, does that not point back to some docetic error in Christology, to a transubstantiation of the human nature of Christ, leaving only a *species* to remain?'[192] For Torrance christology dictates that in the sacramental union God maintains 'a real presence' of each reality to the other, not of someone less than the Creator, nor something more than the created.

(c) Roots of the Problem: The Philosophical/Theological Difficulties in Medieval Sacramental Theology

(i) The Augustinian Dualism

That the doctrine of transubstantiation obviously dismantles created reality is the result of the problem, not the cause of it. In our chapter

---

[191] 'Dispossessed' (*de-substantiatio*) is Trent's own phrase. The created substances in Schillebeeckx's words, 'lost their natural independence as things of nature – they had been dispossessed of themselves' (Schillebeeckx, *The Eucharist*, 69). Thomas Aquinas puts it: The reality of Christ's body in the sacrament demands, then, that 'the substance of the bread cannot remain after the consecration' (*Summa Theologica*, Pt III, Q75, Art 2).

Pope Paul VI in his 1965 encyclical *Mysterium Fidei* restates the Tridentine dogma, stressing it as still normatively binding upon the Church: '[The Council] informs us that Christ becomes present in this sacrament precisely by a change of the bread's whole substance into his body and the wine's whole substance into his blood.... Since on the conversion of the bread and wine's substance, or nature, into the body and blood of Christ, nothing is left of the bread and wine but the appearances alone' (Paragraph 46 of the Encyclical).

[192] *R/st*, 184.

on sacramental signification we observed what Torrance understands as indirectly the root of all the problems of medieval sacramental theology, viz. an underlying Augustinianism obtruding an irreconcilable dualism between things invisible or spiritual and things visible or material, between God and the world. It was this which conditioned sacramental theology in the West, separating on false ontological grounds the unobservable *Res* from the observable *signum* in the Eucharist. It set the stage for all sorts of unorthodox attempts at holding the natural and the 'supernatural' together. Transubstantiation was one of the well-meaning, albeit artificial, attempts to mend the gap, or in Torrance's words, 'to tame the dualist and idealist tendencies in a rampant Augustinianism'. The solution it posed, however, raised other problems just as insoluble and every bit as devastating to christology as the error it sought to correct.[193]

(ii) The Aristotelian Attempt at Synthesis

The resolution of Augustinian dualism proposed by medieval theology was a reconstruction within an Aristotelian framework. These categories served well the Church's corrective intentions, since, by their insistence that primal forms naturally participate in material existence, they appeared to contradict the insidious neo-Platonism underpinning Augustinianism. However, this inherent participation did not imply a real, personal participation. Indeed, the inert concept of deity in Aristotle meant that the Church had to make certain creaturely actions ('effects') 'move', as it were, for God (their incipient 'Cause') in the world. As a result the dualism inherited from Augustine was not so much overcome as hardened by this context of causality. 'This was particularly apparent in the conception of the sacraments as "causing grace", which was further aggravated (as in the doctrine of the "real presence") by the acceptance of Aristotle's definition of place as "the immobile limit of the containing body".'[194] The erroneous Aristotelian concept of space which the Fathers of Trent inherited was the most serious problem in the development of their eucharistic theology. As we have noted, Aristotle defined space as '*terminus continentis immobilis primus*'.[195] All substances were seen to have their own peculiar space, indeed space was perceived as an accident of substance, essentially

---

[193] *R/n*, 123; cf. *C & A* II, 139.
[194] *CFOM*, 25.
[195] *STI*, 25.

inseparable from it, only abstractly distinguishable. In Aristotelianism, Torrance points out, 'the container is not independent of what it contains – space is not different from a spatially perceived object'.[196] Such a view caused a variety of problems for those seeking to formulate a doctrine of the real presence in the sacrament. We will mention three of these.

First, the 'immobility' necessarily predicated for space 'in' a sacrament as such led to a similar inactive connotation being ascribed to the one present 'in' that place. We have already discussed this difficulty philosophically with reference to the medieval doctrine of God. With respect to sacramental theology, if God is conceived as truly the 'unmoved mover' and 'outside' the world of space and time then it is virtually impossible for him to be understood as truly and actively present within the world, not only because of his inert stance in relation to space and time, but also because of the 'limits' of mobility ascribed to him within the sacrament. This led to the need for 'created intermediaries' acting between God and man, particularly ecclesiastical ones. Though scholars of the period hardly spoke of God's presence in such quiescent terms, 'this receptacle notion of space', Torrance insists, could not but 'exercise conceptual control over whatever is conceived by means of it'.[197]

Second, Aristotle's definition could only lead the medievals to think of the presence of God in the sacrament in a spatial manner. Although orthodoxy has never ascribed to God's substance 'space' as such, existing as he does outside space and time, when defining his presence in the world, and especially in the sacraments, medieval theologians were for the most part incapable of thinking of presence without space or of space except in a local sense. Thus, God's general presence in the world was always conceived in terms of 'omnipresence'. With regard to the sacrament, the presence of Christ, although never formally understood as being confined there, was generally thought to be particularly present as the *transubstantiated* host. This lent itself to the misunderstanding that God was contained *in* the host.[198] Even Luther's doctrine of the real presence is for

---

[196] Ibid. 27.

[197] Ibid. 26.

[198] In an attempt to safeguard the human dimensions of the ascended Christ, Thomas Aquinas strictly denied local or spatial dimensions being ascribed to his sacramental presence: 'A [natural] thing cannot be where it was not before except by being brought in locally or by something already there being changed into it. Now it is clear that the body of Christ does not begin to exist in this sacrament by being brought in locally... because it would thereby

Torrance conditioned by this misunderstanding. Officially Luther denied that the presence of Christ in the sacrament was a spatial one; however, since Christ's human dimensions after his ascension were given to participate in the 'omnipresence' of God, his whole polemic was engaged toward securing one particular 'place' in creation where God's presence could be identified and effective in space and time.[199] These 'spatial' definitions of the real presence inevitably reduced Christ's presence to an abstraction, as he says, 'a mathematical point' on an indefinite continuum.[200]

Finally, the ambiguity over ontological distinctions between the container and the contained also clouded the reasoning of the medieval sacramental theologians over the distinction between God and his creation within the sacrament. If God is present in the 'space' of another object, then he must somehow take on the substance of that thing as well, since space is an accident of created substance. The doctrine of transubstantiation, of course, worked in the other direction: Christ is not made bread, bread is made Christ. Nevertheless, with all the accidents of bread still intact and the Aristotelian axiom that 'space is not different from a spatially perceived object' still in mind, the popular misconceptions of God's

---

cease to be in heaven, since anything that is locally moved begins to be somewhere only by leaving where it was.... Now the body of Christ in this sacrament begins simultaneously to be in different places.' 'It begins to be there because the substance of the bread is changed into it' (*Summa Theologiae*, 3a, 75, 1; *Summa Theologiae*, article 4. Cited by Heywood Thomas, 'Logic and Metaphysics', 156–7).

[199] STI, 32ff.

[200] Ibid. 28. It is helpful to compare Luther's understanding of Christ's presence 'in, with and under' the sacrament with Torrance's view that Christ is present 'in, through and over' the sacramental action of the Church. Torrance does not hesitate to say with Luther that Christ is present 'in' the *unio sacramentalis*, but meaning by this that he is present in his people's action, not in their bread, as Luther would insist. On the other hand, Torrance prefers 'through' to Luther's 'with', no doubt underlining the sacrament's instrumental character. His choice of this preposition further accentuates the dynamic nature of the eucharistic presence as well as the referential nature of the sacramental analogy. Torrance would likewise hesitate from using the term 'with' for fear of its synergistic implications. By saying that Christ is present 'under' the bread of the sacrament, Luther highlights Christ's universal presence in all creation as that which undergirds his presence 'in' the bread *pro me*. Torrance's emphasis in contrast is upon the transcendence of that presence, infinitely above and beyond the sacrament, yet from which all his action 'upon creation' is said to progress; hence his choice of the term 'over' (*R/n*, 128; *RP*, 76).

substance being mingled with created substance were inevitable.²⁰¹ The fact is that in the Tridentine sacrament God supervenes upon the created substance in such a way that the creature is made to transcend its own contingency at the expense of its natural existence. It was this sort of thinking, as Torrance sees it, that gave rise to the Roman teaching on 'created grace'.²⁰²

(iii) Created Grace

Torrance defines 'created grace' broadly as 'grace actualizing itself in the creature and elevating it to supernatural existence'.²⁰³ It can be identified in the Tridentine conception of what happens to the transubstantiated elements of the Holy Eucharist and in the Eastern Orthodox understanding of what transpires within the lives of sacramentalized saints. As Torrance sees it, such an idea of grace is the result of the coalescence of two ideas – the Augustinian/neo-Platonic notion of an immaterial, rational correspondence of formal reason in God with its ordering by the mind of the Church, and the Aristotelian understanding of divine causes operating necessarily as divine effects immanent to created reality. In both Augustinianism and Aristotelianism there is an assumed *natural* relation between the uncreated and created which fails to distinguish clearly between the two realities. In Augustinianism the reason of man or the enlightened reason of the Church is confused with the Spirit of God, whereas in medieval Aristotelianism the created facility for divine efficacity is mistaken for the act of God itself.²⁰⁴ With regard to the sacraments, Torrance identifies 'created grace' with transubstantiation and its 'recreation' of things created into things divine in order to effect divine things in the world.²⁰⁵

However, there is another expression of 'created grace' which we have referred to above, one that is more personal and at the same time more 'mystical'. It has to do with 'the interiorizing of the divine

---

²⁰¹ *STI*, 27.
²⁰² Cf. *R/st*, 179–80.
²⁰³ Ibid. 180.
²⁰⁴ Ibid. 177ff.
²⁰⁵ Cf. ibid. 179–80. Schillebeeckx, interpreting Trent, confirms Torrance's definition: 'This aspect may be regarded as "created grace" which is implicit in all God's communication of himself in grace, but which has an unexpectedly profound ontological density in this particular gift of himself in the Eucharist, since it takes hold of the secular reality of the bread creatively and is not simply a transcendent "naming from outside" which leaves the *secular* reality as it was before' (Schillebeeckx, *The Eucharist*, 81).

power within us', with 'grace actualizing itself within the physical as well as the spiritual, metaphysically heightening and exalting creaturely existence' 'elevating [it] for its participation in the divine'.[206] To this way of thinking created being 'participates' in the divine nature, not through a simple creature/Creator relation (*koinonia*) in which neither reality compromises the other but by God literally impregnating our being with his, as one substance permeates another. Torrance distinguishes clearly between what he understands as 'participation' and this 'participation as divinization'. In line with Reformed theology, he states:

> Through a relation of mutual indwelling between Christ and us, we are enfolded within the infinite dimensions of the love of God. The Greek Fathers used to speak of that experience as *theopoiesis* or *theosis* which does not mean 'divinisation', as is so often supposed, but refers to the utterly staggering act of God in which he gives *himself* to us and *adopts us* into the communion of his divine life and love through Jesus Christ and in his one Spirit, yet in such a way that we are not made divine but are preserved in our humanity.[207]

To 'think of grace as deifying man' or heightening his being until he attains the level of a supernatural order can mean nothing but the confusion of created contingency with divine necessity, which results in a 'docetic violence' being done to our creaturely, human being.[208] Torrance links these two ideas of so-called 'created grace' thus:

> Grace was regarded as acting within the recipient in much the same way as the divine power in transubstantiation of bread and wine in the Mass into the realities of the Body and Blood of Christ.... It is almost like a supernatural potency that is infused into human beings, enlightening their minds, strengthening their wills, and conferring upon them beyond any natural state a divine quality which more and more transmutes the sinner into a saint, a being of earth into a being of heaven.[209]

---

[206] *R/st*, 173–4, 179–80.

[207] *MOC*, 75. Torrance comments similarly in another place: 'This is a participation in which the human nature of the participant is not deified but reaffirmed and recreated in its essence as human nature, yet one in which the participant is really united to the Incarnate Son of God partaking in Him in his own appropriate mode of the oneness of the Son and the Father and the Father and the Son, through the Holy Spirit' (*R/st*, 186).

[208] *R/st*, 180.

[209] Ibid. 179–80.

(iv) The Reformation's Reversion to Augustinianism

Torrance is strongly opposed to what he calls transubstantiation's formal 'Eutychian' destruction of the created reality in the sacrament, that is, the dissolution of created substance precisely by its divinization.[210] All the same, he opposes with equal vigour 'the humanists of the Reformation' – viz. Zwingli, Hoen, etc. – and their present-day disciples.[211] Their great error, judged as equally damaging to the sacrament, also arises from Augustinianism, not this time as a reaction to it, but as a form of its resurgence, formulated to counter the misguided Aristotelian attempts at modifying its dualism. These Reformers rightly saw the Tridentine doctrine as destroying the essential, natural 'transcendence' of both the creation and the Creator without actually facilitating God's real act in the world. However, Torrance suggests that their discarding of the Aristotelian synthesis only re-introduced the earlier Augustinian bifurcation. They 'held... the two sides of the sacramental relation [to be] disparate and separable', and thus in their sacramental analogy denied an orthodox, christological analogate, suggesting at best a kind of 'Nestorian christology'.[212] The Eucharist was thus rendered purely a rite of historical memorial of the death of Christ, to be practised principally out of a sense of duty to a dominical command. Such a notion for Torrance contradicts the very spirit of the Eucharist to say nothing of its ontological barrenness.[213] He observes that

> the Churches of the Reformation have never been able to overcome the Augustinian dualism embedded in their foundations, so that in spite of the Reformation stress on the reality of Christ's presence (i.e. the real presence of the whole Christ including his body and blood) in the Eucharist, the ontological relation gave way to a symbolical or to a phenomenological

---

[210] The Eutychians were Monophysites who held that there were 'two natures before, but only one after, the Union' in the Incarnate Christ. In Torrance's mind this amounted to a 'transubstantiation' of Christ's humanity, so that in the whole of his existence among us we only encountered the *species* of an incarnation (cf. 'Eutyches', *The Oxford Dictionary of The Christian Church*, eds F.L. Cross and E.A. Livingstone, 2nd edn revised (London, OUP, 1983), 484).

[211] Cf. *GT*, 6–7; *C & A* II, 139.

[212] The Nestorians denied the *hypostatic union* and thus rejected with it the *inseparabiliter* of orthodox christology. Hence Christ's humanity had only a symbolic association with the Divine Word but could never be formally identified with him. Christ's human being was thus reduced to the 'outward sign' of a 'divine grace' and not itself consubstantial with it.

[213] Cf. *RP*, 3–7; *GT*, 6–7.

relation so that symbolist and existentialist notions of the sacraments have been wide-spread in Protestant theology.[214]

He sees himself as standing on that side of the Reformed tradition which in turn stands,

> upon Chalcedonian Christology [and] repudiates both Nestorianism and Eutychianism in its doctrine of the sacramental union, denying that there is either separation or fusion between the elements of bread and wine and the reality of the body and blood of Christ.... Just as the humanity of Christ remains true humanity even after the resurrection and ascension and is no docetic phantasm, so the bread and wine remain true bread and true wine and are no mere species, though by consecration they are converted into instruments of the real presence.[215]

8. The Manducatio Impiorum

The manner in which Torrance treats what he calls the 'old problem posed by the *manducatio impiorum*' illustrates still again how he can avoid a traditional quandary in sacramental theology by refusing to be drawn into the metaphysical debate usually associated with it.[216] Since medieval times the questions raised by the *manducatio impiorum* have been the ultimate test in determining belief in the objective presence of the soul *and* body of Christ in the sacrament. The problem concerns Paul's interdiction against 'whoever... eats the bread or drinks the cup of the Lord in an unworthy manner'. That person, Paul says, 'will be guilty of profaning the body and blood of the Lord'.[217] If *unbelievers* in fact do eat and drink Christ's body and blood, though to their own condemnation, as Paul seems to

---

[214] *GT*, 10.

[215] *Inter*, 336. Torrance says similarly in another context that the 'Christological mystery must be respected in the communion of the Lord's Supper. That means that the relation between the sign and the signified is to be understood in terms of *inconfuse* and *inseparabiliter*, so that both Eutychian and Nestorian heresies are to be repudiated in a true doctrine of Holy Communion. In terms of the Reformation movements this meant for Calvin a double battle, championing the *inconfuse* against Roman transubstantiation and Lutheran consubstantiation, championing the *inseparabiliter* against humanists and others' (*K & C*, 144).

[216] 'Arnoldshain', 10.

[217] 1 Cor. 11:27f.

be saying, then the point is made that Christ's presence is truly there independently of the faith or appropriation of the communicate. Especially during the Reformation period the question 'do unbelievers eat?' was raised to impeach those eucharistic theologians who conceded only a purely 'spiritual' association of Christ's humanity within the sacrament or who attributed the sacrament's power to 'make' Christ present to the faith of the believer rather than to the power of the Word of God or the priesthood of the Church.

Torrance criticizes Luther and the Lutherans for making the *manducatio impiorum* the 'decisive test' as to the real presence. However, when his own eucharistic theology is put to this test it emerges clearly on the 'realist' side of the debate. When he discusses the problem he turns the matter round, saying that the question of 'whether or not believers eat' is not a question addressed to the matter of the sacrament but to the nature of the gospel. The question asked is not primarily whether all eat, but whether all may eat. For after all, 'the action in the Supper is not another action than that which Christ has already accomplished on our behalf, and which is proclaimed in the Gospel'.[218]

This is reminiscent of Torrance's understanding of the sacrament as the Word's active sign in the world, as the lively extension of the gospel in the Church. We should recall that for Torrance there is no *substantial* difference between our 'eating the flesh and drinking the blood of Christ' by the Word and our doing the same by the Word *and* the sacrament. In both cases the substance and strength of the sacramental action belongs to the Word. Torrance approaches the question not by asking whether or in what way Christ is present in the sacrament but rather by ascertaining if Christ in the gospel offers himself to all. He thus takes the occasion to 'reject the heresy of limited atonement'.[219] However, in so doing he counters not only Calvin's faulty soteriology but his way of begging the question by contending that God only gives himself to the elect.[220] Since the Word embodies a humanity common

---

[218] *C & A* II, 152.

[219] 'Arnoldshain', 11.

[220] Ernst Kinder asserts that the Lutheran affirmation and the Calvinist denial that the unworthy receive the body of Christ is the greatest difference between the two traditions. This is not just because the *manducatio impiorum* undeniably demonstrates the distance between Lutheran and Calvinist sacramental theologies, but by the fact that it underlines the basic differences that lie in Calvin's and Luther's understanding of the gospel. On this score Torrance stands with Luther, for Luther insists that God's forgiveness is offered to all who come to him and that God is therefore present to all, believers and

to all men, Torrance argues, it is assumed that Christ 'does not withhold himself' from anyone wherever the gospel is preached and the sacraments of the gospel are administered.[221]

Christ is present in the whole of the sacramental action by his Word and Spirit to all who are participant, without exception. This 'presence of Christ in his Body and Blood' in the sacrament, like the gospel which Christ embodies, is light and life to some, darkness and judgement to others. All hear the same gospel: it is not objectively different to the believer and the unbeliever because it is rejected by the latter. Torrance therefore reasons, 'there would be no judgement in the Supper if the Body and Blood were not extended to or partaken of by the unbelieving recipient'.[222] While Torrance nowhere suggests a physical presence of Christ's body and blood in the sacrament, the fact that unbelievers do truly receive Christ by virtue of their participation in the sacramental action is salutary witness to just how objectively real he conceives Christ's spiritual presence to be there. '*Jesus does not need to be made real*', he insists. 'We need no existential decision, no sacramental operation, we do not even need faith to make Him real to us.'[223] The fact that Christ is shown to be present in the sacrament independently of the Church's faith makes the point conclusively that no subjective element procures the real presence; rather the mystery of the real presence of Christ and its procession in the Church belongs totally to the agency of God. Nevertheless, while he is clear that the unbeliever may actually partake of Christ's presence by virtue of his participation in the Church's sacramental action, this 'is not to say that [he] will partake of the *saving fruit* of that body and blood'.[224] Christ does not dwell in his heart because he does not feed on Christ by faith.[225]

For Torrance, the questions all this raises are not metaphysical ones, as we have indicated. There is no debating whether or not the body of the ascended Christ is corporeally present in

---

unbelievers alike (cf. McDonnell, *John Calvin*, 64–5. McDonnell cites Ernst Kinder, 'Die lutherische Kirche', *Und Ihr Netz Zerriz*, ed. Helmut Lamparter (Stuttgart, 1957), 254).

[221] Torrance states: 'Because it is the incarnation that constitutes the range of the blood of Christ, we must affirm that in the Supper the body and blood are extended to all within that range.... Jesus Christ does not withhold Himself from anyone in the Holy Supper' ('Arnoldshain', 10–11). 'It is the same Christ giving Himself in His Body and Blood who is extended to all' (*C & A* II, 152).

[222] 'Arnoldshain', 11.
[223] Ibid. 12–13.
[224] Ibid. 10–11.
[225] *C & A* II, 152.

the bread of the sacrament to be 'chewed' by the teeth of the blasphemers. But he is certainly present, by his Word and Spirit, according to the nature of his ascension. Christ's presence is determined by the gospel alone. The offer of God's love is made to all persons in the sacrament and Christ is present there as the embodiment of that love, but *truly* there, not just offering himself to be there. The way Torrance answers what he feels ought to be the questions posed by the *manducatio impiorum* gives added integrity to his statement quoted in the last section:

> while we can only eat and drink the body and blood of Christ through faith, that, by the power of the eternal Spirit, the Church is given through the Eucharist a *relation in being*, beyond its relation to Christ through faith.[226]

What Torrance means by 'a relation in being' here is now shown to mean unquestionably a relation which includes a spiritual presence with real and profound ontological density.[227]

---

[226] *Inter*, 335.

[227] Calvin's preoccupation in discussions such as these was to dismiss what he deems 'the crass notion' of a 'material substance' in the sacrament. The Reformer wanted to avoid at all costs the idea that there is 'anything earthly or material' there (cf. *CR*, 55:110). The bond between the real presence and the eating is not 'a substantial bond' for Calvin, rather a real joining by which the 'substance' of Christ, and by this he means 'the virtue' of Christ, is received. (Christ, he insists, only 'descends to us by his virtue' *CR*, 9:72, 73.) For Calvin, as for Torrance, the eucharistic presence is a spiritual presence, though by this neither means a *pure* spiritual presence. It is a presence realized by the Spirit. Unlike Torrance, however, Calvin insists on addressing the presence of Christ in the Spirit in 'non substantial' terms. Torrance has no hesitancy in this regard, suggesting an intensely substantial, though non-corporeal, ontic presence which Calvin would not allow. Even if Calvin could have entertained the real presence of Christ being offered to all in the sacrament, it is doubtful that the presence he would have understood as being there – 'no other... than that of a relationship' – would have been the kind of objectively constituted presence which unbelievers could have received without the facility of faith (*CR*, 2:1011).

THE EUCHARISTIC SACRIFICE WITHIN THE CHURCH'S SACRAMENT

1. Torrance's Realistic Claims for Sacrifice within the Eucharist

When looked at superficially, Torrance's claims for sacrifice within the Eucharist are indeed bold. Here we 'offer Christ to the Father', he says. In this sacrament, 'we set Christ before God's face in order to propitiate Him'.[228] He is citing Calvin directly in both cases here, making the point that 'no interpretation of the Supper is biblically sound which does not rest upon a doctrine of atonement involving the aspect of sacrifice'.[229] Defending his use of such provocative, cultic language, he says,

> we must not allow these fears [which the choice of terminology might incite] to hinder us from listening to what the Biblical witness has to say about sacrifice.... No doctrine of Eucharistic memorial is adequate unless it corresponds to that fulness in the atonement. We cannot and must not seek to avoid the notion of Eucharistic sacrifice.[230]

There is no doubt that for Torrance the Church's eucharistic offering 'itself partakes of sacrificial character'.[231] Clearly, the notion of sacrifice lies at the very heart of his eucharistic theology.

2. The Essential Difference Between the Sacrifice of the Church and the Sacrifice of Christ

In stark contrast to statements such as these, Torrance unequivocally marks out the distinction between the Church's offering and that of Christ. 'That which distinguishes Christ's atoning sacrifice from the Church's sacrifice', he says, 'is the bearing of judgement'.[232] The difference is between a 'propitiatory sacrifice' and a 'eucharistic

---

[228] *C & A* II, 150.
[229] 'Arnoldshain', 15.
[230] Ibid. 15.
[231] *C & A* II, 178–9.
[232] *Inter*, 329.

sacrifice', or a sacrifice of praise.²³³ This does not mean, however, that Christ's obedient self-offering is not also eucharistic or that the Church's praise is not inclusive of 'all the offices of charity' in obedience.²³⁴ The difference lies in their posture before God. Christ's offering is piacular and vicarious, having strength and appeal before God in its own right. The Church's sacrifice, on the other hand, makes no such pretence. It is purely responsive, answering that sacrifice appropriately in the orientation of 'all that we have and do in the name of Christ *to the Glory of God*'.²³⁵ We will discuss the rationale for the doxological disposition of the Church's sacrifice later; it is sufficient now to say that, for Torrance, Christ alone

> has offered to God a propitiatory sacrifice in the sacrifice of Himself in obedient life and obedient death once and for all, and we can only offer to God praise and thanksgiving for what He has done and finished forever on our behalf and in our stead and for our sakes.²³⁶

At this point several things need to be stressed regarding the nature of Christ's propitiatory sacrifice. When Torrance denies a propitiatory prerogative to the Church's Eucharist he is wholly consistent with his overall theological method. Indeed, as we have seen, even within the incarnation the human element of Christ *per se* has no such power. The redeeming work is not that of Christ's human nature, acting independently or in some equal partnership with the divine nature. The Word is always the predominant principle of movement within his own humanity. Therefore, the atonement which is made through Christ is 'God's act'.²³⁷ In Torrance's theology, man *as man* does not propitiate God; God brings to himself the necessary oblation, albeit in a perfect human offering. Torrance speaks of 'God propitiating Himself', of 'God reconciling Himself to man and reconciling man to Himself in Jesus Christ'.²³⁸ God, he says, 'bears in Himself our judgement'.²³⁹

What of Torrance's understanding of propitiation itself? In the words of John McLeod Campbell (one of Torrance's mentors in these matters) that which is required before 'the mind of God in relation to

---

²³³ *C & A* II, 148; *Inter*, 329.
²³⁴ Cf. *C & A* II, 148; *R/n*, 211.
²³⁵ *C & A* II, 149.
²³⁶ Ibid. 148–9.
²³⁷ *Inter*, 332.
²³⁸ *TS*, 157; *SOF*, XC.
²³⁹ *Inter*, 332.

sin' (the wrath of God) is not just the death of the one for the many. That is merely the negative side. The meaning of propitiation must never be truncated at Christ's passion. For while the propitiation of God certainly includes Christ's obedience through death, and though his substitutionary work includes his assuming our place in death, that death by itself does not effect reconciliation between God and man. What God requires in the face of Adam's disobedience is a life lived justly for all, a second, obedient Adam. Accordingly, from 'the depths of [his] divine humanity' the Word brings to the 'divine justice' a human response that 'has all the elements of a perfect repentance *in* humanity for all the sins of man – a perfect sorrow – a perfect contrition', all within a perfect obedience to the law of love offered in the spirit of love to God and for man.[240] As Torrance puts it: 'It is the whole human life of Jesus, in his active as well as His passive obedience, that we are to see as the one perfect and sufficient sacrifice for the sins of the world once and for all offered through the eternal Spirit to the Father.'[241] Thus, the offering which God seeks, God forms and makes himself in his own humanity.[242] The offering and the offerer are identical in God's propitiation of himself.[243]

Christ's offering is thus seen as the total act of his person, and so is both mental and physical. It is shaped, however, not purely in the ideal world, but at the centre of the human mind itself, so that it is renewed in the knowledge of God. We must, says Torrance, 'think of Christ in his vicarious humanity as Mediator of our salvation *in mind* as well as body'.[244] Indeed, for Torrance the mind of Christ is the fulcrum of all mediation, the locus where God shapes into human categories 'the things of God' to be given to men and likewise where he refines and renews 'the things of men' to be presented to God.[245] Man is justified as the Word returns him in a rational, worshipping mind to God. This worship, as we have said, is not incidental or ancillary to the salvation of man but substantive to it, for man is not

---

[240] John McLeod Campbell, *The Nature of Atonement and its Relation to Remission of Sins and Eternal Life*, 6th edn (London, MacMillan, 1895), 116ff.; cf. *Inter*, 329–30.

[241] *SOF*, XCI, cf. LXXXIV; *Inter*, 329–30.

[242] Torrance says, 'It was the humanity of all men that He presented in Himself to the judgement of the Father and in the humanity of all men that He made expiation for our sins' ('Arnoldshain', 10).

[243] *Inter*, 330; *R/n*, 152.

[244] 'New College', 27, italics mine.

[245] 'In the Incarnation the Son of God ministered not only of the things of God to man but ministered of the things of man to God' (*R/n*, 228; *MOC*, 83. Torrance cites Athanasius, *Contra Arianos* I:41ff.).

rationally whole until he is taught to worship his Creator.[246] Neither is man's knowledge of God complete except in the context of the worship of God. Only in the 'reasonable service' of the ascended Christ is man finally, perfectly restored in relation to God. For Torrance any violation of the integrity of Christ's human mind is to invalidate his high priestly office and consequently to make impossible his mediation of the Church's prayer. As we will see presently, this has profound implications for Torrance's understanding of the eucharistic sacrifice.

3. Historical Compromises of this Differential by the Western Church

(a) The Heretical Background to the Worship of the Western Church

Torrance perceives two christological heresies underlying the Western Church's recurrent misunderstanding of divine worship, particularly that within the Eucharist. The juxtaposition of these underlines the careful balance in Torrance's emphasis between the divine and human dimensions in christology and consequently in the doctrine of atonement. On the one hand, there is the tendency towards Apollinarianism in the Church's understanding of worship, a 'liturgical Apollinarianism', he calls it, i.e. a virtual or total diminishing of the importance of the Word's distinctly human mind as the mediating principle for all human prayer.[247] This results from the Church having pushed 'the humanity of Christ more and more into the sheer majesty of God', and amounts to what Torrance calls 'a docetic destruction' of the integrity of the ascended Christ.[248] This disintegration in turn leads worshippers to lose sight of the 'integral and essential' place of 'Christ's humanity in its vicarious and priestly role in human worship of the Father'. Furthermore, it leaves 'the poor creature at worship... confronted immediately with the overwhelming majesty', and compelled to devise for himself the mediation of his salvation.[249] For something has to be 'interposed between [God] and the sinner'.[250]

---

[246] 'New College', 27.
[247] *R/n*, 115, 193, 201, cf. 191ff., esp. 201, 204.
[248] Ibid. 142.
[249] Ibid. 116; cf. Jungmann, *The Place of Christ*, 251.
[250] 'New College', 26; cf. *Inter*, 332.

Historically, the piety of the Church has turned to its cult of saints in order to compensate for the absence of the human priesthood of Christ, particularly to that of the Blessed Virgin Mary. At a more sophisticated level, however, the Church has interposed its sacramental system between itself and God. Torrance cites the eminent Roman Catholic patristic and liturgical scholar, J.A. Jungmann, who admits this, demonstrating how, in Latin eucharistic theology, 'the Eucharist, the Body of Christ, is [made]... a third factor between the suppliant and the Lord Christ', who has himself become, by the diminution of the human side of his mediatorship before 'the resplendence of his divinity', more the object than the agent of mediation.[251] Hence, Torrance says, 'the consecrated bread

---

[251] *R/n*, 203; cf. Jungmann, *The Place of Christ*, 258, 269. Jungmann says that the tendency of the Church has always been 'to bring out the Godhead in Christ, to honour in him God pure and simple' (Jungmann, *The Place of Christ*, 84). He shows how the Western Church failed to maintain the tension implicit in a divine-human mediation: 'As Christ's mediatorial role in his glorified humanity receded more and more into the background... instead our Lord was contemplated on one hand in his bitter passion (or purely in his humanity), on the other hand in his divinity' (Jungmann, 222-34). Therefore, Christ's divine nature was made to stand over against the act of atonement (which was seemingly perceived as predominantly a human offering), even receiving the act of propitiation.

Torrance points out how 'stress upon the deity of Christ, in reaction to Arianism, prompted incorporation into the liturgies of formal prayers to Christ who as Lord receives our prayer and as Mediator bestows divine gifts upon us' (*R/n*, 115-16). Jungmann, however, indicates that the earliest formal prayers of the Church – viz., the sacerdotal, liturgical prayers, the *anaphora* of the Eucharist – universally addressed the Father through Jesus Christ. They were not offered to Christ as such, rather through him (Jungmann, cf. 3, 34-5, 191). This does not mean that private prayers have not always been addressed to Jesus, or that the worship of the Word and Spirit is not implied in the worship of the Father. Even when Christ is worshipped formally, as in the ancient *Testament of Our Lord* (c. 150), 'the address to [him] prefers to denote his divinity alone' (Jungmann, cf. 3, 131). This was the case also in St Augustine who wrote: It is Christ 'who is praying for us, is praying in us and is prayed to by us. He prays for us as our priest, in us as our head, he is prayed to by us as our God' (St Augustine, Ps. 85, 1; P2, 37, 1081. Quoted by Pope Paul VI, *The Holy Eucharist*, Encyclical Letter *Mysterium Fidei* (London, Catholic Truth Society, 1965), 17). Jungmann's recurring theme is that as long as the Word's human nature and deed remain distinct within the Godhead, his place and role as divine-human Mediator will remain integral to the economy of the Church's worship. For it is only in the Word's humanity, that is, as 'the man Christ Jesus, that he can be the mediator, redeemer and high priest' (Jungmann, 155). Jungmann sees the monophysite view, which made 'the humanity of our Lord vanish into his

and wine, identified with the awful mystery of the Lord's body and blood in the Eucharist, could (even) take on the role of "intercessors" in the worship of the faithful'.[252] This has become most blatantly evident over the recent centuries in the Roman Church's devotion to the *corpus Christi*, that is, to the body of Christ under the 'species' of bread *outside* the sacramental action of the Church. In all such deviations in sacramental theology Torrance contends that the

---

divinity', and the imbalanced stress upon Christ's nature as God arising out of the Arian controversy, which over the decades led to an 'evaporation of the humanity of Christ' in the mind of the Church, as both 'sponsoring' other mediators (cf. Jungmann, 52ff., 62ff., 102, 162, 220, 228, 230). Consequently, the distinctly human mediatiorship of the divine Lord was 'suppressed, [and] the intercession of the saints, automatically became all the more prominent' (Jungmann, 102-3). In the History of the Church he says, 'Christ's intercession [was] pushed back so far into the Godhead that there was no longer any scandal when God was appealed to through' other intermediaries. Kenneth Leech cites Theodore of Mopsuestia (*Cat.* 6) who in the fifth century calls the priest, 'the mediator of the sacrament' (Kenneth Leech, *True God: An Exploration in Spiritual Theology* (London, Sheldon Press, 1985), 275). Even the Eucharist itself was deemed an 'intercessor' for the Church (cf. *R/n*, 192; Jungmann, 258, 268, 84-5). In fact, the Arians had pointed to the orthodox formula of prayer – to the Father, through the Son, and in the Spirit – as teaching tacitly the subordination of the Son (Jungmann, 162). Nevertheless, in spite of the Church's contention with Arianism, even at the height of that controversy, in Athanasius and others 'there was an unwillingness to relinquish the right to pray as one always had prayed: 'Jesus Christ our Lord, *through* whom and *with* whom... to the Father *with* the Son himself, in the Holy Spirit' (Athanasius, *De Incarnatione*, 57. Cited by Torrance, *R/n*, 187; cf. Jungmann, 162).

As late as the Council of Carthage in 397, with St Augustine in attendance, formal prayer to Christ in divine services was not permitted (Jungmann, 164). 'Even at the end of the fourth century', Jungmann says, 'we find hardly any trace of another mode of liturgical prayer' save that directed 'to the Lord God through Jesus Christ' (Jungmann, 144). Formularies both East and West, which made 'Christ's mediatorship... object rather than the constitutent element of the Eucharistic prayer', which made 'Christ appear as receiver of the sacrifice' instead of the offerer of it, belong clearly to post-Augustinian christology (Jungmann, 112, 120, 144, 164). However, long after Augustine's day the eucharistic prayers of the Church for the most part remained faithful to the primitive pattern. It was at first only in the fore-mass prayers and in the prayers of Baptism that Christ was invoked in a manner appropriate only to the Father, that is, in a way which did not acknowledge his unique relation to God and to man as mediator of the Church's prayer (Jungmann, 164). Jungmann concludes: 'Prayer to Christ... has therefore no heritage from the Catholic Church... not from its official liturgical practice' (Jungmann, 169).

[252] *R/n*, 203.

Eucharist has been denigrated to a kind of 'substitute Christ', even a 'rival' to him.[253]

As in the christological theory, so in such a eucharistic theology the redemptive role of Christ's humanity is negated altogether. In an Apollinarian doctrine of worship not only is the function of Christ's human mind usurped by the divine Logos, but that rationality is itself displaced by the mind of its Creator.[254] In this view it is Godhead *qua* Godhead that atones, without a genuine interior relation to real humanity. Torrance shows how this misconception prevents the possibility of Christ's saving anything but man's mortal body, since it disallows the possibility of God taking up our mind to heal it or, for that matter, any divine operation truly from the side of man toward God. Doxologically as well as soteriologically, the mediatorial agency of Christ's divine humanity, God-manward and man-Godward, is lost.[255]

The second heresy is Pelagianism, the corresponding overemphasis on Christ's humanity as against his divinity. Here the primary saving factor is the human act, as such, as though 'it were the man, Jesus, appeasing God'. In this view 'man in Christ' is seen as himself 'acting upon God' to redeem his own life. With regard to sacramental theology, this view would erroneously esteem the Church's human act within the sacrament as having saving significance in itself before God.

The Church, Torrance insists, must mediate in its eucharistic theology between these two extremes by stressing both the predominance of the divine act and the necessity of the human element within the economy of salvation. This balance is found when we speak of the divine action being 'translated... into terms of

---

[253] Ibid. 203; *GT*, 11; 'New College', 26; cf. Jungmann, *The Place of Christ*, 269. For examples of the use of this phrase 'substitute Christ' note John McLeod Campbell, *Christ, the Bread of Life*, 2nd edn (London, MacMillan, 1868), 49, 52, 57.

[254] The whole question for Torrance centres upon the integrity of Christ's human mind. Here is the acid test of his real humanity, for it is only if the distinctly human rational faculty is in place in the Word's incarnation and ascension that the validity of Christ's human priesthood can be guaranteed. This alone determines if the Church really does have in heaven a 'high priest chosen from among men', that is, one who through ontological and existential identity with man has acquired 'fellow feeling with us' and is now 'appointed to act on behalf of men in relation to God' (Heb. 4:15; 5:1; Jungmann, *The Place of Christ*, 137).

[255] 'New College', 26-7.

human action'.²⁵⁶ It was neither the human initiative acting separately from the divine, nor the Word acting in only a tangential relation with his humanity that saved humankind.²⁵⁷ Torrance, echoing F.W. Camfield, says 'it was the God-manhood' that atoned 'and that means, not simply God *in man* but God *as* man. The manhood was integral and essential and not merely instrumental.'²⁵⁸

(b) The Sacrifice of the Mass vis-à-vis the Personal Priesthood of Christ in the Eucharist

Apollinarianism's influence left the Church's image of Christ 'starved for real humanity' and, consequently, the sign of Christ in its sacraments wanting for vital christological content and mediation. Pelagianism, on the other hand, conveniently compensating in this vacuum, lay behind the imposition of the Church's institutional priesthood in place of Christ's mediatorial and divine humanity. Add to this what Torrance contends is the mistaken cosmology of Augustinianism (providing as it does the ground for an inherent agreement between divine and created rationality, and therefore

---

²⁵⁶ *Inter*, 332.

²⁵⁷ In his chapter 'The Atonement and the Oneness of the Church' in the first volume of *Conflict and Agreement* Torrance discusses the soteriological implications of Chalcedonian christology (*C & A* I, 239ff.). He points to the distinction in 'classical christology' between the conceptions of *anhypostasia* and *enhypostasia*. By *anhypostasia* was meant 'that in the *assumptio carnis* the human nature of Christ had no independent subsistence *per se* apart from the event of the incarnation, apart from the hypostatic union'. In other words, Christ was only a man by virtue of the Word's act in the incarnation. By *enhypostasia* it asserted 'that in the *assumptio carnis* the human nature of Christ was given a real and concrete subsistence within the hypostatic union – it was enhypostatic in the Word' (*C & A* I, 242-3). This meant that Christ was in fact a real man in relation to the predominant Word. These are inseparable. To separate them produces grave consequences for the atonement: 'If *anhypostasia* alone were to be applied to the atonement (without *enhypostasia*)... that would mean that the deed of the atonement would be a pure act of God over the head of man, and not an atoning act involving incorporation... [on the other hand] if *enhypostasia* alone were to be applied to the atonement without *anhypostasia* then atonement would have to be understood as a Pelagian deed placating God by human sacrifice. The inseparability [of these conceptions]... is thus supremely important for it means that while atonement is throughout act of God for us, we are to understand it as act of God done into our humanity, wrought out in our place and as our act' (*C & A*, I, 243).

²⁵⁸ *Inter*, 332. Torrance quotes F.W. Camfield's article, 'The idea of Substitution in the Doctrine of the Atonement', *SJT* 1 (1948), 292ff.

between the order of God and the ordering of the Church) and one has the basis for the doctrine of the sacrifice of the Mass.

The amalgamation of these misconceptions fostered the implicit synergism at the heart of the Roman doctrine.[259] Of the three, however, it was the Pelagian heresy which Torrance singles out as the most vicious, specifically its doctrines of the atonement and of man. Predictably for Torrance, any soteriology which does not understand redemption as 'altogether a divine act', albeit in and through a fully human identity, or, from the other side, any anthropology which would allow man to encroach upon God's unique prerogative to save his creation, is a direct offspring of Pelagianism. On both counts the so-called sacrifice of the Mass is culpable.

We noted in our last chapter how Torrance rejects 'a doctrine of identity' in his eucharistic theology. This holds as well with respect to any equivalence of the created act of the Church with the uncreated act of God. In the Eucharist, he says, there is involved 'a continuity of action' between God and his Church, but in such a way that the essential nature of each as well as the essential difference between them is not compromised. The Being and Act of the word is always 'prior to and transcendent to the Church'.[260] In the Mass Torrance sees this integral distinction being imperilled and a reciprocal relation between the earthly and heavenly actions contrived.

This wholesale rejection of the 'doctrine of identity' in the Mass not only applies to the exact equation of our offering with the sacrifice of Christ but to any facsimile of this.[261] The difference between Christ's sacrifice and that of the Church is one of kind, not of degree. Therefore, any notion that the Church's act as such might sustain or bring to fulfilment God's saving act, must be resisted. 'This is neither a Pelagian offering of the immolated Christ by man, nor a Pelagian offering of ourselves in addition to the sacrifice of Christ.'[262] Our Eucharist is not to be seen as that which 'invests the deed of Christ with its sacramental nature or validity', neither is it that which 'continually presents the sacrifice of Christ to the Father'.[263] The *paliggenesia* needs itself no re-generation; the

---

[259] *Inter*, 332.

[260] *RP*, 76.

[261] *Inter*, 331.

[262] *STR*, 117.

[263] *Inter*, 332. He says, 'That sacrificial act of Christ once for all performed and enduring in His endless life in the presence of God, is realised in the life of His people, not by repetition of His substitutionary sacrifice, but by their dying

perpetual self-oblation of the ascended Christ before the Father cannot be improved upon.[264] Neither does the risen Christ need our industry to make him historically relevant. The Church's sacrament, therefore, must not be regarded as a 'making present' of past historical events which we 'do'.[265] Such a uniquely divine act as the Christ-event has no need to be nor can it be 'prolonged in a ceremonial cultus'.[266] The very nature of the Church's sacraments, as 'sacraments of the finished work of Christ', dictates that they can 'add nothing' in either content or efficiency to the Christ-event.[267] At the same time the act of Christ in the sacrament does not add itself to ours so as to perfect it, thereby endowing it with some efficacy to claim for itself. 'The radical significance of Christ's substitutionary Priesthood', he insists, 'does not lie in the fact that His perfect Self-offering perfects and completes our imperfect offerings.'[268] God will never reckon or remake *man's* offering in the Eucharist as anything more or less than simply that, viz. man's offering. In short, Torrance will no more entertain 'transactionation' than he will transubstantiation.[269]

---

and rising with Christ in faith and life, and by the worship of self-presentation to God' (*RP*, 17).

[264] *SOF*, XXXVIII.

[265] *GT*, 7.

[266] *Inter*, 329; cf. *RP*, 31, 37. At the same time, however, he rejects the sacramentarians' view that the sacrament comprises merely 'a recollection of the historical passion of Christ' (*GT*, 7). Torrance's understanding of the way the corporate humanity of the Church is united to the humanity of Christ in the Spirit disallows any thought of a substantial identification of the two and a consequent 'prolonging of the vicarious and atoning work of Christ' through the life and work of the Church (Mary Barbara Agnew, *The Concept of Sacrifice*, 221).

[267] *MOC*, 100.

[268] *RP*, 14.

[269] In our chapter on the objective christological ground of the sacrament we stressed that, corresponding to the predominant relation he maintains with his own humanity, 'the Word exercises supreme authority... in the sacraments' (*RP*, 101). This anticipates the ascendency of his priestly role in the Eucharist. He says, 'it is only on the basis of the divine act... that the priestly work of Christ has its proper place' (*SOF*, XCI). The Word is present in the sacrament as one who mediates himself through his own humanity. The fact that in the Mass the unique nature and place of Christ's priesthood is not upheld, even thought to be shared with the Church, is, in Torrance's view, not only a weakness of Roman sacramental theology, but also of its christology. As he puts it, 'a mutilated humanity in Christ could not but result in a mutilated Christian worship of God' (*R/n*, 150).

It is the confusion of priestly roles within the theology of the Mass that is most intolerable to Torrance. The sacrifice of Christ is not 'of the same genus' as that of the Church, because 'the identity between the Offerer and the Offering' in Christ and then Christ's identity with God 'makes Christ's sacrifice absolutely unique'.[270] For the Church to usurp for its own 'priesthood' that which belongs exclusively to him is equivalent to severing Christ from himself, since mediation is not merely a function of Christ but a personal attribute corresponding to the unity of his being and act.[271] It is the nature and the duty of sacraments, he insists, to represent 'the indivisible oneness of Christ's Word and Act and Person as Mediator between God and man'. This is accomplished, as we shall see, when the Church's sacramental theology gives way to the Incarnate Word's sole mediatorial authority.[272]

Torrance points out that when the Incarnate Word's supreme priestly role is lost in sacramental theology, 'the Church inevitably begins to obtrude inherent causality upon its sacraments'.[273] They are presumed to have a source of energy in themselves, their own movement, even operating in a causal relationship upon God. While this might appear to honour the sacrament, in reality it has the opposite effect, distancing Christ and his real agency from the Church and its sacrament. The attribution of real and propitiatory causality to the Church's eucharistic sacrifice, personified in the power of its priesthood, led naturally to the idea that in the sacrament '*something is done to Christ...*, even to the notion of a sacramental re-enacting of [his] immolation'.[274] Alternatively, Torrance insists that we meet Christ in the Eucharist, not because the sacrament mediates him to us, not even on the basis of the unique kind of sacramental 'mediation' which Christ effects through it, but solely by his will and act to make the sacrament his meeting place with man.

This makes the point again that the whole sacrament, including its eucharistic sacrifice, depends upon the real presence of the Great

---

[270] *Inter*, 330.

[271] It is equivalent to 'detaching... the Offering from the Offerer', Torrance says (*GT*, 10).

[272] *MOC*, 100.

[273] Cf. *RP*, 77, fn. 1; *GT*, 9.

[274] *GT*, 9. Jungmann traces this notion to Thomas Aquinas, pointing out that in scholastic sacramental theology 'The holy sacrifice comes about if "something is done" to the object offered up' (J.A. Jungmann, *The Mass. An Historical, Theological, and Pastoral Survey*, ed. Mary Ellen Evans (Collegeville, MN, The Liturgical Press, 1976), 75).

High Priest. The Eucharist does not give us his presence, his presence gives us the Eucharist. The presence given in the Eucharist is that of Christ who gives himself. The sacrament does not proceed 'with a movement of impetratory ascent leading to the descent of Christ in the real presence'.[275] Furthermore, Christ does not make himself present there only to be offered up by the Church to God. That would make the Church the Master of his presence.[276] The divine presence in the Eucharist will not be manipulated; it cannot be managed. The Church does not act upon her Lord; he acts upon her.[277] In the Church, Torrance insists, 'it is just because He does not come under our control that He remains our Saviour'.[278] The fact that the sacrament of the word made flesh enshrines the real presence of Jesus Christ, ensures that it stands above the institutional continuity of the Church and can never be made relative to it.[279] Christ the High Priest is present and presiding at every Eucharist; his priesthood is inimitable and non-transferable: '*sacerdotium Christi non est in genere*'.[280]

Torrance thus retains the language of 'sacrifice' in his eucharistic theology, but he will not ascribe to it any nuance of human initiative. We do not make sacrifice in the Eucharist, rather we meet in the presence of the One Sacrificed. As we will see more clearly later, it is finally this presence of Christ within the Church's sacramental action, with his offering in him, that allows Torrance to deem the latter a 'sacrifice in itself'. Such a retention of cultic idiom in his eucharistic theology must always be understood in the light of his radical redefinition of the concept – a redefinition which negates all Pelagian overtones and underlines the primacy of Christ's priesthood. Torrance would certainly agree with Sr Mary Agnew's

---

[275] *GT*, 7.

[276] *RP*, 101.

[277] Indeed, Torrance has said that even in the sacrificial system of ancient Israel 'God is not acted upon by means of priestly sacrifice. Priestly action rests upon God's Self-revelation in His Word and answers as cultic sign and action to the thing signified' (*RP*, 3).

[278] *SOF*, CV. Pope John Paul II in his Apostolic Letter, *The Mystery and Worship of the Holy Eucharist*, presents the antithesis to Torrance's thought: 'Over and above our commitment to the evangelical mission, our greatest commitment consists in exercising this mysterious power over the Body of the Redeemer' (23).

[279] *RP*, 101.

[280] Ibid. 36. 'As High Priest of our souls Jesus Christ presides through the Spirit in all our liturgical acts in his name' (*R/n*, 184). 'The Risen Lord Himself is the true Celebrant' (*Inter*, 327).

summation of his notion of sacrifice: 'Man, apart from God's act, has no means of reaching God and if sacrifice seems to give him that power it can be allowed no role in Christian Worship.'[281] All this being said, however, the way Torrance persists in ascribing the title 'sacrifice' to the Church's sacramental rite, without ascribing to the term itself its usual meaning, is one of the most intriguing anomalies of his eucharistic theology.

4. The Church's Sacrifice – Offered and Anticipated in Christ's Sacrifice

What the full implications of Christ's high priestly presence are for the Church's worship cannot be comprehended without another, yet deeper, look into what Torrance calls Christ's 'vicarious human response'. When he says that Christ has taken upon himself total accountability for every aspect of man's relation to God, he is not excluding its doxological dimension. As we have already noted, Torrance perceives worship as an essential part of Christ's saving work.[282] Not only has Christ brought to God's judgement of grace a sacrifice in his obedient life worthy of God, but one suited to God in praise. Not only has he taken upon himself that task in its entirety, but he has brought it ultimately to completion in heaven.

Before the worship of God can be properly performed in the Church, it must be rightly understood as already offered in the completed reciprocity or, as Torrance puts it, in the 'fulfilled liturgy' of Christ's rational service between God and man. In the unity of his divine–human person God's 'Word of Truth and Grace is enacted' and interpreted to man in terms of his created rationality. This is what Torrance calls the 'liturgy of word'. Likewise Christ performs the liturgy of man's answer to God's Word, that is, he brings to God in his own human rationality man's offering of 'filial obedience, faith, trust, love, *worship, prayer* and *praise*'. This is the 'liturgy of... Oblation'.[283] Christ is 'himself... the Word of God come down into our midst, and himself the perfect response of man to that Word in his obedient self-offering in life and death'.[284] Torrance sets out just how conclusive he understands this to be:

---

[281] Mary Barbara Agnew, *The Concept of Sacrifice*, 210.
[282] 'New College', 27.
[283] *RP*, 12–13; *STR*, 115, italics mine.
[284] *STR*, 114.

> As High Priest in our humanity, [Christ] has done for us what we could not do. He has once for all offered to God our obedience, our response, our witness, our amen. He became our brother man and He offered on our behalf a human obedience, a human response, a human witness, and a human amen so that in him our human answer to God in life, worship and prayer is already completed.[285]

As this implies, the 'response' brought to God for man was not made in detachment from man. It was not God's will that simply a response *per se* should be brought, but that man himself come to God responding to his love.[286] To this end the Word in his humanity brings to God not just man's bare created proportion but man himself in every vital dimension of his human personality – thinking, willing, praying man. The response which Christ makes is not so many isolated deeds, or even prayers, but 'his whole life... formed into worship'. Christ has brought to God that acceptable worship-response out of a pure mind in an unsullied offering of his life. This is the sacrifice which God has provided for man, one prepared in the unity of Christ's person and prayer.[287]

However, before this true, noetic response could be made to God for us the capability for its offering had to be created within us, or within the human rationality of Christ. Hence, as we have seen, the worship of the Incarnate Son belongs not only to the content but to the very process for the formation of that human response. Taking this into account, the actual ascension of Christ and its attendant worship means both that Christ's historical response in life and death has been received and that the mind of man has been re-conditioned and, consequently, his rational worship 'accepted and honoured' by the Father.[288] The unending worship of Christ in heaven represents God's completion of his substitutionary work and the realisation of his covenant will for eternal relationship with man. So it is that the vicarious worship of Christ, as Torrance says, 'fulfilled in the flesh throughout [his life]' has now been 'fulfilled in his heavenly mode in his heavenly priesthood'.[289]

By virtue of Christ's ontological/substitutionary relation with us the Church already participates implicitly in Christ's heavenly worship. Torrance illustrates this by pointing to our solidarity with

---

[285] *RP*, 14.
[286] Ibid. 14.
[287] *R/n*, 210–11.
[288] *STR*, 120.
[289] *R/n*, 113.

Christ in his ascension: 'It is the ascension of representative Man in whom all humanity is gathered up and made participant in his self-offering'.[290] It is on the basis of this vicarious participation that the Church's worship shares experientially in Christ's worship. However, what Torrance envisages is not simply a fellowship of two independent worshipping entities. For Christ's offering of himself, both in his historical life and now before the Father in heaven, fully anticipates man's offering. He says this explicitly: 'All our responses, physical and spiritual, are upheld by Christ from within our existence and are enfolded in His one all-embracing response to the Father on our behalf.'[291] What the Church awaits then is not so much the creation within us of our own response as such, that is, as something distinct from the vicarious response of Christ but rather the 'unfolding' of a response from within us already 'enfolded' in Christ's 'all-embracing' response. Torrance confirms this, saying

> As substitute as well as representative he acts in our place and offers worship and prayer which we could not offer, yet offers them in such a vicarious way that while in our stead and on our behalf they are made to issue out of our human nature (in this context, that human nature proper to his own person) to the Father as our own worship and prayer to God.[292]

We will see presently how Torrance works this out in his theology of worship. This is in fact the kind of thinking which lies behind his statement: '[Christ] makes himself the true content and sole reality of the worship and prayer of man'.[293] Christ not only supplies the reality of our devotion but antecedently constitutes that worship in himself. The Church's prayer discovers itself in the prayer of Christ.

5. The Church's Sacrifice – Framed in Doxology and Enacted as Proclamation

The exhaustiveness of Christ's worship is determinative in Torrance's discussion of the Church's sacramental offering. When he says 'the *eucharistic* sacrifice [is] entirely analogous in character to the *substitutionary* act of Christ' he means that the 'all-embracing' character of Christ's work requires that the worship within the New

---

[290] STR, 112.
[291] G & R, 161.
[292] STR, 116–17.
[293] Ibid. 116.

Covenant be 'essentially eucharistic'.[294] Christ's incomparable sacrifice 'invokes from us a corresponding sacrifice of thanksgiving'.[295] This is the 'only mode appropriate to such a substitutionary offering'.[296]

Torrance goes so far as to say that the Church's offering is 'nothing but a sacrifice of praise'.[297] This is not to imply, however, that it is purely and simply praise; that would not be enough. How could the Church offer 'only a sacrifice of praise' and at the same time 'propitiate God' by setting Christ before him? Torrance mitigates this apparent contradiction, suggesting that 'we offer Christ eucharistically'.[298] Those statements of his which suggest that the Eucharist is exclusively 'a thank offering' qualify that aspect and disposition of the sacramental action which is properly ours, while those that point to an expiatory element qualify that aspect which is uniquely Christ's. It is Christ's unique sacrifice, not some supposed sacrifice equated with the Church's sacrament, that is at the heart of Torrance's eucharistic theology. As for the Church's sacrifice, all is to be understood 'in terms of the finished work of Christ', that is, as arising out of and referring back to that.[299] It is the fact that the Church's worship has been accepted and brought to completion in Christ which sets us 'free to worship God in true fear and love'.[300] For this kind of worship does not grow out of anxiety over the inadequacy of our own response to God, rather it issues out of an unassuming awe at the extent to which God has gone to bring us to himself. The worship of the Church which honours God is that which 'rests in his [Christ's] vicarious prayer'.[301] This kind of worship does not entail having to look 'over our shoulders to see if our response is good enough'.[302] The Church's worship is thus 'disinterested' – that is, it is not preoccupied with making itself 'worthy', but altogether intent upon the objective glory of God. Its 'whole centre of gravity',

---

[294] *Inter*, 330, italics mine; *RP*, 12, 14.

[295] *Inter*, 330-31; *C & A* II, 144-5.

[296] *RP*, 14.

[297] *C & A* II, 149.

[298] *R/n*, 118. What the Church offers it frames in praise. He says 'only on the basis of thanksgiving for what Christ has already done for us in his finished work can we really and fully speak about our living and active faith in Christ' (*SOF*, CIX).

[299] *RP*, 19; *R/n*, 110, 109.

[300] *RP*, 19.

[301] *MOC*, 98; *RP*, 19.

[302] *G & R*, 159.

Torrance says, is no longer in itself but in Christ.³⁰³ Consequently the prevailing frame of mind in the Christian life is, broadly speaking, 'eucharistic', with its praise focused and consummated in *the* Eucharist itself. When Torrance says 'the divine self-commitment invites us to approach him on the grounds of love' (his eternal love for us, not our meagre love for him), the Holy Eucharist comprises that active, doxological response of the Church which answers God's invitation.³⁰⁴

If doxology is the disposition in which the Church's offering is framed, it is actually made or enacted as 'proclamation'.³⁰⁵ 'It is', as Torrance puts it, 'not the actual and literal offering of the sacrifice, but an action proclaiming a sacrifice once offered', in effect an action proclaiming another action.³⁰⁶ He equates the Church's sacrifice with its *anamnesis*, its act of eucharistic memorial. He envisages this to be, as we have suggested, as much a declaration of the Christ-event as a recollection of it.³⁰⁷ The eucharistic *anamnesis* proclaims the whole offering of Christ, not only that made in his earthly life and death, but that which now endures in his eternal life with God. It is in its proclamation of the self-oblation of the ascended Christ, the fulfilment and acceptance of his high priestly liturgy, that the Church's Eucharist witnesses to the ultimate truth of its own offering, viz. that every gift of love and worship which it might conceive has been fabricated, indeed already offered within the self-offering of Christ.³⁰⁸ The Eucharist is at its heart a recitation of the

---

³⁰³ Cf. *Inter*, 331.

³⁰⁴ *MOC*, 95.

³⁰⁵ I am indebted to Sister Mary Agnew for this notion of 'Proclamation as Sacrifice', as it is the title of a chapter addressing Torrance's eucharistic theology in her thesis *The Concept of Sacrifice* (194ff.). She says, 'Torrance thus concludes that when we see the Eucharist as proclamation we see that it cannot be a sacrifice in itself; it is an action proclaiming a sacrifice' (Agnew, *The Concept of Sacrifice*, 237).

³⁰⁶ *Inter*, 328.

³⁰⁷ Torrance only once refers to Jeremias' peculiar eschatological understanding of *anamnesis*, viz., that the subject who 'remembers' is not the Church but God, that the Eucharist is an appeal to God actively to 'remember' his Church in the fulfilment of his promise and her longing 'by the *Parousia*'. It was in this vein, Torrance suggests, that 'the early Church prayed at the Eucharist: "Remember, Lord, thy Church"' (*Inter*, 325. He cites *Did*. 10:5). Torrance therefore neither concurs with nor denies Jeremias' view (*Inter*, 325. Torrance cites J. Jeremias, 'The Last Supper', *JTS* Jan–April (1949), 9).

³⁰⁸ For all his insistence that we in our Eucharist should 'dedicate ourselves, soul and body, to be a holy temple to the Lord... [Christ being] the altar on which we lay our gifts', he cautions against any idea that the sacrament's

gospel, a means by which the Church 'continually represents to itself... the atoning sacrifice of Christ', but not only to itself, ultimately also to God.[309]

The Eucharist has no evangelical substance or strength for Torrance apart from its association with God's speaking his own word. 'Through the Spirit', he says, 'the proclaiming activity of the living Lord stands behind the Church's proclamation'.[310] When he suggests that the sacrament is best understood 'under the rubric of proclamation' he means that it fulfils its mission as part of God's witness to himself, that is, demonstrating God's Word as *action*. In the Eucharist God speaks his word of reconciliation and communion in Christ, then acts within the context of the sacrament to bring that word to personal fulfilment within his Church. This act of God which the Church proclaims and anticipates in the sacrament it also heeds and answers there in its own response as *action*. Torrance puts it: 'This Word proclaimed as divine event becomes event... and [thus] is fulfilled as Word in the sacramental ordinances given by Christ for this very purpose.'[311] There is thus no clear distinction between the Church's act of proclamation and its act of response, for its response is in itself a proclamation of the nature of God's Word. The word which the Church hears God speak in the Eucharist is restated and redirected towards him in its act of communion.[312] In effect what Torrance has done at this point is once again to remove the initiative from the Church in relation to its Creator. Consistent with all other aspects of its knowing relation with God, which he says arises in answer to the questions which God's word poses, the sacramental relation unfolds as itself an 'answering', a personal returning to God in praise of his own word of grace.

Thus it is that we in our eucharistic *anamnesis* 'turn our proclamation of Christ's death upwards to God'.[313] This is ultimately what it means for the Church to make sacrifice. She does not

---

emphasis might be upon the 'bringing of our offerings to the Eucharist... the fruit of our labour as represented by the bread and wine' (*C & A* II, 183, cf. 149). Obviously the formal Offertory of the liturgy retains little significance for Torrance, disregarded for its irrelevance before the comprehensive and primary gift of Christ himself (cf. Chapter 5, section G below).

[309] *Inter*, 328; cf. *MOC*, 97.
[310] *Inter*, 328.
[311] *RP*, 76.
[312] J.D. Crichton makes the point that 'Word and sacrament are inseparably united [in that] man's worship is his embodied response to God' ('A Theology of Worship', 3-29, esp. 11).
[313] *Inter*, 330-31.

propitiate God herself, rather in praise she proclaims and thereby offers Christ's sacrifice which does. In order for the Church to offer herself to God she must offer him who offers her in himself.[314] 'We can only offer what has already been offered on our behalf'. Therefore, 'we... draw near to worship the Father with no other oblation than that of Christ himself'.[315] It is this kind of offering, this kind of worship, which our eucharistic act enshrines as proclamation. In its sacramental act the Church at once extols his sacrifice and declares it as its own. It is in this 'derivative way', Torrance asserts, that the offering of Christ 'becomes our offering'.[316] We will further expand the implications of this kind of thinking presently under our discussion of 'eschatological substitution'.

The highest duty of our worship then is to reckon Christ's worship as all sufficient. Therefore, the doxological, proclamatory act embodied in the Eucharist comprising this acknowledgement constitutes the central event of the Church's devotion. It is with this in mind that Torrance sees the sacrament as *the* service of worship. However, this is only part of the reason. The Eucharist is the paragon of the Church's worship, not finally because of anything man does in it, but because Christ has promised himself to it and, in himself, communion with his Father. The sacrament is the formal, appointed way and place of worship for the Church because of Christ's presence there. Hence, all other worship experiences in the Church must return to this one, all others be ordered to it. The true worship of God, Torrance insists, quoting John McLeod Campbell, transpires 'within the circle of [Christ's] life'. Torrance himself says that 'we... worship, adore and serve God within... Jesus Christ'.[317] The Eucharist therefore affords the Church the true worship of God inasmuch as it facilitates our being brought within that 'circle'. The economy of this is our next topic.

---

[314] 'In that which she [the Church] offers, she herself is offered' (cf. Augustine, *City of God* (Harmondsworth, Penguin, 1972), 10, 6, 380).

[315] *RP*, 14; *R/n*, 212.

[316] *Inter*, 331.

[317] *R/n*, 109, 209, 211. *GT*, 7. Jungmann says, '"ἐν χριστῷ" always marks off... the area in which the salvific plans of God operate' (Jungmann, *The Place of Christ*, 137).

6. The Vital Participation of the Eucharistic Sacrifice of the Church in the Self-Oblation of the Ascended Christ

It should not be thought that the Church only relates to the worshipping, ascended Christ through praise and proclamation as to one 'afar off'. Our eucharistic *anamnesis* is not enacted in isolation from its heavenly subject. Indeed, Torrance warns against 'a Platonic dualism between the heavenly and the earthly' which renders the eucharistic sacrifice only a 'symbolic and spiritual pointing to heavenly realities beyond' or to historical realities sequestered in the past.[318] The memorial which we make, Torrance insists, is 'filled with the real presence of the crucified, risen and glorified Lord'.[319]

In the first part of this chapter it was shown how everything of divine significance which happens in the Eucharist does so because of Christ's presence there. What provides the basis for the sacrament's operation is not Christ's presence in the sacramental relation *per se*, but rather the formal ground of the christological relation. The resolution of any contradiction between these two ideas lies in the fact that the risen Christ, embodying that divine–human relation, is present in the Eucharist. It is Christ, Torrance says, who 'carries in Himself the vicarious actuality and conveys in himself the active possibility of true and faithful response on the part of all men to God's Word'.[320] This is a fact which precedes and transcends any sacramental manifestation but is also that which underpins the reality of the sacrament. Christ in his real presence thus brings the sacrament's formal ground into the immediate ground of the Church's celebration.

It is the ascended Christ's own worship of the Father which is the particular aspect of the christological objectivity responsible for conditioning the content and efficacy of the Church's sacrifice. Torrance says explicitly that this *kerygmatic* and 'eucharistic *anamnesis* is... to be understood in the same dimension of depth as the whole mystery of the Eucharist, in which Jesus Christ constitutes himself in his paschal mystery its objective reality'.[321] Just as the incarnate Christ's removal of all noetic and ontological distance between the Holy God and his people determines the operation of the real presence in the sacrament, so the ascended Christ's fulfilment of

---

[318] *R/n*, 129.
[319] *GT*, 7.
[320] *G & R*, 138.
[321] *GT*, 8.

all mediation between man and his God orders the Church's eucharistic sacrifice.

This worshipping relation which the ascended one upholds between God and man, however, should never be conceived as a kind of 'static fixture' in heaven. For inasmuch as that relation is integral to the person of the risen and present Christ it remains a working, mediating factor. Torrance says, 'Christ's priestly sacrifice and oblation of himself are [not] over and done but rather... in their once and for all completeness they are taken up eternally into the life of God and remain prevalent, efficacious, valid or abidingly real.'[322] Thus the 'fulfilled liturgy' of Christ, understood from this transcendent perspective, is made the presiding principle over the Church's worship from its heavenly as well as its historical fulfilment.

> Jesus Christ constitutes in his own self-consecrated humanity the fulfilment of the vicarious way of human response to God provided under the old covenant, but now on the ground of his atoning self-sacrifice once for all offered this is a vicarious way of response which is available for all mankind.[323]

The remainder of this chapter will delineate just how Torrance sees Christ's vicarious response as an active means by which our response is made to God, how our response is made to correspond in its own way to the vicarious character of his response.

In the first place Torrance insists that Christ's substitutionary response in union with us requires the Church's response in union with him as its corollary.[324] Torrance states,

---

[322] *STR*, 114–15.

[323] *MOC*, 86. The acceptance of Christ's perfect oblation for us by God in eternity removes it forever from 'out of the sphere of mere cult or liturgical action' (*RP*, 13). It attests its uniquely divine character, that as it was not the work of man it can never be subject to him. This demonstrates once again how Torrance repeatedly enlists the doctrine of the ascension to distance the christological reality, in this case Christ's sacrifice, from man's control. In the ascension of Christ, all cultic designs within the Church's sacrifice are rendered superfluous. The uniqueness of the 'fulfilled liturgy' determines the nature of the Church's liturgical action as 'only witness to concrete reality' (*RP*, 13).

[324] Christ's work is, as Alasdair Heron says, 'vicarious but also inclusive, substitutionary but also incorporating' (Heron, *Table and Tradition*, 169). It is not contradictory, therefore, that we should personally be included in Christ's sacrificial act since his vicarious relation to us within that act is itself a personal relation, already inclusive of our humanity. Indeed, that relation invites us to share experientially in it. Torrance says, 'In order to fulfil its end in restoring

The union of Jesus Christ with us in body and blood by virtue of which he became our Priest and Mediator before God demands as its complement our union with him in his body and blood, in drawing near to God and offering him our worship with, in, and through Christ, while his continuous living presentation of us before the Father... calls for our continuous living communion with him.[325]

This correlative union of the Church with Christ (and her response within that union) is not realized in the Church simply by the compelling fact of its objective heavenly counterpart, nor purely on the authority of Christ's mandate to 'do this'. It is the presence of the Great High Priest himself in our midst who enables that response. It is he who designates its manifest form in the sacrament and then joins himself to it. In this way the Eucharist incorporates the true worship of God, for to be joined to Christ is to be joined to him in his worship of the Father.

As might be anticipated, the economy of this involves the work of the Holy Spirit, hence the *epiclesis* in the liturgy. In our chapter on the objective christological ground of the sacramental relation we spoke of the Spirit as the one who brings into experiential reality the communion of the people of God in Christ. However, it would be incorrect to impose upon the Eucharist a view of the Church's invocation of the Spirit which would suggest a precipitating of the divine action. Torrance disowns any impetratory element within the sacrament, whether it be the presumptuous ascent of the Church's prayer to heaven so as to retrieve Christ's presence, or the more subtle assumption that the Church's prayer somehow dispatches the Spirit. The whole attitude of the Church's sacrament is one of reception, not of initiation.[326] His view of the *epiclesis* in the

---

human beings to proper sonship in the image of God, it has to be translated into terms of human life and activity. Hence the Son of God... so shared our human being and life from birth to death that what he accomplished in us and for us he accomplished as issuing forth from our human being and life as our own act toward God, consecrating himself for us that we might be consecrated through him, offering himself in holy obedience and atoning sacrifice to God for us that we, through sharing in his self-offering, may offer to God through him a holiness from the side of man answering his own' (*R/n*, 117; cf. *STR*, 117).

[325] *R/n*, 111.

[326] Cf. *GT*, 7. Torrance would concur with Dom O. Casel's statement: 'The only thing that was in the power of the Church was to initiate the celebration of the rite' (Crichton cites Casel, *The Mystery of Christian Worship* in 'A Theology of Worship', 15). Torrance says this also in so many words: 'The broken bread and poured-out wine... Christ Himself *puts into our hands*' (*C & A* II, 148, italics

Eucharist is consistent with this. The household of faith 'appropriates' the act of God in its midst, it does not bring it about. 'The presence of the living Lord in the Church', he says, is 'the living action appropriated by the Church'.[327] The Spirit's presence in the liturgical celebration, however, is not to be perceived simply in terms of the *epiclesis*, as if he joins the sacramental act only at a certain point. 'The liturgy is always celebrated in the power of the Holy Spirit.'[328] In its appeal to the Spirit, the Church acknowledges the spiritual economy of its prayer. Torrance states that

> All things take place in and through the Spirit as essential bond of connection between us and the Holy Trinity, [thus] we see the immense significance of the epiclesis, not only at the Eucharist but in all liturgy, in worship of the Father through his only begotten Son Jesus Christ, whenever and wherever the faithful offer their sacrifice of praise and thanksgiving in the oneness of the Spirit.[329]

In Torrance's theology the Holy Spirit is the nexus between what is general or implicit in Christ's humanity and that which is made particular or explicit in ours. Furthermore, in the light of his profound conception of participation, delineated in the last chapter, we are able to see how Torrance perceives the Spirit's presence in the Church as that of Christ, and the 'connection' which we have with the ascended Christ as an immediate encounter in the Spirit. It is from this understanding of a sacramental presence in the Spirit that he can speak of the Word's *parousia* in the Eucharist as equivalent to the Church's effectual participation in his self-offering, for the presence of the Spirit in the Church is the presence of the ascended one in his worship.[330] 'At the Lord's Supper', he says, 'feeding upon the body and blood of Christ [the real presence] and worshipping the Father [the eucharistic sacrifice] are inseparable'.[331]

---

mine). Even the initiation of the rite Torrance would see as arising from the will of God.

[327] *Inter*, 327.

[328] Crichton, 'A Theology of Worship', 16.

[329] *R/n*, 183.

[330] *GT*, 8.

[331] *R/n*, 212. These are inseparable quite simply, as we have shown, because they are two aspects of the same thing, two sides or dispositions of the presence of Christ in the sacrament and consequently of our participation in them. That which is set towards us Torrance identifies in terms of 'Christ's union with us'; that which is set towards the Father as 'our union with him', the latter unfolding out of the former (*MOC*, 101). He continues: 'The celebration of the Lord's

It is the Holy Spirit, then, who facilitates and, by virtue of the *perichoresis* of the persons of the Trinity, constitutes our 'living communion' with Christ in the sacrament. Implicit in the Son's vicarious mediation of our response to God by the Spirit is the Spirit's mediation of our personal response to him. Worship in the Spirit thus takes the form itself of an assumption of the praying Church into Christ's vicarious human prayer. This ingathering of the Church by the Spirit has its objective ground in Christ's incorporation of all men in his ascended flesh. Indeed for Torrance the gathering action of the Spirit and Christ's high priestly 'activity from mankind towards the Father' are but a single operation.[332] Torrance says that Christ 'takes up' our eucharistic offering as the appointed expression of his own as he 'confers his own *parousia* upon it'.[333] In another place he states that Christ 'interpenetrates and gathers up all our faltering, unclean worship and prayer into himself'.[334] Either way the point is the same: It is by Christ's 'descent' in the Spirit that the Church is 'elevated' to share in his heavenly worship. For the whole heavenly reality is present in the Spirit who is in Christ who is in the Father. Christ's 'interpenetrating' our prayer and his 'taking it up' therefore are seen as two aspects of the same thing. There is no actual 'transport' of the Church's prayer as such involved. Our prayer being gathered up to Christ's heavenly prayer simply means that the Church prays in the Spirit.

What Torrance means by 'prayer in the Spirit' reveals the full implications of Christ's substitutionary work and once again the total christological orientation of everything that the Spirit effects in the Church; for the Spirit's prayer actually involves a reiteration of Christ's heavenly prayer in our own.[335] He is emphatic that the only prayer to which the Spirit can give voice is that which has its origin in Christ. This should not be thought to imply an exact *reproduction* of Christ's heavenly prayer in the Church, but he has so identified with us in his incarnation, and now in his ascension, as to 'make his prayers and worship ours'.[336] Christ's worship-response is thus quite

---

Supper means that we through the Spirit are so intimately united to Christ, by the communion in his body and blood (the real presence) that we participate in his self-consecration and self-offering to the Father made on our behalf and in our place (the eucharistic sacrifice)' (*MOC*, 101).

[332] *R/n*, 117.
[333] *GT*, 8.
[334] Cf. *Inter*, 327.
[335] Cf. Heron, *Table and Tradition*, 168.
[336] *STR*, 117; *MOC*, 99.

literally inclusive of ours, vicarious not only in the sense that it is *pro nobis* but, more importantly, in the sense that in its own act it embodies the very act of our response. This explains his suggestion above that the Spirit's mediation of the Church's response to God is implied in Christ's vicarious response to the Church. In fact, the reality of the Church's response already exists in Christ's prayer. His relation to us is, he says, 'so profound that through the Spirit [his] prayer and intercession are made to echo in our own'.[337] Consequently,

> Even as act of the Church the Eucharist is not to be regarded as an independent act on our part in response to what God has already done for us in Christ, but as act towards the Father already fulfilled in the humanity of Christ in our place and on our behalf, to which our acts in His name are... identified through the Spirit.[338]

Properly speaking, then, our prayer is not 'something apart from', 'something other' or 'something more' than the prayer of Christ, but a further, extended expression of his prayer created and brought forth from within us by the Spirit. Prayer in the Spirit can best be understood as Christ's own human response forming itself in us. Therefore, Torrance can boldly state that 'in the strictest sense Jesus Christ is himself the prayer and praise and worship with which we appear before God'.[339]

---

[337] *STR*, 117.

[338] *R/n*, 109.

[339] 'New College', 27; cf. *R/n*, 109. John McLeod Campbell, whom Torrance cites repeatedly in these matters, puts it: 'Thus is Christ, who, through the Eternal Spirit, offered Himself without spot to God, and was accepted as the one and sufficient sacrifice for sin, presented anew in all prayers of Christians, in so far as these are a participation in the spirit of Christ – a form of the life of Christ in them' (Campbell, *Christ The Bread of Life*, 51-2).

It must be stressed that for Torrance the prayer of Christ for man is not constituted in specific utterances or acts of prayer, but in his own identity as man before the Father. This corresponds of course to the unity of Christ's word and being. This is 'prayer... identical with the personal self-offering and self-oblation of Jesus Christ to the Father on our behalf', 'prayer identical with his life as incarnate Son' (*R/n*, 212). He says Christ 'stands in our place where we cry in prayer to God and makes himself our prayer, a prayer not in word or even in act *only* but a prayer which he is in his own personal Being' (*MOC*, 97, italics mine). The substance and strength of his prayer is not in its specificity or correctness, that is, not in the fact that Christ prays exactly the right thing or the right way (though he does that), but in the appeal of his perfect life before the Father in which he maintains the relation between reconciled man and God. We

It is within this kind of framework that Torrance contends that the meaning of the eucharistic sacrifice is our participation through the Spirit in Christ's self-consecration and self-offering to the Father in worship. This is the way it appears from the side of the Church. However, from God's perspective it is seen as that self-consecration of Christ participating in our worship through the Spirit and thus bringing itself to expression there. Hence, the eucharistic sacrifice is, he says,

> the self-consecration and self-offering of Jesus Christ in our nature ascending to the Father from the Church in which he dwells through the Spirit he has poured out upon it, uniting it to himself as his Body, so that when the Church worships, praises and adores the Father through Christ and celebrates the Eucharist in his name, it is Christ himself who worships, praises and adores the Father in and through his members....[340]

What we have said thus far helps to clarify Torrance's statement that as the Church makes its *anamnesis* of him, Christ blesses 'what we do on earth at his command... accepting it as his own act done in heaven'.[341] The nature of that relation, however, is a more precise identification, for the prayer which we offer in Christ's name on earth cannot formally be separated from the prayer which Christ offers in our name in heaven. So, then, what Christ accepts from us 'as his own act' is precisely that – 'his own act' – realizing its identity in our prayer through the Holy Spirit. Hence Torrance's assertion of the converse – 'what he does in our stead is nevertheless effected as our very own, issuing freely and spontaneously out of ourselves'.[342]

---

indicated earlier in this chapter that Christ's offering to God of his renewed mind, was not some isolated thought or series of thoughts but rather that mind itself, the quiddity of our human being, renewed in the knowledge of God. Likewise, we suggested that it was in the constitution of Christ's pure mind and heart, set toward the face of God, that his perpetual worship inheres, i.e. 'his whole life... formed into worship' (*R/n*, 211). Consistent with this, Torrance will speak of the Church's prayer and worship as reiterating that of Christ, not as an exact reproduction of his prayer, but as 'a form of his life' (*R/n*, 109; cf. comments by John McLeod Campbell above). Christ's life-prayer is thus said to call forth a corresponding life-prayer in us and from us. The Church's worshipping life, not just its 'eucharistic memorial' as such, is finally 'the concrete form and expression of [Christ's] own self-giving and self-offering' (*R/n*, 118).

[340] *R/n*, 134.
[341] Ibid. 109.
[342] *MOC*, 98.

A different and more metaphorical expression makes the same point: The Spirit's prayer in us is said to be 'inarticulate'.[343] In other words, 'the Holy Spirit does not speak of Himself but listens to Christ who ever lives to make intercession for us, and what He hears He *echoes* in the *anamnesis* of the Church'.[344] When Torrance speaks of the Spirit 'interceding for us' he always has in mind his ministry of forming Christ's prayer in us. *Mediatorial* intercession as such belongs only to the priestly office of the Son. This is illustrated at the heart of the liturgy 'in the Lord's prayer which we take into our mouths at his command'.[345] It is because of this primal, formative relation between Christ's prayer and the eucharistic prayer of the Church that Torrance calls the latter the 'utmost act of prayer'. The Church's 'profoundest confession of sin is made, he says, as it echoes Christ's confession of our sins before God. The 'supreme act of thanksgiving' is performed in union with Christ as we share by the Spirit in the worship of the Lamb round the Throne.[346] 'And when the Church at the Eucharist', he states, 'intercedes in his name for all mankind it is Christ himself who intercedes in them, doing in them what he has done for all mankind in his own Person'.[347] For Christ's

---

[343] Ibid. 99.

[344] *C & A* II, 176.

[345] *MOC*, 98–9; *STR*, 116–17.

[346] 'Arnoldshain', 16–17.

[347] *R/n*, 134; cf. *STR*, 116. It is by the Spirit's 'intercession' that the Church knows the mind of Christ so as to present it to the Father. We can only speak like this because the will of God is translated into human categories for us through the worshipping mind of Christ. Already it has been shown how essential the human mind of Christ is to Torrance's incarnational soteriology and, consequently, foundational to his doctrine of worship. Without the interposition of the human mind of Christ in heaven, man's prayer is lost to infinity, left alone to mediate itself. And looking at it from the other direction, except for the human mind of Christ, how can man's prayers be informed of God's will; how can we be taught to pray as we ought, except by one who has 'ranged himself among us worshippers as himself a worshipper' (*R/n*, 113). In a reference which illustrates just how interwoven the economies of epistemology and the sacraments are in his theology Torrance cites Cyril of Alexandria's reoccurring appeal to St Paul's statement in Phil. 2:5: 'Let this mind be in you which was also in Christ Jesus' for it is through sharing our human mind and sanctifying it through his vicarious self-consecration and oblation on our behalf, that *we are enabled to share with him his mind*, and be associated with him in his priestly presentation of us in and through himself to the Father' (*R/n*, 113, italics mine. Torrance gives no specific reference in Cyril's works).

Similarly John McLeod Campbell stresses how by the Holy Spirit the will of God, manifest in Christ's rational and spiritual worship, is restated through

prayer actually to take shape in our prayer in this way is the most concrete manifestation of what Torrance means by the Spirit's giving the Church participation in Christ's self-oblation.[348]

7. Divergence and Convergence of the Church's Worship with Christ's Heavenly Worship within this Participation

Discussing the participation of uncreated, heavenly realities in created, earthly ones, we contrasted in our last chapter a kind of mystical fusion of these identities, which tended to blur their distinction, with a *koinonia* of distinct identities. In this vein, with respect to the doxological aspect of this *koinonia*, Torrance emphasizes divergence as well as convergence between the prayer of Christ and that of his Church. In 'sacramental *anamnesis*', he states, these 'involve each other' but, like the christoform of Chalcedon, 'they cannot be fused or separated'.[349] There is in the sacramental

---

our prayer: 'We are *born of the will of God*, (Jn 1:13) and we, therefore, *ask things according to His will, and He heareth us* (1 Jn 5:14, 31). Thus it is the mind of Christ which we present to the Father' (Campbell, *Christ the Bread of Life*, 51, brackets mine).

It is in this way that Christ quite literally in our prayers 'makes himself the true content and sole reality of the worship and prayer of man' (cf. *R/n*, 111).

[348] The necessity for this kind of active 'intercession' between Christ and his people by the Spirit is rooted in the impotence of man to offer anything to God. Torrance says the prayer of the Church as such 'has nothing to bring... nothing to offer'. He calls it 'The prayer that knows not how to pray.' Man's prayer must thus be 'energized by the Eternal Spirit who himself makes intercession for us with groanings that cannot be uttered'. 'And what can His [the Spirit's] intercession be [?]' he asks, 'but the echoing in the Church of the intercession of the great High Priest' (*C & A* II, 176-7). The doctrine of total depravity conditions as well as clarifies how he regards man's prayer and sees him regaining the capacity to pray. The fact is that for Torrance man's 'prayer' as such does not exist by itself, since man, engaged as he is in 'active perversity' against the will of God does not initiate true prayer, but rather bargains for his own ends (cf. *R/st*, 107). That element of prayer in our Eucharist then which does truly rise up to God must of necessity *not* be originally ours but Christ's. It is put into our hearts, or, as he says, 'taken into our mouths' by Christ and never loses its formal connection with him. All Christian prayer then must necessarily be prayer in his Spirit. As we have said, implicit in Christ's vicarious prayer are all our prayers which are finally 'united' to his by the Spirit in this way, since our prayers are not properly prayers other than his, rather his prayers shared with us.

[349] *C & A* II, 176, cf. 163.

relation, he insists, 'a union between the divine action and human action, between the *actio* of Christ and the *re-actio* of the Church', but such that neither action can be identified formally or disengaged one from the other. There is no substantial *metousiosis*, no *communio consubstantialis* as in the hypostatic union. There is rather a *communio substantialis*, a *koinonia* of actions, a union of the two 'in the *koinonia* of the eternal Spirit', an 'interpenetration' of the divine act within the human act, but all in such a way that neither integrity is compromised.[350]

No matter how intertwined and concurrent these become in the sacrament, the Church's worship on earth can never for Torrance be 'a transcription of the heavenly reality, but (rather) a pointer in observable form to a higher reality'.[351] Although having human identity, in that it has its source in a human mind like ours, that which is Christ's and of divine initiative is one thing and that which is ours quite another. The formal christological reality, though manifest in the midst of our prayer, can never be said to be synonymous with it. As he says so clearly:

> The action of the Church is the *anamnesis* of an act that is once and for all, and enduring before the Face of the Heavenly Father; but it is no more than the *anamnesis* for it is *not the act itself*. It is the living echo of that act which Christ alone performs as Mediator and Saviour, 'The splintered reflection on earth of Christ's presentation of his sacrifice in heaven'.[352]

This should control our interpretation of any statement of Torrance's that apparently implies more than a *koinonia* of actions between Christ's prayer and that of the Church. The only 'formal identity' that obtains between Christ's prayer and ours belongs to the vicarious worship of his divine-humanity.

(a) A Simile of Distinction: the Echo

The simile of the 'echo' used above is the most common way Torrance refers to the relation between Christ's worship and that of his Church. While demonstrating the contingent relation between the two, it serves also to underline the innate distinction between the

---

[350] Ibid. 163, 178.

[351] *RP*, 20.

[352] *C & A* II, 176, italics his, then mine. The final quotation is a citation by Torrance from D.M. MacKinnon's *Report of the Sixth Anglo-Catholic Congress*, 134.

divine and human act.³⁵³ The echo, like the sign in Torrance's concept of analogy, depends for its content upon its referent. As a mirror depends for its reflection upon its subject, so an echo – itself 'a sound reflection' – depends for its 'voice' upon the one who produces the original sound. Since, as we have noted, created being is integrally incapable of speaking of its Creator, there can be therefore no '*natural* correspondence' between our eucharistic oblation and that of Christ. God can sound his word through his creatures but they are powerless to speak *for* him. 'The relation between God and the creation is irreversible'; the Eucharist is not the one exception.³⁵⁴ Indeed, as we noted in our definition of a sacramental relation, there can be no correspondence at all except through an immediate relation between the divine and created realities. Likewise, since the true worship of God is formed and emanates from within Christ's own humanity, the Holy Spirit must inform and relate our worship with his for it to have any divine import. The Church truly prays therefore only by the gift of the Holy Spirit. Just as God must personally erect all analogies to himself and speak himself through them in order to provide their 'word', so after appointing the sacrament as active witness to Christ in the Church, he must likewise join himself to the eucharistic action and speak, or pray, within it. Christ through the Spirit thus makes his prayer 'to echo in us. Just as there can be no echo of Christ's prayer in the prayer of the Church except by sustained relation with Christ in his self-oblation so too it must be said that Christ's prayer is not heard in the world except in association with the prayer of the Church. As God has chosen to speak his word in conjunction with the word of man so he has chosen to pray, as it were, within our meagre acts of prayer.³⁵⁵ Hence the Eucharist remains the place of Christ's prayer on earth until the end of time.

(b) A Simile of Consonance: Musical Counterpoint

Torrance walks the line between extremes, maintaining the presence of Christ's prayer within that of the Church, but without identifying the two or even saying when or where Christ's prayer might be recognized. While insisting that that which is of significance before God is not our prayer but Christ's, the fact that his prayer is only to

---

[353] Cf. *C & A* II, 181.
[354] *TS*, 67.
[355] *C & A* II, 175–6.

be found in association with ours guarantees for all time that the Church's prayer, despite its infirmity and limitation, will be upheld.

When Torrance speaks of the interrelatedness or consonance between the prayer of Christ and that of his Church he employs a musical simile, saying that these two have a contrapuntal relationship with each other. 'The Eucharist is the *Amen*, the counterpart on earth, to the eternal oblation in heaven, and the eucharistic Thanksgiving the counterpoint on earth to the New Song, "Worthy is the Lamb", of the saints in the Church triumphant.'[356] The eucharistic *anamnesis* or proclamation exists in the Church as counterpoint, he says, to its 'eternal *canto firmo*, the Self-consecration of the Mediator before the face of the Father in His intercession for the Church'.[357] Here in the objective 'life and action of the Church on earth' the Christ-event forms its own 'objective proclamation' and finds 'objective duration'.[358] Torrance stresses that the Church's sacrament is 'more than a parable; it is the actual *homoioma* of the Christ-event'. The eucharistic action of the Church is the appointed similitude (*homoioma*), the prescribed 'sacramental counterpart' on earth to that of Christ in heaven.[359] There is consonance between the two because Christ's own word and presence permeates the Church's eucharistic witness and there bears witness to himself.[360] It is because of the presence or the *totus*

---

[356] Ibid. 176.

[357] Ibid. 178.

[358] Ibid. 177. The 'objective duration' which the life of Christ finds within the life of his Church is a matter of co-existence, never an absorption of his life in ours. Torrance is emphatic: 'The Church is other than Christ' (*RP*, 46). 'While the Church is one Body with Christ it is in no sense an extension of His Personality, an extension of His Incarnation, not to speak of a reincarnation of the Risen Lord' (*RP*, 31). The actual vivifying of the Church as the Body of Christ, that which gives it its identity with the ongoing life of Christ, is his active presence within it; not anything exclusively which the Church does. Torrance puts it: 'He bodies Himself forth in the Church and makes the Church His Body, incorporates it into Himself, so that He can identify Himself with His Church on the ground of His servant-ministry on the Cross' (*RP*, 83).

[359] 'It is sacramentally and analogically derivative from [Christ's sacrifice], but as such it is analogically different' (*C & A* II, 178).

[360] *C & A* II, 180. As we noted previously, Torrance insists that 'the proclaiming activity of the living Lord stands behind the Church's proclamation'. Actually, Torrance's presuppositions regarding the nature of analogy – viz. that no created reality, least of all fallen man, has any natural capacity to speak for or about its creator – requires that God makes his own word to sound forth in the eucharistic act of the Church in order for it to make a conclusive reference to him, i.e. *that God form his own witness to himself there*.

Christus in the sacrament, present as it were in his self-oblation before the Father in heaven, that our Eucharist 'partakes of sacramental character'.[361] 'The Church in its eucharistic liturgy does not participate in the sacrifice', i.e. it has no part in the actual material content or offering of the sacrifice.[362] Nevertheless, because of the sustained relation of the christological *canto firmo* with its ecclesiological counterpoint, because of the strength and ingenuity of the former in relation to the latter, supplying as it does the dominant and integrative theme, these two are brought into some semblance of harmony.

In another context Torrance speaks of God's breaking in upon man's life as an intersection of 'a symmetry on a lower level by a symmetry on a higher level'. The notion of 'symmetry' on our level, however, he insists is an illusion. Therefore, God 'breaks into the *apparent* symmetries of our life with all their harsh dissonance' and, like the *canto firmo* in intentional association with its counterpoint, shatters these symmetries while at the same time 'takes them up' with all the dissonance which appears to remain. He thereby calls them into such contrapuntal relation with himself that they are 'given a harmony beyond what they are capable of in themselves at their level alone'. He thus 'redeems and transforms them in a profound re-ordering of the whole' in which the earthly counterpoint 'is made to serve another pattern of musical events'.[363]

In a discussion of 'the closest relation between the eucharistic worship of the Church on earth and the eternal intercession of Christ at the right hand of God' Torrance employs this same kind of imagery, but exchanges the more complex musical simile for a less complicated one. He explains how the 'ineffable New Song of Heaven keeps breaking in and opening up the ordered liturgical forms of earth'. The very presence of that new song in our midst brings to judgement our earthly liturgies, 'no matter how beautiful and adequate we may make them', revealing them for what they really are, 'fragmentary... and essentially imperfect'. However, God's judgement upon our earthly song is not the final word, for the presence of 'the liturgy of heaven' among the liturgies of the world continually renews the earthly counterparts, 'making them point above and beyond themselves', while at the same time equipping them to echo more adequately that heavenly prayer of Christ.[364]

---

[361] Ibid. 179.
[362] *RP*, 95–6.
[363] Cf. *G & G*, 134–5.
[364] *RP*, 95–6.

In the sacramental relation Christ does not discard the Church's prayer, but seeks to cleanse it, refine it and enrich it in association with his own.[365] The christological *canto firmo* with its sacramental counterpoint comprise the 'reordered whole' mentioned above. This is an ensemble which is 'wholly Christ's but wholly ours' as well.[366] Just as in a mature musical composition one cannot, without destroying the whole piece, extract the *canto firmo* from the counterpoint written as its complement, so the prayer of Christ cannot be disentangled from its sacramental context, at least not in this world.[367] Neither can there be nor should there be an attempt on this side to separate that which in our prayer has its origin and inspiration in the Spirit from 'our weak and stammering and altogether unworthy acts of devotion'.[368] Indeed in the world the latter is always the frame for the former. The 'Christian liturgy holds the new wine in old wineskins'.[369] In the same way that the *signum* cannot be divided from *Res*, or the *kerygma* from the living Word, so the prayer of the Church cannot be separated from the prevailing prayer of Christ. 'These may be distinguished from each other in thought, but are actually inseparable.'[370] In Torrance's thought there are not discernible parts, words or phrases in our liturgy which can be definitively ascribed to Christ.[371] He says in fact that 'through the Spirit the heavenly intercession of Christ is echoed *unutterably* in the stammering intercession of the Church on earth' – and he reiterates 'unutterably'.[372] 'It is impossible to score that New Song', he says. Christ's prayer is unutterable not only because the mystery involved is too great to be expressed but also because our capacity to receive and enunciate such exalted things is gravely limited by our sin. The Church's prayer is always mitigated by our worldly place and weighted down by the flesh. The heavenly prayer of Christ is never in such harmony with our own that it can actually be heard, except in

---

[365] Cf. 'New College', 27.
[366] *MOC*, 90.
[367] *STR*, 117.
[368] Ibid. 117.
[369] *RP*, 96.
[370] *Inter*, 309.
[371] Torrance thus guards against any thought that the intercession of the Church actually itself constitutes Christ's intercession. He says, 'To think that his intercession is always made through the prayers of the liturgy is rank blasphemy and folly. For even if it is true that Christ performs the sacrifice, we cannot attribute everything that is said and done through the liturgy to him' (*R/n*, 194).
[372] *RP*, 95, italics mine.

'broken snatches'.[373] Nevertheless, as the High Priest of heaven descends to his Church, assuming the Church's worship to his own, arranging and sanctifying its prayers in harmony with his, there is heard in the midst of the Church's prayer 'the living echo' of the prayer of Christ.[374] While 'our prayers are in no sense transcriptions in the language of earth of the heavenly liturgy around the throne of God, nevertheless, they are related to that inexpressible mystery in the Spirit'.[375]

8. The Assimilation or Final Identification of the Sacrifice of the Church in the Sacrifice of Christ

For Torrance the 'disentangling' of Christ's doxological activity from ours is possible only within his high-priestly mediation.[376] Christ comes, Torrance says, 'through his union and communion with us taking up and sanctifying our prayer in himself, *assimilating* them into his vicarious prayer, and presenting us in and through his own self-offering to the Father, which he makes on behalf of all humanity'.[377] When he says that Christ 'assimilates' our prayer into his he is suggesting more than that our prayers are simply conjoined with his. This is their final perfection by virtue of their identity with his prayer in heaven. Although the earthly and heavenly dimensions of Christ's *koinonia* with our prayer clearly transpire simultaneously, the assimilation of our prayer to his belongs exclusively to the unobserved side. He says,

> It is as our High Priest, with all His human conditions in body, mind and soul which He took from us, with His human worship and prayer into which He assimilates our worship and prayer in His name, that He appears in the presence of His Father and fulfils His heavenly worship.[378]

It should be recalled that everything the Church ought to pray, indeed, everything it does *truly* pray by the inspiration of the Spirit exists already in the prayer of Christ. With this in mind Torrance speaks of Christ the High Priest 'associating us with himself in

---

[373] Ibid. 96.
[374] *C & A* II, 176; 'New College', 27.
[375] *RP*, 95.
[376] *STR*, 117.
[377] 'New College', 27, italics mine.
[378] *R/n*, 114.

assimilating our prayers to his which has already ascended to the Father and continues to avail for us in his presence'.[379]

Precisely what Torrance means by the assimilation of the Church's prayer to Christ's is not easily established. His uses of the word 'assimilation' in other contexts conform to both meanings usually associated with the term – 'to be incorporated with' (though without necessarily the loss of either identity), and the more common meaning: 'to be absorbed into'.[380] Torrance uses the word in its first connotation with reference to Christ's having assumed our human identity and 'assimilated himself to us in our actual condition'.[381] From all that we have concluded thus far we know that assimilation in this case would not mean that the divine reality actually loses its integrity in Christ, but rather incorporates human identity and being into his experience. In another place, using the word pejoratively, Torrance implies the second meaning. He refers to the extinction of the biblical concept of grace by the Western Church's acquiescence to sacramental causality as 'an assimilation of grace to causality'. Yet again, this time assigning the term transitive action, he speaks of the destruction of divine–human dialogue by the Church's 'assimilating into theology a general philosophy of nature'.[382] In both cases the assimilation by the Church of an alien factor has led to the gospel being integrally compromised.

When referring to the assimilation of our prayer to Christ's, however, Torrance does not seem to be using the term with either of these connotations. For Torrance Christ's assumption of our peculiarly human worship could not mean that the human element is annihilated, lest the final end of his saving work – 'restoring human being to proper sonship in the image of God' – be undermined.[383] Neither, as has been said, could it simply mean that our prayer is gathered 'alongside' Christ's, that is, as a separate entity; for at its very best our worship cannot stand by itself.[384] There does appear, however, to be a reasonable alternative between these two extremes, one that we have already indicated. It is that when Christ assimilates our prayer to his own vicarious prayer he identifies in our worship

---

[379] Ibid. 182.
[380] Chambers 20th Century Dictionary (Bath, Pitman, 1981), 77.
[381] R/n, 111.
[382] Ibid. 123.
[383] Cf. Ibid. 117.
[384] Christ's sacrifice, Torrance says, was a 'lonely sacrifice' so that ours might not have to stand alone in the vacuity of its 'own significance', or lack of it (cf. Inter, 330; G & R, 153).

that which is primally his, separating as it were 'the wheat from the chaff'.[385] Thus, although Christ receives the whole of our prayer, he only 'keeps' or incorporates into his perfect, heavenly prayer that which has arisen from it. From our perspective, assimilation is Torrance's way of showing how God receives the prayer of Christ *once* from Christ himself but *again* in the echo of that prayer in the worship of the Church. However, this is only how it would appear to us, for he makes the point that from God's perspective (or in heaven) our prayer is not heard as a *separate* prayer from that of Christ, either in its origin or in its utterance.[386]

---

[385] Cf. *R/n*, 213.

[386] Torrance says, 'Really to pray to God, therefore, is to pray with Christ who prays with us and for us and to pray with him is to pray his prayer, the prayer of his life which he offered in our place and on our behalf, and in which through union with Christ in the one Spirit we are made continually participant' (*R/n*, 209). The point of the Church praying 'with Christ' then is not that our prayer necessarily exists as a separate entity in relation to his, but that Christ prays to God for man from our humanity, 'with us', and that our prayer finds its highest reality in its identity in Christ's heavenly prayer, i.e. 'with him'. He says, 'we are with Jesus beside God, for we are gathered up in him and included in his own self-presentation before the Father' (*STR*, 135). He decries Apollinarianism's deficiency: 'Because the incarnate Logos is not actually consociated with us in the wholeness of our humanity, then worship cannot be thought of as taking place *with* Christ any more than through or in him' (*R/n*, 150). 'Our worship of God the Father is *with*, *in* and *through* the mind of Jesus Christ', he says (*R/n*, 117, italics mine). Stressing Christ's purposive, unbroken relation with sinful, though worshipping man, Torrance cites Cyril of Alexandria: Christ has 'ranged himself along *with* us as himself a *worshipper* of God the Father. He *worships for he has assumed the nature that pays worship*' (*R/n*, 176. Torrance cites *Thesaurus*, MPG LXXV, 117 CD; cf. Jungmann, *The Place of Christ*, 30). Torrance insists upon what he calls a 'doxological with' as well as a 'mediatorial with' in Christ's relation to the worshipping Church. He means that the Church not only offers its prayer 'with Christ' or 'through Christ', that is, simply on the strength of his agency as a mediating factor between God and man, but in personal, doxological *koinonia* 'with' its worshipping Head, 'with' him who 'prays and worships the Father as one of us, with us and on our behalf' (*R/n*, 196-7). Such distinctions as these underscore once again the supreme importance to Torrance that the Word's identity and work as man be safeguarded. He comments: 'The retention in a liturgy of an unambiguous mediatorial "*with whom*" along with a mediatorial "*through whom*" may well be taken as an indication that the old classical understanding of Christian worship... ['to the Father, through the Son, and in the Holy Spirit' rather than 'to the Father and to the Son and to the Holy Spirit'] remains intact' (*R/n*, 187-8). He means that the juxtaposition of these suggests a necessary abstraction construed between Christ's mediatorial agency as such and Christ's abiding

> When he [Christ] presents himself as the worship and prayer of all creation, our worship and prayers are presented there also. When the Father accepts us in Jesus Christ his beloved Son, who then can distinguish our worship and prayer from Jesus' worship and prayer, for they are one and the same, wholly his and wholly ours in him?[387]

In this way Christ offers our prayers 'as assimilated to his vicarious acts of faith and love'.[388] The assimilated prayer then is the 'prayer which is trained away from its own cry and taken up into the cry to the Father that ascends from the incarnate Son, in whom the Father is well pleased'.[389]

As our prayer is thus assimilated it finds its anterior christological identity and in that its authenticity before God. Hence,

> The worship and prayer which we offer in the name of Christ is the worshipping form of the life and sonship which we have received in Christ and which ascends from us through Christ to the Father. It is in fact the eternal life of the incarnate Son in us that ascends to the Father in our worship and prayer through, with and in him, in the unity of the Holy Spirit. While they are our worship and prayer, in as much as we freely and fully participate in the Sonship of Christ and in the whole course of his filial obedience to the Father, they are derived from and rooted in a source beyond themselves, in the economic condescension and ascension of the Son of God.[390]

This means that when we 'gather together in Christ's name' in the Church to 'offer Christ to the Father', the obverse is happening concurrently in heaven, viz. Christ, 'who has united us to himself [and] gathered up and sanctified all our worship and prayer in himself' is actually offering *us* to the Father in his own self-offering.[391] Although economically our prayers might appear to be 'a response to his response', as we have suggested in an earlier chapter, in its 'dimension of depth', as Torrance calls it, ours is not another response from his, rather his 'all embracing response' formed in us

---

personal and human identity – not that they exist except in relation to each other – ruling out an assimilation of one to the other.
[387] *MOC*, 98.
[388] *R/n*, 211.
[389] Ibid. 213.
[390] Ibid. 212.
[391] Ibid. 212.

by the Spirit and returned through him to the Father in the Spirit.[392] He says this explicitly: 'The Eucharist is not to be regarded as an... act on our part in response to what God has already done for us in Christ, but as an act towards the Father already fulfilled in the humanity of Christ... to which our acts in His name are assimilated and identified through the Spirit.'[393]

This not only demonstrates the total christocentricity of Torrance's eucharistic theology but once again its interior dynamic. Reality for Torrance, as we have noted, is never only what it appears; there is always an inner structure and movement fundamental to external reality. In this case the doxological act of the Church is seen to inhere in the very form and saving operation of the Trinity itself. 'The movement of worship and prayer in which we are engaged', he says, 'to the Father through the Son and in the Spirit, is essentially correlative to the movement of divine love and grace, from the Father, through the Son and in the Spirit'.[394] A final comparison of these in the light of Torrance's concept of assimilation will not only illustrate this active, trinitarian formation inherent in the Church's worship but also allow us to observe his eucharistic theology brought to its conclusion.

All movement of saving love, Torrance insists, 'even the mediation of Christ', 'flows from the Father'.[395] It is by the will of the Father and the 'power of the Holy Spirit', that the Son 'came down from heaven', 'took our human nature, healed and sanctified it in himself that he might offer it up to God'. In so doing he 'made our distorted sonship and worship his own and... transformed them in union with his own'.[396] From the ontological reconstitution of our

---

[392] Cf. ibid. 108. Crichton comes very near to this, saying that our 'yes' in and through Christ in the Eucharist 'endorses' Christ's positive fulfilment – his 'yes' of all the will of the Father: 'The response of Jesus Christ is the correlation of the "faithful love" of his Father, or in other words the whole meaning and intent of his life is to do the will of the Father who sent him. But the radical change for the Christian is that now he is able to make the response of faith, to say Yes to God in and through *the response of Christ, whose Yes we endorse with Amen "to the glory of God"'* (Crichton, 'A Theology of Worship', 9).

[393] *R/n*, 109. Torrance will even go so far as to say that 'Christ takes the Eucharist for us' (Lectures, 27/2/86, No. 4, Nottingham, 'On the Eucharist').

[394] *R/n*, 212; cf. Crichton, 'A Theology of Worship', 19.

[395] *R/n*, 185. However, with Cyril of Alexandria, he rejects any idea of an '*independent* centre of priestly activity' in Christ – that is, one separate from the act of the Father – which reiterates his position as to the unity of operation within the Trinity.

[396] Cf. ibid. 208.

nature, by his ascension and likewise through the eternal Spirit, Christ offers our renewed humanity and its prayer back to the Father as his own.

The movement of the Church's worship parallels this. For, 'while they are our worship and prayer... they are derived from and rooted in a source beyond themselves, in the economic condescension and ascension of the Son of God'.[397] On the ground of his incarnation and the renewal of our minds in his obedient worship, Christ continues to come in his Spirit 'to take up our prayer into himself [and] moulds and shapes them'. Thereby he facilitates the reverberation in our worship of his own.[398] Finally, on the basis of his ascension and likewise in the Spirit, Christ returns our worship to the Father, or rather his worship formed in us, as assimilated to his own. Thus our eucharistic worship is 'taken up (ultimately)... to share in the inner relations of God's own life and love'.[399] Torrance summarizes this, emphasizing that it is the Spirit who co-ordinates the operation of the Church's worship with that of Christ.

> Christ now sends to dwell in us the same Holy Spirit who inheres in his divine and incarnate Being and is operative in all his vicarious activity, it is in the Spirit coming to us through his humanity that we are united to Christ and share in his self-presentation before the Father. He is the bond of unity in all our prayer in Christ's name. Thus Christ comes to dwell in us through his Spirit, associating with us as worshippers of God, while remaining our mediator, advocate and high priest in the heavenly sanctuary, and associating us with himself in assimilating our prayer to his which has already ascended to the Father and continues to avail for us in his presence.[400]

---

[397] Ibid. 212; cf. *GT*, 6–7.
[398] *R/n*, 208.
[399] *MOC*, 74.
[400] *R/n*, 182.

This can be demonstrated as follows:

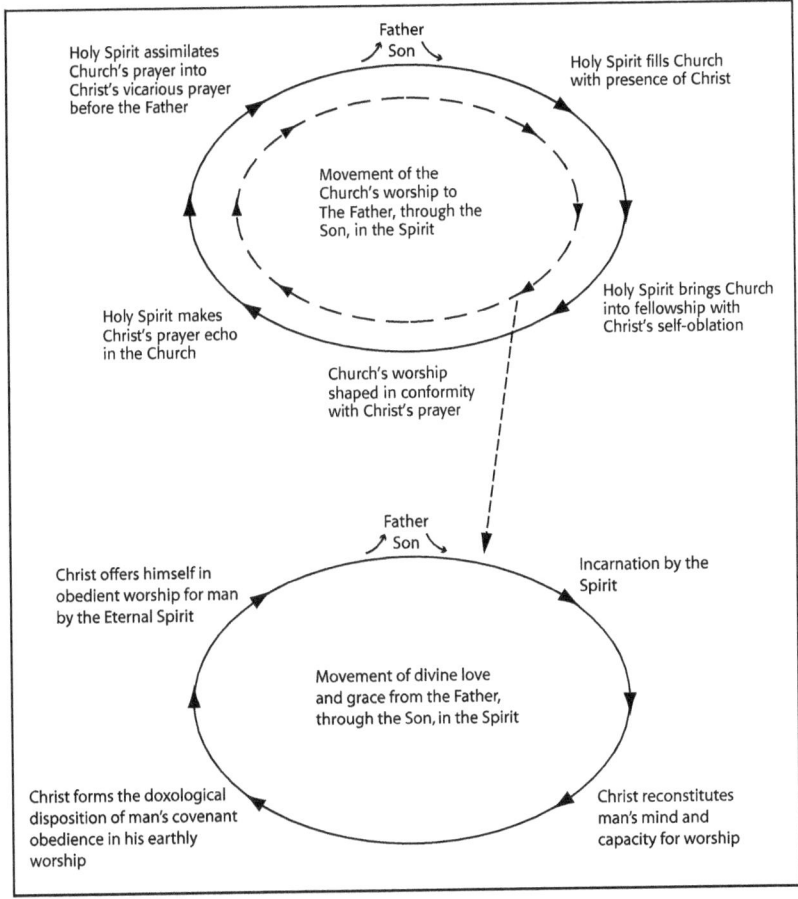

The concept of assimilation is clearly the loftiest metaphor in Torrance's eucharistic theology. The presence of the Incarnate Son before the Father, with our eucharistic worship assimilated to his, represents the deepest point of that closest of all possible unions between God and man which the Eucharist represents.[401] In the assimilation of the Church's prayer to Christ's heavenly prayer the will and love of God 'come full circle', but not without the free and loving response of man. Christ, he says, refuses 'to be alone or without us'.[402] This portrays the quintessence of the fulfilment of the Covenant in Jesus Christ.

---

[401] *Inter*, 337.
[402] *The Incarnation*, XV.

9. The Eschatological and Counter-Substitution of the Sacrifice of Christ for the Sacrifice of the Church

Since Christ comprehensively and personally embodies the fulfilment of God's purposes, his presence in the Church's Eucharist is seen as equivalent to 'that future supper in the kingdom of God' interpenetrating the present action of the Church. Implicit, therefore, in the Church's sacrificial act is an eclipse of our *anamnesis* by Christ, 'The *Eschatos*' himself, an overtaking of the remembrance by the reality.[403] The Eucharist, he says, 'enshrines an essential displacement of the action of the Church by the action of Christ'. Whether or not the Church acknowledges or yields to the fact, the presence of the High Priest, among us as the fulfilment of our liturgy, virtually 'suspends the liturgical action' of the Church. It is not only in his historical life, not only before the Father's throne, that Christ 'substitutes' or interposes his saving act for ours, but in the sacrament as well. 'The liturgical *re-actio* of the Eucharist', he says, 'is displaced by the immediate *action* of Christ Himself'. This is the divine side of what Torrance calls an 'eschatological substitution', foreshadowing the final suspension of all liturgical action at the *Eschaton*. As far as the Church is concerned, Christ's eschatological presence in the Eucharist calls for a deliberate act of deference in the sacrament, acknowledging the exclusive prerogatives of the Great High Priest to act on our behalf.[404]

Our part in this 'eschatological economy' corresponds to the 'epistemological repentance' mentioned earlier by which the Church was said to admit to her own incapacity to aspire to the knowledge of God, while at the same time submitting to God's sole right to speak to her for and about himself.[405] This so-called 'substitution' belonging to our worship is incumbent upon us by the overbearing presence of the Heavenly Priest who asserts every right to soteriological sovereignty in his Church. When Torrance says that the Eucharist incorporates an 'essential displacement' of the Church's action by Christ's action, he does not mean that the Church no longer acts, but that the whole attitude and nature of its act is changed.[406] The Church

---

[403] *Inter*, 327, 324.

[404] Ibid. 326–7.

[405] What is said here concerning 'epistemological repentance' as well as what follows regarding the Word making his sacrament 'transparent' and finally redundant' recalls our discussion of 'sacramental images' in Chapter 2, part 2, section 2.

[406] *Inter*, 326–7.

in its worship, whether explicitly or not, must deny to its own action any and all right of appeal to God, ascribing that exclusively to Christ. In effect the voice of the Church's act is changed from active to passive. It can be said that the New Testament Church makes her sacrifice by 'sacrificing' her privilege to do so herself, by relinquishing all need, right and worthiness to offer anything to God. She does, in fact, truly 'set Christ before... [God] in order to propitiate Him', but not by her own act as such, not as a constitutive part of *her* eucharistic sacrifice; she offers and is offered herself 'by the right hand of Christ'. The Church's offering always concedes primary action to Christ's offering and in that concession her offering is made.[407]

Torrance envisages the whole eucharistic sacrifice as a kind of substitutionary exercise – an offering up of our prayer 'in his name' on the basis of the prayer which Christ makes before God 'in our name'.[408] Because Christ's substitutionary act is 'complete', that is, inclusive of our response to God in its entirety, the most essential aspect of our sacramental act is its expressed acquiescence before his. He cites F.W. Camfield again, who highlights this substitutionary aspect of the gospel: 'all that constituted atonement was... wrought *for us* and *as our* act'. Torrance suggests that the Church's sacrifice 'answers' the vicarious act of Christ in a way appropriate to it, viz. '*as our act*' of acceptance of his sacrifice for us. This is the Church's way 'to let Jesus Christ take our place', a kind of substitution in reverse.[409] He calls it a 'sacramental sacrifice', a 'counter-sacrifice' to the sacrifice of Christ.[410] Thus is demonstrated in the Church's Eucharist the 'substitutionary kind of response' obliged of a sacramental act said to be 'entirely analogous to Christ's substitutionary act' viz. one that is itself 'radically vicarious' or 'in the acutest sense substitutionary'.[411]

It is on account of the deference of the Church's eucharistic theology before the all-sufficient sacrifice of Christ that the

---

[407] *C & A* II, 150; *R/n*, 212. It is only 'by the right hand of Christ' that we offer anything to God at all', Torrance says with Knox (*C & A* II, 149). 'He is the priest, on whose behalf they [the Church's priests] perform the sacred act of the Eucharist; it is he who is ever standing at the Throne of God; it is through his hands that all offerings and prayer make their way to God' (Jungmann, *The Place of Christ*, 148).

[408] *MOC*, 97.

[409] *Inter*, 330; *MOC*, 98.

[410] *Inter*, 330, 328.

[411] Ibid. 330; *MOC*, 99; *Inter*, 332; 'New College', 27.

people of God are said to offer up 'spiritual sacrifices'.[412] Christ alone, as we have indicated, exercises the proper rights of priesthood in his Church. His is a 'royal priesthood' by virtue of 'the coincidence of Grace and Omnipotence' in his own person, that is, by the fact that in him God in his divine humanity is at once both the one who offers and that which is offered in sacrifice. It is a priesthood which arises out of Christ's Sonship, in which apostleship from God and priesthood from man are hypostatically united. The Church is said to share his title in as much as Christ himself 'displaces' the content and action of its offering with his own.[413] The Church's priesthood, like the Church's sacrifice, is one of derivation. As Torrance puts it, 'this is priesthood in a secondary sense, not another priesthood than that of Christ... but a humble participation of the Church in His Priesthood in terms of service'.[414] Christ's priestly prerogatives in Torrance's view are not delegated as such to the ministry or agency of the Church but faithfully preserved through the ministry of the Spirit. Sacerdotal function in the Church never loses its direct, formal connection with Christ himself. Since it is within the Eucharist that Christ's word and deed are formally substituted for ours, it is from the 'office of sacrificing' inherent within that sacramental act that, as Calvin says, 'all are called "a royal priesthood"'.[415]

---

[412] 1 Peter 2:5, 10.

[413] *STR*, 112, 114; cf. *RP*, 14; *STR*, 112ff.

[414] *RP*, 99.

[415] *C & A* II, 149; cf. *Inter*, 344. While certain members are assigned by the Church to be ministers of the word and sacraments, 'priesthood' as such belongs to the whole Church. In the same way that 'the office of sacrificing' in the Eucharist was said to invest the title of 'royal priesthood' upon the Church, the Eucharist itself is said finally to confirm the vocation of those chosen for its ministry. It was stated earlier that all worship experiences within the Church are ordered to the Eucharist. In fact, divine orders are themselves ordered to this sacrament. 'Church order', he says, 'is taken from the Eucharist' (*RP*, 72). He quotes Thomas Aquinas: 'The Sacrament of Order is ordained in order to the Eucharist which is the Sacrament of Sacraments' (*Summ. Theol. Suppl.* q. 27.4.2–3; *RP*, 77). What Torrance means is that, since the Word is nowhere so manifestly present as in the Eucharist, here 'becoming event' as he unites his Church to himself, any one appointed to preside at his Table finds himself 'ordained' not by that appointment as such, but by the one whose presence he is appointed to serve. Torrance says, 'Thus in, through and over the sacraments the ordering power comes from the Real Presence of Christ' (*RP*, 75–6). This illustrates the point that in Torrance's ecclesiology Christ's priesthood never loses its immediate influence upon the Church. In this case, it is the Great High Priest, present to his Church in word and sacrament, that directly validates

Torrance once again makes the determining factor the presence of Christ.[416]

The ramifications for the Church's liturgical life of the substitution of Christ's personal action for ours bring to mind our study of the meaning of 'sacramental images'. The presence among us of one who incorporates in his own mediation and prayer the 'fulfilled liturgy' of the Church requires of our worship a willingness at any moment or at any point of its execution to be 'broken in upon by the Risen Lord', at his word to be 'broken up' or 'set aside', so as to 'leave room' for this 'eschatological substitution'.[417] 'All order and liturgy has validity and truth' only in so far as they do this.[418] There can therefore be no place in the Church's liturgy for intransigence or legality of form. Instead, he insists that there must be a *Maranatha* at the heart of the Holy Eucharist, an expressed anticipation of Christ's supervening presence, not only in his sacramental *parousia*, but perhaps even in his final unlimited epiphany. In this context it must be remembered that the difference between these two is not a qualitative but a quantitative one.[419] Reflecting his belief in the transcendence as well as the immanence of Christ's *parousia*, that the sacramental presence in fact contains the full reality of Christ's presence, though not the fullness of its disclosure, he recommends the Church's liturgy to point away from itself to that one who 'indefinitely transcends' it.[420]

For Torrance this reality 'beyond' is the divine reality within, which infinitely surpasses the sacrament's capacity to contain or manifest. The witness of the sacrament to this transcendent reality,

---

ministry within his Church. 'New Testament ordination', he says, is properly not 'the laying on of hands' by the Church but the 'filling of the hands' by God with the bread and wine of the Presence. He concludes: 'In the last analysis it is Christ Himself who is the one Priest, and men are ordained only in the sense that He gives them to share in His Priesthood, but to share in it... in a mode appropriate to those who are but stewards and servants' (*RP*, 81).

[416] 'It is because he who is Priest, Altar and Offering indivisibly in himself dwells in the Church through the Spirit who unites us to him, that the Church of believers is constituted the temple or sanctifying sphere in which Christ fulfils his ministry as Apostle and High Priest of our Confession' (*R/n*, 183).

[417] *Inter*, 327; *MOC*, 98. As Torrance puts it: 'It is because the Church incorporates through the Word and Sacraments the everlasting continuity of the Christ-event travelling through and under the visible and historical continuities that the latter are disrupted, and will finally break up at the *parousia*' (*Inter*, 323).

[418] *Inter*, 327.
[419] *MOC*, 98.
[420] Cf. *Inter*, 328.

however, is not finally the task of its liturgy. For no deferential act on the Church's part is sufficient in itself to make that reference. The Word himself must finally come and join his voice and act with that of the Church in order for its Eucharist to speak definitively of the things of God. As we noted earlier, it is only as God appropriates the sacramental signs to function within God's revelatory purposes that they are made 'transparent' or means through which the Church apprehends Christ. They are made transparent precisely as they are made sacramental or communicative of the reality they signify. It is Christ, acting in continuity with the Church's liturgical action, who '*makes it point* beyond itself' to himself.[421] We stated earlier that sacramental images realized their purposes by this kind of living lucidity. Now we can see how this is actually accomplished. For it is by the light of God's word that the Church is enabled to 'see through' its Eucharist to Christ's 'all-embracing' sacrifice and thus to allow him to 'take our place, replacing our offering with his own self-offering'.[422]

Whether or not Christ comes in the sacrament is not dependent upon the sincerity or quality of the act of the Church. Torrance insists that in every Eucharist he comes in association with the sacramental word of proclamation and its corresponding sacramental act to make conclusive reference to himself. When Christ's presence is acknowledged in relation with the sacramental action of the Church and his word discerned there two things should happen simultaneously. In the first place the Church must reckon Christ's worship as incomparable, encompassing not only all that is worthy in its own worship, but infinitely more. In this association the halting inadequacy of our liturgical worship is obvious and its transitory nature accentuated. There must then transpire what Torrance has called a radical 'conversion of analogies' in the Church's worship, a shifting from a preoccupation with the relation with God it has in its own worship to that which it has in the worship of Christ.[423] We must remember here that Torrance never sees the

---

[421] Ibid. 327, italics mine.

[422] *MOC*, 98.

[423] *TS*, 133. Reflecting this kind of thinking, John McLeod Campbell asks, 'Does the ordinance of the Lord's Supper, in your meditation of it, speak to you of Christ? or does it commend itself? Does it suggest what altogether apart from it you possess in Him? or does it promise as to what of Him you are to receive through it? Does it turn your thoughts to Christ as the true interest of all things, the meat which endureth unto Eternal life, to be discerned and fed upon in all occupations of your being? or does it concentrate your interest on itself as the specially appointed medium of your participation in Him?' (Campbell, *Christ the Bread of Life*, 62).

sacramental analogy as a statement about itself or about the Church's experience of God within the Eucharist. It is rather a declaration of the gospel, that all men have been restored to communion with God in Christ. The sacraments, he says, 'by their nature direct us away from ourselves to Jesus Christ in whom all God's blessings are embodied, out of whose fullness we receive grace for grace'.[424]

This reorientation of the mind of the Church away from its own manifest experience to what God says is its higher reality in Christ compares in Torrance's thought with the transition which occurs when visual signs are interpreted by the spoken word, viz. a redirection of our attention from the observable to what cannot be observed but only heard. So the sacramental relation must finally yield to Christ, acknowledging its own emptiness and impotence except that Christ appropriate it to sound through his own worship. In this disposition the Church understands its worship to be, indeed always to have been in its deeper reality, wholly the Spirit's echoing of Christ's own praise to the Father. It is with this in mind that Torrance persists in speaking of the Church's worship as 'displaced' by the worship of Christ. This is not to say that the Church's prayer is lost, or that it is not praying its own prayer. The worship of the Church is truly its own, as he says, 'issuing freely and spontaneously out of ourselves', yet truly his as well, arising out of his humanity in a primal sense. The prayer of Christ does not actually displace ours, in the sense of dispossessing it of its own identity. The Church's prayer is no less ours for being his, no less his for being ours. On the contrary, it is all the more authentically human for having its origins in God's New Man.[425] Furthermore, the fact that Christ's prayer can be heard in the Church's prayer is evidence that our hearts and minds have been freed enough from those dehumanizing elements in ourselves and in the world to hear and respond to God's Word in our worship.

Our prayer is thus displaced as it loses its solitary identity. It is filled with the worship of Christ, discovering in that interrelation its higher, enduring reality. This compares with the 'making redundant' or 'dispensing' of sacramental signs, observed earlier in Torrance's theology, as the living Word was said to realize within them precisely that which they signified. The Church's worship is displaced as it surrenders its place before the altar to him who is the altar and the sacrifice all in one as well as 'the true Celebrant at the holy table'.[426]

---

[424] *MOC*, 100.
[425] *RP*, 45.
[426] *C & A* 11, 150; *Inter*, 327. Torrance identifies the phrase 'the Altar is

Our prayers do not cease materially; they 'cease' volitionally. In this act of surrender the Church demonstrates that its worship has not only its origin but also its destiny at the very throne of God with him.[427] Thus, the Church's worship is not to be discarded, neither is it to end in some self-effacing dirge or lonely silence but rather in an eternal fellowship with its Lord. Indeed Christ's prayer honours and supports the prayer of the Church, calling it into union with his own. He will never allow the Church's prayer to 'fall to the ground' in its own insignificance, but holds it up in perpetual relation to his own heavenly worship.[428] For 'He took our place that we might take His place before God'.[429] Our worship therefore is only displaced in order to find its proper place in Christ. The Church's worship must lose its life in order to find it. Like Calvin Torrance refers to this as a *mirifica commutatio* or a 'wonderful exchange'.[430] It is the final stupendous outworking of the substitutionary atonement.

Until the end of the age, then, the Eucharist is the place in time where the worshipping Church is given real and renewed participation in the worship of Christ. In each Eucharist our earthly worship is brought to culmination in a heavenly one which infinitely surpasses it. This juxtaposition in the sacrament witnesses to the fact that one day every limitation to our worship, excepting our created nature, will be removed, as Christ himself finally brings the worship of heaven to earth, thereby making all Scripture and sacraments redundant or 'no longer necessary'.[431] Each time the Church communes in Christ it foretastes the day when the full reality of its sacramental relation will be unveiled in the plenary disclosure of the christological relation.

Christ' as from Calvin. Its origins, however, are not from the Reformation but much earlier in the 'Roman Pontifical' (noted by Bishop Martin B. Hellriegel, *The Holy Sacrifice of the Mass*, St Louis, MO, Pio Decimo Press, 1963, 24).

[427] Sister Mary Agnew says correctly that for Torrance 'in so far as the Eucharist does what it is meant to do, it is itself inactive'. However, she then resorts to terminology which reflects her wholly different frame of reference, one alien to Torrance's thought: 'As act of the Church *it makes present* the action of Christ and in so doing, it displaces itself' (Agnew, *The Concept of Sacrifice*, 235, italics mine).

[428] *MOC*, 98.

[429] *RP*, 33. 'What Christ does he does "in our place"... in order that we may come to be in his "place" before the Father' (cf. C.F.D. Moule, *The Sacrifice of Christ*, London, 1956, 31-58. Quoted by Rowan Williams, *Eucharistic Sacrifice - The Roots of a Metaphor*, Liturgical Study, No. 31, Bramcote, Grove Books, 1982, 32).

[430] *Inter*, 327, 330.

[431] *STR*, 158; cf. *Inter*, 326.

CHAPTER 5

An Appraisal of Torrance's Eucharistic Theology with Open Questions

A GENERAL ASSESSMENT

A proper appraisal of T.F. Torrance's eucharistic theology should begin by marking some of its positive features and achievements. We must be careful to judge it by the way it differs from and improves upon its sources and also by how successfully it realizes its own aspirations. Only after that ought the questions and problems it poses to be considered.

Looking back on the main body of this dissertation what becomes especially apparent is the inward coherence of Torrance's thought and its faithfulness to its presuppositions. His eucharistic theology emerged as a microcosm of his theology as a whole, with every part of his theology proving to be germane to his understanding of the sacrament. This was evident not just because his sacramental doctrine drew broadly from other areas of theological discussion but because it genuinely belonged to every part. The sacrament in Torrance's theology was not seen to be an anomaly (as he thinks it was for Luther) or a mere supplement to preaching (as it apparently became for Barth). Rather, eucharistic theology lies at the very heart of his theology. It was for this reason, as we stated in the introduction, that we chose to delineate it within a broader discussion of his theological method. Subsequently, we found that Torrance's sacramental thought was entirely congruous with his theological framework as well as consistent within itself.

Let us examine Torrance's eucharistic theology first in the light of what he desires his overall theology to be: 'a theology in reconciliation', stressing the common ground at the intersecting point of three concentric circles – the Orthodox, Roman Catholic and Evangelical traditions.[1] It is especially in his sacramental theology that Torrance discerns a possible bridge between East and West. This is not because of anything novel but rather because of roots already shared. As Torrance sees it, Calvin's theology and Reformed Theology in general, have much in common with the East. This is especially true with respect to sacramental theology. Residual links with the Eastern tradition are evident in the Reformed emphasis upon the role of the Spirit in the sacrament and, at least in theory, in the eucharistic disposition of the rite.[2] Common ground is also detected in common sources. As we will discuss in more detail presently, Torrance makes a great deal of Calvin's reference in his sacramental writings to the works of Cyril of Alexandria. He discerns a profound influence upon Calvin's eucharistic theology by Cyril, particularly with respect to the doctrine of the real presence.[3] For making these kinds of associations and seeking to reclaim previously neglected Eastern roots for the Reformed tradition, Torrance's own sacramental theology must be commended. Indeed, Ronald Lunt esteems Torrance's contribution in this regard as 'piles driven down deep into history on which there could begin to rise the solid structure of a united Christendom'.[4] This undoubtedly expresses Torrance's own hopes for the ecumenical contribution of his theology.

Let us observe in more detail Torrance's dialogue with Eastern sacramental theology. When asked in 1985 what he would change if

---

[1] *R/n*, 6ff., esp. 9.

[2] Cf. 'Comments on Eucharistic Practice in the Church of Scotland Today', *ChSSR* 5 (1983), 18.

[3] T.F. Torrance (ed. and intro.), *Theological Dialogue between Orthodox and Reformed Churches* (Edinburgh and London, Scottish Academic Press, 1985), 4, 13.

[4] Ronald Lunt, 'Collected Papers of T.F. Torrance', review of *Theology In Reconciliation* by T.F. Torrance, *Exp Tim* 87 (1975–76), 379.

his earlier works on the Eucharist could be rewritten, Torrance stated that he would like to alter their context, i.e. not to discuss the issues so much from the perspective of the Reformation, as from that of the Eastern Fathers.[5] Torrance certainly quotes patristic sources widely, especially their works on the doctrine of God and christology, and he draws from them all sorts of implications for his eucharistic theology. Curiously, however, in those studies specifically on the Eucharist, Torrance makes only tangential references to Eastern sacramental theology as such.[6] Although his eucharistic thought clearly aspires to be more Eastern in its orientation, the majority of its annotations are still from Reformation and more recent sources.

The question remains, then, whether Torrance's sacramental thought finally offers the Church an ecumenical alternative to the polarisation of East and West. On the affirmative side, we have observed how he disclaims the mechanistic, Western concept of a sacrament ('means of grace'), preferring the more biblical, Eastern notion of 'mystery', i.e. the distinctly divine and hence inexplicable act of God upon his people under created signs. Furthermore, we have seen how, consistent with the East, he forgoes any metaphysical speculation regarding the real presence, deferring instead to the power of the Spirit. The 'mood' of the Eucharist in his theology of worship is also characteristically one of praise, as it is in the Eastern Church, without the slightest hint of the penitential preoccupation that has dogged the Western Eucharist since the middle ages.[7]

---

[5] Personal Interview, 23/12/85, Edinburgh. Gustav Aulén already appraised Torrance's early work on the Eucharist as addressing the subject much more broadly than the writings of the Reformers. He states: 'A presentation of the Lord's Supper such as the Scottish theologian Torrance has given in *Intercommunion* cannot be incorporated within the framework of the Reformation controversies' (Gustav Aulén, *Reformation and Catholicity* (Edinburgh and London, Oliver & Boyd, 1962), 191).

[6] This is not to say that there are not in his eucharistic theology numerous general references to the Eastern Fathers, even in some of his earliest works. For example as early as 1956 in his article 'The Place of the Humanity of Christ in the Sacramental Life of the Church', *Church Service Society Annual* 26 (1956), 3-10. Torrance speaks of Cyril of Alexandria's influence on Calvin ('Humanity of Christ', 4; cf. *Inst* IV.17.9).

[7] Brilioth comments on the heaviness which characterized medieval worship: 'The element of Thanksgiving, which had once found its chief expression in the *Anaphora* as a whole, had now disappeared from the Canon [proper, and]... was completely ousted by that of Sacrifice' (Yngve Brilioth, *Eucharistic Faith and Practice, Evangelical and Catholic* (London, SPCK, 1934), 78-80).

On the other side, however, when Torrance's concept of the Eucharist is examined more carefully in the light of the very least which Eastern sacramental theology requires, it is found to be severely lacking. Some beliefs which the East would consider absolutely essential he disowns outright. For example, he rules out any substantial 'conversion' (*metaballein* or *metapoiein*) of the bread and wine into the divine body and blood of Christ and therefore any substantial, corporeal presence of Christ in the sacrament. Such a change and such a presence the Eastern Fathers universally require.[8] Torrance will speak of a 'conversion' of the elements by the Holy Spirit but this denotes a change of instrumentality, not of substance.[9] He also notes, as an example of Eastern influence upon Reformed sacramental theology, Calvin's use of the phrase 'the vivifying flesh of Christ' from the sacramental writings of Cyril. Yet, the way the Reformer, and Torrance too for that matter, re-deploys the idea does not at all correspond with the

---

[8] Schillebeeckx cites as an example an excerpt from Theodore of Mopsuestia: 'Christ did not say, "This is the *symbolum* of my blood", but "This is my blood", a *change* of the wine takes place' (Schillebeeckx cites Theodore of Mopsuestia, 'Fragmenta in Mt. 26, 26', *PGM* 33, 1113 and 1116, in *The Eucharist*, 66–7). Another example is to be found from Cyril of Jerusalem: 'We call upon the benevolent God to send out the Holy Spirit upon the gifts which have been laid out: That he may make the bread the Body of Christ, and the wine the Blood of Christ; for whatsoever the Holy Spirit touches, that is sanctified and changed' ('Catechetical Lectures', 5, 7, from *The Faith of the Fathers*, selected by W.A. Jurgens (Collegeville, MN, The Liturgical Press, 1970), vol. 1, 363). Still another example can be taken from Cyril of Alexandria: 'He states demonstratively: "This is My Body", and "This is My Blood", lest you might suppose the things that are seen as a figure. Rather, by some secret of the all-powerful God the things seen are transformed into the Body and Blood of Christ, truly offered in a sacrifice in which we, as participants, receive the life-giving and sanctifying power of Christ' ('Commentary on Matthew', 26, 27, from Jurgens, *The Faith of the Early Fathers*, vol. 3, 1979, 220).

[9] Torrance says, 'By consecration [the bread and wine] are converted into instruments of the real presence' (*Inter*, 336). What is then 'transubstantiation' for the Council of Trent, 'transignification' for Schillebeeckx, might be termed 'transinstrumentation' for Torrance. Cf. Calvin: 'Christ followed the ordinary custom in such a manner as to draw away the minds of his followers to another object, by changing *the use of the bread* for a different purpose.... So then the *bread*, which had been appointed for the nourishment of the body, is chosen and sanctified by Christ to a different use, so as to begin to be spiritual food. And this is the conversion which is spoken of by the ancient doctors of the Church' (John Calvin, *Commentary on a Harmony of the Evangelists, Matthew, Mark, and Luke*, ed. William Pringle (Grand Rapids, Eerdmans, 1957), vol. 3, Matthew 26:26, 204, 206, italics mine, then his).

patristic usage.[10] According to both Calvin and Torrance, Christ's divine humanity is the giver of the Spirit and the principle of all divine activity in the sacramental action, but corporally present only in heaven. For Cyril, on the other hand, the flesh of Christ is all these things and also present in heaven, but no less corporally present in the sacrament to 'vivify' his church.

Another basic difference between Torrance and the East centres around the concept of the *epiclesis* and the role of the Spirit in the Church's sacrament. In the East, the *epiclesis* constitutes an appeal to the Spirit to 'bring about' the presence of Christ in the sacrament as well as to unite the Church's praise with that of its Great High Priest. While the *epiclesis* in Torrance's eucharistic theology is a similar invocation toward similar ends, what actually transpires by the Spirit's coming is entirely different from what the East perceives. For Torrance the Spirit's presence in the sacrament itself constitutes (by virtue of the *perichoresis*) the presence of the worshipping Christ and causes the prayer of Christ to echo in the prayer of the Church. For the East the Spirit's presence will not suffice for the presence of Christ, nor will an 'echo' of Christ's prayer in the Church's liturgy pass for genuine participation of the earthly liturgy in that of heaven. Torrance, of course, teaches that our 'worship and prayer' have their place in heaven, but by the fact that we 'freely and fully participate in the ascension of Christ'. The substantive factor is the incorporation of our humanity in Christ's divine humanity, and thereby our participation in his heavenly worship, and not the Church's participation in the Spirit.[11] In Eastern thought the Spirit affords the Church's eucharistic liturgy such real participation in the worship of heaven that it is even said to transpire there. A reflexive echo of the heavenly liturgy as delineated in Torrance's eucharistic theology would be hardly concrete enough for the Eastern Church.[12]

---

[10] We will see presently that Torrance's use of the phrase does not exactly correspond with that of Calvin either.

[11] *R/n*, 212.

[12] Cf. Torrance's statement: 'The Church in its eucharistic liturgy does not participate in that (Self-presentation of the Lamb of God before the Father) except by echoing it in the counter-sacrifice of praise and thanksgiving. He, the Lamb, is upon the altar-throne.... The saints are given to pray *beneath* the altar. In other words, the eucharistic sacrifice in the liturgy of the Church on earth belongs to a different dimension' (*RP*, 95–96). Compare this with Timothy Ware's appraisal of Orthodox Worship: 'Worship, for the Orthodox Church, is nothing else than 'heaven on earth'. The Holy Liturgy is something that embraces two worlds at once, for both in heaven and on earth the Liturgy is one

In the light of these inadequacies, as the East would reckon them, Torrance's eucharistic theology finally ought not to be judged by what it aspires to be, but by what it actually is, a Eucharist in the Reformed tradition operating from a highly developed christology richly informed by patristic sources. It would seem appropriate at this juncture therefore to examine Torrance's thought more closely *vis-à-vis* that of Calvin, particularly noting those points of variance. Asked how he saw his own eucharistic theology 'improving upon that of Calvin', Torrance, presupposing a profound influence upon Calvin from the East, insisted that virtually everything he has written on the Eucharist was implicit in the Reformer's understanding of the sacrament and had been inspired by it.[13] If this is the case, then it might be said that Torrance's sacramental theology carries through the implications of Calvin's teaching in the Eastern direction to which it has pointed us.

Regardless of Torrance's claims to have Eastern sources in common with Calvin, their sacramental theologies certainly have different internal starting points. For his part Torrance develops his thought from a distinctly Alexandrian understanding of the hypostatic union, in contrast to the more Antiochene view held by Calvin. He also proceeds from a decidedly Cappadocian soteriology, as opposed to Calvin's undeniably Augustinian mould.[14] The

---

and the same – one altar, one sacrifice, one presence' (Timothy Ware, *The Orthodox Church*, revised edn (Harmondsworth, Penguin, 1972), 270).

[13] Personal Interview, 23/12/85, Edinburgh.

[14] Torrance acknowledges in Calvin a '"Nestorian" appearance' with all the signs of a duality still existing between divine and created being, particularly in Calvin's doctrine of the incarnation (*Orth & Ref'd*, 13). By employing the term 'Antiochene' and 'Alexandrian' we refer to the broad characterization and contrast between christologies that highlight the distinction of Christ's natures (the former) and those which stress the unity of his person (the latter). This caricature was popularized in the 1940s by R.V. Sellers in his *Two Ancient Christologies: A Study in the Christological Thought of the Schools of Alexandria and Antioch in the Early History of Christian Doctrine* (London, SPCK, 1940).

In contrasting Cappadocian with Augustinian soteriologies we have in mind the difference between salvation perceived as transpiring by the vicarious healing and reorientation of our fallen nature which the Word has actually assumed, and salvation accomplished purely by redemptive acts of obedience and expiation performed by the Word in our *pre-fallen* humanity. In the former salvation has roots in the ontological framework and reconstitution of Christ's human nature, in the latter it does not. A point Torrance never makes is the difference these soteriologies presume as to the doctrine of original sin. The very fact that Augustine and Calvin after him equated original sin with original guilt, both of which were understood to inhere within man's fallen flesh, precluded the

difference this makes for their respective sacramental theologies becomes apparent with respect to their understanding of the 'vivifying flesh of Christ' already mentioned. Calvin says with regard to the life-giving quality of Christ's flesh: it is not Christ's 'material body, or of what belongs to the body as such, but of the spiritual efficacy which emanates from it to us. For as far as Christ's flesh is quickening, and is a heavenly food to nourish souls, as far as his blood is a spiritual drink and has cleansing power, we are not to imagine anything earthly or material as being in them.'[15] We have already noted a disagreement over this concept between Calvin and Cyril, now a basic difference can be seen existing between Calvin and Torrance. Contrary to Calvin's way of thinking illustrated above, the flesh of Christ for Torrance is 'life-giving', not just because it was the vessel through which the Word accomplishes his saving deeds, not just because it is filled with the 'life-giver' – viz. the Spirit who emanates efficaciously upon the Church – but because it is itself causative of our salvation. In suggesting this, of course, Torrance only speaks of the flesh of Christ in hypostatic union with the Word; in other words, he means the divine humanity. Whereas in Calvin's thought, the humanity of Christ in its innocence is the vehicle of the saving reality, for Torrance salvation itself inheres within it. Christ's human nature – his mortal body, mind and spirit – is in Torrance's theology that which is healed, that which is presented in obedience to the Father and by virtue of that fact, it is that through which the Word by his Spirit continues to act and heal us.[16] The divine

---

Word's assumption of our Adamic nature. Calvin says, for example: 'Therefore good men, and beyond all others Augustine, have laboured to demonstrate... that we derive an innate depravity from our birth.... Every descendant, therefore, from the impure source, is born infected with the contagion of sin; and even before we behold the light of life, we are in the sight of God defiled and polluted.... Original sin, therefore, appears to be an hereditary pravity and corruption of our nature, diffused through all the parts of the soul, rendering us obnoxious to the Divine wrath' (*Inst* II.1.5, II.1.8, trans. John Allen).

[15] John Calvin, *Commentaries on the Epistles to the Hebrews*, ed. John Owen (Grand Rapids, Eerdmans, 1949), Heb. 9:11, 203.

[16] Contrast Torrance's views with those of Calvin who understands the life-giving factor of Christ's flesh as purely the presence of the Word giving himself from that context: 'The flesh of Christ, however, has not such power in itself as to make us live, seeing that by its own first condition it was subject to mortality, and even now, when indued with immortality, lives not by itself. Still it is properly said to be life-giving, as it is pervaded with the fulness of life for the purpose of transmitting it to us. ... Accordingly, he shows that in his humanity also fulness of life resides...' (*Inst* IV.17.9). Although Torrance could undoubtedly agree with the 'words' Calvin writes here, he could not agree with

humanity of Christ is the *Palinggenesia* of our salvation; it is that which is saved and now that which saves. For all his insistence upon the abiding integrity of the hypostatic union in Christ's ascension, Calvin knows no relation between the divine and human natures with comparable salvific implications.[17] Although for Torrance, as for Calvin, the Word is the principle of action within his humanity, that divine humanity itself is for Torrance the principle of salvation. In Calvin it is the Word alone that is the saving principle, though not the Word disconnected from his flesh.

With regard to the doctrine of the real presence, Torrance's unique association of the Eastern idea of the *perichoresis* with Calvin's *extra Calvinisticum* serves to fill out a concept left largely undeveloped by the Reformer himself. It also provides an ontological and trinitarian framework, unapparent in Calvin's thought, for understanding the link between the Spirit and the Son. This in turn offers a fuller rationale than Calvin possessed for speaking of the Spirit's presence in the sacrament as 'the life-giving virtue of Christ's flesh – poured into us' and hence 'reduces the distance' even more between the Church in its sacrament and the ascended Christ.[18] There is also evidence, particularly in the way Torrance answers the question of the *manducatio impiorum*, that he would ascribe to the presence and act of Christ continuous with the Church's sacramental action a given, objective 'ontological density' which Calvin would not. Whereas Calvin, with Torrance, will affirm that Christ is 'presented (in the sacrament) to the wicked no less than to the good', the latter will go so far as to speak of Christ's body and blood being 'partaken of by the unbelieving recipient'.[19] For Torrance Christ not only 'indiscriminately' gives himself in the sacrament but is

---

what Calvin means. For while the Word in Calvin does not save us apart from his flesh, his saving acts can be abstracted from that humanity, so that it is the Word and not his flesh that saves. In Torrance's thought that 'abstraction' is both inconceivable and undesirable. It is the Incarnate Word who saves us by virtue of the fact and from the fact of the redemption of our integral humanity.

[17] Calvin comments: 'Thus, so skillfully does [Paul] distinguish Christ from the common lot that he is true man but without fault and corruption. ... For the generation of man is not unclean and vicious of itself, but is so as an accidental quality arising from the Fall. No wonder, then, that Christ, through whom integrity was to be restored, was exempted from common corruption' (*Inst* II.13.4, trans. F.L. Battles).

[18] Cf. *CR*, 49:487.

[19] John Calvin, *Commentary on the Epistles of Paul the Apostle to the Corinthians*, vol. 1, 1 Cor. 11:27, 385–7; 'Arnoldshain', 11.

'indiscriminately' received as well.[20] Would such a view be conceived by Calvin as 'degrading to the dignity of Christ', as it was in its Lutheran form? It almost certainly would, since the universal grace it suggests contradicts his doctrine of limited atonement.[21]

In his doctrine of the eucharistic sacrifice Torrance elaborates upon an idea latent in Calvin's thought, one which largely lay dormant because of his preoccupation with the question of the real presence in his ongoing debate with the Lutherans. We have become familiar with texts originating in Calvin which indicate that the Church 'offers Christ' to the Father 'by faith and prayers' in a spontaneous response of praise.[22] There are also texts which speak of the Church being 'elevated to God' in the Eucharist, of Christ's presence found there in a 'mode of descent by which he raises us up to himself'.[23] However, Calvin never connects these thoughts in any systematic way so as to suggest that the Church's prayer is formally conjoined or participates in Christ's prayer in heaven. Scholars generally concur that Calvin was so intent upon stressing the natural disjunction between Christ's expiatory sacrifice and the wholly eucharistic sacrifice of the Church that any possibility of actual participation in his self-offering was ruled out altogether.[24]

---

[20] 'Indiscriminately' is Calvin's word. 'For some were led, by the heat of controversy, so far as to say, that it [the presence of Christ] was received indiscriminately by the good and the bad' (Calvin, *Commentary on the Epistles of Paul the Apostle to the Corinthians*, vol. 1, 386).

[21] Cf. François Wendel, *Calvin: The Origins and Development of His Religious Thought* (London, Collins, 1965), 339; McDonnell, *John Calvin*, 64-5; Ronald S. Wallace, *Calvin's Doctrine of the Word and the Sacrament* (Edinburgh, Oliver & Boyd, 1953), 212f.

[22] 'In order that we may be partakers of ablution, it is necessary that each of us should offer Christ to the Father. For, although He only, and that but once, has offered Himself, still a daily offering of Him, which is effected by faith and prayers, is enjoined to us, not such as the Papists have invented, by whom in their impiety and perverseness, the Lord's Supper has been mistakenly turned into a sacrifice, because they imagined that Christ must be daily slain, in order that his death might profit us. The offering, however, of faith and prayers, of which I speak, is very different, and by it alone we apply to ourselves the virtual fruit of Christ's death' (John Calvin, *Commentary on the Last Four Books of Moses Arranged in the Form of a Harmony*, ed. C.W. Bingham (Grand Rapids, Eerdmans, 1950), vol. 2, Numbers 29:2, 39).

[23] *Inst* IV.17.16, IV.17.42, cf. IV.17.1, 2 & 3; *K & C*, 144, fn. 5.

[24] Cf. e.g. Heron, *Table and Tradition*, 168-9; Francis Clark, *Eucharistic Sacrifice and the Reformation* (London, Darton, Longman & Todd, 1960), 105ff.; Gustav Aulén, *Eucharist and Sacrifice* (Edinburgh, Oliver & Boyd, 1958), 80ff.

Although Torrance takes exception to this view, he would agree that Calvin certainly never worked out his doctrine of participation to any degree in this direction.[25] Kilian McDonnell comments on what the Reformer has said and yet failed to say in his embryonic doctrine of eucharistic sacrifice: 'It is possible to construct a rather remarkable theology of sacrifice from texts, and not isolated texts from Calvin's writings.... The texts are there, as are the beginnings of a more complete theology of sacrifice as applied to the Eucharist, but they are left undeveloped.'[26] From what we have observed, Torrance has in fact explicated that which was implicit in Calvin and filled in at points where nothing is said, and all in a way that would not compromise Calvin's wholly substitutionary, non-expiatory premises. Indeed over half Torrance's eucharistic writings are devoted to developing the concept of eucharistic sacrifice for the Church. Kenneth Stevenson expresses his own desire for the Church in this regard: 'Would that Calvin's emphasis on *epiklesis* of the Spirit and eucharist as latreutical (as opposed to expitiatory) sacrifice had been fully digested into the piety of all branches of Western Protestantism.'[27] For their part, Torrance's writings bear witness to this emphasis being integrated into a concept of 'eucharistic devotion' at the heart of his theology. Indeed, after studying his idea of eucharistic sacrifice alongside Calvin's, one wonders how any Reformed eucharistic theology could take the idea much further, that is and remain faithful to the Reformer's utterly non-piacular stance. Perhaps it might all be stated differently, or still more clearly, but undoubtedly Torrance has stretched the concept to its limits.

Working from a different world-view Torrance is also able to avoid the pitfalls of a spirit/body, spiritual/physical dichotomy which Calvin inherited from Augustine. Calvin had regarded as sacrosanct Augustine's conception of sacrament, viz. 'a visible sign of a sacred thing, or a visible form of an invisible grace', and with it, no doubt,

---

(Aulén centres his comments primarily around the Lutheran Reformation); McDonnell, *John Calvin*, 285-6.

[25] In an interview with Torrance the question was raised as to the accuracy of Alasdair Heron's statement that Calvin 'is so anxious to avoid any idea of repeating or adding to Christ's sacrifice that he also seems to rule out our *participation* in his self-offering' (Heron, *Table and Tradition*, 169). Torrance took exception to this (Personal Interview, 23/12/85, Edinburgh).

[26] McDonnell, *John Calvin*, 285.

[27] Kenneth Stevenson, review of *Table and Tradition: Towards an Ecumenical Understanding of the Eucharist* by Alasdair Heron, *SJT* 38 (1985), 246.

most of its cosmological assumptions.²⁸ While never taking this dichotomy to its full-blown dualist conclusions, as did the more radical Reformers, Calvin still spoke of the sacrament in terms of spiritual things being fed by spiritual means to the spirits of men.²⁹ Likewise, the corporeal constituents associated with the sacrament – the physical body and blood of Christ, our own corporal bodies, and the material elements – are generally depreciated in Calvin's arguments *vis-à-vis* their spiritual counterparts.³⁰ Torrance simply does not think like this. For Calvin the sacrament fails to lessen, indeed it accentuates, the opposition of things physical to things spiritual. According to Torrance, the sacrament, while underlining the natural 'tension' existing between the physical and the spiritual until the end of the age, enshrines a 'two way relationship' and 'a conjunction' between the two.³¹ This only follows since, at the same time, the sacrament enshrines the healing in Christ of 'the rift between spiritual and physical existence which characterizes our fallen nature'.³² The Eucharist, he says, is 'a sacrament of God's interaction with our physical existence in Jesus Christ' and hence anticipates eschatologically the 'interaction of the spiritual and physical... of the new creation'.³³

Furthermore, in contrast to Calvin and to the Reformation in general Torrance does not set the sacrament over against preaching, determining the former's significance purely by its service as

---

²⁸ *Orth & Ref'd*, 4; *Inst* IV.14.1. Torrance rejects this definition out of hand with all its dualist 'spiritualistic' presuppositions (Lecture, no. 4, 27/2/86, Nottingham).

²⁹ Calvin, *Commentaries on the Epistle to the Hebrews*, Hebrews 9:11, 203. (For a most helpful and comprehensive overview of the Augustinian roots and framework for Reformed thought, particularly its insidious tendency towards a purely 'spiritualistic understanding of the Sacrament' cf. Sasse, *This Is My Body*, 19f., esp. fn. 10.)

³⁰ Calvin thus introduces his sacramental theology, equating man's earthbound, and therefore unspiritual way of thinking, with his need for sacraments: 'In this way God provides first for our ignorance and sluggishness, and, secondly, for our infirmity.... But as our faith is slender and weak, so if it be not propped up on every side, and supported by all kinds of means, it is forthwith shaken.... And here, indeed, our merciful Lord, with boundless condescension, so accommodates himself to our capacity, that seeing how from our animal nature we are always creeping on the ground, and cleaving to the flesh, having no thought of what is spiritual, and not even forming an idea of it, he declines not by means of these earthly elements to lead us to himself...' (*Inst* IV.14.3).

³¹ *C & A* II, 151-2.

³² *G & R*, 160.

³³ Ibid. 159-61.

illustration, pledge or token to the latter; rather he sets preaching and the sacrament in relation to the Living Word, with both finding their meaning and efficacy in service to him. While Torrance chooses, particularly in his earlier writings, to discuss the Eucharist in association with preaching, and makes the point that the message *heard* is more appropriate to God's Word than the sign *seen*, he never fails to emphasize how the sacrament corresponds naturally to the character of the Divine Word as action, while facilitating at the same time an appropriate response as action on our part to him. This aspect of Torrance's sacramental theology can be seen as an enlarging of the Reformer's insistence on the inseparability of preaching and the sacrament, but guided by an 'actualist' concept of God's Word, for God himself always retains an objective and determinative relation to both.[34] In this Torrance is highly indebted to Barth. However, even in his earliest writings Barth backed away from giving the sacrament anything approaching joint centrality with preaching in the Church.[35] Although he will say that the sacrament illustrates the nature of God's word as action, it does so only in a secondary sense, that is, as it relates to the Word's primary action in preaching. Barth hesitates to speak of the sacraments as directly acts of God themselves.[36] After reading Barth we are still obliged to ask the question which François Wendel addresses to the whole of Reformation's sacramental theology: 'What exactly does the Supper give us that we cannot obtain otherwise? Under these conditions, is there still good reason for the existence of the Supper alongside the preaching of the Word?' He goes on to elaborate: 'This problem touches the very nerve of the nature of the sacrament as it was elaborated by the reformers; and the mere fact that it can present itself shows that they did not manage to integrate the sacrament organically into their theological system.'[37]

Torrance's theology more than most, and certainly more than Calvin's, gives reason for the sacrament. He will not hesitate where Barth in fact shies away. Torrance sees the sermon and the sacrament as partners in the Church, as both servants of God in his word and act. His teaching on the sacraments as the miraculous signs of God's presence, which accompany the preaching of the

---

[34] Cf. Chapter 1, part 1, section 1 above.
[35] Cf. fn. 39 below.
[36] Cf. Chapter 2, fn. 48.
[37] Wendel, *Calvin*, 353.

gospel, illustrates this.[38] What the Living Word proclaims and promises in the sermon he effects through the sacrament.[39] Although Torrance leaves no doubt that God acts in the Church's preaching, it is the sacramental act of the Church (though not disassociated from preaching) which principally and formally witnesses to the active nature of God's Word. In this Torrance's sacramental theology provides a central place for the sacrament in the Church which Calvin's thought could not warrant, and which Barth's teaching would not pursue.[40] In the final analysis, this probably comprises the single most profound contribution of Torrance's eucharistic theology.

---

[38] When queried as to whom he would attribute his 'sacramental interpretation' of Mark 16:20, Torrance replied: 'I cannot recall if I owe this interpretation, the application of miraculous signs to the sacraments, to another: but it is likely that I have been influenced in this by something in Calvin – it was probably an adaptation on my part of a thought in Calvin' (Correspondence, 2/7/86). Clearly, Torrance did not get this understanding of Mark 16:20 directly from Calvin. If he had then his own views would have been toned down considerably. Calvin says of the relation of miracles to the preaching of the Word in this text simply, 'they aid the gospel'. They cannot be 'separated from the Word of God, to which they are appendages' (Calvin, *Commentary on a Harmony of the Evangelists, Matthew, Mark, and Luke*, vol. 3, Mark 16:20, 395).

[39] In this he is working out in active terms an idea already implicit in Calvin. When Calvin contrasted his own views regarding symbol with those of the sacramentarians he did so dynamically: 'For what is the nature of a sacramental union between a thing and its sign? Is it not because the Lord, by the secret power of his Spirit, fulfills what he promises?' (*Calvin, Commentary on a Harmony of the Evangelists, Matthew, Mark, and Luke*, vol. 3, Matthew 26:26–28, 209).

John M. Barkley comments on Calvin's views in a way that would confirm Torrance's dynamic interpretation. 'The term "symbol" in Reformed Theology is used, not in a popular but in its biblical sense, as constituting an act of God in the sacrament. It is not a symbol of things absent, but of things present' (John Barkley, *The Worship of the Reformed Church* (London, Lutterworth Press, 1966), 70).

[40] When asked, 'Do you think communion should be administered every Sunday[?]', Barth answered affirmatively saying that 'it should be the climax of every service', recalling Calvin's frustrated wish in this regard. Immediately following this statement, however, he suggested that the sermon, even in the communion service, should never be less than thirty minutes, usually between thirty and forty-five minutes! He stressed that 'we must help men and women to meet God', which is facilitated it would seem not so much by the Eucharist as by preaching. Barth then attributed to preaching as it were the power of the Roman sacrament. 'When we preach', he said, 'we do the same thing as the Roman Catholic priest when he is celebrating the transubstantiation'. One wonders how the sacrament in Barth's mind could ever merit comparable time, place or efficacy to the sermon (Barth, *TT*, 21–2).

Prologue to a more Critical Assessment

The more critical part of this appraisal deals with questions which, in the author's estimation, Torrance's eucharistic theology itself raises. Some will be grappled with in dialogue with scholars who have taken issue at various points with Torrance's sacramental thought or with matters closely related to it. There are other major issues which critics have raised, however, that we have avoided altogether, simply because of their irrelevance to our subject.[41]

As to the questions themselves, a number relate directly to Torrance's doctrine of the Eucharist, but most to theological matters much larger than simply the sacrament. Although some of these broader subjects will appear at first to be only peripherally relevant to the Eucharist, they all emerge as fundamentally or strategically important to it. Several issues are so vital in fact, that if handled differently they would substantially alter the sacrament's meaning. The initial question on the doctrine of God, for example, addresses a matter at the heart of Torrance's eucharistic theology, one which determines whether or not the Incarnate Word can be understood as truly present to the Church. The length of our treatment of this question reflects its significance. Another decisive debate centres around the meaning of grace and whether Torrance has misunderstood the issue altogether. If he has, then his eucharistic theology should be amended at its starting point. Yet another issue raised toward the end of the section asks if Torrance's view of sacramental analogy, indeed, his whole concept of analogy, really affords the Church a knowing experience of God as he is in himself, or if in the final analysis the radical demarcation fixed between our knowledge of God and our knowledge of the world prevents it. This, of course, is the ultimate question, touching as it does the *homoousion* upon which everything in Torrance's theology hinges.

Three other questions are entertained in this appraisal which pertain to the integrity of various responses to God: one concerning the validity of man's personal response over against that of Christ, a second involving the designation of a response within the Trinity which is identifiably proper to the person of the Spirit, and a third having to do with Christ's response as an individual human being,

---

[41] For example, Torrance's hermeneutical use, or abuse, as James Barr would see it, of 'biblical language'. James Barr's strategic study and dismissal of so-called 'Biblical Theology' popular in the middle decades of last century singled out Torrance's writings for criticism (cf. James Barr, *The Semantics of Biblical Language* (London, OUP, 1962)).

i.e. if that response is compatible with the universal requirements and claims of his vicarious role. These matters are all interconnected in that they bear directly or indirectly upon whether or not the response of man *qua* man has genuine value to God. There are also questions concerning style, aesthetics and choice of metaphor which, although relatively superficial to the inner integrity of Torrance's sacramental thought, are important if it is to gain wide acceptance in the Church. A final question is posed in the form of a suggestion as to how Torrance's eucharistic theology could be developed to facilitate a 'common altar' where scientist and theologian already said to work 'at the same bench' – might offer together the praise of all creation.[42] This treatment is also a lengthy one due, interestingly enough, to the fact that it was prepared for Torrance himself to evaluate. His own appraisal of this possible expansion to his thought is included in the final footnote.

Although this introduction could suggest that the questions which follow all fit neatly together, this is not the case. Indeed, they comprise such a mixture that any natural succession superimposed upon them would be wholly artificial. Nevertheless, when an obvious sequence or association can be deduced our arrangement will reflect it. Undoubtedly, an appraisal of any aspect of Torrance's thought could quite literally be extended into a dissertation itself, such are the formidable theological issues raised. However, the nature of the material we are examining, particularly the fact that Torrance's eucharistic theology is not all in one place, neatly headed and argued systematically, but is instead scattered throughout his writings, has meant that we have been required in this thesis to spend more time imposing order upon the subject than criticizing it. Certainly there are other questions that could be asked, and some which deserve still more thorough investigation, but our task is not to exhaust the questions but rather to appraise Torrance's eucharistic theology in their light.

A QUESTION OF THE DOCTRINE OF GOD AND A LATENT AUGUSTINIANISM

In spite of Torrance's repudiation of things Augustinian and Western in deference to the theology of the East – 'All great theology', he says, 'has its roots in the East' – is not his doctrine or

---

[42] *TS*, VIII.

the real presence dependent precisely upon an understanding of the Trinity peculiar to the West?[43]

Every aspect of Torrance's eucharistic theology has underlined his rejection of Augustinian/Neo-Platonic cosmology and dualism. Behind the misconception of the world which this system advocates lies an 'immutable', 'impassible' deity which Torrance perceives as the crux of the problem.[44] It is a deity which cannot truly act 'outside of itself' and therefore cannot create reality totally free from itself. This 'unchanging triad', as he calls it, is seemingly incapable of incarnation in the fullest sense, in view of its inability to experience human suffering. It is a God that cannot freely move in the world, being bound by its own static necessity to communicate itself through secondary means.[45] In this regard, Torrance's theology decisively removes the possibility of a remote or static relation adhering between divine and created reality, as it posits nothing less than an immediate relation between the Being/Act of God in his self-disclosure and the Church in its knowing and receiving.

Curiously, Torrance's understanding of the Trinity, and consequently his doctrine of the Eucharist, is still grounded upon Western or Augustinian presuppositions. It must be stated straight away that Torrance would adamantly deny this. He prefers to think of his understanding of God as primarily an Eastern one. From at least the late sixties he has sought to model his doctrine of God after

---

[43] Personal Interview, 23/12/85, Edinburgh.

[44] T.F. Torrance, 'Toward an Ecumenical Consensus on the Trinity', *ThZ* 31 (1975), 337–50, esp. 339.

[45] By 'secondary means' Torrance refers to intrinsic, uncreated 'forms of immutable reasons of... things', the *rationes aeternae*. The universe of Augustinian cosmology carries in its make-up numerous traces of its Creator. These 'triadic patterns', as Torrance refers to them, are not only structurally manifest within creation in general, but functionally innate to the human intellect, playing 'an essential role in our knowledge of God from the very start' ('New College', 24–5; *G & G*, 148–9; cf. Caroline Eva Schuetzinger, *The German Controversy on Saint Augustine's Illumination Theory* (New York, Pagent Press Inc., 1960), 21–9, 76–81). Torrance resists at every hand the static implications of the Augustinian monad. Referring to Athanasius, *Ad Serapionem* 1:17, he says, 'It is not something strange to the Being of God, but God is so wonderfully and transcendentally *free* in his own eternal Being that he can do something new without changing in his own *ousia* and can go outside of himself in the Incarnation without ceasing to be what he is eternally in himself in his own ineffable Being, for his *energeia* inheres in his eternal *ousia*' (*R/n*, 224). Or more succinctly stated: 'In the creation of the world and above all in the Incarnation of the Son something *new* has taken place in God' (*R/n*, 223).

Athanasius and the earlier Greek Fathers.⁴⁶ If, however, Torrance's doctrine of God has been, as he admits, strongly influenced by that of Karl Barth, who shaped his own thought on the Trinity after the West, and if his theology has remained consistent through the years, as he claims, then his earlier understanding cannot be said to have been significantly altered by Athanasius.⁴⁷ What in fact he appears to have done is to have found an Eastern source for what is generally acknowledged as a Western notion of the Trinity.

The Western disposition of Torrance's doctrine of God can be demonstrated also by the fact that most of his conceptual formulations concerning the Trinity, while having their immediate equivalent in Barth, are to be found incipiently in Augustine. For example, by his insistence upon using the classical term 'person' applied to the hypostases of the Trinity, he in fact departs from Barth though not from Augustine.⁴⁸ Yet, following Barth, he refers to the divine hypostases as 'modes of divine activity', which could indicate little more than economic sequences of the divine operation. He avoids any Sabellian implications, however, as does Barth, suggesting that these modes obtain in God's eternal being. They are more than varying temporal dispositions of the divine economy, being three eternal ways that he is God.⁴⁹ Employing Augustinian terminology, he refers to the divine persons as 'relations immanent in God himself' or as 'intratrinitarian relations in God'.⁵⁰ In line with Barth,

---

⁴⁶ Torrance refers to these earlier Fathers as the 'impeccably Orthodox'. He contends that they were generally more unitary in their emphasis with respect to the Trinity, that is, in contrast to the later Cappadocian and Byzantine Fathers who tended to think more partitively on this subject. (Torrance, *Orth & Ref'd*, 16; cf. *R/n*, 246, 252.)

⁴⁷ Cf. *CD* I.1, 408ff., 548. Torrance confirms the consistency of his own views in these matters through the years (Personal Interview, 23/12/85, Edinburgh).

⁴⁸ Barth insists that the term 'person' belongs properly to the doctrine of God and only derivatively to the doctrine of the Trinity. It is the way the Church addresses 'the one personal God' not the different modes of his being. 'This one God is to be understood not just as impersonal lordship, i.e. as power, but as the Lord, and so not only as absolute Spirit but as Person, i.e. as an I existing in and for Itself with a thought and will proper to it' (*CD* I.1, 412). Barth also refrains from using the word 'person' for its possible anthropomorphic implications (cf. Richard Roberts, 'Karl Barth', in *One God In Trinity*, ed. Peter Toon and James D. Spiceland (London, Samuel Bagster, 1980), 85).

⁴⁹ *G & G*, 157; cf. *CD* I.1, 407. 'Father, Son and Holy Spirit are not just operational modes', he says (*R & E*, 23). Rahner says the divine persons are 'three relational ways in which God subsists' eternally in himself (Torrance cites Rahner, 'Trinity', 343-4).

⁵⁰ *G & G*, 157, 168. What Torrance seeks to explain by reference to 'onto

but contrary to the procedure of Augustinian/Western thought, Torrance requires hermeneutically that the doctrine of God be determined, not abstractly from the unity of divine essence to the opposition of persons, but the other way round after the method of the East, since in the economy of revelation God manifests himself in the distinction of his persons.[51] The immanent Trinity must be considered by reflection upon the economic Trinity. The way we think and speak of God must be informed by the way God discloses himself. The Trinity, Torrance says, is 'the basic grammar of theology'.[52] However, the fact that Torrance adopts an Eastern approach to God does not mean that he operates from an Eastern conception of him.[53] For, as we will see, after having approached the subject by the method of the East, he actually discusses it from the framework and in the idiom of the West.

---

relations', viz. that the 'relations between persons (in the Trinity) belong to what persons really are in their own beings', appears to have its counterpart in Augustine: e.g. 'Father, Son and Spirit are three relations in the sense that whatever each of them *is*, He *is* in relation to one or both of the others' (J.N.D. Kelly, *Early Christian Doctrines* (London, A & C Black, 1958), 275, italics mine. This is actually Kelly's concise summation of Augustine's thought). Cf. Augustine, 'Homilies on the Gospel of John', NPNF 1, 7, 222-4. Cf. Augustine, 'City of God', XI, 10, 440-42. Cf. Augustine, 'On the Trinity', *On the Holy Trinity. Doctrinal Treatises. Moral Treatises*, NPNF 1, 3, 87-114.

[51] 'Trinity', 346; cf. *G & G*, 150. Colin Gunton in his study of 'Barth's Trinitarian Theology' comments, 'We require the concept (of the Trinity) because of the way in which men have actually come to know God, and because it is required for the rational description of the reality of the revealed God' (Colin Gunton, *Becoming and Being: The Doctrine of God in Charles Hartshorne and Karl Barth* (Oxford, OUP, 1978), 146).

[52] *G & G*, 155, 158-9; *MOC*, 65.

[53] Indeed, contrary to Eastern thought, what Torrance perceives in the light of this triune and personal revelation of God is the three-fold definition of a single, self-appropriating subject, the Person of God-head. Barth arrives at the same point by the same route. We are led from distinction within God's revelation of himself to conclusions affirming his unity, i.e. the knowledge of the one God; the three-ness in God must be conformed to his oneness. Richard Roberts comments on Barth's reasoning: The act of God in revelation occurs 'simultaneously and unitedly in all his three modes of existence.... God is fully trinitarian but any such assertion is subordinated to the demands of singularity posited in the act of revelation, in which the eternal antecedence of God in Trinity is given temporal realisation in this "single act"' (Roberts, 'Karl Barth', 84-5). Barth himself concludes: 'For none [of the persons] exists as a special individual, all three "inexist" in one another, they exist only in common as modes of the existence of the one God and Lord who posits Himself from eternity to eternity' (cf. *CD* I.1, 425).

Our study has revealed that for its own coherence as well as for its interpretation Torrance's eucharistic theology requires a traditional, Western concept of God. This became apparent especially in the way he interprets the doctrine of the real presence, in which the presence of the Incarnate Son in the sacrament is defined in terms of the presence of the Spirit, and the act of the Spirit in the sacrament identified substantially with the 'grace of the Lord Jesus Christ', which, by his definition, means nothing less than Christ's own being and act.[54] As we have observed, Torrance builds his argument around the late Eastern doctrine of the *perichoresis* of the persons of the Trinity, but not without giving it a decidedly Western slant.

Before we delineate exactly how Torrance arranges, or re-arranges this doctrine, we should look at the way it was originally formulated by John of Damascus in the eighth century. It was enunciated initially not so much on the basis of the identity of persons within the Trinity, or the sameness of the essence of those persons, but on the coherence of their operation. They are said to 'empty themselves into each other and receive each other's fulness'.[55] The Son and the Spirit emanate out of the person of the Father and return in a unity of love to him. *Perichoresis* inheres within this self-giving and receiving of the persons of the Trinity.[56] Although for Eastern theology each of the divine persons exists of the same essence and shares a common life, that essence or life as such is never given personal definition except as Father, and 'after' him as

---

[54] *SOF*, LXXIX.

[55] Cf. Geoffrey Wainwright, *Doxology. The Praise of God in Worship, Doctrine and Life: A Systematic Theology* (London, Epworth, 1980), 23. Moltmann makes the point that in the Eastern doctrine of the *perichoresis* 'the very thing that divides' the persons of the Trinity, viz. their 'difference' from each other, 'becomes that which binds them together' viz. their freedom and capacity to give themselves to each other (cf. J. Moltmann, *The Trinity and the Kingdom of God* (London, SCM, 1981), 175). As an aside, Torrance has described Moltmann's concept of the Trinity as delineated in the work cited above as 'tritheism' pure and simple (Lecture, no. 1, 27/2/86, Nottingham).

[56] Torrance would not agree with this as it is stated, since according to his presuppositions, God's essence is identical with his operation. However, the Eastern definition is not based *primarily* on the singularity of God's essence and operation, but rather on 'the part of each person in the operations performed in the community of action', each belonging to the other and all together to 'the whole' by virtue of their giving and receiving of themselves one to the other and each to all. As we will see, this is not what Torrance means by *perichoresis* (cf. E. Portalie, *A Guide to the Thought of Saint Augustine* (Westport, CT, Greenwood Press, 1975), 132-3).

Son and Holy Spirit. The whole trinitarian doctrine of the East is founded upon the distinct relations of the Son and the Spirit to the Father, and *vice versa*. All originates and coalesces in the Father.

The East's rejection of the *filioque* underlines this distinction. In the West the unity and commonality of essence within the Trinity determines the procession of the Spirit. The Spirit is given by the Godhead and comes among us as the presence of the Godhead. In Eastern theology there is no Person of a Godhead as such, only persons within the Godhead. John of Damascus can thus conclude: 'It is impossible to say that the Three Persons are one person.'[57] The Godhead does not appropriate itself as Father, Son and Holy Spirit, rather the Father begets the Son and 'emits' the Spirit. The Fathers of the East certainly affirmed the unity of the divine nature but it was, as Eugene Portalie says, 'the fruit of reflection, for in their direct description of the Trinity they emphasized, on the contrary, the part of each person in the operations performed in community of action until it became almost a distinct role'.[58] The persons of the Trinity represent for the East 'distinct but interpenetrating centres of consciousness'.[59] As John of Damascus puts it, 'each of the three has perfect distinct subsistence', 'each is subsistent in itself, that is to say, is a Perfect Person and has its own property and distinct manner of existence'.[60] It is, therefore, to stress the distinction of the persons within the Trinity as much as their unity that he says, 'for they are united... so as not to be confused, but to adhere closely together, and they have their *circumincession* (*perichoresis*) one in the other without any blending or mingling and without change or division in substance'.[61]

Let us turn now to consider Torrance's own way of understanding this ancient Eastern doctrine. Although he can refer to it in terms reminiscent of John of Damascus – e.g. as 'the consubstantial communion of Father, Son, and Holy Spirit as distinct persons co-existing and co-inhering in mutual love and life and activity' – he approaches the matter from a wholly different

---

[57] John of Damascus, 'An Exact Exposition of the Orthodox Faith', *Saint John of Damascus*, TFOC 37 (Washington, DC, The Catholic University of America Press, 1958), 278.

[58] Portalie, *Saint Augustine*, 132-3.

[59] H.E.W. Turner, 'Person(s)', in *A Dictionary of Christian Theology*, ed. Alan Richardson (London, SCM, 1969), 256.

[60] John of Damascus, 'Orthodox Faith', 184, 277.

[61] Ibid. 187. Barth's description of the Eastern Trinity is helpful here: 'Three persons just alike (like a superimposed picture)' (*TT*, 59, brackets his).

orientation.⁶² He insists that the Spirit cannot be what he is without the Son, neither can the Son be present without the Spirit. This is because they are both co-essential, co-extensive manifestations of the one God and cannot be more or less than that.⁶³ With reference to the sacrament he argues that, since the Spirit exists within the Son and the Son within the Spirit by virtue of their common identity, the presence of the Spirit cannot be essentially a different presence from that of the Son. Following Barth, Torrance therefore understands the community of the persons within the Trinity as 'modes of (the) existence' of God which participate in each other, which

---

⁶² 'Trinity', 347.

⁶³ Torrance's position on the *filioque* clause is thus already decided, or at least the point which he understands the *filioque* as upholding, viz. 'the inseparable relation of the Spirit to Christ in creation and redemption' (*R/st*, 217–18). It would be thoroughly inconceivable for Torrance that the Spirit's proceeding upon the Church be reckoned as something qualifiably other from the being and person of the Son, since by his own reasoning 'person' does not 'emit' person, but rather Godhead (in this case, Father and Son) issues in what can be only a repetition of himself (in this case Spirit), or in Augustine's terminology 'as whole God from whole God' (cf. Augustine, 'On the Trinity', NPNF 1, 3, VI, 10). Alasdair Heron insists that Torrance 'believes that much of the Eastern criticism of Western theology is justified and also that the unilateral insertion of the *filioque* in the creed should be revoked' (Alasdair Heron, 'The "filioque" in Recent Reformed Theology', *Spirit of God, Spirit of Christ*, ed. Lukas Vischer (London, SPCK, 1981), 115). What Torrance actually objects to in the formal statement of the *filioque* is its language, which he perceives as contrary to the order of revelation, viz. 'from the Father and through the Son' (cf. *R/st*, 218). Furthermore, Torrance concedes that an ecclesiastical coup was manoeuvred to get the clause inserted into the creed: 'It was', he states, 'entirely wrong to introduce it into the Ecumenical Creed without the authority of an Ecumenical Council' (*R/st*, 219). For Torrance the *filioque* clause within the creed as such is expendable, but what it confesses is not, viz. 'the inseparable relation between the Spirit and Christ, and that the Spirit proceeding from the Father operates in and through the Son and thus proceeds from the Son as well as the Father' (*R/st*, 187, cf. 219). Torrance restates what he calls Anselm's argument that 'if the Holy Spirit proceeds from the *ousia* of God who is the Father, he proceeds from what is common to the Father with the Son and the Holy Spirit', viz. Godhead. He insists that the whole *filioque* 'problem' would be resolved 'if we could agree that... the Son is from his Father, i.e. from God who is his Father, and the Holy Spirit proceeds not from God his Father but only from God who is his Father' ('Trinity', 340). This statement, with little subtlety, posits the priority and principle of Godhead rather than that of the person of the Father in the Trinity, which of course is wholly unacceptable to the East and therefore could never be a basis for dialogue. Torrance rejects outright a 'causal priority or superiority of the Father over the Son and the Spirit' as 'a relic of subordinationism' ('Trinity', 340).

'interpenetrate one another interchangeably' and 'inexist interchangeably in one another'.[64]

After saying this, however, Torrance, unlike Barth or Karl Rahner who follows him, conceives of the *perichoresis* more dynamically than simply the inner, relational arrangement of 'an absolute subject', or of 'one self-presence'.[65] In other words, he gives the notion of 'self', implicit in any serious concept of hypostasis, somewhat more import than do either Barth or Rahner. In order to make sense of the communion of love within the Trinity, Torrance thinks it necessary to give '*consciousness* some real place in the notion of person as applied to the three persons in God', that is, that the 'three persons [must be] conscious of one another in their distinctive otherness and oneness'. To this degree he has certainly moved East of Basel. However, he denies explicitly three 'separate centres of consciousness' in the Godhead, suggesting instead a single divine consciousness but one 'shared in... differently and appropriately' by each of the divine persons.[66]

Nevertheless, Torrance's qualification of Barth and Rahner is itself qualified by the fact that he ascribes personhood principally to 'God himself', albeit manifest in a three-fold way.[67] No person of the Trinity exists 'entire' apart from what it is in relation to the Person of the whole, that is apart from what it is in the one God.[68] Expressed

---

[64] *CD* I.1, 424–5, 455.

[65] Rahner rejects the notion of three 'spiritual centres of activity, of several subjectivities and liberties' within the Godhead. 'There are not three consciousnesses; rather, the one consciousness [which] subsists in a threefold way.' God is 'only *one* essence... one self-presence.' Hence there can be 'properly no *mutual* love between Father and Son, for this would presuppose two acts' (K. Rahner, *The Trinity* (New York, Seabury Press, 1974), 106). Barth, similarly, cannot conceive of individual centres of self-awareness, or self-activity within the one God. He says flatly, 'If we have three distinct centres of consciousness, then we are not meeting the one God' (Barth, *TT*, 59; cf. *R & E*, 43).

[66] 'Trinity', 347. Although Torrance qualifies Rahner's refusal to ascribe reciprocity of love to the persons of the Trinity, his resolution of the difficulty differs little from Rahner's. Rahner says, 'There is only one real consciousness in God, which is shared by Father, Son and Spirit, by each in his own proper way' (Rahner, *The Trinity*, 107).

[67] Cf. fn. 63 above.

[68] Cf. 'Trinity', 342, 346 (Augustine, 'On the Trinity', NPNF 1, 3, V, 10f.; VIII, 1). Persons are for Torrance, to borrow a phrase of H.E.W. Turner's, describing Barth's concept: 'permanent styles of God's being God' (H.E.W. Turner, 'Person(s)', *A Dictionary of Christian Theology*, ed. Alan Richardson (London, SCM, 1958), 256; cf. *R & E*, 42). However, Torrance speaks negatively of the tendency in classical Roman Catholic theology to address the one essence of

from the side of unity this means there is 'one Person... existing and meeting us in the triunity of persons in one God'.[69] From the side of distinction, there are 'three persons of one and the same Being in God'. 'God is three persons but he is the infinite and universal Person in three distinct modes of subsistence'.[70] It is thus clear that, regardless of what Torrance says about distinct consciousnesses of the *hypostases* having 'some real place' in the divine *ousia*, all is still being thought out from the uniquely Western notion that the Godhead itself is the principle of the Trinity and not, as the East would require, that that principle is peculiarly the person of the Father.[71] He insists with Hilary that revelation is 'not of the Father

---

God as though it were something distinct from his three personal modes of subsistence, viz. 'a neutral, undifferentiated fourth' person (cf. 'Trinity', 346; *CD* I.1, 455). Nevertheless, his own system encourages him to speak of any one of the persons of the Trinity simply as 'God-himself', that is, as comprising in himself – i.e. in his intrinsic inner-relations, and as a person-constituting-relation himself – the whole Person of the one God (*R/n*, 246, 252; *STI*, 15). Berkouwer speaks of the tendency in the Church, particularly around the theopaschitist controversy, to address God, according to his unity, as 'God himself' and not as Father, Son and Holy Spirit (G.C. Berkouwer, *The Work of Christ* (Grand Rapids, Eerdmans, 1965), 280).

Although Torrance intends no theological mischief by it, one is impressed in reading his theology how consistently God is referred to simply as 'God himself', the 'divine reality', or the 'uncreated Objectivity', etc., with the oppositions within that reality hardly given equal time. With Berkouwer's comment above in mind, the following quotation from Torrance illustrates the point: 'But put God on the Cross, let Jesus Christ be *God himself* incarnate, who refused to be alone or without us, but insisted on penetrating into the heart of our sin and violence and unappeasable agony in order to take it all upon himself and to save us, and the whole picture is transformed' (*The Incarnation*, XV, italics mine).

[69] 'Trinity', 347. The full quotation: 'We must think of God himself as Person, but of this one Person as existing and meeting us in the triunity of persons in one God'.

[70] Ibid. 347; cf. *R & E*, 23. It is interesting in the light of our discussion that Augustine hesitates where Torrance and Barth do not, viz. in the use of the term 'person' with reference to the Godhead (cf. Augustine, 'On the Trinity', NPNF 1, 3, VII, 11; *CD* I.1, 412).

[71] *R/n*, 251-3. Cf. the insightful study on 'Personhood and Being' by John D. Zizioulas in *Being As Communion: Studies in Personhood and the Church* (London, Darton, Longman, and Todd, 1985), 27ff.) in which he discusses the evolution of the concept of *hypostasis* in relation to *ousia*. In pre-Christian antiquity these words had an equivalent and impersonal connotation. However, Zizioulas shows how the early Eastern fathers rescued the terms from abstraction 'personalizing' their meanings according to the nature of God the Father. Zizioulas says therefore 'among the Greek Fathers the unity of God, the

manifested as God, but of God manifested as the Father'.[72] There is, he says, 'one Fountain and Principle of Godhead'.[73]

It is from this kind of thinking that Torrance formulates what we have shown to be his peculiarly Western style *perichoresis*. In the final analysis, Torrance's insistence upon the priority of the Person and principle of Godhead, the modalistic meanings he prescribes to both person and consciousness, as well as his understanding of *perichoresis* as a 'communion in [a] mutual love' rather than *of lovers*, all militate against his aligning himself conceptually with the East. Clearly, the strength of the mutual 'indwelling' or 'involution' of the persons of the Trinity in Torrance's doctrine lies in their consubstantial subsistence within the Godhead or in the essential unity of the one God that is Love. Although Torrance would undoubtedly prefer a more dynamic interpretation of his own views, he would, conceptually at least, be more at home with Augustine's kind of '*perichoresis*' than that of John of Damascus: 'He [the Son] is in the Father, and the Father is in him; as one who is equal is in him whose equal he is.'[74]

Neither the ontology nor the idiom of the Eastern *perichoresis* will allow the virtual '*communicatio personae*' between the Son and the Spirit demonstrated within Torrance's eucharistic theology. Although in the East the fellowship of the Spirit and the Son is never broken, the Son is one 'thing' (John of Damascus' word) and the Spirit an 'other'. There is a 'mutual permeation' of the persons of the Trinity by virtue of *perichoresis*, a definite unity of action between them, but such that their distinct subjectivities are never 'mingled', neither in actuality nor as a matter of speech.[75] For unity of action, given all the *perichoresis* imaginable, would never suggest to the East the near equation of Christ and the Spirit that Torrance's approach appears to permit.

One God, and the ontological "principle" or "cause" of the being and life of God does not consist in one substance of God but in the *hypostasis*, that is, *the person of the Father*.... Thus God as person – as the hypostasis of the Father – makes the one divine substance to be that which it is: the One God.... This point is absolutely crucial... the substance never exists in a "naked" state, that is, without hypostasis' (40–41).

[72] 'Trinity', 340. In other words, Godhead 'appropriates' himself as Father.

[73] *R/st*, 224.

[74] Augustine, 'Homilies on the Gospel of John', NPNF 1, 7, XLVIII, 10, 269. 'In the highest Trinity... each are in each, and all in each, and each in all, and all in all, and all are one' (Augustine, 'On the Trinity', NPNF 1, 3, VI, 12, 103).

[75] Cf. Otto Heick, *A History of Christian Thought* (Philadelphia, Fortress Press, 1965), vol. 1, 164–5.

It must be stated that Torrance is not unaware of this tendency in his system. For all his stress upon the co-incidence of the being and act of the Son and the Spirit, he seeks to ward off the possibility of a 'blurring' of the distinct hypostatic properties of the Father, Son, and Holy Spirit 'which would make them no more than modal aspects of an undifferentiated oneness of divine Being'.[76] By Torrance's own definition, however, 'differentiation' within the Godhead lies in mode or disposition of God's being, though obtaining in him eternally. Persons, as we recall, are 'distinctly personal modes of divine activity and ways of being'.[77] In other words, they are different ways the Person of God manifests who he is. He states, 'the divine operation is not divided between the Persons, but there is a distinction of mode of operation indicated by the prepositions *ek, dia,* and *en*'.[78] The question is: can differing modes of a perfectly identical Being/Act, coinherent 'consciousnesses' in a single divine consciousness, or varying dispositions of the uncompounded operation of the Person of the Godhead really have any more genuine personal distinctness than that which Origen posited, viz. 'being, begottenness and procession', and that understood in a modalistic sense? By appealing to the prepositions '*ek, dia* and *en*' is Torrance really suggesting more than this? If it is true that the *act* and *being* of God are absolutely identical, and that the persons of the Trinity are 'modes of divine *activity*' or 'ways of [his] being', is it possible that the 'One *from* whom' and the 'One *through* whom' and 'the One *in* whom', could be any other than the one indiscerptible Godhead in a threefold repetition of itself? The principle applied to attributes of the simple deity of Augustinianism seems appropriate here: 'things equal to the same thing are equal to each other'.[79] For Augustine 'whatever is affirmed of God is affirmed

---

[76] *MOC*, 59; cf. *G & G*, 157.

[77] *G & G*, 157.

[78] *R/st*, 216.

[79] Rev. Dr Theodore Williams, *Augustinianism; An Interpretation*, printed but unpublished lecture notes, Patristics Seminar, TAE 6733, Oral Roberts University School of Theology, Tulsa, OK., Spring, 1981. Augustine affirms that the Persons of the Trinity are 'equal, equal in all things, on account of the absolute simplicity [*aequalis, in omnibus aequalis propter summam simplicitatem*] which is in [their] substance' ('On the Trinity', NPNF, 1, 3, VI, 7); 'De Trinitate', *Opera Omni post Lovaniensium Theologorum Recensionem* (Paris, Gaume Brothers, 1837), vol. VIII/I, col. 1295). Such an 'absolute simplicity' allows, indeed requires, the Church to 'confess the *absolute* equality [*fateamur summam aequalitatem*] of the Father, Son, and Holy Spirit' ('On the Trinity', NPNF, 1, 3, VI, 10; 'De Trinitate', col. 1299).

equally of each of the three Persons'.⁸⁰ 'There exists within the Trinity an equality so absolute... that no one person of the Trinity [can be said to be] less than the Trinity itself.'⁸¹ Torrance makes statements almost exactly like this, but appealing to Athanasius instead of Augustine. With Athanasius he can say that the 'whole Godhead' is complete in the Son and in the Spirit as much as it is in the Father', or that 'the whole being' of any one person of the Trinity is 'proper to the essence' of the other two.⁸² It is this kind of thinking

---

In discussions such as these, however, Torrance appeals to Athanasius not Augustine, but always affirms 'the simple uncompounded and undivided nature or being of God' (*R/n*, 246; cf. Augustine, 'On the Trinity', NPNF, 1, 3, VII, 10; 'City of God', XI, 10).

⁸⁰ Kelly, *Early Christian Doctrines*, 272; cf. Augustine, 'On the Trinity', NPNF 1, 3, V, 9.

⁸¹ Augustine, 'On the Trinity', NPNF 1, 3, VI, 12, 103; VIII, 1-2, 115-16.

⁸² *R/n*, 252; *STI*, 15. Torrance makes a similar statement, referring to Athanasius' teaching: 'The being of the Godhead is whole or complete not in the Father alone but in the Son and in the Holy Spirit as much as in the Godhead' (*R/n*, 246. Torrance cites Athanasius, *De Decretis*, 16ff., 22f. Elsewhere (*R/n*, 252), but in the same kind of discussion, he cites Athanasius, *Contra Arianos*, 2:33ff., 41, 49; 3:1ff., 21; 4:1). Superficially, Torrance's appeal to Athanasius would seem to be justified in that the Alexandrian's doctrine of God is manifestly more 'unitary' than the later Eastern Fathers. However, any commentary on Athanasius' doctrine of the Trinity must be made in the light of the fact that, as Jürgen Moltmann points out, Athanasius ascribes 'The one divine personality to the Father' (Moltmann, *The Trinity and the Kingdom of God*, 143). In other words, Athanasius formulates his doctrine of God from the standard Eastern assumption of the Father's 'priority' as the 'principle of the Godhead'. This can be illustrated from his arguments 'Contra Arianos': 'The Father is the source... of the Son' (1:14). 'The Son [is]... proper to the substance of the Father.... The Son is eternally the proper offspring of the Father's substance' (1:29). 'The Son is the Image of the Father's Godhead' (3:6, cf. 3:3). And from Athanasius' 'Letter Concerning The Councils of Rimini and Seleucia', 51: 'He [the Son] is the Father's Wisdom and Word' (All quotations immediately above and below taken from *The Faith of the Early Fathers*, vol. 1, 327-9). Contrary to Torrance's opinion, statements such as these make it apparent that Athanasius is following the method of the East and therefore understands the Son as invested with deity that is 'derived' (albeit eternally) from that of his Father (cf. *R/n*, 252). 'The Begotten is... from the Father and is proper to His essence' ('Contra Arianos', 2:56). The Son is 'of His [own] essence, the Divinity and Image of the Father' ('Letter Concerning The Councils of Rimini and Seleucia', 51). Reading Athanasius with this in mind puts the texts to which Torrance appeals in a very different light: e.g.

'Nor is this Shape of the Godhead (which is the Son) merely partial, but the fullness of the Father's Godhead is the Being of the Son, and the Son is whole God. Although He was equal to God, He did not estimate being equal to God a

which allows him, without the slightest contradiction, to posit the presence of the Spirit as that of the Son in the sacrament.[83] Although Torrance usually invokes the *perichoresis* when making assertions such as these, he criticizes at the same time the 'partitive language' used by John of Damascus in delineating the concept.[84] Already from what we have observed by his interpretation of the doctrine, it is clear that Torrance is saying exactly the same thing and from the same presuppositions as Augustine.

In the light of what we have said, Torrance's eucharistic theology offers us an opportunity to observe him seeking to identify as much as possible with the East, with their hermeneutic as well as their language. It represents an attempt on his part to distance himself as far as possible from the dualistic cosmology and the idea of an inert deity intrinsic to Augustinianism.[85] Indeed, his doctrine of the sacrament evidences a conclusive bridging of the dualistic gap, a completely open universe and a God who acts immediately within it. It further witnesses to a God who comes 'out of himself', out of his solitariness, to be joined to man in his estrangement and hence to join us to himself at his table, so as to realize among men the fruit of the fulfilled work of Christ. However, for all his ability to discard Augustinian conclusions on some fronts, it is nowhere evident that Torrance is finally able to free himself from basic Augustinian or Western predilections, particularly with regard to the doctrine of the Trinity. Indeed, as we have seen, at the most crucial point – viz. concerning the real presence of the Incarnate Son within the sacrament – Torrance's assertions hinge entirely upon Augustinian presuppositions. He appeals to the East, but from a Western frame of reference. Although this thesis cannot deal with the full implications of this, Torrance's eucharistic thought certainly carries with it many of the difficulties inherent in an Augustinian doctrine of God.

---

thing to be eagerly retained; and again, since the Godhead and the Image belonging to the Son is that of none other than the Father, this is what He says: 'I am in the Father.' Thus, 'God was reconciling the world to Himself in Christ;' for the propriety of the Father's essence is the Son, in whom creation was being reconciled' ('Contra Arianos', 3:6).

[83] Torrance refers to what he calls 'Athanasius' great principle', viz. 'we say of the Son everything we say of the Father, except 'Father' (*Orth & Ref'd*, 15). If Torrance is saying, as all his presuppositions would allow him to, that the only difference between the persons of the Trinity is nothing more than a nominal one then our point is made.

[84] Cf. *R/n*, 246, 252; cf. *MOC*, 57.

[85] Cf. 'Trinity', 339.

QUESTIONS AS TO THE LEGITIMACY OF VARIOUS RESPONSES TO GOD

I. As to the Abiding Integrity of Man's Individual Response vis-à-vis the All-Embracing Vicarious Response of Christ

The question remains: In Torrance's theology of worship, does the distinctly individual prayer of man finally obtain before God? There is no doubt that *Christ's* own prayer does, that prayer which shares ontological identity with us and which, by the Creator's identity with it, prevails for all men. Furthermore, it is certain that that aspect of 'our' prayer which is the approximate echo of Christ's, which is called forth from man by the Holy Spirit and offered for man by Christ, assimilated to his own prayer, is there as well. However, in both these cases, though all men are heard *as Christ*, in the final analysis only Christ's prayer is heard.

Thomas A. Smail queries the extreme implications in Torrance's theology arising from Christ's comprehensively vicarious response: 'If Christ acts so decisively on our behalf in regard to our response to God what room is left for our own response to God?' He asks further whether Torrance, in his attempt to distance himself from 'an Arminian autonomy' with respect to man's personal response to grace, has in fact adopted 'a christological objectivism' that usurps the reality of man's response altogether.[86]

---

[86] Thomas A. Smail, review of *The Mediation of Christ* by T.F. Torrance, *SJT* 38 (1985), 241-4. Smail's comments are in dialogue with Torrance's statement that 'our faith is implicated in his faith, and through that implication... it is made to issue freely and spontaneously out of our own human life before God.... If we do not allow him to substitute for us at that point, we make his atoning substitution for us something that is partial and not total, which would finally empty it of saving significance' (*MOC*, 94). Smail takes this proposition to its extreme conclusion: 'But if our faith is so implicated in his, why is it important that we should ourselves believe? Why are not all men saved through Christ's believing on their behalf...? How is Christ's believing for us related to the Gospel demand that we believe if not *by* ourselves at any rate *for* ourselves?' (Smail, 243).

In another place Torrance in fact attempts to answer objections such as this saying, 'We are not saved *by* the act of our believing but saved *in* the very act [but] by the faithful and obedient life of Jesus Christ on whom we rely' (*SOF*,

There is no suggestion in any of these questions that man's prayer can or should exist independently of the prayer of Christ. Torrance's point is well taken, that our prayer cannot stand alone and by God's grace will not. The prayer of man in question is not a prayer offered on any other ground or by any other agency than Christ's. There is no prayer save that which is 'through him'. But what of the prayer of man which is said to be 'with Christ'? In contending for the abiding integrity of man's prayer in heaven Torrance does not answer this question. What he contends for is not the distinction of our prayer in relation to Christ's, but the distinctly human prayer of Christ in relation to the Godhead, in other words, for the continuing integrity of his human mediatorship. For Torrance, then, to say that we pray 'with Christ' is equivalent to his saying that our prayer 'in Christ' never loses its essential human identity.[87]

As to the relation of Christ's prayer to that of the Church, we have observed Torrance employing the similes of echo and counterpoint. Although in an earlier context we referred to the latter as indicating consonance, its purpose being to provide a 'coherent texture' in relation to the dominant theme, it could have been understood just as easily to denote difference. Counterpoint by definition is a distinct part set over against the controlling melody, the resolution of which is not found in the absorption of one by the other but in their complementary relation.[88] Indeed, counterpoint has no independent identity as such, no reason for being by itself, no beauty to display except in its contrapuntal association with the theme. With this in mind, our question might be phrased: is there an enduring human counterpoint to Christ's predominant prayer? Torrance clearly allows for such among the asymmetries of this world, but what of heaven?

To use another musical metaphor, is there no place, no pause, in the sublime heavenly score offered by the Incarnate Son for a *cadenza* by the redeemed themselves? A *cadenza* properly owes its origin to the piece it serves. Indeed, it is inspired by it, belongs to it and is freely dependent upon it. It is as it were 'composed' not to enhance so much as to acclaim that ascendant score. Yet for all its

---

CIX, italics mine). His point is that personal faith facilitates salvation, it does not cause it.

[87] Cf. Chapter 4, fn. 387 above.

[88] 'The term ['counterpoint'] derives from the expression *punctus contra punctum*, i.e. point against point' (Michael Kennedy, 'Counterpoint', *The Concise Oxford Dictionary of Music* (London, OUP, 1980), 151).

indebtedness to the original piece and its utter lack of independence in relation to it, a *cadenza* is a spontaneous expression which also belongs to the individual performing it.[89] Is there no place then in heaven for just such a response on the part of the Church, for our prayer 'with his', that is, for our prayer at his side, offered as a doxological answer to his prayer on our behalf? Christ's worship is heralded by Torrance as the all-sufficient and prevailing doxological expression of our obedience. Will there be after all no place before God purely for the Church's own doxological response, having no salvific connotations, but rather offered freely in celebration of his accepted vicarious work?

Everything in Torrance's theology militates against a positive answer to these questions. All human response is offered by Christ, even our response to his response: our 'amen', he says, belongs as well to his prayer. There is nothing left unsaid, therefore nothing left for us to say.[90] His view of sacramental analogy corroborates this conclusion. That analogy has no word of its own, nothing finally to say about itself, no purpose except to point worshippers away from itself to the work of Christ. At the end of the day, the joyful duty of the Church's sacrament is to render itself speechless, emptied of all self-assertion before the total adequacy of his work. Such a disposition is required not only by the nature of man's salvation in Christ, but by the nature of man himself. He says, 'as fallen human beings we are quite unable through our free-will to escape from our self-will, for our free-will is our self-will.'[91] The only posture proper therefore for the imperfect prayer of man before the perfect prayer of Christ is one of 'acquiescence'. The apex of our dialogue with God, he says, is 'silence before the depth and majesty of [his] objectivity'.[92] This corresponds exactly with what Torrance says should be our attitude in the larger knowing-relation: 'The activity of the knower does not enter into the content of his knowledge *at all*.'[93] Instead, we 'allow [God] to impose himself upon our mind' or to 'put into our mouths' questions appropriate to the given revelation.[94]

---

[89] This is the definition of a *cadenza* belonging to the classical concerto (e.g. Mozart, Beethoven), i.e. an improvisation by the performer, usually one of 'planned spontaneity'. Later (post Beethoven) the *cadenza* would be written entirely by the composer himself as an integral, formal part of the composition.

[90] *RP*, 14.

[91] *MOC*, 95.

[92] *TS*, 161, 292.

[93] Ibid. 85, italics mine.

[94] Ibid. 138, 124, 120.

Torrance's theology of worship is couched in almost identical language. He says Christ puts his prayer 'into our mouths' as he 'makes himself the true content and sole reality of the worship and prayer of man'.[95] There would appear then to be little prospect for the Church's being enabled or given the right to 'compose' its own prayer to the glory of God. 'In theology', he says, 'we are concerned with statements that are pronounced primarily by God and only pronounced after Him by human subjects as hearers of His Word.'[96] From what has been said it would appear that our lot in heaven will be something between a 'holy hush' before the matchless prayer of Christ and a 'holy mime' of it. Torrance, with Wotherspoon and Kirkpatrick, has implied as much:

> What He then does personally in the Upper Sanctuary, He echoes in us on earth as we fulfill His command in making this Memorial: uniting us to Himself by His Holy Spirit and ministering also in and through us before God. We are united with Him in His heavenly priesthood, *sacramentally enacting here in His Name that which in the actuality is proper only to Himself.*[97]

James Quinn has masterfully pinpointed the questions that must be asked of Torrance's theology, questions which it appears inadequate to answer. Does this way of thinking make God 'so absolute that man is relativized to the point of vanishing[?]. What is the Christian response to God, if it is not a real response of the Christian, albeit in and through Christ? Is our communion with God a real possession?'[98] In his attempt to separate the subjectivity of God from our own, to make the subjectivity of Christ and not our own that which is determinative, and finally to remove all assertiveness from our own subjectivity, has Torrance in effect removed not only our significance salvifically speaking, but our significance altogether?

---

[95] *STR*, 116.

[96] *TS*, 98.

[97] *Manual*, 40, italics mine.

[98] James Quinn, review of *Theology in Reconstruction* by T.F. Torrance, *ThSt* 28 (1967), 389ff., esp. 390. Alasdair Heron cites C.S. Lewis who characterizes 'Barthianism' similarly as amounting to 'the flattening out of all things into common insignificance before the majesty of the Creator' (Alasdair Heron, *The Holy Spirit: The Holy Spirit in the Bible in the History of Christian Thought and in Recent Theology* (London, Marshall, Morgan & Scott, 1983), 124).

2. As to the Distinction of the Holy Spirit's Personal Response within the Immanent Trinity Over Against that of the Incarnate Son

Does not the difficulty of the depreciated place which Torrance assigns in his theology of worship to the personal, individual response of man in the sacramental relation *vis-à-vis* the objective response of the Incarnate Word ultimately repose in the lack of clear differentiation assigned to the Spirit's work *vis-à-vis* the completed work of Christ?

Torrance warns explicitly against the reduction of all doctrines to christology.[99] Yet, from what we have observed in his sacramental theology, a real question remains if he is not guilty of precisely this error with respect to the doctrine of the Spirit. One can hardly say that Torrance's thought is lacking in pneumatology. However, upon careful examination, it is extremely difficult to conceive of it as more than an appendage to his doctrine of Christ. Although the Spirit appears to have a crucial role to play in Torrance's theology, it is not certain that the distinction which Torrance observes in function between the persons of the Trinity constitutes more than an economic re-distribution of identically the same thing. The Holy Spirit in Torrance's thought appears to have no unique characteristics, no 'source and centre of personal action', that are peculiarly his in distinction from the other persons of the Trinity.[100]

This can be observed clearly in the relation Torrance perceives prevailing between the Son and the Spirit. The Spirit of God is 'formed Spirit'; which is to say, the Son is the 'form' of the Spirit.[101] 'The doctrine of the Spirit', he asserts, 'has Christology as its content'.[102] This might suggest that the Son in his saving work simply 'forms' the vital content for that which the Spirit effects within the Church, that the former is the formal cause of that which the latter is the efficient cause. This, however, is ruled out by Torrance's christological equation of the matter and action of salvation, which we saw underlined in his asserting the identicality of the matter and action of the sacrament. Such an understanding is also highly

---

[99] *SOF*, LXIII.

[100] This is T.A. Smail's definition of *hypostasis* given in the article 'The Son-Spirit Relationship – Modern Reductions and New Testament Patterns', *IrBSt* 6 (1984), 85–102.

[101] *RP*, 23.

[102] Ibid. 24.

untenable in the light of his insistence upon the absolute coincidence of the operation of the Son and the Spirit. The Godhead, as Torrance understands it, subsists in single, unitary and indivisible movement, but one negotiated economically in a three-fold manner. There would seem to be little possibility in such a view for the Spirit's act to have any real definition of its own over and against the act of the Son. This is confirmed in Torrance's theology of worship when he suggests that the Spirit's intercession in the Church is but a recital of the intercession of Christ, that he has no 'utterance' of his own, only that which the Word affords him.[103] The Spirit 'continues to utter Christ the Word', he says.[104] From all this one surmises that the Holy Spirit of the Trinity has little more to say to the Father in his worship relation than does man, sharing with man a generally passive posture before the completed response of Christ. This raises the even more basic question relative to the immanent Trinity (which Torrance says is identical to the economic Trinity): has the Holy Spirit 'his [own] knowing and loving response to the Father and to the Son'?[105]

What seems to be lacking in Torrance's pneumatology, and consequently in his eucharistic theology, is a formal doxological and revelatory function proper to the Spirit *vis-à-vis* the praise and word of Christ. Torrance appears not to be taking fully into account the biblical material which accords the Spirit's role a dignity of its own. Paul states that it is by the Spirit that believers confess 'Jesus is Lord' (1 Cor. 12:13). John records that Christ said of the Spirit 'He will glorify me' (John 16:14).[106] Surely Christ does not confess his own name, or glorify himself in order to provide the Spirit 'material' to reiterate in the Church! For his part, Torrance has formulated his theology of worship strictly by the patristic pattern – 'To the Father, through the Son and in the Spirit'. He has shied away from the emphasis, also in early patristic theology, that Christ is, with his Father, also the recipient of worship from his Church.[107]

---

[103] Ibid. 95.

[104] *SOF*, CIII.

[105] Sabbas J. Kilian, 'The Holy Spirit in Christ and Christians', *AmBenR* 20 (1969), 99–121.

[106] Smail, 'The Spirit–Son Relationship', 92f.

[107] We observed Torrance citing Jungmann who made the point that it was because of the Church's overreacting to the Arian's denial of the divinity of the Son that this historic trinitarian pattern of worship was altered to 'Glory to the Father and to the Son and to the Holy Spirit'. However, Jungmann never denies that the Church always ascribed and encouraged worship to the Son, particularly in its private devotion (cf. Jungmann, *The Place of Christ*, 170–75).

Pannenberg finds in both these texts cited grounds to differentiate personally and functionally between the Spirit and the Son. He states:

> Was Jesus not the recipient partner with regard to his glorification as it was granted to him by the Father in the exultation of the crucified and resurrected Lord? And is he not the recipient partner in his glorification through his believers' confession? Is not the glorification something that happened to Jesus from outside himself? If this notion proves itself sound, then one can perhaps justify the step to the dogma of the Trinity in 381 that called the Holy Spirit the third 'Person' in God alongside the Father and the Son.[108]

Traditionally it has been the theology of worship which has required a clearly defined and differentiated doctrine of the Spirit, one which postulates the Spirit's standing on the side of the Church over against the Son, who is to be glorified. T.A. Smail in a study of 'The Son–Spirit Relationship', comments on how that relation within the Trinity conditions the Church's view of worship: 'The one who acts in the Church and enables [Christ] to be confessed and worshipped is the Spirit.' In the worship relation it is the Spirit, he states, who is 'at work with us on our side of the relationship, enabling us to receive, to confess and to give glory to the Lord [Christ]'.[109] The Church's prayer 'in the Spirit' is thus shown to be not just the echo of Christ's worship of the Father facilitated among us by the Spirit, although that is certainly an essential part of it, but the Church's praise called forth by the Spirit and conjoined with his own praise of the Father and the Son.

The problem posed in the last section – the integrity of the Church's subjectivity in its relation to the subjectivity of Christ – can now be seen to be closely aligned to the first major question raised – the integrity of the subjectivities of the members of the Godhead in their relations to each other. What we are suggesting is that the way Torrance answers the trinitarian question inevitably conditions the way he answers the doxological one. In saying this we thus keep to his own rule, that the Trinity itself prescribes our way of thinking

---

[108] Pannenberg, *Jesus – God and Man*, 179. Pannenberg is not suggesting that either Paul or John actually have a fully developed doctrine of the Trinity engaged or even conceived in their theology. He concludes the paragraph cited: 'But even then one must clearly understand that this step leads beyond the concepts expressed by Paul and probably John too.' He calls the Holy Spirit the 'third independent movement in God's essence' (179).

[109] Smail, 'The Spirit–Son Relationship', 93, 98f.

about God and his relations with men, that the Trinity is the 'grammar of theology'. Concisely stated, the doctrine of the Trinity, as Torrance conceives it, projects only the act of a single subject, albeit an act proceeding in a three-fold manner. There does not exist within his understanding of the Trinity a true counterpart to our response, only Christ's wholly substitutionary response which ultimately displaces ours. The lack of a response immanent to the person of the Spirit *vis-à-vis* the person of the Son affords no formal place as it were within the divine economy for the distinct identity of the Church's prayer 'in the Spirit' *vis-à-vis* the prayer of Christ.

In our discussion of Torrance's epistemology we noted what he calls 'the supremacy of Christology' in his doctrine of revelation.[110] Admittedly, pre-eminence must belong to Christ in the economy of revelation, since it is in the particularity of Christ's human word and deed that the very knowledge and wisdom of God is manifest. But has this christological supremacy become a kind of christological monarchianism? Has, in fact, Torrance's pneumatology finally collapsed into christology? Torrance's doctrine of the Eucharist, which perhaps as much as any other area of his thought juxtaposes the work of the Spirit with the work of the Son, has not indicated otherwise.

3. As to the Unimpaired Condition of the Individual Human Person and Response of Christ vis-à-vis the Particular Christological Gifts of the Sacrament

The question must still be asked how Torrance can reconcile his insistence, on the one hand, that Christ's vicarious human response fully anticipates and embodies the response of each of us and, on the other hand, that Christ's response as such, determined as it is by his individual human integrity, is itself of particular and not universal proportion.

For this discussion it is crucial that we look again at what Torrance means by the vicarious humanity of Christ. It is that particular and historical human being united to the person of the Word in his incarnation. Torrance, like Calvin, never thinks of the humanity of Christ apart from its hypostatic relation to God. Indeed, it has its universal vicarious significance precisely because of the

---

[110] *TS*, 137–8.

union of God and man which inheres within it.[111] The Incarnate Word is the one who acts on behalf of the many, one with man in that he shares a genuine human identity in common with each of us, while related to all men as their Creator. The vicarious act is therefore not the act of God *qua* God as such, nor is it the act of man *qua* man.[112] Neither is it purely the act which relates these two proportions in Christ. The saving deed is that which God enacts as a human being. It is his act from within his human nature, while at the same time his act upon it. For *in man* the Word rectifies our noetic perversity and in so doing reconciles us to himself; *as man* he presents us to the Father whole and in obedience even to the cross. In his resurrection and ascension the Word brings that humanity to its glory and to its heavenly service for all men. Christ's vicarious humanity is at once a renewed humanity in which a new creation is reconstituted and a renewing humanity from which a new creation is conferred.

Because our new life consists in this new creation in Christ's flesh and blood, and because all God's saving activity continues to cohere there, Christ's humanity is said to be the gift of the sacrament.[113] However, corresponding to his vicarious humanity, the sacramental gift is neither Christ's human nature nor his divine nature *per se*. In the sacrament, Torrance says, we are concerned with 'a third dimension, … with the new humanity in Christ who is God and man…. It is His new humanity risen from the dead and eternally in union with God which is the *substance* or the *matter* of the Sacraments'.[114] Christ's risen flesh is itself 'vivified' by the eternal life of God which permeates it and consequently is said itself 'to vivify'. Torrance declares with Calvin that 'without equivocation… the flesh of Christ gives life'.[115] The imparting principle of grace is Christ's divine humanity, but not statically so; that humanity imparts because it is imparted to. The flesh of Christ does not itself give of

---

[111] Wendel, *Calvin*, 224. 'This humanity of the Christ has value for [Calvin] only by its union with the divine nature' (Wendel quotes Max Dominice, *L'Humanité de Jésus d'apres Calvin* (Paris, 1933), 48).

[112] Cf. Lecture, no.2, 27/2/86, Nottingham.

[113] T.F. Torrance, 'Humanity of Christ', 3. 'Jesus Christ is *the New Adam* and it is in Him, in our sharing of the humanity of the New Adam, that our salvation and our new life consist' (p. 3).

[114] Ibid. 3. 'Christ's own human nature is risen and exalted to the right hand of the Father, and it is in that incorruptible human nature that we are given to participate so that we have perpetual reconciliation and communion with God' (*C & A* II, 144).

[115] *C & A* II, 143.

itself. Rather it is the Word *made flesh* who gives himself to the Church in the sacrament and thereby makes us 'to partake in that eternal life which abides in him.'[116] The gift of the sacrament then is God's own eternal life, but not apart from or around his own individual human life. This indicates the inner meaning and dynamic of Christ's breathing the Holy Spirit upon the Church out of his humanity.[117] Keeping this in mind, the gift of the sacrament must therefore never be thought to reside in the Spirit himself, but in the divine humanity from whence he comes. Nor is that gift purely our communion with Christ facilitated by the Spirit – not 'any mystical event', Torrance says – but the eternal life of God which inheres for the Church in Christ's flesh.[118] It is in this sense that Torrance can say that we 'draw life from the flesh once offered'.[119] Furthermore, it is from this kind of thinking that Torrance would have us interpret his extremely realistic statements regarding the Church's participation in Christ's humanity.[120]

---

[116] 'Humanity of Christ', 5. Torrance resists any tendency, as we have indicated, to reduce the conferring agent in the sacrament to Christ's divine nature *simpliciter*. At the same time, he takes issue with William Cunningham's negative appraisal of Calvin's attempt 'to bring out something like a real influence exerted by Christ's human nature' in the Lord's Supper ('Humanity of Christ', 7. Torrance is citing David Cairns, *The Reformers and the Theology of the Reformation*, 240, who has referred to William Cunningham. The latter is quoted as saying of Calvin's effort to attribute to Christ's flesh potential to confer grace as 'the greatest blot in the history of Calvin's labours as a public instructor'). Torrance's own position represents a middle way between these extremes, one that would posit 'an influence exerted by Christ's human nature' to be sure, but not separated from its own 'vivifying' and controlling principle, the Divine Word.

[117] Cf. John 20:22. Calvin stated it thus: 'From the hidden fountain of the Godhead life was miraculously infused into the body of Christ, that it might flow thence into us' (Calvin, 'Mutual Consent in Regard to the Sacraments', from *Tracts and Treatises*, notes and introduction by T.F. Torrance (Grand Rapids, Eerdmans, 1958), vol. 2, 238).

[118] *C & A* II, 142.

[119] Calvin, 'Mutual Consent in Regard to the Sacraments', 219.

[120] 'The sheer realism' Torrance accords to the presence of Christ in the sacrament he attributes to the influence of John Calvin and Robert Bruce upon his sacramental theology. However, he also credits indirectly the Greek fathers by virtue of their formative influence upon Calvin, e.g. Irenaeus, Athanasius, and Cyril of Jerusalem, but especially Cyril of Alexandria. Torrance cites Calvin's particular indebtedness to Cyril for his concept of 'the vivifying flesh of Christ' (Personal Interview, 23/12/85, Edinburgh; 'Humanity of Christ', 4; cf. *Orth & Ref'd*, 13; Ezra Gebremedhin, *Life-Giving Blessing: An Inquiry into the Eucharistic Doctrine of Cyril of Alexandria* (Uppsala University Ph.D., Uppsala

We should rightly qualify statements which at face value would imply that it is Christ's human life as such which is conferred in the sacrament, or his human nature that is the universally given property within it. However, Torrance persists in speaking of that which is given to man in the knowing relation, and its doxological equivalent in the sacrament, in terms of 'human particulars'. Our thoughts are said to be 'informed by His thinking of the Father' and our prayers and intercessions by his.[121] This difficulty can be resolved by identifying those thoughts and prayers of Christ conveyed to us, not as so many ideal entities actually transferred from Christ's mind to ours, but rather in terms of their approximate repetition in us by the Spirit. A more serious problem arises,

---

University Press, 1977), 48ff.). He says, 'Calvin learned from Cyril of Alexandria (specifically from Oecolampadius' Latin edition of Cyril's works) the enormous emphasis, which he made his own (including Cyril's vocabulary) on the servant obedience of the incarnate Son' (*Orth & Ref'd*, 13). As we indicated, Torrance has referred to the term ζωοποιός as specifically one which Calvin borrowed from the Alexandrians. Whatever might be said as to how Calvin's understanding of the term parallels that of Cyril, Torrance's own view does. For example, Cyril says: 'For he [the Word] is life by nature, in as much as he was begotten of a living Father: no less quickening is his holy body also, being in a manner gathered and ineffably united with the all-quickening Word. Wherefore it is accounted his, and is conceived of as one with him. For, since the Incarnation, it is inseparable; except [it is]... not indeed the same in nature (for the body is not consubstantial with the Word from God), yet they are one by that coming-together and ineffable concurrence. And since *the flesh of the Saviour has become life-giving* (as being united to that which is by nature life, the Word from God), when we taste it, then we have life in ourselves, we too united to it as it to the indwelling Word.' 'But when the mystery of the Incarnation is carefully considered, and you then learn who it is who dwells in the flesh, you will then surely feel (he says) unless you would accuse *the divine Spirit* itself also, that it can impart life, although of itself *the flesh profits* not a bit. For since it was united to the life-giving Word, it has become wholly life-giving, hastening up to the power of the higher nature, not itself forcing unto its own nature him who cannot in any wise be subjected. Although then the nature of the flesh be in itself powerless to give life, yet will it effect this, when it has the life-working Word, and is replete with his whole operation. For it is the body of that which is by nature life, not of any earthly being, as to whom one might rightly hold, *the flesh profits nothing*. For not the flesh of Paul (for instance) not yet of Peter, or any other, would work this in us; but only and especially that of our Saviour Christ in whom dwell *all the fulness of the Godhead bodily*' (Cyril of Alexandria, 'Commentary on St. John' in *The Mass: Ancient Liturgies and Patristic Texts*, ed. Andre Hamman (Staten Island, NY, Alba House, 1967), 136, 151-2, italics mine, then his).

[121] *TS*, 159-60.

however, when Torrance states that 'all our responses' to God are already embodied 'in his one all-embracing response to the Father on our behalf'.[122] It is a difficulty not so easily unravelled by an appeal to the Spirit. For in this case Torrance is not suggesting a particular in Christ (his thoughts and prayers) which can be as it were multiplied to the number of like kind (our thoughts and prayers) in the Church, but an *exact* correspondence in quantity and quality between the responses of Christ and those of his people. According to this view, for every genuine and particular response to God in the Church which the Spirit calls forth, there exists in Christ its perfect but also particular counterpart. If this is the case, then for all practical purposes the *individual* creaturehood of Christ over and against our own is rendered meaningless.

This conclusion, however, would seem to be precluded by one of the most important determining factors we have observed in Torrance's sacramental theology, viz. the continuing integrity of the real human person of Jesus, inclusive of all the dimensional limitations belonging to his individuality. We have seen how this concept, delineated in his doctrine of the ascension, radically conditions Torrance's understanding of the real presence. It was from this basis also that he refuted Luther's sacrifice of Christ's human distinctiveness in relation to his divine nature in order to gain Christ's corporeal presence as a universal constituent in the sacrament. If the interpretation of Torrance's view above is correct, has he not made Christ's rational mind, at least in its doxological service, a universal principle of a sort? How else can we make sense of 'all our human responses' being anticipated and implicated in Christ's prayer?[123] Has Torrance after all committed the Lutheran heresy in Calvinist disguise? Even if this is not the case, does there remain the possibility that there is in heaven after all something still missing, viz. that response to God which is unique to man and which he may offer 'through him, and with him, and in him', a response which God desires, not only for his love of Christ, but for his love of man?

---

[122] *G & R*, 161.
[123] Ibid. 161; cf. *RP*, 14.

A QUESTION OF THE MEANING OF GRACE

Torrance's concept of grace has been called into question in the context of an ongoing debate with Roman Catholic scholars over the nature of 'created grace'. Is the conflict a legitimate one, or purely perpetrated by misunderstanding?

Although he now admits that his earliest work, *The Doctrine of Grace in the Apostolic Fathers* was prejudiced by a Barthian point of view, what Torrance outlined in that work as the New Testament concept of grace is consistent with definitions indicated in all subsequent writings.[124] Grace is God's self-bestowal upon man, 'identical with the person of Christ'.[125] As he sees it, any detachment of grace in the mind of the Church from the Incarnate word has the gravest consequences in the Church's theology, particularly in its understanding of the sacraments. When grace is interpreted as an independent, sub-personal or purely pneumatic principle inevitably another material base for its operation must be devised. This has been most commonly construed in the sacraments. For Torrance any concept that purports grace to be something other or apart from the immediate act of God in Christ, any notion in which grace is 'made to inhere in creaturely being', including those contingent elements and/or actions proper to the sacraments, is what he calls 'created grace'. God's acts only inhere in God.[126]

---

[124] Torrance acknowledged this weakness in his doctoral dissertation in a personal interview, 23/12/85, Edinburgh.

[125] *DOG*, 139.

[126] *R/st*, 182. Torrance says: 'Grace is whole and indivisible because it is identical with the personal self-giving of God to us in his Son.... Between its going forth from God and its coming out upon the creation grace at no point ceases to be what it is within the Trinity, in order to become what it is not, some impersonal entity or causality. Grace can never be regarded in an instrumental sense, for from beginning to end in grace God is immediately present and active as living agent' (*R/st*, 183, 187).

The Council of Trent spoke of grace 'inhering' in the soul. Fransen points out how 'very vague and theologically uncommitted' the Council's choice of terms was (Fransen cites Trent, D.800, 821, *Intelligent Theology*, 95). Rahner insists that even in its 'inhering' in man grace is not compromised in its integrity as purely the grace of God, that is, as purely God's act. The point Trent was making, he says, was that grace is 'constitutive' to the new creation. At the same time, Rahner admits that unofficial, popular interpretation of Tridentine thought on the matter made grace and its 'created partner' mutually

All Torrance's theological presuppositions militate against any other interpretation than this. His doctrine of God perceives nothing inherent in the Creator preventing him from speaking and acting immediately toward us out of his own Being. Correspondingly, his doctrine of creation denies that created reality has any necessity or capacity to speak for God. God can and will speak for himself. Torrance's rejection of a sacramental universe is at its heart a rejection of a lesser doctrine of grace than this one. Furthermore, the 'finished work of Christ', the operating centre of his soteriology, by its very definition, needs no supplementation by any external agency to bring itself to fruition among men. Likewise, his understanding of the Church, remaining ontologically distinct in its word and deed from that of its Lord, though always dependent upon him, leaves no suggestion that its worldly life and work might become itself a source of grace or a 'prolonging of the vicarious and atoning work of Christ' in the world.[127] It is, however, primarily the *homoousion* that prevents a different understanding of grace.[128] Torrance states, 'God has freely and irreversibly communicated *himself* to us in the Incarnation once and for all in such a way as to make any other possibility unentertainable by us.'[129]

In the light of this it can be clearly seen why Torrance's doctrine of the Eucharist depends entirely upon just such a concept. No other interpretation of grace will assure that the gift to the Church in the sacrament is anything less than the Giver, that the offering in the sacrament is none other than the Offerer, Jesus Christ, the Royal Priest.[130] Torrance will go so far as to say that it would be just as wrong to speak of a 'sacramental grace' as a 'sacramental Christ'.[131] He means that to identify the source and strength of the grace given through the Eucharist in the sacrament itself would be commensurate to saying that Jesus Christ is himself somehow reincarnate there, and that consequently his power is either usurped

---

conditioning in a 'reciprocal causality' (Karl Rahner, 'Grace', *Sacramentum Mundi*, ed. Karl Rahner and others (London, Burns & Oates, 1968), vol. 2, 418).

[127] So stated in a personal letter to Mary Agnew by Torrance, cited in her doctoral dissertation (Agnew, *The Concept of Sacrifice*, 221).

[128] *R & E*, 112; *R/St*, 182.

[129] 'Trinity', 338, italics mine. 'God is already in Christ what he will be' (*DOG*, 35).

[130] As Torrance has affirmed, 'The matter [of the sacrament] is not any mystical event but Jesus Christ Himself... [and] the action of the Sacrament... none other than... the one saving action of Christ effectively extended to us' (*C & A* II, 142, 144; cf. *Manual*, 19).

[131] *R/st*, 183.

altogether or necessarily supplemented by the sacrament's creaturely operation.[132]

The Roman Catholic theologian Piet Fransen in his series *Intelligent Theology* has sought to dialogue with Torrance regarding his doctrine of grace.[133] He seeks primarily to temper Torrance's view of 'created grace', pointing out that the Roman Catholic Church never officially subscribed to any view of grace as quasi-divine corporality or an independent principle of causality. He concedes, however, that these notions have been held broadly among Roman Catholics from the Middle Ages.[134] 'Created grace' for Fransen is that divine operation not immediately 'in' God *qua* God but 'in' us, in other words, that act of God *ad extra*.[135] He asks: 'Why then is it [grace] called "created"? For the reason that, in so far as we consider it in us, and not in its source which is God, it cannot be God himself, and therefore it has to be called "created".'[136] This, of course, underlines precisely the point Torrance is making. For in Torrance's view, as well as Rahner's, the act of God 'in himself' and the act of God 'in us' is co-extensive. 'The *ad extra* and *ad intra* is identical, because the self-communication of God to us in the Son and in the Spirit would not be a self-communication of God to us, if what God is for us in the Son and in the Spirit were not proper to God himself.'[137]

---

[132] Such a crude manifestation should not be thought remote. For example, cf. Paul VI's statement in *Mysterium Fidei*, encouraging the 'reservation of the Eucharist' in the Churches: 'It is not only while the sacrifice is being offered, the sacrament constituted, that Christ is truly Emmanuel, "God with us". He is so after the offering of the sacrifice, the making of the sacrament, as long as the Eucharist is kept in Churches and oratories' (Pope Paul VI, *The Holy Eucharist*, 28).

[133] The third volume of this study written with T.F. Torrance includes Torrance's article 'The Roman Doctrine of Grace from the point of view of Reformed Theology', as well as Fransen's critical reply to it. This article by Torrance originally appeared in *Eastern Churches Quarterly* 16 (1964), 290–312, and was later published as Chapter 10 in Torrance's *Theology in Reconstruction*, 1965.

[134] Cf. Fransen, *Intelligent Theology*, 95. Philip Watson observes: 'In Catholicism, the main emphasis has been on grace as a power, conveyed primarily through the sacraments, and often described in terms suggestive of a metaphysical substance, not to say quasi-physical force' ('Grace', *A Dictionary of Christian Theology*, 147f.).

[135] Fransen, *Intelligent Theology*, 95.

[136] Ibid. 95.

[137] 'Trinity', 338–9; cf. *G & G*, 158f. Torrance refers to an independent monograph, *The Trinity* by Rahner and discussed by the Colloquy of the

An Appraisal of Torrance's Eucharistic Theology 281

While acknowledging that no aspect of grace can be 'for one moment separated from its divine source', Fransen goes on to identify grace precisely in the way Torrance would anticipate, i.e. as renewed human character. Fransen says, 'Grace is life, is faith and love, inseparably embraced by and engulfed in the love of God.'[138] His very defence reveals the root of the problem as Torrance would see it, highlighting as it does the subtle distinction in Roman Catholic theology between grace and the direct act of God in his own being.[139]

Similarly in her dissertation on Torrance's doctrine of eucharistic sacrifice, Mary Agnew insists that the question of created grace consists in 'whether there is any effect of the Redemption in man or whether Christ's merits are "imputed" to him'.[140] By such a statement she appears not to be fully abreast of the issues Torrance is raising. The concern is not whether grace effects real substantial change in man – Torrance never suggests otherwise – but whether that act of grace in man remains the act of God himself irrespective of the secondary or sacramental objectivity which he might requisition in order to effect it.

Finally, another Roman Catholic, John Quinn, in a review of *Theology in Reconstruction*, suggests that Torrance often treats very complex issues all too perfunctorily, failing to grapple with the full scope of the problem.[141] Undoubtedly, Torrance does sometimes abbreviate the historical compounding of a question in its development so as to get directly at what he thinks is the root of the matter. If the Roman Catholic critics cited here are representative, however, it might be said that for their part they are unable to 'see clear' of their own abstract, metaphysical ideas on grace in order to confront the basic questions Torrance is raising. Even Rahner, as

---

'Academie Internationale des Sciences Religieuses' (Bethanien, Switz.) of which he was a part.

Contrast Torrance's and Rahner's thought with later Eastern thought: 'Byzantine thought affirms the full and distinct reality of the Triune hypostatic life of God *ad intra* as well as His "multiplication" [in the divine "energies"] as creator, *ad extra*. These two "multiplicities" do not however coincide' (John Meyendorff, *Byzantine Theology* (New York, Fordham University Press, 1974), 187).

[138] Fransen, *Intelligent Theology*, 96.
[139] Cf. 'New College', 24.
[140] Agnew, *The Concept of Sacrifice*, 212.
[141] James Quinn, review of *Theology in Reconstruction* by T.F. Torrance, *ThSt* 28 (1967), 389. Actual quotation: The work 'is strewn with assumptions that demand closer scrutiny than they receive'.

Torrance points out, is sometimes 'found expressing the Economic Trinity as immanent, that is as it is in God, in such a way that it prescinds from God's free self-communication, and so a moment of abstraction appears to be introduced between what God is in himself and the mode of his self-revelation and self-communication to us'.[142] That, of course, is for Torrance the fatal mistake. However, he feels that this difficulty in Rahner's thought is probably either our 'confusion... in reading him' or merely an anomaly out of character with his overall position. For, as he notes, 'Rahner like Barth insists, the self-communication of God in his revelation and the self-giving of God in his Being are one and the same.'[143]

QUESTIONS OF STYLE, METAPHOR AND APPEAL

Will the abstractness and complexity of concept and style in which Torrance delineates his eucharistic theology inhibit its being generally understood and therefore widely accepted in the Church?

---

[142] 'Trinity', 338.

[143] Ibid. 339. Rahner in fact says: Grace is 'God's self-communication in his own divine life [and is], both as given, and accepted by man... essentially God's free, personal gift'. Any relation with nature which 'the divine self-communication creatively posits for itself' is accomplished in such a way so that that 'communication does and can remain what it is' (416, 417). In commenting specifically on 'Uncreated and created grace', Rahner says, 'it is readily intelligible that "grace"... as such and as strictly supernatural is first and foremost God himself communicating himself with his own nature: Uncreated grace'. And while 'there is no agreement in Catholic theology on how exactly the relation between created and Uncreated grace is to be determined... it is at all events quite possible to regard Uncreated grace as primary and as *the* grace which is the essential basis of the whole of man's grace-given endowment and as what alone renders intelligible the authentic and strictly supernatural character of grace' (418). In other words, Rahner interprets that grace which Trent says 'inheres' in the soul as always retaining its own being, its own 'self-inherence', so that in all its relation to man in the Church and its sacraments grace never loses its uniquely divine character. Grace may be said to 'inhere', that is, to subsist, in created substance (e.g. in man) but not without continuing to 'inhere' in its own uncreated being in its own divine way, that is, never forfeiting its own nature as the Being and Act of God in contradistinction to the being and act of creation. (All quotations above from Rahner, 'Grace', *Sacramentum Mundi*, vol. 2, 409–24, italics mine).

The lack of specificity which we have noted in Torrance's thought with regard to the exact moment of the occurrence of Christ's presence within the sacrament corresponds to a lack of definiteness as well with regard to what is the unique benefit conferred by Christ through the sacrament. Kilian McDonnell observes that for Calvin, as for Luther, there was 'no specific eucharistic gift', that is, nothing given in the Eucharist peculiar to that sacrament as such.[144] This was generally the case in the eucharistic theologies of the Reformation. He states, 'The gift of Christ in the Eucharist is the same gift given in baptism and in the preaching of the Word: the whole presence (of Christ) in his divine and human totality, the whole living Christ.'[145] For Luther, however, Christ was seen extending in the sacrament specifically the forgiveness of sins. Forgiveness in Lutheran sacramental theology is a kind of secondary gift, the gift of the Gift himself. For Calvin and for Torrance, on the other hand, this 'secondary gift' lacks concreteness. Some might suggest that 'participation in Christ' is the Church's special bequest in Reformed sacramental tradition.[146] This would only be true, however, so long as participation is not conceived as something separate from Christ. In other words, it must be understood to encompass both the christological end and means all in one.

No matter how one interprets it, 'participation' is in itself an exceedingly abstruse concept, and our study has not revealed Torrance's eucharistic theology as having made it any less so. For example, he was shown to perceive the Church's sacramental participation as a re-presentation in time of a 'moment' of our eternal participation in Christ. For all the theological profundity conveyed by such a notion, it is not one that is easily grasped or communicated. The abstractness of the idea was only compounded by Torrance's choosing to unpack its significance almost exclusively in ecclesiastical terms. The Eucharist, he says, is a 'corporate sacrament', corresponding to Christ's substitutionary incorporation of all men in his flesh.[147] Sacramental communion is at once the

---

[144] McDonnell, *John Calvin*, 179; cf. Wendel, *Calvin*, 353.

[145] McDonnell, *John Calvin*, 71. Torrance concurs with John McLeod Campbell, who speaks of the legacy of the sacrament as 'Christ, the Bread of Life', i.e. as one who is 'the Divine Life in man', the source of Eternal Life (cf. Campbell, *Christ the Bread of Life*, 7–12, esp. 9).

[146] Cf. *Inter*, 320.

[147] *C & A* II, 151ff. In this emphasis Torrance follows Calvin. Scholars generally highlight the corporate nature of the Reformed Eucharist (cf. Wallace,

ingathering act of God and the gathering act of man in which the Church takes manifest and corporate shape. Although Torrance can say that God's 'human partner' in the sacramental relation 'is both the Church and the individual believer within the Church', sacramental participation has relevance for the individual only inasmuch as individuals belong to the Church which shares in Christ as one.[148] No doubt, the Eucharist does have deep significance for the Church as a whole; this emphasis has always been a hallmark of Reformed sacramental theology. Torrance's emphasis at this point is an understandable one as a counterweight to the excessive individualism of modern evangelical pietism. Nevertheless, after all the corporate meanings of the Eucharist have been elucidated by him, do those for the individual ever really come into view, that is, except by implication? He further expounds the significance of sacramental participation for the Church in extremely remote eschatological images. In this feast, he asserts, by virtue of the presence of one in whose divine and glorified humanity the whole creation and history partake in eternity, the Church itself partakes of 'fulfilled time and incorruptible creation'. Here, Torrance says, is a foretaste, after the nature of the Spirit and of the sacrament, of a 'new creation', and a 'new time', of 'time in the form of the Spirit'.[149] These are lofty thoughts indeed, but virtually inaccessible except to those prepared to unravel his densely complex metaphors.

Torrance's writings are characterized not only by a conceptual obscurity but equally by a very laborious style. Reviewers have consistently criticized his presentation. The Canadian chemist and author, Walter R. Thorson, although in general agreement with Torrance's philosophy of science, describes great portions of his

---

Calvin's Doctrine of the Word and Sacrament, 154f.; McDonnell, *John Calvin*, 184f.). The views of Gregory Dix are enigmatic at this point and wholly unconvincing. He says, 'the real eucharistic action is for Calvin individual and internal, not corporate' (Gregory Dix, *The Shape of the Liturgy* (Westminster, Dacre Press, 1943), 633).

[148] *R/st*, 181. One such implication for the individual within the sacrament's predominantly corporate meaning is that life in Christ is always a shared experience. It belongs to the nature of the sacrament that members of the Church, after the example of him who washed our feet, should serve each other the body and blood of Christ. Here, he says, Christ makes 'each... a deacon to the other at [his] Holy Table' (*C & A* II, 151, cf. 151-4). The Eucharist then for Torrance is a feast for the whole Church, a 'corporate act', as he calls it, 'in which all join in' (*C & A* II, 152).

[149] Cf. *RP*, 59f.

work as 'stylistically turbulent'.[150] Donald M. McKay refers to Torrance's compositions as a 'verbal jungle'. 'One need not be a rabid linguistic analyst', he says, 'to long here for more semantic discipline in the use of words'.[151] Similarly, Ronald Lunt, reviewing one of Torrance's works, remarks, 'He plies us with sentences of complex structure and inordinate length – seldom less than ten lines – with clause and phrase piled like Pelion on Ossa. They are great intellectual constructions, but they make hard going and by the end seem to have lost their bite.'[152] Most agree that Torrance's works are 'difficult to read', requiring 'scholarly hard work to be really understood'.[153]

The intricacy of Torrance's style and concepts is made even more problematic by the convoluted progression of his ideas. In order to master his theology, including his theology of the Eucharist, one is required to follow a circuitous interweaving of presuppositions and exercise a theological exactitude clearly beyond the level of most. Nevertheless, for those who will 'take the trouble' Torrance's sacramental theology offers a fresh and insightful interpretation of the Reformed Eucharist.[154] Hopefully this study has shown that his concept of sacramental participation, despite its complexity, reveals the Holy Eucharist at a most profound christological depth, so that for those who can grasp it, the sacrament can never again be thought of simply in terms of 'external relations' between Christ and the sacrament or the sacrament and the Church.[155]

Faced with the peculiar complexity of Torrance's eucharistic theology, however, one wonders whether his contribution, any more than Calvin's, will have any general influence in the Church. The fact is that in every generation Reformed theologians have taken Calvin's teaching on the sacrament seriously and sought to reinterpret it for the Churches, usually without diminishing its claims to sacramental realism. However, in view of the ancillary place which the sacrament has always occupied *vis-à-vis* preaching among Reformed Churches,

---

[150] W. Thorson, review of *Reality and Scientific Theology* by T.F. Torrance, *PSCF* 38, 2 (1986), 212–14.

[151] Donald M. McKay, review of *Divine and Contingent Order* by T.F. Torrance, *ChrG* 35, 2 (1982), 38–9.

[152] Ronald Lunt, review of *Theology in Reconciliation* by T.F. Torrance, *ExpTim* 87 (1975–76), 379; for 'Pelion on Ossa' cf. Shakespeare, *Hamlet*, final act.

[153] W. Thorson, review of *The Christian Frame of Mind* by T.F. Torrance, *USCF* (Winter 85/86), 43–6; W. Thorson, review of *Reality and Scientific Theology*, 212.

[154] Ibid. 212.

[155] *GT*, 6.

there is no reason to believe that any of them has ever been convinced.[156] Generally speaking, Churches which hold a high view of

---

[156] Some would view Calvin's doctrine itself as ascribing only a 'secondary significance' to the sacrament, that is, in relationship to the preached word. James S. McEwen takes this position (James S. McEwen, *The Faith of John Knox*, The Croall Lectures, 1960 (London, Lutterworth, 1962), 46). There is certainly this tendency in Calvin, however, Geddes MacGregor gives a much more theologically considered appraisal: 'The Reformers' natural suspicions of all pseudo-sacramentalism that is separated from the proclamation of the Word ought not to mislead us into the erroneous and quite unrealistic view that the Sacrament itself is considered to have an attenuated importance. For the contrary is the case: The insistence upon the association of Word and Sacrament is calculated to exalt the latter no less than the former' (MacGregor, *Corpus Christi*, 181). Kilian McDonnell reaches a similar conclusion. He says, 'Though Calvin will speak of the Eucharist as an appendix to the Gospel, this must be understood against the background of sacramental imperialism. He would hardly have expended so much effort on a matter that lacked centrality' (McDonnell, *John Calvin*, 74). McEwen also contends that the Church of Scotland did not merely 'follow Calvin' in its sacramental doctrine, but, by starting with him 'at his best', it went 'beyond him to something still better' (McEwen, 45, 59). In explaining what this 'something... better' is, McEwen appeals more to Scottish sacramental practice than to their sacramental theology. 'A change of emphasis', he calls it, 'and a remarkable change of practice' (McEwen, 54). The Kirk he insists gave to the sacrament more dignity than did Calvin. He cites the fact that, whereas the Eucharist was the last thing which Calvin instituted in the life of the Church, it was the first thing which Knox did. In short, the sacrament in Scotland is perceived as more 'foundational' to the Church as an institution; it manifests the visible Church (McEwen, 55-7). In contrast to this Torrance contends that in fact the Church in Scotland 'followed Calvin' more closely than any other church in Europe. Brilioth confirms this: 'The purest representation of Calvinism (in this context, Calvin's sacramental doctrine) in the Anglo-Saxon world is the Church of Scotland' (Brilioth, *Eucharistic Faith and Practice*, 186). Torrance shows how, at least in its emphasis on the importance of the humanity of Christ for sacramental theology, the Church of Scotland 'stands decidedly nearer to the teaching of Calvin than any of our sister Reformed churches on the Continent' ('Humanity of Christ', 6). McEwen stresses the great solemnity and time the Church of Scotland has traditionally given to the celebration of the rite – 'communion seasons', etc. (McEwen, 46; cf. Barkley, *The Worship of the Reformed Church*, 75-6). While Torrance acknowledges that these so-called 'seasons' in their earlier form evidence a remnant in the Scottish rite of the preeminent place given to thanksgiving in early Christian liturgy as well as in Calvin's sacramental theology, he thinks that much of the solemn ordeal surrounding sacramental observance in Scotland since the seventeenth century, rather than a sign of awe engendered by the sheer presence of Christ and an expression of praise, has been the result of the heavy burden of repentance laid upon the Church by Federal Theology ('Comments', 18; cf. Basil Hall, '*Hoc Est Corpus Meum*: The Centrality of the Real Presence for Luther' in *Luther:*

Christ's presence, priesthood and sacrifice in the Eucharist will make the sacramental celebration an essential and regular part of their worship-life.[157] Within the Reformed Tradition, besides a few local exceptions, no Church celebrates the Eucharist more than monthly. Moreover, when queried with regard to their sacramental doctrine, most Reformed Christians will, unknowingly, answer as Zwinglians rather than proper Calvinists.[158] Certainly this state of affairs will not

---

Theologian for Catholics and Protestants, ed. George Yule (Edinburgh, T & T Clark, 1985), 139). Furthermore, Torrance is convinced that there has been an unhealthy preoccupation upon penitence in the Scottish Church since the Middle Ages, probably originating at the time of the imposition of severe and aesthetic Latin piety upon the Celtic Church by Queen Margaret at the time of the 'Normanization of the Scottish Court' (c. 1068-1093) (Personal Interview, 23/12/86, Edinburgh; cf. John Prebble, *The Lion of the North: A Personal View of Scotland's History*, London, Book Club Association, 1974, 35-7).

[157] Cf. McEwen, *The Faith of John Knox*, 52.

[158] This is incongruous of course with the teaching and admonition of Calvin in his time and that of T.F. Torrance today. Calvin himself sincerely desired a weekly celebration of the Eucharist (MacGregor, *Corpus Christi*, 181, esp. 53, fn. 1). This, as John Barkley points out, 'was one of the points on which he quarrelled with the Geneva magistracy and which led to his banishment from the city in 1538' (Barkley, *The Worship of the Reformed Church*, 75). Calvin himself went so far as to declare infrequent communion to be 'an invention of the devil' and held that 'once a week at the very least the Lord's Supper should be celebrated in the Christian congregation' (William Maxwell, 'Reformed Worship' in *A New Dictionary of Liturgy and Worship*, ed. J.G. Davies (London, SCM, 1986), 459; cf. Brilioth, *Eucharistic Faith and Practice*, 176-7). Torrance, with Wotherspoon and Kirkpatrick, suggests the 'desirability of weekly celebration'. He states, 'Indeed, the practice of our Church in this respect has always been below its own standard; but repeated Acts of Assembly have enjoined or pointed to reformation in the matter' (*Manual*, 47). John M. Barkley, himself a Professor in Church History at Presbyterian College Belfast, echoes the cry of so many Reformed theologians through the centuries: 'The great service of the Lord's Day must itself include communion of the people' (Barkley, 76). Barkley also points out that neither weekly nor 'monthly Communion (ever) seems to have been the practice in Scotland, this apparently being determined, not only by the shortage of ministers... but by the Act of the General Assembly in 1562, which ordained, 'that the Communion be administered four times in the year within the burghs, and twice in the year toward landward' (Barkley, 75).

An exception to this is St Giles, The High Kirk of Scotland, Edinburgh, where a regular Sunday Eucharist seems long to have been celebrated. Barkley, however, criticizes, as would Torrance, the place and form which the service took for several decades, viz. 'After the Sunday Morning Service... in the Moray aisle' (Barkley, 76). Happily, this 'aisle service' has now been abandoned with two of the three Sunday morning services being eucharistic celebrations

be remedied among Reformed Churches until the laity at large are persuaded as to the vital importance of the Eucharist for the Church's life and that, of course, depends upon theological indoctrination. Such a task, however, and this reiterates the point made above, will be an arduous one because of how difficult Calvin's doctrine is to explain. What is required theologically is to convince the people of the equivalence of participation and presence, that there is no 'distance' or difference between communing in Christ and communing in him by the Holy Spirit. This dissertation among other things underlines just how extremely complicated this can be. Our study has provided little evidence that Torrance's commendable attempt at interpreting Calvin's doctrine for the Church has made it any less difficult to understand.

Given all the obvious deficiencies of Lutheran sacramental theology which Torrance has identified – viz. its virtual destruction of the doctrine of the ascension, its propensity to subjectivism, underpinning, as he sees it, the later idealism of Kant and Protestant Liberalism, and its failure to stress the doxological element – Luther's doctrine has two strengths sorely lacking in Reformed eucharistic theology in general and in that of Torrance in particular. The first is the explicit meaning it carries for the individual Christian. Being associated more directly with the forgiveness of personal sins, the sacramental theology of the Lutheran tradition tends to foster a desire in Christians for regular attendance at the sacrament corresponding to the perpetual need of all for God's mercy.[159] It is a matter of real question if any eucharistic theology

---

(Correspondence with the senior minister, Rev. Gilleasbuig MacMillan, 27/6/86). He writes:

'St. Giles' is not typical of the Church of Scotland, although there has been a considerable increase in the frequency of the Sacrament in most churches, and monthly celebrations are not uncommon. In St. Giles' there has been fairly continuous development, at least since the time of Dr. Arnot in the 1860's. Weekly Communion in a side chapel after the 11 am morning service ran from around 1930 until 1974, when the weekly celebration was moved to 9, as a morning service without choir. Since 1983 the present custom of two mid-morning services, each with choir, has been our practice. I would attribute our relative distinctiveness partly to those who have been Minister here, and partly to the "Cathedral" or metropolitan aspect of our life, both in our own eyes, and in the eyes of many Scottish people.'

[159] It must be said that virtually everything stated here would be hotly debated by scholars from both sides, particularly the positive way that I have handled Luther's individualistic approach to the sacrament. This aspect of the German Reformer's sacramental theology has always been contested, not least of all by Lutheran critics themselves (cf. Brilioth, *Eucharistic Faith and Practice*,

131f.; Dix, *The Shape of the Liturgy*, 635, 638; D.H. Hislop, *Our Heritage in Public Worship*, Kerr Lectures, 1933 (Edinburgh, T & T Clark, 1935), 167). They point out that Luther's predominant stress upon the personal implications of the Eucharist was rooted in the very penitential piety that had originally, albeit indirectly, given rise to infrequent communion in the practice of the medieval Church. Lutheran Protestants, particularly early on, have struggled against these tendencies. Eugene Brand notes this:

'In spite of heroic efforts to restore frequent communion among the people and thus balance sermon and sacrament, old habits prevailed [in early Lutheranism]. Awe of the presence and the need for solemn self-preparation, the individualism resulting from an almost exclusive emphasis on the forgiveness of sins as chief fruit of the sacrament and a strong stress on the importance of preaching all contributed to infrequent celebrations. This did not result, as it did in England, in the ascendancy of mattins. Lutherans used antecommunion as their preaching service with the result that, in spite of the infrequency of the eucharist, their devotion remained oriented to the mass' (Eugene Brand, 'Lutheran Worship' in *A New Dictionary of Liturgy and Worship*, 345–6).

Brilioth even goes so far as to suggest that it was the Lutherans' 'individualism' which directly caused their infrequency at communion in the past (cf. Brilioth, *Eucharistic Faith and Practice*, 134).

Certainly the Lutheran emphasis is not enough. There is a need to balance their narrow personal focus with the broader corporate implications of the sacrament. However, whatever might be said about the questionable sources of Luther's individualism in medieval piety and the inherent, long-term weakness of the forgiveness of sins as a principal motivating factor toward eucharistic communion, history has evidenced a progressive triumph of Luther's doctrine of grace over all these encumbrances. *In contrast to the practice of so much of the Reformed Church, in which Federal Covenant Theology has historically gained predominance, the eucharistic feast in the Lutheran Church is kept for the mercy it offers and celebrates rather than the repentance it obliges.* D.H. Hislop comments that, despite the 'Lutheran Sacrament [dwelling] too exclusively' upon 'the receiving of forgiveness by the individual worshipper', 'the God of Lutheran Worship is the God revealed in Christ who pardons. Other aspects of the Divine Being that belong also to worship may fail to receive full recognition, but the centre and the core of the Christian experience find expression in the worship of God in this service. There is also a richness and a warmth in this worship that are sometimes lacking in the worship of the other reformed churches' (Hislop, *Our Heritage in Public Worship*, 167, 176; cf. Bryan Spinks' conclusion that Luther repositioned the *Sanctus* after the Institution in his *Deutsch Mass* in order to supply a fittingly doxological climax and reply to the testament of grace. It is this emphasis that is being reclaimed in present-day Lutheran sacramental theology. Bryan D. Spinks, 'Luther and the Canon of the Mass', *LitR* 3 (1973), 43–4).

There is no other tradition within mainline Protestantism that has given comparable place to the sacrament and their worship as have the Lutherans. All the impairing tendencies of individualistic piety and their own failings being

will ever be broadly accepted which does not have such personal concerns demonstrably at its heart. If Luther's doctrine can be justly criticized for its predominantly individualistic focus, Torrance's theology can be faulted for having so little to say directly to the individual. In the opinion of the author, Torrance's theology cries out for a healthy *pro me* to balance its corporate preoccupation.

Secondly, though certainly not without its metaphysical paradoxes, indeed relishing them, Lutheran sacramental theology has always been more plainly presented, more easily understood, and hence more simply believed than that of the Reformed tradition. For this reason Lutheranism has generally proven highly resistant to sacramental reductionism, like that of the sacramentarians and quite resilient in the face of ritualism. In contrast to this, after our study of Torrance's eucharistic theology, one is inclined to think that Torrance's doctrine, like Calvin's before him, might ultimately be disregarded not for its sheer realism, but for its sheer complexity. Basil Hall, writing in a recent collection of articles compiled to mark the occasion of the five hundredth anniversary of Luther's birth, makes several of the points raised here as well as underlines other manifest weaknesses in Reformed eucharistic theology to which Torrance has drawn our attention.

> In spite of the sacramental realism of Calvin, whose theme was the sursum corda so that our souls are fed with the body and blood of Christ through the power of the Holy Spirit when we eat the bread and wine, the Reformed Churches in their varieties like other forms of Protestantism (whatever the degree of official recognition of Calvin's legacy) are in practice Zwinglian at the Communion. The tendency to Nestorianism at least latent in Reformed Theology has played its part here. Also, remembrance has been given the further dimension of sealing and fulfilling the new covenant to which promises for obedience are attached. In the seventeenth century and later this covenant or federal theology brought back again what Luther had sought to abolish, the trust in works righteousness which led to emphasizing that moralism which reduces the sacrament to being an appendix to or recognition of moral virtues attained. All the varieties of federal theology are destructive of sacramental theology. Whatever modifications to Reformed Theology were brought about through Anglican

---

acknowledged, the fact remains that through the centuries the Lutherans have more consistently centred their worship around the eucharistic celebration and likewise communed more regularly than any other Protestant body. What I am commending in Lutheran faith and practice is the fact that among these Christians the sacrament shares with the preached word an importance at the centre of the Church's worship unparalleled elsewhere.

evangelicism, through the Methodist movement, or through the post-Ritschlian Theology, the Zwinglian remembering and not sacramental realism has essentially triumphed for the majority of non-Lutheran Protestant laity. That Lutheranism could fall into the narrowness of [sic] excess of dogmatizing and other defects including some loss of Luther's original freshness of approach will be plain to non-Lutherans at least, but it is still possible to find behind the denominationalism the quickening theology of Luther himself which could change for the better the sacramental aridity just mentioned.[160]

QUESTIONS OF 'IMAGELESS IMAGES' AND AESTHETICS

Is Torrance's general depreciation of anything other than 'reflexive' images in the created order consistent with his appeal to the divine humanity as the Image of God? Furthermore, is his overwhelming preference for audible images, as well as for unobservable and abstract so-called 'imageless images', compatible with a sacramental theology which claims to assign the sacrament central respect in the Church alongside the spoken word? Finally, do these invisible signs really pay enough respect both to the manifestly palpable correlates belonging to the incarnation and to the aesthetic need in the Church's worship for visible and tangible correlation with that aspect of the christological mystery?

Because God's Living Word can be heard and not seen, and since, therefore, the spoken word obviously lends itself more to the nature of God in this respect, Torrance as a rule defers to the medium of hearing in the communication of divine truth. Although never denying that perceptible images 'have their place in our knowledge of God', in that the visual attribute belongs necessarily to the creaturely content of revelation, these best serve the Word by themselves deferring to what God is speaking, by pointing away from themselves to a reality which they cannot describe.[161] The lack of

---

[160] Hall, *Hoc est Corpus Meum*, 139.

[161] *TS*, 19–20. Torrance comprehensively devalues 'picture thinking' about God or speaking about him in 'the language of vision'. 'Observable concepts', he says, are inappropriate to the divine reality; they are 'primitive and pre-scientific'. Since God is invisible reality it follows that any appropriateness at the visible level of created reality is precluded. 'Picture models' when referred to

'significance', properly so-called, which Torrance attributes to the visual dimension within the Eucharist, illustrates this. While recognizing that the sacrament carries an element of perceptual expression, he insists that the sacrament's principal role is not to reproduce the truth in pictorial form, but to demonstrate the nature of the truth as action.[162]

We have observed how Torrance, operating from these premises, has tended progressively towards purely intellectual or mathematical images when referring to God. These are deemed more appropriate to him by the very fact that they connote ideas in our minds that do not inhere in observable reality. Similarly, out of the formal matter of revelation and in the history of dogma Torrance discerns certain primary models of this kind which have been intuitively given and received by the Church, e.g. the doctrines of the Trinity and the hypostatic union. These he calls 'disclosure models', not just to underline the fact that they have no parallels in the created order and hence their obvious God-givenness, but because they are not themselves *directly* representative of that which they disclose. It is their referential element which is most important. The purpose of these images is not to set themselves up to be intellectually contemplated, but to direct our attention beyond themselves to the divine reality which transcends comprehension.[163] This is not to say that such models are 'thoughtless', that would be nonsense, but that the concepts which they designate are non-visual ones and resist, by their faithfulness to the divine object, any attempt to be stylized, even mentally.

Since we are 'not allowed to have any imaginative or pictorial representation of [God] in our thought', the desirable goal for the Church is to be able to apprehend him without their assistance altogether.[164] Torrance thus prefers 'images' which refer to the divine

---

him, therefore, have only symbolic value, their significance being based not upon what God has revealed about himself, but upon the relativity and subjectivity of man's representative frames of reference (cf. *G & G*, 124–5; *TS*, 23–4).

[162] The 'co-ordination [of] perceptual and auditive images' suggested by the co-centrality which Torrance assigns the Word and sacrament in the Church 'provide us with the cognitive instruments we need for explicit theological understanding of God's interaction with us' (*R & E*, 49).

[163] Torrance cites Tillich's definition of a symbol: 'a symbolic expression is one whose proper meaning is negated by that to which it points. And yet it is also affirmed by it, and this affirmation gives the symbolic expression an adequate basis for pointing beyond itself' (*TS*, 19; Paul Tillich, *Systematic Theology* (London, James Nisbet & Co., 1953), vol. 1, 265f.).

[164] *TS*, 20.

reality without the aid of pictorial impression – 'imageless images', as he designates them.[165] Acknowledging the difficulty that this poses, since all images have an element of the representative in them, he nevertheless wants the visual element to play as little part as possible. The Church's task is steadily to refine its thoughts about God in the light of his Word so that the 'observational significance is reduced to a minimum'.[166] What Torrance seeks is truly 'transparent images', as we suggested earlier, viz. images which by their appropriateness to the christological object lend themselves readily and easily to his self-disclosing power, that obtrude themselves as little as possible, so that the Word can quite literally 'show himself through' them.[167]

The question must immediately be asked if the kind of 'imageless imaging' about God which Torrance thinks preferable is actually possible. Do not even the purely cognitive models which he has chosen, whether out of the sciences or theology, give rise to mental 'pictures' 'representative' of divine reality, though, admittedly of a kind more distant from surface phenomena? Can man really think without images as Torrance says the Jews learned to do?[168] Does not all thinking require 'images' of a sort, that is, correlates in our created context, albeit some only on a highly abstract or mathematical plane? Sallie McFague comments on the wholly interdependent relation between thoughts and images: 'Images without concepts are blind', she says, 'concepts without images are sterile'.[169] Do not words themselves belong to the world of creaturely imagery? It is a maxim of linguistics that conceptualist and imagistic language can never be utterly divorced. In any event, even the most abstract, theoretical words had pictorial origins.[170] If

---

[165] *G & G*, p.126.
[166] Ibid. 123ff., esp. 126.
[167] Cf. ibid. 126; *R/st*, 89; *TS*, 19.
[168] 'Israel', 5.
[169] Sallie McFague, *Metaphorical Theology: Models of God In Religious Language* (London, SCM, 1983), 26.
[170] Numerous philosophers and philologists have remarked on the radically metaphorical nature of all, even abstract, language. Owen Barfield – now greatly respected as a theorist of metaphor – has called language a 'tissue of faded metaphors'. In the same essay, he identified Max Muller (the nineteenth-century philosopher) as the pioneer of this way of thinking. He also quotes Ernest Weekley: 'Every expression that we employ, apart from those that are connected with the most rudimentary objects and actions, is a metaphor, though the original meaning is dulled by constant use.' Weekley then proceeds to illustrate this from the words he has just used. 'Thus, in the above sentence, 'expression'

imageless words are impossible then so too are imageless images in the Church; for Torrance, with Barth, has dismissed 'wordless' images as 'a-logical' and meaningless.[171]

The subtle implication of Torrance's reasoning might be that the further one gets from the outward visible nature of created reality, or the more one patterns his thoughts away from that which is concretely imaginable, the more appropriate to God the attributes of that reality, or at least our thinking about him at that level, becomes. But surely this is not true. For though certain qualities might be more or less apposite – by their invisibility, audibility, even unimaginability in observable categories – what they qualify are nevertheless infinitely distinct proportions. Admittedly, with respect only to the bare proportion, audible or purely intellectual images are more appropriate to God, more applicable to his Word, but they still share the same inherent difference from him as do visual ones. 'Images' of God drawn from the theoretical depths of matter/energy do not belong any less to the created order just because they are more abstract. A mental or mathematical image is not any more an image of God because it is not manifest to the visual sense. The devil is also invisible. Torrance's tendencies in this direction need to be checked by his own unequivocal rule: no created thing bears any likeness to God whatsoever.[172]

The main contention Torrance has with any supposed image of God from this natural order is its being projected back into the nature of God. This is the great sin of the *ikon*, that men are invited to 'follow the cue' of manifestly created being so as to contemplate the uncreated.[173] But are even the most abstruse 'images' – onto

---

means 'what is squeezed out', to 'employ' is to 'twine in' like a basket-maker, to 'connect' is to 'weave together', 'rudimentary' means 'in the rough state', and 'object' is 'something thrown in our way' (Owen Barfield, 'The Rediscovery of Meaning' in *The Rediscovery of Meaning and Other Essays* (Middleton CT., Wesleyan University Press, 1977), quotations, 14–15).

[171] Cf. *KBI*, 98.

[172] Cf. *CDOM*, 142.

[173] The Dominican, Aidan Nichols, cites a Russian Orthodox commentator's rather more sophisticated evaluation of 'theological art'. 'The icon is a visible sign of the splendour of invisible presence. The space granted us when we follow the cue of the icon in no sense imprisons anything. Rather, it shares in a presence and is hallowed by it. The icon has no existence of its own. It simply guides us to what really is.' Torrance, of course, is not uninformed or wholly adverse to iconology as such, but when he refers to it it is the spiritual, invisible depth highlighted behind the visual medium which is all-important. The presupposition for Torrance is always that such visual images must 'take their

relations, energy fields, etc. – any less iconic in this sense? Certainly conceptual 'icons' arising from the world of philosophy, are just as dangerous as three-dimensional statuary, with the more obscure being all the more insidious.[174] Has Torrance not just exchanged images proper to the outward character of created reality for images proper to its internal character?

We are not suggesting that Torrance ever claims for created reality, however exalted, the capacity to image God; but we have established a definite tendency engendered by his preference for abstract models which expose him to criticisms such as those noted.[175] Let us then try to make his point more clearly than he himself does by this massive stress upon the Church getting as far away as possible from ideas about God which can be facilely conceptualized. His point is surely that in the end the created order is useless in this context. Our thoughts about God must be formulated exclusively by the guidance of the Word. The analogy of God in the world finally does not arise by natural things being more audible or less visible, more intellectual or less physically accessible, but rather reposes upon the Word's self-initiated association with created reality. Torrance is simply saying that 'images' of this kind are more easily adaptable to the Word.

What then of the image of God in the historical person of Christ? Torrance admits that in the christological revelation 'there is an inevitable and proper element of anthropomorphism in our knowledge of God'. It is important, therefore, that we learn to

---

cue' in turn from the invisible, spoken word of God (Aidan Nichols, *The Art of God Incarnate: Theology and Image in Christian Tradition* (London, Darton, Longman and Todd, 1980), 99, cites Paul Evdokimov, *L'Orthodoxie* (Neuchatel, 1959), 219).

[174] For example, it could be argued that Spinoza's reasoning that things can only exist in the order and manner that they do because God is 'the first and only free cause of the essence of all things and their existence' constitutes no less an act of idolatry than the erecting of effigies (Benedict de Spinoza, *Ethics and 'De Intellectus Emendatione'* (London, J.M. Dent & Sons Ltd., 1910), 26–9).

[175] Oliver R. Barclay criticizes Torrance on a point closely associated with this. He warns of the danger, 'in view of all the metaphysical chaos afflicting contemporary physical theory' of aligning our 'apologetic arguments to fashions in scientific thinking, even when the prestige of Einstein can be invoked in their support'. Torrance, he claims, does this. Barclay cites as an example his 'deterministic' interpretation of Copenhagen quantum mechanics a la Einstein, when in fact the trend now, among the vast majority of physicists, is rather to view 'quantum theory as a departure from classical Laplacean determinism' (Oliver R. Barclay, review of *Divine and Contingent Order* by T.F. Torrance, *ChrG* 35, 2 (1982), 39).

distinguish what is 'properly anthropomorphic' from what is improperly so.[176] Even in Christ the image which God ascribes to himself does not lie in what we see, but in what we hear and perceive intellectually. The *homoousion*, he suggests, will not 'allow us indiscriminately to read back into God' the patently human features in Christ.[177] Ultimately then, even the one whom Torrance refers to as 'He who is the Image of God His Father' is not an image of God according to strict definition, but rather the archetypal, most successfully 'imageless' image of all created images, i.e. with all that is human in Christ surrendering to the controlling impression of the Word.[178] Even in the incarnation, the created element only refers to God because God's Word and Spirit make that reference. Strictly speaking, only the Word *qua* Word is the image of God. In a primal sense it is 'the imageless and invisible eternity of God... [that] is the source of God's revelation in Jesus Christ'.[179] Our humanity becomes the Word's humanity, and therefore the instrument of his revelation, by 'adoption and grace', not by metamorphosis. The virginal conception underscores this fact, it does not alter it. Torrance has said, quoting Hilary, that all images are 'helpful to man rather than... fitted to God'.[180] For all its uniqueness, the christological image is not the one exception.

---

[176] *G & G*, 163-4.
[177] Ibid. 163.
[178] *K & C*, 150.
[179] Newell, *Participatory Knowledge*, 222; cf. *CDOM*, 141-2.
[180] *TS*, 20. Torrance cites Hilary, *De Trinitate*, 1:19. The entire quotation reads: 'If in our study of the nature and birth of God we shall cite some examples for the sake of illustration, let no one imagine that these are in themselves a perfect and complete explanation. There is no comparison between earthly things and God, but the limitations of our knowledge force us to look for certain resemblances in inferior things as if they were manifestations of higher things, in order that, while we are being made aware of familiar and ordinary things, we may be drawn from our conscious manner of reasoning to think in a fashion to which we are not accustomed. Every analogy, therefore, is to be considered as more useful to man than as appropriate to God, because it hints at the meaning rather than explains it fully. And the comparison should not be regarded as presumptuous in placing the natures of the flesh and the spirit, the invisible and the tangible, on an equality, since it declares that it is necessary for the weakness of the human understanding and bears no ill-will because it is only an unsatisfactory illustration. We proceed, therefore, to our task and shall speak of God in the words of God, but at the same time we shall come to the aid of our understanding by analogies drawn from circumstances in our own life' (Hilary of Poitiers, *The Trinity*, TFOC 25, reprinted with corrections (Washington, DC, The Catholic University of America Press, 1968), 18-19).

The question then must be asked, can this reflexive image of God in Christ, as Torrance conceives it, be considered a true image of God? Donald S. Klinefelter, in a broad but thorough critique of Torrance's epistemological method, expresses his conviction that Torrance has posited so radical a disjunction between the nature of the knowledge of God and the nature of the knowledge of the world that they cannot possibly be, as Torrance puts it, 'co-ordinated within the same universe of knowledge', not even in Christ.[181] Likewise, Roger Newell fears that the unyielding ontological dissimilarity between the divine and the contingent maintained in Torrance's theology, underscored as it is by citations of statements such as the one above by Hilary, is so comprehensive as to jeopardize an authentic Creator/creation analogy. Newell questions if Torrance has not left open, even in the incarnation, the possibility for a 'difference to still exist between God as he is and God as he is revealed'.[182] Both these critics detect a latent dualism in Torrance's theology which they think he has not successfully overcome.

In reality, Torrance is walking a line between duality and dualism. He argues, predictably, from the *homoousion*. In the christological analogy, which rests upon the hypostatic union, none of the essential rules of analogy Torrance has laid down is broken. The created reality remains the passive element; the divine reality is that which predominates and appropriates it to his revelatory purposes. By his association with the created element and by its instrumentality, the Word makes reference to himself and his sovereign will in the world. However, while the christological analogy is like all the rest in its proportions and, as we say, in the rules it keeps it contains a great difference too. For unlike any other Creator/creation relation the natural element in this analogy – viz. our own humanity – is not merely passive but willing, not only appropriated but assumed. The Word does not just speak in simple conjunction with created being in Christ, as he does in other analogies, but from within our human being. Hence, when the Word directs our attention to the Eternal God by this Living Sign which he effects in our humanity, it is not as it were to something outside the incarnation but to himself in his own infinite recession in God which inheres within it. The christological analogy, for all it might have in common with other analogies, is erected at such depth and grounded in such an intense interpenetration of *phuseis* that it is said to be one

---

[181] Donald S. Klinefelter, 'God and Rationality: A Critique of the Theology of Thomas F. Torrance', *JRel* 53 (1973), 117–35. Klinefelter cites *STI*, 51.

[182] Cf. Newell, *Participatory Knowledge*, 219, 220.

of a kind. Indeed, Torrance refers to it as 'the sole, exclusive image of God'.[183] In Christ the Image and the Imaged have a common identity. He says, 'there is a perfect identity and fidelity between all that God has manifested of himself in Jesus Christ and what he is inherently in himself and ever will be'.[184] What Torrance is advocating is not an *absolute* identity between the divine and created factors in the revelation of God's Word, which would destroy either its divine source or its genuine human expression, but rather an *exact* identity, which would affirm equally both factors.[185]

Although theology must always acknowledge an ontological distinction in Christ between divine and created being, the nature of the ontological union, as well as the unitary nature of the divine-human revelation, will not allow us to abstract beyond this simple distinction. When Torrance instructs us to learn to distinguish the 'properly anthropomorphic' in the revelation of God in Christ from the 'improperly anthropomorphic', he is not suggesting that we think of Christ's two natures except in terms of their union in him. For in the person of Christ 'the divine and human are interlocked in one particular historical life'. The Word has so closely co-ordinated himself with created being in Christ that we do not have two words, one human, one divine, being synchronized together, but rather one divine-human Word. In Jesus of Nazareth God lives as man, thinks as man, speaks as man and therefore cannot be apprehended except in that 'actual context of space and time in which [he is] found'.[186] In Christ the divine and human natures are 'indivisible' and, accordingly, must be thought of inseparably.[187]

---

[183] *R/st*, 182; *R/n*, 221.

[184] *The Incarnation*, XVIII. 'The Incarnate Word and Truth of God in Christ in his own personal Being is identical with the Revelation which he mediates' (*MOC*, 19).

[185] The Chalcedonian delineation of parameters within the *unio hypostatica* is thus upheld: 'One Person in two natures, which are united unconfusedly, unchangeably, indivisibly, inseparably (ἀσυγχύτως, ἀτρέπτως, ἀδιαιρέτως, ἀχωρίστως)' ('The Definition of Chalcedon', *The Oxford Dictionary of the Christian Church*, 262–3).

[186] *TS*, 326.

[187] This fact makes all the more puzzling Torrance's talk of distinguishing that which is proper to man from that which is proper only to God in the Incarnate Word. A formal distinction, of course, is presupposed, but the actual exercise of separating the properties and/or natures of Christ would seem inconsistent with Torrance's rule that the Church must not divide that which the hypostatic relation unites forever as one. Admittedly, this kind of reasoning in Torrance's writings is infrequent and inconclusive; however, by engaging in it at all he approaches Zwingli's and sometimes Calvin's tendency to separate in

The 'difference' which Newell fears and the 'disjunction' which Klinefelter perceives preventing God's Word from truly being heard in the world is, in actuality, only the ontological demarcation between God and the world which Torrance insists must obtain even at the innermost point of the hypostatic union. What neither seems fully to appreciate is that distinction and union in Torrance's theology cannot be considered as mutually exclusive ideas. For however radical the difference is between the Creator and his creation, this is counter-balanced and set in perspective by the equally radical union demonstrated in the incarnation. Although God in Christ does not become something he is not, he does become immanent to what he is not. In Christ the person of the Word assumes our human being as his own. There is therefore nothing in Torrance's doctrines of God or creation that would imply discrepancy or distance, as Newell thinks, between what God says and what he says by his human life and word in Christ. Such qualifications must be made, not according to the measure of difference between the divine and human natures in Christ, but according to the measure of their union in him. Indeed, the theme of the incarnation is not one of substantial difference but of consubstantial synthesis.

In contrast to the christological analogy (*communio consubstantialis*), difference is as much the point as correspondence in the sacramental analogy (*communio substantialis*). Torrance's stress upon the prevailing dissimilarity between the created and uncreated elements within the sacramental relation has inevitable implications as for the importance he is willing to ascribe to the visual, concrete factor in the sacrament itself. It is precisely in a discussion of the relevance, or irrelevance, of this dimension in the sacramental analogy that one is confronted with the most aesthetically barren aspect of Torrance's theology. He says that in the context of eucharistic worship the perceptual and auditive elements are 'stereoscopically' co-ordinated and made to complement each other.[188] However, in the light of the overbearing diminution in his theology of the visual medium, one is left to think that, if it were possible to deduce such from the biblical record, Torrance would

---

Christ's person that which they considered the operation of the divine nature as opposed to the operation of the human nature. Torrance's understanding of the solidarity of Christ's person will not finally allow such partitive thinking (cf. *Inst* II.17.1; Ulrich Zwingli, 'An Exposition of the Faith', *Zwingli and Bullinger*, ed. G.W. Bromiley, LCC 24 (London, SCM, 1953), 251–3).

[188] Cf. *R & E*, 49.

have preferred a sacramental word and act without corporeal, visible co-ordinates. The question might be raised at this point if he has, after having so firmly repudiated neo-Platonic dualism, finally taken on board a fundamental characteristic of it, not just in a preoccupation with mathematical entities resembling Plato's similar preference over and against 'sensuous particulars', but in a basic undermining of the material element.[189] Has he gone so far towards reinstating the material on the basis of the hypostatic union, only to put it firmly in its place by asserting that the invisible and intangible alone really matter? Such a criticism is only partly relevant. It is clear that Torrance is much more at home when relating the truth of God to the unobservable attributes of material reality, but that reality itself is not the problem, only certain characteristics of it. While Torrance's theology invites the interaction of God with creation on every plane, within the analogy of grace the 'surface level' of contingent reality is always lacking in significance. Even when God directly refers material things to himself – e.g. in the sacrament – it is the *function* within the sacramental act which is appropriate to God and not the elements themselves. This has the desired effect of removing their meaning with reference to God one step away from their quality as visible reality. At the same time, there is no question of Torrance depreciating the material element as such in the sacramental relation in deference to the spiritual element. Torrance never sets these qualities in contradistinction to one another. His whole non-dualistic orientation militates against it.

This, however, is the nearest Torrance comes to Calvin's disparaging of the creaturely elements within the sacrament. Although he never belittles the created factor as such in the sacramental action, nor regrets the need for man to receive the communication of God's word by the created medium, still the 'language of vision' has virtually no role to play in the sacrament except as 'the set' for the all important word/act of the sacrament to which God unites himself.[190] After all Torrance has said about the inseparable relation of word and sacrament, the question still must be asked if he has given the auditory such ascendancy in the worship of the Church that the sermon will not finally displace the sacrament

---

[189] Frank Thilly, *A History of Philosophy*, 3rd edition revised by Ledger Wood (New York, Holt, Rinehart and Winston, 1961), 78; cf. Plato, 'Theory of Art' in *The Republic*, 2nd edn revised (Harmondsworth, Penguin, 1974), 421–39.

[190] Cf. Calvin's typical comment: 'We ought indeed to grieve and lament, that the sacred truth needs assistance (by the sacraments) on account of the defects of our flesh' (*Commentary on the Prophet Isaiah*, vol. 1, 241).

in importance, as it has, for all practical purposes, in the Reformed churches. Although Torrance would undoubtedly object, since the sacrament is necessary to facilitate the nature of the word as action, is there any reason to believe that after a time those who have taken his sacramental theology seriously will not replace the sacrament, with its wholly 'inappropriate', 'cumbersome' and finally 'redundant' liturgies, with para-sacramental responses in the Church more generally adaptable as well as more directly associated with the preached word, such as 'altar calls', 'covenant services' and 'pledge Sundays'?

Although Torrance will not go as far as Barth, who states flatly that 'pictorial and symbolic representations are out of place in the Protestant Church', his undergirding presuppositions leave little place for them.[191] When he says that 'God is not imaginable', the direct inference he draws is that any pictorial impression of God which might arise in our minds is latent or at least potential idolatry.[192] The fact remains, however, that Christ has not left created reality 'unassumed' at any level; Torrance is quite emphatic about this. Undoubtedly, even its most outwardly observable features also now belong to God. If this is true, then has not God evoked his own blasphemy by feeding our imagination with ὁ λόγος σὰρξ ἐγένετο? On the contrary, God has conveyed an immeasurable worth and dignity upon every aspect of material reality – the visual, tangible dimension no less than the unobservable and intangible – precisely by assuming it. Surely, if this is the case, no aspect of our humanity is really inappropriate to him now, the incarnation having superseded every contradiction. Did the Johannine Christ say, 'if you have heard me you have heard the Father'? Did he say, 'if you have seen through me you will be able to hear the Father'? Or did he in fact invite our eyes to look upon him and 'see the Father' (John 14:9). Does not Jesus' going home with Zacchaeus, the tax collector, depict in a very perceptible yet profound way the same embrace of man by the Father which the hypostatic union discloses imperceptibly? Certainly, as Torrance would insist, the latter is required for the fullest interpretation of the former, but is not the former, or its equivalent, required for the explanation of the latter in this world of sight and sound where sinners live? Likewise, when Jesus took bread and wine at the table, declaring that he was, like these elements, to be consumed, or when he referred to himself as 'The Bread of Life', did not the naturally symbolic association of these staples with

---

[191] Cf. Busch, *Karl Barth*, 474.
[192] *R/st*, 19–20, 90.

sustenance for life carry considerable weight for the meanings of the statements themselves? Torrance, while acknowledging the eucharistic orientation of John 6, never recognizes this kind of significance. John of Damascus dealt with the whole question of the imagery in the light of the incarnation, and in a way sensitive to the aesthetic needs of man. He wrote:

> Now, however, when God is seen clothed in flesh, and conversing with men, I make an image of the God whom I see. I do not worship matter, I worship the God of matter, who became matter for my sake, and deigned to inhabit matter, who worked out my salvation through matter... but as I am human and clothed with a body, I desire to see and [to deal with... holy things in a bodily way.][193]

Torrance's theology needs to reckon more graciously and less apologetically, with the manifestly visible and tangible character of the *totus Christus*.

Torrance's repeated appeal to the iconoclastic inter-dictions of the Old Testament against eidetic images and his general denigration of 'models of vision' has left a sacramental theology overrunning with words and concepts defined to precision, but all in 'black and white'.[194] In failing to elicit the service of the imaginative capacity in man he has left to starve or to atrophy a vital aspect of man's personality, one which also waits to worship God.[195] Torrance's eucharistic theology definitely is not a help towards aesthetically renewing Reformed worship in this regard. Indeed, D.H. Hislop's sweeping censure of the worship of the Reformed Church could be addressed to Torrance's doctrine of worship as well.

---

[193] John of Damascus, *Holy Images Followed by Three Sermons on the Assumption*, 1:16; 1:36 (London, Thomas Baker, 1898), 15–16, 36.

[194] Paradoxically, a visit to Torrance's study reveals icons on every wall. Directly over his prayer desk hangs a Coptic cross, with pictures of Christ crucified and Christ at prayer on either side.

[195] Philosophers of education in recent years have been keen to stress the importance of the imagination in the learning and knowing process. Philip H. Phenix's comments are typical: 'Imagination belongs to the active inner life of a person. It is the conscious centre of his psychic existence. It is the power that renders his experience vitally meaningful. By contrast, unimaginative aspects of experience are routine, dull, and unexciting. They do not grasp one at the core of his personal being. They are essentially meaningless' (Philip H. Phenix, *Realms of Meaning* (London, McGraw-Hill, 1964), 345).

There is in [Reformed worship] in the main a repudiation of all symbolism which appeals to the eye. Two things result from this: the first is the peril that the service may become intellectualistic or moralistic and the sense of worship be reduced to a vanishing point. Yet even when this danger is averted because of its intellectual character the range of the service is limited. It makes its appeal too exclusively to one side of human nature. The second limitation is that by ignoring the symbolic it sacrifices a dramatic appeal. It has no movement that can be appreciated and felt by those who do not possess conscious faith. It therefore tends to lack the power which the dramatic liturgies have of inducing the spirit of worship.[196]

Roger Newell, in his comparative study of Torrance's approach to theology and that of C.S. Lewis, speaks of the former, with his appeal to 'imageless images' in mind, as the 'Christian mathematician', the latter, for his liberal exploitation of the imagination, as the 'theological poet'. Newell concludes that they could learn from each other, but, recognizing especially the aesthetic poverty of Torrance's theology, reckons that he has a greater deficiency to balance. Of course, criticisms which involve judgements of beauty arguably tend to vary with the critic's tastes. However, Newell writes as a researcher very sympathetic to Torrance's overall position. He contrasts Torrance's and Lewis' theologies as an exact map would be compared to a landscape painting. Certainly the former is necessary to know where one is going, but the latter provides the believer with a preview of the loveliness of the land. Theology is obliged before its Object to be as beautiful as it is correct.

---

[196] Hislop, *Our Heritage in Public Worship*, 90. On Hislop's latter point we have noted that for all Torrance's contempt for the symbolic overtones in the rite, he does seek to retain the historic Reformed 'dramatic rubric'. We pointed out, however, that by stressing this it was to draw attention to the element of action which directly, albeit visually, reiterates the meaning of the words spoken in association with the acts, viz. 'broken for you', 'poured out for you'. Hislop notes this element in Reformed worship: 'Yet [Reformed worship] is not wholly lacking in the dramatic sense. In the service of Holy Communion the attempt is made to reproduce and to represent the circumstances and the situation of the first Supper. The Roman priest at no point of the service is anything but the offerer of the sacrifice; in the Calvinistic service the presbyter at certain points represents and personifies our Lord Himself. Something of the mystery drama is here' (Hislop, *Our Heritage in Public Worship*, 190).

A FURTHER QUESTION

Does not Torrance's eucharistic theology invite a further development which would unite the 'eucharistic' dimension of man's priesthood of creation with the Eucharist itself? Is there not provided here the appropriate material and facility for the Eastern emphasis along this line to be reclaimed as well as qualified christologically?

For Torrance man stands in a unique place spanning, as it were, both the created and uncreated orders, belonging to the first by nature and to the second by election.[197] He is *imago mundi* and *imago Dei*. Man and the universe are 'profoundly bracketed together', not just by the fact that man is made of the same stuff as the world – 'man with the world', he says, 'constitutes what we mean by world' – but by virtue of the position in which he has been placed vis-à-vis the world.[198] For only man among creatures can reason, not only for the world but with God at his invitation.[199] He therefore is the 'primary constituent' within the world 'through whom it is destined to know itself', both from out of itself as well as from the Creator's knowledge of it.[200]

---

[197] *CFOM*, 33.

[198] *TL*; *R & E*, 25. Jürgen Moltmann in his published Gifford Lectures describes man as 'a creature in the fellowship of creation'. He is '*imago mundi*... a microcosm in which all previous creatures are to be found again, a being that can only exist in community with all other created beings and which can only understand itself in that community' (186). He comments further: Man is 'the embodiment of all other creatures. The complex system "human being" contains within itself all simpler systems in the evolution of life, because it is out of these that the human being has been built up and has proceeded. In this sense they are present in him, just as he is dependent on them' (J. Moltmann, *God in Creation: An Ecological Doctrine of Creation*, The Gifford Lectures 1984–1985 (London, SCM, 1985), 189–90).

[199] There exists, Torrance insists, 'A profound harmony between the rationality of the human understanding and the rationality of the universe, and indeed a congruence between the stratified structure of science and the stratified structure of nature' (*DCO*, 129). The difference between man and the world at large does not consist primarily, however, in the fact that he alone has rational faculty or the unique capacity among creatures to relate to God, but rather in the relation God elects to have with him. It is in that relation and purely by that relation that man reflects the image of God: 'It is not that there is any distinction of "quality" between man and the beast, but that God relates Himself to us in a special way' (*CDOM*, 29).

[200] *R & E*, 26.

Man is 'the instrument under God' through which the universe unravels and develops the secrets of its own vast range of intelligibility and discloses the beautiful patterns of its being.[201] It is through man's activity 'as a rational, articulating agent under God, [that] the inherent intelligibility of the universe, in its stratified structures and multivariable order and harmony comes to expression and articulation'.[202] By man's rational endeavour the natural order is brought to orderly self-expression, something it cannot do without him.[203] He is its rational head, 'the culminating point of rational order'.[204] This is one aspect of what it means for man to be 'the mediator of order'. He is 'nature's midwife', Torrance says. As he sees it, 'man as scientist' has a unique role to play in this. For, whether he acknowledges it or not, the scientist occupies the office of 'priest of creation' interpreting the 'book of nature written by the finger of God'.[205]

This 'mediation of order' which is man's charge, as we have suggested, is more than just his own intelligent demonstration of the inherent rationality and structures of order in the universe. There is another side to man's priesthood of creation called for not by what the contingent order discloses at his investigation as such but by what it cannot disclose. For 'in the intrinsic order of the universe' man is confronted with 'a depth of intelligibility which reaches indefinitely beyond anything our finite minds can comprehend.[206] This is not, however, just a matter of our rational impotence before that which is indefinite. The universe *itself* contains a rationality that is finally incapable of self-explanation and remains stubbornly

---

[201] *CFOM*, 33; *R & E*, 26.

[202] *R & E*, 25.

[203] Torrance lets the solidarity of rational man with the created order as well as his own unitary nature say a word about the character of his knowledge of the world. There is nothing in man to suggest a matter-mind dualism. He is 'soul of his body and body of his soul'. So 'it is possible for the human mind, in reliance upon the inner connection between its laws and laws of nature to penetrate intuitively into the intelligibility embedded in nature and grasp its natural truth' (*CFOM*, 33).

[204] *DCO*, 130. 'From the perspective of natural science man must also be recognised to be a focal point of significance in the universe, both because he represents the culmination of its development to ever higher levels of reality and order and because all we know of the universe, even of the universe and its structure billions of years before man emerged is correlated – to the rationality of man' (*DCO*, 129).

[205] *TL*; cf. *CFOM*, 29ff.

[206] Ibid.

transcendent over against the mind of man, defying any absolute understanding or control.[207] By its own silence it cries out to be informed by a rational 'word' from outside itself, or as Torrance says, for completion and explanation beyond itself.[208] It is in this way that 'God has made the universe to develop and express itself as the creation of God.'[209] It belongs to man's sacerdotal responsibility to express what Torrance calls this 'implicit meta-reference to God' in

---

[207] Cf. *DCO*, 29; Lecture, no. 3, 27/2/86, Nottingham. Torrance puts it: 'In these processes (of nature) there becomes revealed an intelligibility beyond man's artifice and control, something absolutely given and transcendent, to which as man he is and must be rationally open and obedient, for that is his nature as a rational agent'(*R&E*, 26).

[208] *R & E*, 26; *CFOM*, 42. Torrance never varies from his precept that 'nothing can be established about contingence except through divine revelation', contingence being understood paradoxically as the freedom of the world in its own rationality *vis-à-vis* the divine rationality precisely by virtue of creation's continuous dependence upon its Creator (*DCO*, 26). He says, 'The contingence and order which our science presupposes and which it cannot account for within the frame of its own conceptual systems, carry us back to their ground in God the Creator' (*DCO*, 29). The contingent order can take us there but it cannot itself tell of its Creator. Torrance, however, sometimes speaks of the implications of this profound silence of the world as though it were 'speaking' of God, e.g. 'We find ourselves grasped by its [the world's] inherent relations in such a way as to be caught up in a reference of these relations beyond themselves' (*DCO*, 29). The world refers, it implies, it indicates 'a regulating principle, transcendent to itself', by the very fact that it cannot finally account for itself. There is 'a zero point', as Torrance calls it, at which the inherent intelligibility of the world can say no more, and it is precisely at that point where its 'sheer contingence' is most clearly manifest ('There becomes starkly disclosed the sheer contingence of the cosmos, although as such it is not demonstrable', *DCO*, 28). He says, 'In the prosecution of our scientific inquiries we can only move along the intelligible relations and their sequences latent in the world until we reach the boundaries where they break off, and where we find it scientifically illegitimate to extend intramundane connections and possibilities beyond our actual world' (*DCO*, 27). Therefore, 'Divine creation [itself] requires us to investigate the contingent world out of its own natural processions alone; without including God in the given' (*DCO*, 26). Nevertheless, at this so-called 'zero point', 'we find ourselves grasped by a commanding rationality, calling for our respect and obliging our assent to it beyond the range of our experience in the empirical world, a rationality of a higher order which makes semantic sense of the contingent universe', in other words, a rationality that finally clarifies and articulates the fact and character of the world's contingence, which it is incapable of accounting for itself (*DCO*, 29). The axiom is for Torrance then always in place: the 'lower level' of rationality is explainable in terms of the 'Higher Level' but not the other way round. (Lecture, no. 3, 27/2/86, Nottingham).

[209] *R & E*, 26.

the universe. If he does not, his scientific investigation will be meaningless.[210] It is rational man's place in the universe then not only to mediate its order to his own curiosity and amazement, but to mediate between the two orders, to express in both directions and in praise the utter contingency of the created order upon the divine order. It is at this point that the vocations of the theologian and the scientist overlap, as both are seen to serve the sanctuary of God.[211]

> Just as man is to be [finally] understood from his relation to God the Creator and Sustainer of the entire creation, so the universe through man at its highest and most advanced level of expression is finally to be understood from its contingent relation to God. That is to say, the secret of the universe or its meaning becomes disclosed through man's interaction with it both as man of science and man of God.[212]

'Without man', Torrance declares, 'nature is dumb, but it is man's part to give it word, to be the mouthpiece through which the whole universe gives voice to the glory and majesty of the living God.'[213] It must be said, however, that when it comes to any explicit reference to God man is virtually as 'dumb' as the rest of the natural order, that is to say, he is totally dependent upon God for a word about God. As he reads 'the book of nature' in the light of God's personal revelation, however, he is enabled to see the world in all its wonder and beauty for what it is ultimately viz. not just something wonderful and beautiful, but the very handiwork of the Creator. Through his priestly service the universe fulfils 'its proper end as the vast theater

---

[210] *CFOM*, 42.

[211] The scientist and the theologian 'work at the same bench', Torrance says (*TS*, VIII; Lecture, no. 3, 27/2/86, Nottingham). He states further: 'Science properly pursued is a religious duty. Man as scientist can be spoken of as the priest of creation whose office it is... to bring it all into orderly articulation' (*TL*; cf. *R & E*, 26-7). 'Regarded in this way natural science and theological science are not opposites, but partners before God' (*TL*).

[212] *CFOM*, 46. Torrance has written as early as 1947: 'It is not from below man that man can be understood but from above man.' 'There is no question of trying to understand man out of himself or from his relation to the world. He must be understood exclusively from the Word made flesh' (*CDOM*, 26, 36).

[213] *TL*. Torrance further expands this thought and that delineated immediately above, suggesting that man's 'mediation of order' within the universe consists essentially in his delegation of ultimate meanings to the world from God. 'Without [man] the various levels of contingent reality in the universe would lapse back into meaninglessness and pointlessness, but with and through him the meaning and purpose of the universe are disclosed and effectuated' (*DCO*, 130).

of glory in which [the] Creator is worshipped and hymned and praised by his creatures'.[214] Man's scientific investigation of nature thus ends not in itself, not in the world as such and not just in man's gaping through the window of indefiniteness, but by his leading creation in praise of its Creator.[215] It is with this in mind that Torrance says, 'man occupies a unique metaphysical place in the universe'.[216]

The sordid fact is, however, that all is not praise and glory. Man, 'the mediator of order', is himself inwardly and noetically

---

[214] *TL*.

[215] In its 'Pastoral Constitution on the Church in the Modern World' the Second Vatican Council reaffirmed man's role in this regard: 'Man, though made of body and soul, is a unity. Through his very bodily conditions he sums up in himself the elements of the material world. Through him they are thus brought to their highest perfection and can raise their voice in praise freely given to their creator' (*Vatican Council II: The Conciliar and Post Conciliar Documents*, ed. Austin Flannery (Collegeville, MN, The Liturgical Press, 1975), 915).

Alexander Schmemann, the Orthodox liturgist and theologian, takes the thought a step further, 'Man is first of all "homo adorans". The first, the basic definition of man is that he is *the priest*. He stands in the centre of the world and unifies it in his act of blessing God, of both receiving the world from God and offering it to God – and by filling the world with his eucharist, he transforms his life, the one that he receives from the world, into life in God, into communion with Him' (Alexander Schmemann, *For The Life of The World* (Crestwood, NY, St. Vladimir's Seminary Press, 1973), 15).

Jürgen Moltmann delineates his juxtaposition of man as *imago mundi* and man as *imago Dei* around the theme of man as priest. He says, 'As microcosm (of creation) the human being represents the macrocosm. As "image of the world" he stands before God as the representative of all other creatures. He lives, speaks and acts on their behalf. Understood as *imago mundi*, human beings are priestly creations and eucharistic beings. They intercede before God for the community of creation. Understood as *imago Dei*, human beings are at the same time God's proxy in the community of creation. They represent his glory and his will. They intercede for God before the community of creation. In this sense they are God's representatives on earth. If human beings stand before God on behalf of creation, and before creation on behalf of God, and if this is their priestly calling, then in a Christian doctrine of creation human beings must neither disappear into the community of creation, nor must they be detached from that community. Human beings are at once *imago mundi* and *imago Dei*. In this double role they stand before the Sabbath of creation in terms of time. They prepare the feast of creation' (Moltmann, *God in Creation*, 190).

Thanksgiving itself is part and parcel of Torrance's notion of the image of God in man, not only by the fact that thanksgiving by definition declares the glory of God, but because it is fundamental to man's relation with God in which the reflexive *imago Dei* inheres. He says, 'In that life of thankful relation to God, man reflects the divine glory in an image' (*CDOM*, 34, cf. 51).

[216] *TL*.

disordered, 'out of gear' as it were with God and hence with the world. Man has become an 'infectious source of disorder in nature' himself.[217] Torrance explains the consequences:

> If man's function in the inter-level connections of nature is to serve their coherent order and harmony, enabling different levels of reality to define and express their rationality through his interaction with them, then any disorder in himself will inevitably be reflected in the way he handles, interprets and explains the orderly structures of nature of which he constitutes an integral and indeed an integrating factor.[218]

Disordered man inevitably tends to 'dominate [nature] and make it serve an alien end'. The Marxists' manipulation of nature to their own ends, their 'substitution of technology for science', as Torrance calls it, is a case in point.[219] This does not mean that sinful man is deprived of his central role in the created universe. What it does mean, however, is that he can only properly 'mediate order' after he has been rationally re-ordered himself.[220] Torrance puts it,

> Man himself needs to be redeemed, put right with God, and saved from his diseased self-reference which alienates him from the rest of creation, if he himself is to fulfil a redemptive function in nature, saving it from pointlessness and disorder and mediating to it meaning and harmony from the Creator.[221]

What all this means is that the ground upon which man is finally established as priest of creation is the ground of redemption in Christ. It is not just the strength of man's original charge by God to oversee creation, for that trust he has betrayed. Neither is it simply the reordering of his mind or his equipment to fulfil the task, for that

---

[217] *R & E*, 26; *CFOM*, 46–7.

[218] *DCO*, 133.

[219] *R & E*, 26; *DCO*, 131. Torrance does not underestimate the effects of sinful man's 'mediation' of disorder. He says 'Scientifically' created disorder in the ecological chaos of nature or of human society can be so sinister and demonic in character' (*DCO*, 133).

Alexander Schmemann comments on the 'original sin' in similar terms, but relating it all to man's failure to fulfil his eucharistic stewardship of creation. 'The fall', he says, 'is not that [man] preferred world to God, disturbed the balance between the spiritual and material, but that he made the world material, whereas he was to have transformed it into 'life in God' filled with meaning and spirit' (Schmemann, *For the Life of the World*, 18).

[220] *CFOM*, 46–7.

[221] *DCO*, 133.

is his standing, but not what he stands upon. The basis of man's priesthood, his reconditioning for its duties as well as his reinstatement to its privileges, is in the renewal of Christ's own rational and created being. It is in Christ in a primal sense where the reordering of creation has taken place and necessarily from him that all mediation of order proceeds. 'The miraculous fact of Jesus', Torrance says, 'is to be regarded as the chosen *locus* within our space and time where the order of redemption intersects and sublimates the order of creation, so as to heal, enrich and advance it to a consummation in God's eternal purpose of Love beyond anything that we can conceive.'[222]

This all takes shape in the world as redeemed man, himself ordered to the divine order in Christ so that there is a 'truthful matching of the order within him and the order outside him', mediates into the world the symmetry of divine and contingent realities in Christ.[223] As Torrance puts it,

> So the role of man reconciled to God in and through Jesus Christ, therefore, must be viewed as one to be fulfilled, not only across the boundary of invisible and visible realities but across the order of redemption and the order of creation where his destiny, under God, is to be the mediator of order.[224]

This means practically that 'in the event of evil erupting into the creation', like that mentioned above, consequently obtruding chaos into it, 'the priestly role of man must take on a redemptive form'.[225] It further means that in a world in ecological disarray he becomes a rectifier of order 'wherever it has been disturbed or corrupted'.[226] Man in Christ will have no part in a 'tormenting of nature'. Instead, he affirms its dignity as God's creation and handles it with appropriate respect.[227] He is creation's servant as well as its priest, intent that the secrets of scientific investigation 'delivered' at his hand should be employed for the healing of the planet and the enrichment of humankind as well as the glory of God.

Torrance's teaching on man's priestly stewardship of the natural world terminates here, the point being made that 'as the priest of

---

[222] *CFOM*, 32.
[223] *DCO*, 133.
[224] *CFOM*, 33.
[225] *DCO*, 130.
[226] *CFOM*, 33.
[227] *R & E*, 26.

An Appraisal of Torrance's Eucharistic Theology   311

creation, [man] is not a means of order in himself, but can only mediate order from the transcendent source of order beyond himself'.²²⁸ It seems obvious, however, that a further word can be extrapolated from Torrance's eucharistic theology, one which would relate man in his sacramental act to the fulfilment of his priesthood of creation, particularly in its doxological expression viz. 'to lead the creation in its praise and glorification of God the Creator'.²²⁹ The *anaphorae* of the Eastern churches have always related these two ideas, whereas in the West such a relation has been largely overlooked until relatively recently.²³⁰ Generally speaking, the

---

²²⁸ CFOM, 46-7.

²²⁹ R & E, 26.

²³⁰ W. Jardine Grisbrooke and Geoffrey Cuming locate, as do many liturgical scholars, the 'starting-point from which the Christian eucharistic prayer... developed' with the ancient *berakoth*, which was characterized for its 'celebration of creation'. Cuming stresses what an important place the whole created world had in the eucharistic prayers of the early Church. Not only was God praised for having created the world, but creation itself was understood as giving thanks through the Church's prayer (Cuming, *He Gave Thanks*, 6-8; W. Jardine Grisbrooke, 'Anaphora' in *A New Dictionary of Liturgy and Worship*, 14).

Grisbrooke comments on the divergent development of the eucharistic prayers East and West: 'During the formative centuries of the liturgy a clear distinction arose between two types of this thanksgiving: the one variable, stressing from day to day one part or aspect after another of the saving work of Christ, and the other fixed, longer, and presenting a general view of the whole history of salvation at each celebration of the eucharist. The first type came to predominate in the West, and the second in the East. Each has its advantages and disadvantages: the variable Thanksgiving, or "proper preface", makes it possible to think more deeply and appositely of the mystery appropriate to the day or season than does the invariable type, while the latter enables thanksgiving to be at one eucharist for the whole action of God in creation and redemption more fully than does the variable type' ('Anaphora', 16).

Cuming decries the West's 'relegation of thanksgiving to a preface', and hence its virtual removal from the canon proper, as symptomatic of the general 'down-grading of Thanksgiving' in the West ('Anaphora', 12).

Among early Christian liturgies which highlight creation's 'role' in the thanksgiving of the Church, Cuming cites particularly the Clementine Liturgy of the Apostolic Constitutions (? AD 360-80) and the later Jerusalem Liturgy of St James ('Anaphora', 9-10; cf. also Brilioth, *Eucharistic Faith and Practice*, 22). This was 'a deep insight', Cuming states, which, although sorely neglected in the West, 'the East never lost' (*We Gave Thanks*, 15).

Irenaeus is said to be an exception, as exemplifying in his writings this emphasis in the early West (cf. Ralph Martin, *The Worship of God* (Grand Rapids, Eerdmans, 1982), 61-2; Charles Gore, *The Body of Christ*, 2nd edn (London, John Murray, 1901), 171-2). Noting the significant place given to 'the

eucharistic liturgies of the Reformation offer little room for manoeuvre around a solidly soteriological and didactic

---

fruits of the earth' in Christian worship as recalled by Irenaeus and other 'early canons', Bishop Gore comments, 'A Christian eucharist in the first age must have frequently resembled a modern harvest thanksgiving' (172). Alan Richardson makes a similar observation: 'The Eucharist in the ancient church was a sacrament of creation as well as of redemption.... In the early Church every Lord's Day was not only an Easter Sunday, but a Rogation Sunday and Harvest Festival as well' (Alan Richardson, ed., *An Introduction to the Theology of the New Testament* (London, SCM, 1958), 384f.).

Cuming observes how so 'few modern liturgies display the Jewish delight in the variety of creation' (14) He calls attention to two notable exceptions, the Fourth Eucharistic Prayer of the New Roman Rite and Alternative Rite D of the Revised American Episcopal, *Book of Common Prayer*. The opening section of the former reads:

> Father in Heaven,
> it is right that we should give you thanks and glory:
> you alone are God, living and true.
> Through all eternity you live in unapproachable light.
> Source of life and goodness, you have created all things,
> to fill your creatures with every blessing and lead all men to the joyful vision of your light.
> ...[I]n the name of every creation under heaven, we too praise your glory.

('The Order of the Mass', The Weekly Missal (London, Collins, 1975), 1027).

The latter hymns the cosmos in a way that would undoubtedly suit Torrance's doctrine of creation:

> God of all power, Ruler of the Universe, you are worthy of glory and praise.
> Glory to you for ever and ever.
>
> At your command all things came to be: the vast expanse of interstellar space, galaxies, suns, the planets in their courses and this fragile earth, our island home.
> *By your will they were created and have their being.*
>
> From the primal elements you brought forth the human race and blessed us with memory, reason, and skill. You made us the rulers of creation. But we turned against you, and betrayed your trust; and we turned against one another.
> *Have mercy, Lord, for we are sinners in your sight.*

('Alternative Forms of the Great Thanksgiving', *The Book of Common Prayer* (New York, The Church Hymnal Corporation, 1979), 370).

preoccupation.[231] Torrance's understanding of the sacrament, however, with its distinctly 'eucharistic' disposition, as well as its

---

[231] Cf. D.H. Tripp, 'Protestantism and the Eucharist', in *The Study of the Liturgy*, ed. Cheslyn Jones, Geoffrey Wainwright and Edward Yarnold (London, SPCK, 1978), 260; cf. Brilioth, *Eucharistic Faith and Practice*, 177.

This 'didactic strain' through the soteriological construct of Protestant worship was inevitable in view of the Reformers' 'marriage' of the sacrament with the *kerygma*. Luther himself stated 'The Gospel voice announcing remission of sins [is] the one and most worthy preparation for the Lord's Table' (From his 'Formula of Mass and Communion for the Church at Wittenberg, 1523' cited in *Prayers of the Eucharist: Early and Reformed*, ed. R.C.D. Jasper and G.J. Cuming (London, Collins, 1975), 124).

The liturgies of the Reformation are generally not noted for their great emphasis upon thanksgiving. D.H. Hislop comments on Luther's understanding of worship as 'lacking in the buoyant note of praise so characteristic in Eastern worship' (Hislop, *Our Heritage in Public Worship*, 167). Brilioth in turn notes that Luther 'somewhat grudgingly indeed' brought himself to speak of a 'eucharistic' sacrifice in the sacrament (131). He further explains: 'When the Lutheran Reformation condemned the false popular conception of the eucharistic sacrifice, it failed to restore the act of thanksgiving in its true proportions' (278). Calvin's sacramental theology, as we have observed, in contrast to Luther's, laid great stress upon the eucharistic element, while having a no less soteriological theme. Paradoxically, the early Calvinist liturgies never reflected the doxological disposition of Calvin's sacramental doctrine. Hislop remarks that 'one is sometimes surprised at the scanty place given to adoration and thanksgiving in the prayers of the Calvinistic Rite' (189; Hislop, concentrating too much upon Calvin's doctrine of the sovereignty of God and seemingly oblivious to the central place the *sursum corda* occupied in his eucharistic thought, explains this peculiar lack of praise in Calvin's form for divine service by the fact that it 'did not have the unitive experience of adoration as its goal. The service belongs (exclusively) to what we have already called the descending movement of worship', 189). Bucer's order for the Holy Communion offered little improvement in this regard. Tripp notes how it decidedly 'mutes the tone of thanksgiving'. Cuming's commentary on Cranmer's liturgical innovations denotes a similar deficiency in this respect. 'Thanksgiving', he says, 'seems to have been his blind spot' (*He Gave Thanks*, 12). Two notable exceptions in the period, however, seem to have been the liturgies of Knox and Melancthon. The former included 'a eucharistic prayer with thanksgiving for creation [as well as for] redemption' and the latter stressed the 'value in the liturgical action of the eucharist as a whole, and [treated] the whole service as an act of thanksgiving' (Brilioth, *Eucharistic Faith and Practice*, 186, 131; cf. Tripp, 'Protestantism and the Eucharist', 259).

Cuming attributes this general lack of the doxological element in the liturgies of the West, particularly as it involved the magnitude of creation, to the liturgical reforms of Basil in the East, over a thousand years before the Reformation. It was Basil who originally criticized the tendency of the liturgy to dwell too much on created things and not enough on that which mattered most,

emphasis upon the presentation of a New Creation to God in Christ would easily allow this kind of development; indeed it invites it.

Torrance has made it clear that in Christ we have the fulfilment of all duties incumbent upon man by God. Surely this would not exclude his priestly service rendered for creation. For in Christ the whole Edenic epic is recapitulated and re-enacted. 'He is the New Adam, the restoration of that which Adam failed to be.'[232] He is that New Adam come into fallen creation. By the power of the Spirit Christ restores in his mind and body the natural order, reorienting it to God and returning it to him in himself. The ascended Christ in the fullness of his humanity personally embodies a New Creation and, in his rational prayer, incorporates the creation's praise to its Creator. Christ is himself the high priest of the new heaven and the new earth. Whatever priesthood man has, whether in the Church or more

---

the history of salvation. Cuming's remarks are provocative: 'Once the theme of creation was associated with the Son, it was bound to be subordinated to that of redemption, and deprived of its rich content' (*He Gave Thanks*, 10–11). Brilioth, less pejoratively, notes already a tendency in this direction in the early worship of the Church: 'In the early liturgies we see the Jewish thanksgiving for the creation and for natural gifts making room for, and in part yielding place to, the joy of the New Covenant in the Divine work of redemption and in the fulfilment of the Divine promises' (*Eucharistic Faith and Practice*, 278).

Torrance would contend that only a deficient soteriology could ever have had this effect upon the Church's worship, one that failed to take seriously the involvement of and implications for creation itself in the history of redemption, not only in the incarnation as such, but in the second coming of Christ to this world. We are reminded of his statement: 'With the Incarnation and the finishing of Christ's work, we must think of the whole relation between the Spirit of God and His creation as undergoing a change – but that change has to be interpreted Christologically in relation to Christ the First-born and Head of all creation, i.e. it has to be interpreted eschatologically in terms of the new creation' (*SOF*, CII). Torrance himself criticizes Reformed theology for having failed to work out the broader meanings of this: the implications of the operation of the Spirit in creation which 'Reformed theology has never fully faced or worked out, depends upon the doctrine of the relation of the incarnate Word, crucified, risen and ascended, to the whole creation, and that... has never been fully worked out' (*SOF*, CII–CIII).

Our proposal here of a way to reintroduce creation itself into the constitution of the Church's Eucharist, according to the firm christological principles of Torrance's sacramental theology, is intended to modify Cuming's statement above, as well as carry through, at least in part, Torrance's own suggestion that the Church must develop the implications of christology for its doctrine of creation.

[232] Schmemann, *For the Life of the World*, 93.

broadly in the world, it is one necessarily derived from and regulated by that of Christ.[233]

Torrance speaks of our Eucharist specifically as a breaking in of the New Creation upon our order. In the same vein as Calvin, he asserts that as the Church shares in Christ's vivified flesh by the Holy Spirit in the Eucharist it partakes of this New Creation.[234] Does it not follow naturally, then, that we should also share in the priestly presentation in that New Creation with Christ?[235] Indeed, taking into

---

[233] Schmemann speaks of the Church being reinstated by Christ in its doxological priesthood of Creation: 'Christ, the new Adam... restores the "eucharistic life" which I, the old Adam, have rejected and lost; who makes me again what I am, and restores the world to me. And if the Church is *in Christ*, its initial act is always this act of thanksgiving, of returning the world to God' (*For the Life of the World*, 61).

[234] *Inter*, 311-12. H.A. Williams indulges in some engaging speculation around the idea of creation in the Eucharist coming to the fullest expression of what it is and can be in union with the risen Christ. He states: 'Ultimately He [Christ] will "fill all things" i.e. the whole of nature will become the vehicle of His Real Presence.... In the new heavens and the new earth... the universe in all its parts will become the perfect organ of Christ's Person, the faultless instrument of His self-expression.' The Church has a foretaste of this new world in the holy Communion. He says that we should therefore 'think of the consecrated bread and wine as being the physical universe made new in miniature so that it becomes (as the whole creation is destined to become) the instrument of Christ's presence and power.... Just as finally in the new heaven and new earth Christ will fill all things, so now in anticipation of that divine act of renewal, He fills the consecrated bread and wine. They do not change into something different from themselves... but (within the context of the Eucharistic celebration) they are transferred into the new world... [i.e.] gathered up fully in Christ. The consecrated bread and wine then... witness to the ultimate destiny of the... physical universe. In them God's promise is fulfilled, "Behold, I will make all things new" (H.A. Williams, *Jesus and the Resurrection* (London, Longmans, Green and Co., 1954), 17-20).

From this it can be quickly discerned what would make such theological thinking wholly unacceptable to Torrance. Williams' foremost mistake, as far as Torrance is concerned, would be that he postulates and works from a union of God and creation, not as it is principally in Christ, but as it is in the Eucharist. Although what Williams says might have commendable eschatological implications, Torrance would insist that in fact it preempts the second coming, so that what he says we have in the Eucharist is nothing less than the new heaven and the new earth microscopically perceived, or as he puts it, 'in miniature'.

[235] Schmemann, reflecting the continuity of this kind of thinking with the theology of the East, states this in no less christological categories than would Torrance.

account Torrance's understanding of the eucharistic sacrifice and the dynamic connotation he attributes to the notion of participation, could it be otherwise? For it is here, as we have seen, that man is brought into a *koinonia* of praise with the Great High Priest, and not without a token of the rest of creation either. For in the Eucharist Christ places the bread and wine in our hands, at once the signs of this natural order – always that! – as well as the active signs of its new creation in the flesh and blood of Christ. With gifts such as these (his gifts to us not ours to him) bearing such an analogy at his Word as they do, can we who receive them do anything but exult and glory in him who is the reconciliation of all things and lift up our praise with him who is the praise of all creation.

The Eucharist thus becomes a celebration of the fulfilment by the New Adam of the original Adam's mandate, while, at the same time, affording the Church a most appropriate setting for the fulfilment of at least the eucharistic dimension of our priestly ministry for the world inherited from both Adams. The Eucharist is as Jürgen Moltmann says 'a feast of creation', but not one prepared by man as such.[236] For Torrance the eucharistic feast is spread by Christ and, although man is invited to share in it, all acts of man there must fittingly defer and mirror those of the God-man. What we are suggesting is that man, in a single eucharistic act, might honour pre-eminently the high praise of Christ offered for all creation while at the same time 'give word' as praise to the creation which is his

---

'We offer the world and ourselves to God. But we do it *in Christ* and *in remembrance of Him*. We do it in Christ because He has already offered all that is to be offered to God. He has performed once and for all this Eucharist and nothing has been left unoffered. In him was *Life* – and this Life of all of us, He gave to God. The Church is all those who have been accepted into the eucharistic life of Christ. And we do it *in remembrance of Him* because, as we offer again and again our life and our world to God, we discover each time that there is nothing else to be offered but Christ Himself – the Life of the world, the fullness of all that exists. It is His Eucharist, and He is the Eucharist. As the prayer of offering says – "it is He who offers and it is He who is offered." The liturgy has led us into the all-embracing Eucharist of Christ, and has revealed to us that the only Eucharist, the only offering of the world is Christ. We come again and again with our lives to offer; we bring and "sacrifice" – that is, give to God – what He has given us; and each time we come to the *End* of all sacrifices, of all offerings, of all eucharist, because each time it is revealed to us that Christ has *offered* all that exists, and that He and all that exists has been offered in His offering of Himself. We are included in the Eucharist of Christ and Christ is our Eucharist' (*For the Life of the World*, 35-6).

[236] Moltmann, *God in Creation*, 190.

charge. This, of course, would not be properly another word from that of Christ, but rather the praise of the New Creation in him being made to sound within us. Just as our eucharistic sacrifice either in initiative, content or performance was seen not to be formally another sacrifice from the self-presentation of Christ in heaven, so our priestly service for creation, viewed from this perspective, would not be another service from his, but one fulfilled through him, with him and in him. In this way the fulfilment of man's destiny in heaven in Christ would be decisively linked to the fulfilling of man's destiny on earth.

Torrance has made it perfectly plain that the only act in the Eucharist worthy of the completed work of Christ is praise. He has also adamantly asserted that we do not offer the bread and wine to God after the fashion of certain Anglican liturgical 'transitions' of the nineteenth century.[237] What we are suggesting here does not in any way compromise these standards. Man does not offer creation to God, but he does with Christ offer the praise of creation. The role of man as priest, as Torrance insists, must not be seen as finally fulfilled by man alone, that is, by man attempting himself to mediate between visible and invisible realities, but rather by man in Christ, who takes both his priestly office and offering from him who, by virtue of his belonging naturally to both orders, mediates between them by right. According to this view, the Eucharist – already established as the venue on earth where the praise of Christ is heard – provides for man the formal place to return to God

---

[237] Torrance was emphatic on this point in a personal interview, 27/2/86, Nottingham. He has said, 'There is a way, however, of speaking too easily about the bringing of our offerings in the Eucharist, about bringing the fruit of our labours as represented by the bread and wine, which savours rather much of the sacrifice of Cain' (*C & A* II, 183). A similar opinion is expressed by Colin Buchanan in his study of the history of the Offertory (C. Buchanan, *The End of the Offertory – An Anglican Study*, Grove Liturgical Study No. 14 (Bramcote, Grove Books, 1978), 24-5). In contrast to this view, J.H. Srawley seeks to retain the Offertory, seeing it as a filling out of the concept of the Word as Recreator by the concept of the Word as Creator. He says: The 'association with the Eucharist of the offering of the gifts of bread and wine, as an act of thanksgiving for God's creation, was a fine Christian instinct, which brought the commemoration of Christ's redeeming activity into relation with his creative activity as the Word, and so gathered up in one act of worship the whole conception of God's providence and dealing with men' (J.H. Srawley, *The Early History of the Liturgy*, 2nd edn (Cambridge, CUP, 1949), 215; cf. also Franz Hildebrandt's general comments on the subject in *I Offered Christ: Protestant Theology and the Mass* (London, Epworth Press, 1967), 62-3. This book is particularly helpful for its bibliography).

that which is his trust, his eucharistic stewardship of creation. In this way, the Eucharist presages even more poignantly the eschatological feast of the New Creation in a new heaven and a new earth.[238]

---

[238] In the interview mentioned above we briefly proposed to Torrance a way, such as we have delineated in this section, that his eucharistic theology might be more fully developed so as to 'unite the "eucharistic" dimensions of man's priesthood of creation with the Eucharist itself'. At that time he dismissed the idea, contending that any notion of the Church making offering in the Eucharist smacked of synergism. He reiterated the theme that all offering, both in its act and in its content, belongs exclusively to the office of the Mediator. Nevertheless, he agreed to read my argument when formally prepared and to offer his comments. This was sent to him in late June 1986. His reply of 2 July 1986 was as follows: 'I have read [the] section... of your thesis, in which you relate the eucharistic praise in the Eucharist to the way in which, in Christ, we call upon all creation to praise and glorify God.... I find myself in agreement with what you have written: yes, you do develop it without allowing the Pelagian elements which I dislike to enter into it!! I think you have been theologically sound and acute...'.

BIBLIOGRAPHY

Agnew, Mary Barbara. *The Concept of Sacrifice in the Eucharistic Theology of Donald M. Baillie, Thomas F. Torrance, and Jean-Jacques von Allmen*, The Catholic University of America Ph.D., Ann Arbor, University Microfilms, 1972

Aquinas, Thomas. *Summa Theologica*, New York, Benziger Bros Inc., 1947, 3 vols

Armstrong, A.H. *An Introduction to Ancient Philosophy*, London, Methuen & Co., 1947

Athanasius. 'Ad Epictetum', *Select Works and Letters*, NPNF 2, 4, ed. Philip Schaff and Henry Wace, Grand Rapids, Eerdmans, 1957, 570-74

—. *Contra Arianos* I, II, III, IV, *The Faith of the Early Fathers*, vol. I, selected by William A. Jurgens, Collegeville, MN, The Liturgical Press, 1970, 327-38

—. *Contra Arianos* III, *The Christological Controversy*, ed. Richard A. Norris Jr, Philadelphia, Fortress Press, 1980, 83-101

—. *Contra Arianos* I, II, III, IV, *Select Works and Letters*, NPNF 2, 4 (see above), 306-447

—. *Contra Gentes and De Incarnatione*, ed. Robert W. Thomson, Oxford, The Clarendon Press, 1971

—. 'De Decretis', *Select Works and Letters*, NPNF, 2, 4 (see above), 150-72

—. 'Epistle I, A Letter of Athanasius to Bishop Serapion Concerning the Holy Spirit', *The Letters of Saint Athanasius Concerning the Holy Spirit*, ed. C.R.B. Shapland, London, Epworth Press, 1951, 58-149

—. 'Epistle IV, A Letter from the Same to the Same Serapion Likewise Concerning the Holy Spirit', *The Letters of Saint Athanasius Concerning the Holy Spirit* (see above), 179-89

—. 'Letters Concerning the Councils of Rimini and Selucia', *The Faith of the Early Fathers*, vol. I (see above), 338-9

—. 'Sermon to the Newly Baptized', *The Faith of the Early Fathers*, vol. I (see above), 345-6

—. 'Tomus ad Antiochenos', *Select Works and Letters*, NPNF 2, 4 (see above), 481-6

Augustine. *City of God*, Harmondsworth, Penguin, 1972

—. 'De Trinitate', *Opera Omni post Lovaniensium Theologorum Recensionem*, vol. VIII/I, Paris, Gaume Brothers, 1837, cols 1153-1516

—. 'Homilies on the Gospel of John', *Homilies on the Gospel of John, Homilies on the First Epistle of John, Soliloquies*, NPNF 1, 7, ed. Philip Schaff, Grand Rapids, Eerdmans, 1956, 7-452

—. 'Letter 98', *Letters*, vol. 2 (83-130), TFOC 18, Washington, DC, The Catholic University of America Press, 1953, 129-38

—. 'On the Trinity', *On the Holy Trinity, Doctrinal Treatises, Moral Treatises*, NPNF 1, 3, ed. Philip Schaff, Grand Rapids, Eerdmans, 1978, 1-228

Aulén, Gustav. *Eucharist and Sacrifice*, Edinburgh, Oliver & Boyd, 1958, Reformation and Catholicity, Edinburgh & London, Oliver & Boyd, 1962

Baillie, Donald M. *The Theology of the Sacraments and Other Papers*, New York, Charles Scribner's Sons, 1957
Bamborough, R. (ed.). *The Philosophy of Aristotle*, New York, Mentor Books, 1963
Barclay, Oliver R. Review of *Divine and Contingent Order* by T.F. Torrance, ChrG 35, 2 (1982), 39
Barfield, Owen. 'The Rediscovery of Meaning', *The Rediscovery of Meaning and Other Essays*, Middletown, CT, Wesleyan University Press, 1977
Barkley, John M. 'The Theology of Liturgy', *LitR* 3 (1973) 1–15
—. *The Worship of the Reformed Church*, London, Lutterworth, 1966
Barr, James. *The Semantics of Biblical Language*, London, OUP, 1962
Barrett, C. Kingsley. *The Gospel According to St. John, An Introduction with Commentary and Notes on the Greek Text*, London, SPCK, 2nd edn, 1978
Barth, Karl. *Anselm: Fides Quaerens Intellectum: Anselm's Proof of the Existence of God in the Context of His Theological Scheme*, London, SCM, 1960
—. *Church Dogmatics, The Doctrine of the Word of God*, vols I.1 and I.2, Edinburgh, T & T Clark, 1960 and 1963
—. *Credo. A Presentation of the Chief Problems of Dogmatics with Reference to the Apostles' Creed*, London, Hodder & Stoughton, 1936
—. *The Epistle to the Romans*, ed. Edwyn C. Hoskyns, London, OUP, 1933
—. *God in Action*, Edinburgh, T & T Clark, 1936
—. *The Heidelberg Catechism for Today*, Richmond, VA, John Knox Press, 1964
—. *The Knowledge of God and the Service of God according to the Teaching of the Reformation*, London, Hodder & Stoughton, 1938
—. *Table Talk*, recorded and edited by John D. Godsey, SJT Occasional Paper no. 10, Edinburgh, Oliver & Boyd, 1963
Basil the Great. *Letters and Select Works*, NPNF 2, 8, ed. Philip Schaff and Henry Wace, Grand Rapids, Eerdmans, 1961
Bell, Richard. Review of *Reality and Scientific Theology* by T.F. Torrance, *RSCF* 6 (1986), 50–51
Berkhof, Louis. *Systematic Theology*, London, Banner of Truth, 1958
Berkouwer, G.C. *The Work of Christ*, Grand Rapids, Eerdmans, 1965
Bethune-Baker, J.F. *An Introduction to the Early History of Christian Doctrine To the Time of the Council of Chalcedon*, London, Methuen, 1903
Bonhoeffer, Dietrich. *Letters and Papers from Prison*, ed. Eberhard Bethge, London, SCM, enlarged edition, 1971
The Book of Common Prayer According to the Use of the Episcopal Church, New York, The Church Hymnal Corporation, 1979
Brand, Eugene. 'Lutheran Worship', *A New Dictionary of Liturgy and Worship*, ed. J.G. Davies, London, SCM, 1986, 345–7
Brilioth Yngve. *Eucharistic Faith and Practice: Evangelical and Catholic*, London, SPCK, 1934
Buchanan, Colin O. *The End of the Offertory – An Anglican Study*, Liturgical Study no. 14, Bramcote, Grove Books, 1978

—. (ed.). *Essays on Eucharistic Sacrifice in the Early Church*, A Sequel to Liturgical Study no. 31, Eucharistic Sacrifice, The Roots of a Metaphor by Rowan Williams, Liturgical Study no. 40, Bramcote, Grove Books, 1984

Busch, Eberhard. *Karl Barth*, London, SCM, 1976

Calvin, John. *Commentaries to the Epistle to the Hebrews*, ed. John Owen, Grand Rapids, Eerdmans, 1949

—. *Commentary on the Epistles of Paul the Apostle to the Corinthians*, vol. 1, ed. John Pringle, Grand Rapids, Eerdmans, 1948

—. *Commentary on the Epistles of Paul the Apostle to the Corinthians*, vol. 2, ed. John Pringle, Grand Rapids, Eerdmans, 1959

—. *Commentary on a Harmony of the Evangelists, Matthew, Mark, and Luke*, vol. 3, ed. William Pringle, Grand Rapids, Eerdmans, 1957

—. *Commentary on the Last Four Books of Moses Arranged in the Form of a Harmony*, vol. 2, ed. C.W. Bingham, Grand Rapids, Eerdmans, 1950

—. *Commentary on the Prophet Isaiah*, vol. 1, ed. William Pringle, Grand Rapids, Eerdmans, 1958

—. *Commentary on the Prophet Isaiah*, vol. 3, ed. William Pringle, Grand Rapids, Eerdmans, 1948

—. *Institutes of the Christian Religion*, trans. Henry Beveridge, 2 vols, Grand Rapids, Eerdmans, 1957, 2 vols

—. *Institutes of the Christian Religion*, LCC 21, ed. John T. McNeill, trans. Ford Lewis Battles, 2 vols, London, SCM, 1960

—. *Institutes of the Christian Religion*, trans. John Allen, 2 vols, Philadelphia, Board of Christian Education, Presbyterian Church, USA, 1936

—. 'Mutual Consent in Regard to the Sacraments', *Tracts and Treatises*, vol. 2 (historical notes and introduction by T.F. Torrance), Grand Rapids, Eerdmans, 1958, 199-244

—. 'The CLXXII, Sermon, which is the fourth upon the thirtith Chapter of Deuteronomie', *The Sermons of M. John Calvin upon the Fifth Booke of Moses called Deuteronomie*, London, Printed by Henry Middleton for Thomas Woodcocke, 1583, 1065-71

Campbell, John McLeod. *Christ the Bread of Life*, London, MacMillan, 2nd edn, 1868

—. *The Nature of Atonement and its Relation to Remission of Sins and Eternal Life*, London, MacMillan, 6th edn, 1895

Cannon, William Ragsdale. *The Redeemer*, New York, Abingdon-Cokesbury Press, 1951

Chesterton, G.K. *Saint Thomas Aquinas 'The Dumb Ox'*, New York, Image Books, 1956

Clark, Francis. *Eucharistic Sacrifice and the Reformation*, London, Darton, Longman & Todd, 1960

Crichton, J.D. 'A Theology of Worship', *The Study of Liturgy*, ed. Cheslyn Jones, Geoffrey Wainwright, Edward Yarnold, London, SPCK, 1978, 3-29

Cross, F.L. and E.A. Livingstone (eds). *The Oxford Dictionary of the Christian Church*, Oxford, OUP, 2nd edn (revised), 1983

Cullman, Oscar. *Early Christian Worship*, London, SCM, 1953

Cullman, Oscar and F.J. Leenhardt. *Essays on the Lord's Supper*, London, Lutterworth, 1958

Cuming, Geoffrey. *He Gave Thanks: An Introduction to the Eucharistic Prayer*, Liturgical Study no. 28, Bramcote, Grove Books, 1981
Cyril of Alexandria. 'Commentary on John', *The Mass: Ancient Liturgies and Patristic Texts*, ed. Andre Hamman, Staten Island, NY, Alba House, 1967, 125–52
——. 'Commentary on Matthew', *The Faith of the Early Fathers*, vol. 3, selected by William A. Jurgens, Collegeville, MN, The Liturgical Press, 1979, 219–20
——. 'The Third Letter to Nestorius', *Christology of the Later Fathers*, LCC 3, ed. Edward Rochie Hardy and Cyril C. Richardson, London, SCM, 1954, 349–54
Cyril of Jerusalem. 'Catechetical Lectures', *The Faith of the Early Fathers*, vol. I, selected by William A. Jurgens, Collegeville, MN, The Liturgical Press, 1970, 347–71
Daly, Robert J. *The Origins of the Christian Doctrine of Sacrifice*, Philadelphia, Fortress Press, 1978
Daube, David. *He That Cometh*, London, Diocesan Council for Christian–Jewish Understanding, 1966
Diess, Lucien. *It's the Lord's Supper*, London, Collins, 1980
Dillenberger, John (ed.). *John Calvin: Selections from his Writings*, New York, Anchor Books, 1971
Dix, Gregory. *The Shape of the Liturgy*, Westminster, Dacre Press, 1943
Dowley, Tim (ed.). *Eerdmans' Handbook to the History of Christianity*, Grand Rapids, Eerdmans, 1977
Dugmore, C.W. 'The Eucharist in the Reformation Era', *Eucharistic Theology Then and Now*, Theological Collections no. 9, London, SPCK, 1968, 59–75
Eagleton, Terry. *Literary Theory*, Oxford, Basil Blackwell, 1983
Fenwick, John. *The Eastern Orthodox Liturgy*, Ministry and Worship no. 56, Bramcote, Grove Books, 1978
Ferré, Frederick. *Language, Logic and God*, London, Eyre and Spottiswoode, 1962
Flannery, Austin (ed.). *Vatican Council II: The Conciliar and Post-Conciliar Documents*, Collegeville, MN, The Liturgical Press, 1975
Florovsky, Georges. 'The Iconoclastic Controversy', *Christianity and Culture*, vol. 2, Belmont, MA, Nordland Publishing Co., 1974, 101–19
Fransen, Piet and T.F. Torrance. *Intelligent Theology*, vol. 3, *A Universal Theology*, London, Darton, Longman & Todd, 1969
Gebremedhin, Ezra. 'Life Giving Blessing: An Inquiry Into The Eucharistic Doctrine of Cyril of Alexandria', University of Uppsala Ph.D., 1977
Gore, Charles. *The Body of Christ*, London, John Murray, 2nd edn, 1901
——. *Dissertations on Subjects Connected with the Incarnation*, London, John Murray, 1896
Gregory of Nazianzus. 'Epistle 101, To Cleodonius against Apollinarius', *Christology of the Later Fathers*, LCC 3, ed. Edward Rochie Hardy and Cyril C. Richardson, London, SCM, 1954, 215–24
Grillmeier, Aloys. *Christ in Christian Tradition*, vol. 1, *From the Apostolic Age to Chalcedon*, London and Oxford, Mowbrays, 1975
Grisbrooke, W. Jardine. 'Anaphora', *A New Dictionary of Liturgy and Worship*, ed. J.G. Davies, London, SCM, 1986, 13–21
Gunton, Colin E. *Becoming and Being: The Doctrine of God in Charles Hartshorne and Karl Barth*, Oxford, OUP, 1978

—. Review of *The God of Jesus Christ* by Walter Kasper, Th 89 (1986) 131-2
—. *Yesterday and Today: A Study of Continuities in Christology*, London, Darton, Longman and Todd, 1983
Hall, Basil. '*Hoc est Corpus Meum*: The Centrality of the Real Presence for Luther', *Luther: Theologian for Catholics and Protestants*, ed. George Yule, Edinburgh, T & T Clark, 1985, 112-44
Hanson, R.P.C. *Eucharistic Offering in the Early Church*, Liturgical Study no. 19, Bramcote, Grove Books, 1976
Harnack, A. *History of Dogma*, vols 3 and 5, London, Williams & Northgate, 1897 and 1898
Heick, Otto W. *A History of Christian Thought*, 2 vols, Philadelphia, Fortress Press, 1965 and 1966
Hellriegel, Martin B. *The Holy Sacrifice of the Mass*, St Louis, Pio Decimo Press, 1963
Hendry, George S. *The Gospel of the Incarnation*, London, SCM, 1959
Heron, Alasdair (ed.). *Agreement and Disagreement, The Common Ground and Major Differences in Belief Between the Church of Scotland and the Roman Catholic Church*, Edinburgh, The Handsel Press, 2nd edn, 1984
—. 'The "filioque" in Recent Reformed Theology', *Spirit of God, Spirit of Christ*, ed. Lukas Vischer, London/Geneva, SPCK/WCC, 1981, 110-17
—. *The Holy Spirit: The Holy Spirit in the Bible in the History of Christian Thought and in Recent Theology*, London, Marshall, Morgan & Scott, 1983
—. *Table and Tradition: Towards an Ecumenical Understanding of the Eucharist*, Edinburgh, The Handsel Press, 1983
Heywood Thomas, John. 'Logic and Metaphysics in Luther's Eucharistic Theology', *RMS* 23 (1979) 147-59
Hick, John. *God and the Universe of Faiths*, London, Collins, revised edn, 1977
Hilary of Poitiers. *The Trinity*, TFOC 25, Washington, DC, The Catholic University of America Press, repr, with corrections, 1968
Hildebrandt, Franz. *I Offered Christ*, Protestant Theology and the Mass, London, Epworth Press, 1967
Hislop, D.H. *Our Heritage in Public Worship*, Kerr Lectures, 1933, Edinburgh, T & T Clark, 1935
Holland, J. Angus B. 'Athanasius versus Arius, What Now?', *RefTR* 28 (1969) 16-28
Jasper, R.C.D. and G.J. Cuming (eds.). *Prayers of the Eucharist: Early and Reformed*, London, Collins, 1975
Jeremias, Joachim. *The Eucharistic Words of Jesus*, Oxford, Basil Blackwell, 1955
John of Damascus. 'An Exact Exposition of the Orthodox Faith', *Saint John of Damascus*, TFOC 37, Washington, DC, The Catholic University of America Press, 1958, 165-406
—. *Holy Images Followed by Three Sermons on the Assumption*, London, Thomas Baker, 1898
John Paul II, Pope. *The Mystery and Worship of the Holy Eucharist*, Apostolic letter Dominicae Cenae, Preston, Apostolate of Catholic Truth, 1980
Jungmann, Josef A. *The Mass, An Historical, Theological, and Pastoral Survey*, ed. Mary Ellen Evans, Collegeville, MN, The Liturgical Press, 1976
—. *The Place of Christ in Liturgical Prayer*, London, Geoffrey Chapman, 1965

Kelly, J.N.D. *Early Christian Creeds*, London, Longmans, Green & Co., 1950
—. *Early Christian Doctrines*, London, A & C Black, 1958
Kennedy, Michael. *The Concise Oxford Dictionary of Music* (based on the original publication by Percy Scholes), London, OUP, 3rd edn, 1980
Kerr, Hugh Thomson (ed.). *A Compend of The Institutes of the Christian Religion by John Calvin*, Philadelphia, The Presbyterian Board of Christian Education, 1939
Kilian, Sabbas J. 'The Holy Spirit in Christ and Christians', *AmBenR* 20 (1969) 99–121
Klinefelter, Donald S. 'God and Rationality: A Critique of the Theology of Thomas F. Torrance', *JRel* 53 (1973) 117–35
Knowles, David. *Evolution of Medieval Thought*, London, Longman, 1962
Knox, John. 'The Scots Confession', *The Works of John Knox*, vol. 2, ed. David Laing, Edinburgh, Printed for the Woodrow Society, 1848, 93–182
Kraemar, Hendrik. *A Theology of the Laity*, London, Lutterworth, 1958
Lampe, G.W.H. *A Patristic Greek Lexicon*, Oxford, Clarendon Press, 1961
—. 'The Eucharist in the Thought of the Early Church', *Eucharistic Theology Then and Now*, Theological Collections no. 9, London, SPCK, 1968, 34–58
Lash, Nicholas. 'Up and Down in Christology', *New Studies in Theology*, vol. 1, ed. Stephen Sykes and Derek Holmes, London, Duckworth, 1980, 31–46
Leech, Kenneth. *True God: An Exploration in Spiritual Theology*, London, Sheldon Press, 1985
Leeming, Bernard. *Principles of Sacramental Theology*, Westminster, MD, The Newman Press, 1956
Lietzmann, Hans. *Mass and the Lord's Supper: A Study in the History of the Liturgy*, Leiden, E.J. Brill, 1979
Long, Roy. 'The Ecclesiology of Dietrich Bonhoeffer and its Relationship to the Traditional Lutheran Understanding of the Church', University of Nottingham M.Phil., 1984
Louth, A. 'The Concept of the Soul in Athanasius' *Contra Gentes – De Incarnatione*', *StPatrist* 13 (1975) 227–31
Lunt, Ronald. 'Collected papers of T.F. Torrance'. A review of *Theology in Reconstruction* by T.F. Torrance, *Exp Tim* 87 (1975–76) 379
MacDonald, A.J. (ed.). *The Evangelical Doctrine of Holy Communion*, Cambridge, W. Heffer & Sons, 1933
McDonnell, Kilian. *John Calvin, the Church, and the Eucharist*, Princeton, NJ, Princeton University Press, 1967
McEwen, James S. *The Faith of John Knox*, The Croall Lectures 1960, London, Lutterworth, 1962
McFague, Sallie. *Metaphorical Theology: Models of God In Religious Language*, London, SCM, 1983
MacGregor, Geddes. *Corpus Christi: The Nature of the Church according to the Reformed Tradition*, London, MacMillan, 1959
MacKay, D.M. Review of *Divine and Contingent Order* by T.F. Torrance, *ChrG* 35, 2 (1982) 38–9
McKenna, John H. *Eucharist and the Holy Spirit: The Eucharistic Epiclesis in 20th Century Theology (1900–1966)*, Great Wakering, Mayhew-McCrimmon, 1974

McKinney, R.W.A. (ed.). *Creation, Christ and Culture: Studies in Honour of T.F. Torrance*, Edinburgh, T & T Clark, 1976
—. Lectures, University of Nottingham, Autumn Term, 1983
MacMillan, Gilleasbuig (Minister of St Giles' Cathedral, Edinburgh). Correspondence, 27/6/86
MacNicol, D.C. *Robert Bruce: Minister in the Kirk of Edinburgh*, London, Banner of Truth, 1961
Manschreck, Clyde L. (ed.). *Melanchthon on Christian Doctrine*, New York, OUP, 1965
Martin, Ralph P. *The Worship of God*, Grand Rapids, Eerdmans, 1982
Martos, Joseph. *Doors to the Sacred: An Historical Introduction to Sacraments in the Christian Church*, London, SCM, 1981
Mascall, E.L. *Corpus Christi: Essays on the Church and the Eucharist*, London, Longman, 1953
—. Review of *Creation, Christ and Culture: Studies in Honour of T.F.T.* by R.W.A. McKinney (ed.) *SJT* 30 (1977) 71–3
—. *Whatever Happened to the Human Mind? Essays in Christian Orthodoxy*, London, SPCK, 1980
Maxwell, William D. *An Outline of Christian Worship: Its Development and Forms*, London, OUP, 1936
—. 'Reformed Worship', *A New Dictionary of Liturgy and Worship*, ed. J.G. Davies, London, SCM, 1986, 458–60
Meijering, E.P. *God Being History*, Oxford, North Holland Pub. Co., 1975
—. *Orthodoxy and Platonism in Athanasius: Synthesis or Antithesis?* Leiden, E.J. Brill, 1968
Meyendorff, John. *Byzantine Theology*, New York, Fordham University Press, 1974
Molnar, Paul David. 'A Critical Examination of the Relationship between the Sacrament of the Eucharist and the Doctrine of God in the Theology of Karl Barth and Karl Rahner', Fordham University Ph.D., Ann Arbor, University Microfilms, 1980
Moltmann, Jürgen. *The Church in the Power of the Spirit*, London, SCM, 1977
—. *God in Creation: An Ecological Doctrine of Creation*, The Gifford Lectures 1984–85, London, SCM, 1985
—. *The Trinity and the Kingdom of God*, London, SCM, 1981
Moule, C.F.D. *Worship in the New Testament*, London, Lutterworth, 1967
—. *Worship in the New Testament*, Liturgical Study no. 12, Bramcote, Grove Books, 1977
Muggeridge, M. 'A Line to Reality', Interview in *Viewpoint Magazine*, vol. 32 (n.d.) 7–8
A New Catechism: Catholic Faith for Adults, New York, Seabury Press, 1969
Newell, Roger J. 'Participatory Knowledge: Theology as Art and Science in C.S. Lewis and T.F. Torrance', University of Aberdeen Ph.D., 1983
Nichols, Aidan. *The Art of God Incarnate: Theology and Image in Christian Tradition*, London, Darton, Longman & Todd, 1980
Niesel, Wilhelm. *The Theology of Calvin*, London, Lutterworth, 1956
Obermann, Heiko Augustinus. *The Harvest of Medieval Theology*, Grand Rapids, Eerdmans, revised edn, 1967

O'Donovan, Oliver. *Resurrection and Moral Order: An Outline for Evangelical Ethics*, Leicester, IVP, 1986

Ordinal and Service Book For Use in Courts of The Church, Church of Scotland, London, OUP, 3rd edn, 1962

Origen. *De Principiis*, ed. G.W. Butterworth, New York, Harper & Row, 1966

Ozment, Stephen. *The Age of Reform 1250-1550: Intellectual and Religious History of Medieval Europe*, New Haven, Yale University Press, 1980

Pannenberg, Wolfhart. *Jesus – God and Man*, London, SCM, 1968

Paul VI, Pope. *The Holy Eucharist*, Encyclical letter *Mysterium Fidei*, London, Catholic Truth Society, 1965

Pelikan, Jaroslav. *The Christian Tradition, A History of the Development of Doctrine*, vol. 1, *The Emergence of the Catholic Tradition (100–600)*, Chicago and London, The University of Chicago Press, 1971

——. *The Christian Tradition, A History of the Development of Doctrine*, vol. 3, *The Growth of Medieval Theology (600–1300)*, Chicago and London, The University of Chicago Press, 1978

Phenix, Philip H. *Realms of Meaning*, London, McGraw-Hill, 1964

Phillips, J.B. *Appointment with God: Some Thoughts on Holy Communion*, New York, MacMillan, 1957

Pigott, Graham. 'Christian Liturgy as Education', University of Nottingham M.Phil., 1984

Plato. *The Republic*, Harmondsworth, Penguin, 2nd edn, revised, 1974

Portalie, Eugene. *A Guide to the Thought of Saint Augustine*, Westport, CT, Greenwood Press, 1975

Prebble, John. *The Lion In the North: A Personal View of Scotland's History*, London, Book Club Associates, 1974

Prestige, G.L. *Fathers and Heretics*, The Bampton Lectures, 1940, London, SPCK, 1958

Quick, Oliver Chase. *The Christian Sacraments*, London, Nisbet & Co., 1948

Quinn, James. Review of *Theology in Reconstruction* by T.F. Torrance, *ThSt* 28 (1967) 388-90

Rahner, Karl. 'Grace', *Sacramentum Mundi*, vol. 2, ed. Karl Rahner et al., London, Burns & Oates, 1968, 409-24

——. *The Trinity*, New York, Seabury Press, 1974

——. 'The Two Basic Types of Christology', *Theological Investigations*, vol. 13, *Theology, Anthropology, Christology*, London, Darton, Longman & Todd, 1975, 213-23

——. 'The Word and the Eucharist', *Theological Investigations*, vol. 4, *More Recent Writings*, London, Darton, Longman & Todd, 1966, 253-86

Raven, C.E. *Apollinarianism*, Cambridge, University Press, 1923

Reardon, Bernard M.G. *Religious Thought in the Reformation*, London, Longman, 1981

Richardson, Alan (ed.). *An Introduction to the Theology of the New Testament*, London, SCM, 1958

Roberts, Richard H. 'The Ideal and the Real in the Theology of Karl Barth', *New Studies in Theology*, vol. 1, ed. Stephen Sykes and Derek Holmes, London, Duckworth, 1980, 163-80

——. 'Karl Barth', *One God in Trinity*, ed. Peter Toon and James D. Spiceland, London, Samuel Bagster, 1980, 78-94
——. 'Karl Barth's Doctrine of Time, Its Nature and Implications', *Karl Barth - Studies of his Theological Methods*, ed. S.W. Sykes, Oxford, Clarendon Press, 1979, 88-146
Runes, Dagobert D. (ed.). *Dictionary of Philosophy*, Paterson, NJ, Littlefield, Adams & Co., 1961
Ryder, Sonia. Review of *The Mediation of Christ* by T.F. Torrance, ChrA 37, 3 (1984) 37
Sasse, Herman. *This is My Body: Luther's Contention for the Real Presence in the Sacrament of the Altar*, Adelaide, Lutheran Publishing House, revised edn, 1981
Schillebeeckx, E. *Christ the Sacrament of the Encounter with God*, New York, Sheed & Ward, 1963
——. *The Eucharist*, New York, Sheed & Ward, 1968
——. 'The Interpretation of Eschatology', *The Problem of Eschatology*, ed. E. Schillebeeckx and Boniface Willems, New York, Paulist Press, 1969, 42-56
Schmemann, Alexander. *For the Life of the World*, Crestwood, NY, St. Vladimir's Seminary Press, 1973
Schuetzinger, Caroline Eva. *The German Controversy on Saint Augustine's Illumination Theory*, New York, Pagent Press Inc., 1960
Sellers, R.V. *Two Ancient Christologies: A Study in the Christological Thought of the Schools of Alexandria and Antioch in the Early History of Christian Doctrine*, London, SPCK, 1940
Senarclens, Jacques De. *Heirs of the Reformation*, London, SCM, 1963
Sibley, Brian. *Shadowlands*, London, Hodder & Stoughton, 1985
Smail, T.A. Review of *The Mediation of Christ* by T.F. Torrance, SJT 38 (1985) 241-4
——. 'The Son-Spirit Relationship - Modern Reductions and New Testament Patterns', *IrBSt* 6 (1984) 85-102
Spinks, Bryan D. 'Luther and the Canon of the Mass', LitR 3 (1973), 34-46
——. *Luther's Liturgical Criteria and his Reform of the Canon of the Mass*, Liturgical Study no. 30, Bramcote, Grove Books, 1982
Spinoza, Benedict de. *Ethics and 'De Intellectus Emendatione'*, London, J.M. Dent, 1910
Srawley, J.H. *The Early History of the Liturgy*, Cambridge, CUP, 2nd edn, 1949
Stead, Christopher. *Divine Substance*, Oxford, Clarendon Press, 1977
Stevenson, J. (ed.). *A New Eusebius: Documents Illustrative of the History of the Church to AD 337*, London, SPCK, 1957
Stevenson, Kenneth. *Eucharistic Sacrifice in the Early Liturgies*, unpublished paper, March 1984
——. *Gregory Dix 25 Years On*, Liturgical Study no. 10, Bramcote, Grove Books, 1977
——. Lecture given at St John's College, Nottingham, 8/3/85
——. (ed.) *Liturgy Reshaped*, London, SPCK, 1982
——. Review of Table and Tradition: Towards an Ecumenical Understanding of the Eucharist by Alasdair Heron, SJT 38 (1985), 244-6

Sykes, S.W. 'Barth on the Centre of Theology', *Karl Barth - Studies of his Theological Methods*, ed. S.W. Sykes, Oxford, Clarendon Press, 1979, 17-54

Tappeiner, Daniel A. 'Hermeneutics, the Analogy of Faith and New Testament Sacramental Realism', *EvQ* 49 (1977) 40-52

Thilly, Frank. *A History of Philosophy*, revised by Ledger Wood, New York, Holt, Rinehart and Winston, 3rd edn, 1961

Thorson, Walter R. Review of *The Christian Frame of Mind* by T.F. Torrance, *USCF* (Winter 85/86), 41-3

—. Review of *Reality and Scientific Theology* by T.F. Torrance, *PSCF* 38, 2 (1986), 212-14.

Tillich, Paul. *Systematic Theology*, vols 1 & 2, London, James Nisbet & Co, 1953 and 1957

Torrance, James B. 'Covenant or Contract? A Study of the Theological Background of Worship in Seventeenth Century Scotland', *SJT* 23 (1970) 51-76

—. 'The Vicarious Humanity of Christ', *The Incarnation, Ecumenical Studies in the Nicene-Constantinopolitan Creed AD 381*, ed. T.F. Torrance, Edinburgh, The Handsel Press, 1981, 127-47

Torrance, Thomas F. *The Addresses at the 6th Presentation of the Templeton Foundation Prize for Progress in Religion*, Dublin, Lismore Press, 1978

—. *The Apocalypse Today*, Greenwood, SC, The Attic Press Inc., 1960

—. 'The breaking of Bread', *LitSt* 1 (1971) 18-26

—. (intro.). *A Calvin Treasury*, London, SCM, 1963, v-xiii

—. *Calvin's Doctrine of Man*, Westport, CT, Greenwood Press, 1977

—. *The Centrality of Christ, Devotions and Addresses*, The General Assembly of the Church of Scotland, 1976, Edinburgh, The St. Andrew Press, 1976

—. *Christian Theology and Scientific Culture* (Theological Lectures at the Queen's University, Belfast, 1980), Belfast, Christian Journals Ltd., 1980

—. *The Christian Frame of Mind*, Edinburgh, The Handsel Press, 1985

—. 'The Church in the New Era of Scientific and Cosmological Change', *N Coll B* 7 (1973) 19-31

—. 'Comments on Eucharistic Practice in the Church of Scotland Today', *ChSSR* 5 (1983) 17-18

—. *Conflict and Agreement in the Church*, 2 vols, London, Lutterworth, 1959 and 1960

—. Correspondence, 2/7/86

—. *Divine and Contingent Order*, Oxford, OUP, 1981

—. 'Doctrinal Consensus on Holy Communion, The Arnoldshain Theses', *SJT* 15 (1962) 1-35

—. *The Doctrine of Grace in the Apostolic Fathers*, Edinburgh, Oliver & Boyd, 1948

—. 'Eschatology and the Eucharist', *Intercommunion*, ed. Donald Baillie and John Marsh, London, SCM, 1952, 303-50

—. *God and Rationality*, Oxford, OUP, 1971

—. *The Ground and Grammar of Theology*, Belfast, Christian Journals Ltd., 1980

—. 'Hermeneutics of St. Athanasius', *Ekklesiastikos Pharos* 52 (1970) 446-68; 53 (1971) 133-49

—. (ed. and intro.). *The Incarnation: Ecumenical Studies in the Nicene-Constantinopolitan Creed AD 381*, Edinburgh, The Handsel Press, 1981
—. Interviews, Edinburgh 23/12/85; Nottingham 27/2/86
—. 'Israel, People of God – God, Destiny and Suffering', *ThRen* 13 (1979) 2–14
—. (notes and intro.). *John Calvin's Tracts and Treatises*, Grand Rapids, Eerdmans, 1958, 3 vols
—. *Karl Barth: An Introduction to his Early Theology 1910–1931*, London, SCM, 1962
—. *Kingdom and Church: A Study in the Theology of the Reformation*, Edinburgh, Oliver & Boyd, 1956
—. Lectures, Edinburgh, Michaelmas term, 1963, 'Christian Dogmatics', New College
—. Lectures at Nottingham, 27/2/86: (1) 'Realism and Openness in Scientific Inquiry', at University of Nottingham; (2) 'The Legacy of Karl Barth', at St John's College; (3) 'Time in Scientific and Historical Research', at St John's College; (4) Lecture on the Eucharist at St John's College
—. *The Mediation of Christ*, The 1982 Didsbury Lectures, Exeter, Paternoster Press, 1983
—. (ed. and intro.). *The Mystery of the Lord's Supper: Sermons on the Sacrament Preached in the Kirk of Edinburgh in AD 1589 by Robert Bruce*, London, James Clark, 1958
—. 'The Paschal Mystery of Christ and the Eucharist, General Theses', *LitR* 6 (1976) 6–12
—. 'The Place of the Humanity of Christ in the Sacramental Life of the Church', *Church Service Society Annual* 26 (1956) 3–10
—. *Reality and Evangelical Theology*, The 1981 Payton Lectures, Philadelphia, The Westminster Press, 1982
—. *Reality and Scientific Theology*, Edinburgh, Scottish Academic Press, 1985
—. 'Reason in Christian Theology', *EvQ* 14 (1942) 22–41
—. Review of *Quellen zur Geschichte des Christliche Gottesdienstes* by Joachim Beckmann, *SJT* 12 (1959) 108–09
—. Review of *Sacraments and Worship* by Paul F. Palmer (ed.), *SJT* 12 (1959) 109–11
—. *Royal Priesthood*, *SJT* Occasional Paper no. 3, Edinburgh, Oliver & Boyd, 1955
—. (ed. and intro.). *The School of Faith: The Catechisms of the Reformed Church*, London, James Clark & Co., 1959
—. *Space, Time and Incarnation*, Oxford, OUP, 1978
—. *Space, Time and Resurrection*, Grand Rapids, Eerdmans, 1976
—. (ed. and intro.). *Theological Dialogue between Orthodox and Reformed Churches*, Edinburgh and London, Scottish Academic Press, 1985
—. *Theological Science*, based on the Hewett Lectures for 1959, Oxford, OUP, 1978
—. *Theology in Reconciliation: Essays Towards Evangelical and Catholic Unity in East and West*, Grand Rapids, Eerdmans, 1976
—. *Theology in Reconstruction*, Grand Rapids, Eerdmans, 1975
—. 'Toward an Ecumenical Consensus on the Trinity', *ThZ* 31 (1975) 337–50

—. *Transformation and Convergence in the Frame of Knowledge*, Belfast, Christian Journals Ltd., 1984

—. *When Christ Comes and Comes Again*, London, Hodder & Stoughton, 1957

Torrance, Thomas F. and Ronald Selby Wright, ed. and revised by, *A Manual of Church Doctrine According to the Church of Scotland* by H.J. Wotherspoon and J.M. Kirkpatrick, London, OUP, 2nd edn, 1960

Tripp, D.H. 'Protestantism and the Eucharist', *The Study of Liturgy*, ed. Cheslyn Jones, Geoffrey Wainwright, Edward Yarnold, London, SPCK, 1978, 248–63

Turner, H.E.W. 'Person(s)', *A Dictionary of Christian Theology*, ed. Alan Richardson, London, SCM, 1969, 256–7

—. 'Trinity, Doctrine of the', *A Dictionary of Christian Theology*, ed. Alan Richardson, London, SCM, 1969, 345–51

Vagaggini, Cyprian. *Theological Dimensions of the Liturgy*, vol. 1, Collegeville, MN, The Liturgical Press, 1959

Von Campenhausen, H. *The Fathers of the Greek Church*, London, A & C Black, 1963

Vonier, Anscar. *A Key to the Doctrine of the Eucharist*, Westminster, MD, The Newman Press,1951

Wainwright, Geoffrey. *Doxology. The Praise of God in Worship, Doctrine and Life: A Systematic Theology*, London, Epworth, 1980

Wallace, Ronald S. *The Atoning Death of Christ*, London, Marshall, Morgan & Scott, 1981

—. *Calvin's Doctrine of the Word and Sacrament*, Edinburgh, Oliver & Boyd, 1953

Ware, Timothy. *The Orthodox Church*, Harmondsworth, Penguin, revised edn, 1972

Watson, P.S. 'Grace', *A Dictionary of Christian Theology*, ed. Alan Richardson, London, SCM, 1969, 147–9

—. *Let God be God: An Interpretation of the Theology of Martin Luther*, Philadelphia, Fortress Press, 1947

The Weekday Missal, London, Collins, 1975

Wendel, François. *Calvin: The Origins and Development of His Religious Thought*, London, Collins, 1965

Wesley, John. *The Journal of the Rev. John Wesley, A.M.*, vol. 2, ed. Nehemiah Curnock, London, Charles H. Kelly, 1909

Whitacre, Aelred. Vincent McNabb, A.E. Taylor, Monsignor Gonne, T.F. Tout and Hugh Pope, *St. Thomas Aquinas*, papers read at the celebrations of the sixth centenary of the canonization of St Thomas Aquinas, held at Manchester, 1924, Oxford, Basil Blackwell, 1925

Wiles, Maurice. 'The Nature of the Early Debate about Christ's Human Soul', *JEH* 16 (1965) 139–51

Williams, H.A. *Jesus and the Resurrection*, London, Longmans, Green, 1954

Williams, Rowan. *Eucharistic Sacrifice – The Roots of a Metaphor*, Liturgical Study no. 31, Bramcote, Grove Books, 1982

Williams, Theodore. *Augustinianism: An Interpretation*, printed but unpublished lecture notes, Patristic Seminar, TAE 6733, Oral Roberts University, School of Theology, Tulsa, OK, Spring 1981

Wilson, John. *One of the Richest Gifts: An Introductory Study of the Arts from a Christian World-view*, Edinburgh, The Handsel Press, 1981

Wotherspoon, H.J. and J.M. Kirkpatrick, *A Manual of Church Doctrine According to the Church of Scotland*, London, Hodder & Stoughton, 1920

Zizioulas, John D. *Being as Communion: Studies in Personhood and the Church*, London, Darton, Longman & Todd, 1985

Zwingli, Ulrich. 'An Exposition of the Faith', *Zwingli and Bullinger*, LCC 24, ed. G.W. Bromiley, London, SCM, 1953, 239–79

www.ingramcontent.com/pod-product-compliance
Lightning Source LLC
Chambersburg PA
CBHW052052300426

44117CB00012B/2086